GRAND PRIX

DRIVER BY DRIVER

A compilation of every driver ever to have raced in Grand Prix

WRITTEN BY

PHILIP RABY

GRAND PRIX
PRIX
DRIVER BY DRIVER

CONTENTS

INTRODUCTION

Everyone has heard of the likes of Stirling Moss and Michael Schumacher – true legends of the world of Formula One. However, in the history of this most glamorous of sports, there are dozens of long-forgotten names for every Clark, Hill or Button.

Don't make the mistake of thinking, though, that because a driver isn't well-known today, they must have been a failure. There have been plenty of great Formula One drivers over the years who astonished the world with their skill and bravery. And even those people who didn't perform well at the top of the sport still deserve recognition for making it into Formula One.

Each and every driver who has competed in Formula One has a fascinating story behind his (and occasionally her) name. Stories of bravery, glamour, skill and, more often than you'd wish, tragedy. It's these stories, albeit in necessarily short forms, that I've told in these pages, because I believe that they are, in many cases, more interesting than page upon page of data documenting race results; all of which is available elsewhere.

This book lists all drivers who have entered an FIA Formula One World Championship Grand Prix from 1950 to 2007. In other words, they may not have started the race itself but did attempt to qualify. In fact, in some cases, the driver did not even reach the qualifying stage, for whatever reason, but if their name was down for the Grand Prix, then they have been included within these pages.

The reason this book begins in 1950 is because that was the year that the FIA World Championship series began.

Prior to that, Grand Prix racing wasn't controlled in the same way, and prizes were only given to manufacturers, not drivers as well. Note that non-Championship Formula One grands prix took place in some countries up until 1983, but drivers who took part only in these are not included in this book. Also, for a period in the 1950s, Formula Two cars could drive in World Championship events; drivers of these cars are included because they entered World Championship races.

Furthermore, from 1950 to 1960, the annual American Indianapolis 500 race counted towards the World Championship. Entrants to that race in that period are listed separately at the back of the book.

These days, drivers compete as part of a team, such as Ferrari or Honda. In the past, however, before costs became prohibitive, it wasn't unusual to see privateer entrants – individuals driving their own cars, or ones in a team that didn't construct its own cars. That's why, in the listings, I've included entries for team or manufacturer, so you can see the type of car being used.

Finally, details of some of the more obscure drivers have become lost in the sands of time. I've done my best to ensure that all the information is accurate but, in some cases, no one is a hundred per cent sure of the truth.

I hope you'll enjoy discovering the lost heroes of Formula One as much as I have done!

Philip Raby, 2007

A

Christijan Albers

Carlo Mario ABATE

Nationality: Italian
Born: 10th July 1932
Seasons: 1962-1963
Team/manufacturer(s): Lotus-Climax
Grands Prix: 2
Race wins: 0
Championship wins: 0

Carlo Mario Abate was an accomplished racing driver who had much success racing Ferrari 250 GTOs, as well as competing for other private and works teams, including Porsche, and in 1959 he won the Mille Miglia race.

He turned his hand to Formula One in 1962, entering races in France and Germany with Lotus-Climax but failed to qualify. Abate met with the same lack of success the following year when he entered the Italian Grand Prix.

However, outside Formula One, he won the Targa Florio in 1963, driving a factory Porsche. After this, he retired from motor racing and became the director of a clinic.

George ABECASSIS

Nationality: British
Born: 21st March 1913
Died: 18th December 1991
Seasons: 1951-1952
Team/manufacturer(s): HWM, Alta
Grands Prix: 2
Race wins: 0
Championship wins: 0

George Abecassis began racing in 1935 driving an Austin Seven, and went on to compete in an Alta. In 1939, he won the Imperial Grand Prix but his race career was then interrupted by the Second World War, during which time he flew in the RAF.

After the war, Abecassis became involved with HWM and, after competing in some pre-Formula One Grands Prix, he raced these cars at the Swiss Grands Prix in 1951 and 1952.

He was a more successful sports car racer, competing for Aston Martin and winning his class at Le Mans in 1950.

Abecassis retired from racing in 1956 but continued to run HWM and also imported Facel Vegas, before turning his attention to the grocery business.

Kenneth Henry (Kenny) ACHESON

Nationality: British
Born: 27th November 1957
Seasons: 1983, 1985
Team/manufacturer(s): RAM
Grands Prix: 10
Race wins: 0
Championship wins: 0

Born in Northern Ireland to a race-driver father, Kenny Acheson began racing in Formula Ford, where he won 29 races and three titles. He then moved on to Formula 3 and then Formula 2, where he had less luck. Indeed, a bad accident in 1982 left him with two broken legs.

His Formula One debut was in 1983 but he only succeeded in qualifying once, when he finished 12th in South Africa. Acheson competed again in Formula One in 1985, at the Dutch and Italian Grands Prix, but with no success.

He then moved on to Formula 3000 and sports car racing, before retiring after a bad accident in 1996 and setting up in business in England.

George Abecassis

Philippe ADAMS

Nationality: Belgian
Born: 19th November 1969
Seasons: 1994
Team/manufacturer(s): Lotus
Grands Prix: 2
Race wins: 0
Championship wins: 0

Philippe Adams began racing karts before moving onto saloon cars, where he had occasional success. A move to Japan in 1991 to race in Formula 3 and Formula 3000 netted little success so he tried British Formula 3 in 1992 and finished a respectable second in the championship.In 1994, Adams secured a drive with the Lotus Formula One team, reputedly by bringing some half a million dollars of his own money to the struggling team. Sadly, it wasn't enough to buy him success and he returned to saloon and sports car racing in later years.

Kurt ADOLFF

Nationality: German
Born: 5th November 1921
Seasons: 1953
Team/manufacturer(s): Ecurie Espadon
Grands Prix: 1
Race wins: 0
Championship wins: 0

Kurt Adolff was born in Stuttgart, Germany, and had had some success racing Mercedes 170 saloon cars. However, between 1950 and 1952 he became known for competing in a two-litre Veritas RS, when he achieved two third-place wins at the Nürburgring.

In 1953 he entered the German Grand Prix, driving a specially-prepared Ferrari 166. However, he retired from the race after only a few laps, and never did any more single-seat racing.

Adolff went on to compete in hillclimbs and touring car racing.

Kurt AHRENS Jr

Nationality: German
Born: 19th April 1940
Seasons: 1966-1969
Team/manufacturer(s): Caltex Racing
Grands Prix: 4
Race wins: 0
Championship wins: 0

The son of German Speedway champion – Kurt Ahrens Sr – Kurt Ahrens Jr began racing in Formula 3 and then Formula 2 and touring cars.

Because of the length of the circuit, Formula 2 cars were allowed to compete in the Grand Prix races at the Nürburgring, which is why Ahrens raced in Formula One between 1966 and 1969.

After that, he joined the Porsche works team and took part in long-distance races before retiring from motorsport in 1971. He went on to run a car dealership and a scrap-metal business.

Christijan ALBERS

Nationality: Dutch
Born: 16th April 1979
Seasons: 2005-
Team/manufacturer(s): Midland F1, Spyker F1
Grands Prix: 46
Race wins: 0
Championship wins: 0

Christijan Albers is the son of rallycross driver, André Albers. After starting off in karts, he won the Formula Ford 1800 championship in the Netherlands and Belgium in 1997, and the German Formula 3 series in 1999.

In 2000, he moved to Formula 3000 before spending time in German touring cars, where he made a good impression. At the same time, Albers tested for Minardi and, in Australia in 2005, entered his First Grand Prix for that team. Later that year, he gained his first championship points when he finished fifth in the USA.

Albers moved to the new Midland F1 team (formerly Jordan) for the 2006 season. In 2007 this was renamed

Christijan Albers

Jean Alesi

Spyker F1 and Albers remained with the team until July of that year when lack of sponsorship forced him to be released from his contract.

Michele ALBORETO

Nationality: Italian
Born: 23rd December 1956
Died: 25th April 2001
Seasons: 1981-1994
Team/manufacturer(s): Tyrrell, Ferrari, Larrousse, Arrows, Minardi
Grands Prix: 215
Race wins: 5
Championship wins: 0

Michele Alboreto began his career in 1976 Formula Monza in a car he designed himself. However, his success began in 1978 when he finished third in the Italian Formula 3 series.

He raced for Minardi's Formula 2 team in 1981 and had his Formula One debut the same year, in a Tyrrell at San Marino. Alboreto stayed with Tyrrell until 1983 and then moved to Ferrari. The following year he finished fourth in the championship.

After returning to Tyrrell in 1989 he spent time with other teams before retiring from Formula One at the end of 1994.

Alboreto went on to win Le Mans in 1997 in a TWR-run Porsche. He was killed in 2001 while testing an Audi R8.

Giovanni (Jean) ALESI

Nationality: French
Born: 11th June 1964
Seasons: 1989-2001
Team/manufacturer(s): Tyrrell, Ferrari, Benetton, Sauber, Prost, Jordan
Grands Prix: 202
Race wins: 1
Championship wins: 0

Jean Alesi began as a rally driver but moved to single-seaters and won the 1988 French Formula 3 championship and 1989 International Formula 3000 series.

He finished fourth in his first Formula One race, in France in 1989. After a successful 1990 season, Alesi was in demand but chose to race for Ferrari, which was a bad choice because the team was not doing well and he had little success in five years, although he did gain a large and enthusiastic Italian fan-base.

Despite his skill, bad luck meant that Alesi only won one Grand Prix, at Montreal in 1995. After leaving Formula One at the end of 2001, he went on to race in the DTM German touring cars series.

Philippe ALLIOT

Nationality: French
Born: 27th July 1954
Seasons: 1984-1990, 1993-1994
Team/manufacturer(s): RAM, Ligier, Larrousse, McLaren
Grands Prix: 116
Race wins: 0
Championship wins: 0

Michele Alboreto

Philippe Alliot

Fernando Alonso

Philippe Alliot began racing in Formula Renault in 1976 and, by 1978, he won the championship and moved to French Formula 3.

Alliot's Formula One debut was for RAM in 1984, and he then went on to drive for Ligier in 1986, followed by Larrousse the following year. However, he was a fast but erratic driver and had some spectacular accidents.

Alliot moved to sports car racing in 1991, driving for Peugeot and helped the team to win the World Sportscar Championship in 1992.

He returned to Formula One with McLaren in 1994, but only raced once. Alliot then went back to Larrousse but, again, only competed in one race, before retiring from racing to move to a career in politics.

Henry Clifford (Cliff) ALLISON
Nationality: British
Born: 8th February 1932
Seasons: 1958-1961
Team/manufacturer(s): Lotus, Scuderia Centro Sud, Ferrari
Grands Prix: 18
Race wins: 0
Championship wins: 0

Cliff Allison's family ran a garage in his home town of Brough, in Cumbria. He began racing in 1952, in a Cooper-Norton Formula 3 car. By 1958 he was racing in Formula One, alongside Graham Hill, and showed great potential.

Allison moved to Ferrari the following year but, in 1960, he crashed during practice at Monaco and was thrown from his car. A broken arm and other injuries put him out of racing for the rest of the season.

The following year he crashed again at the Belgian Grand Prix, breaking both his legs. He never raced again after that, choosing to return to run the family garage, which included driving the village bus!

Fernando ALONSO
Nationality: Spanish
Born: 29th July 1981
Seasons: 2001-
Team/manufacturer(s): Minardi, Renault, McLaren
Grands Prix: 105
Race wins: 19
Championship wins: 2

In 2005 Fernando Alonso won the World Drivers' Championship, breaking Schumacher's reign and becoming the youngest driver to win the title, at just 24 years of age.

Impressive stuff, and all thanks to his father's passion for kart racing. José Luis, wanted his children to take on his hobby. So he built his eight-year-old daughter a simple kart but she took no interest in the sport, therefore it was passed onto three-year-old Fernando, who loved the kart.

Before long, the youngster was excelling in the sport and, in 1988, at the age of seven, he won all eight races in the Pola de Laviana championship and took the title. He went on to win the Spanish Kart Championship in 1994, 1996 and 1997, and he was the World Junior Karting Champion in 1996.

At the age of 18, in 1999, Alonso won the Spanish Nissan Open Series, which gained him a place in Formula 3000 for the following season. That year he won at Spa and was asked to drive for the Minardi Formula One team in 2001. Despite putting in a good performance through the season, he failed to score any points in his first year.

Alonso moved to Renault in 2002 as a test driver in advance of his first season of racing with the team in 2003. In his second race of 2003, he won the Hungarian Grand Prix, becoming the youngest driver ever to win a Formula One race. He finished the season in sixth place. The following year, he failed to win any races but nonetheless finished the championship in fourth place. In 2005 Alonso finished third in the first race of the season (in Australia), then he won his next three Grands Prix, in Malaysia, Bahrain and Italy. He also won at Monaco, the Nürburgring, France, Germany and China.

In between, he consistently achieved podium positions and had clinched the Drivers' Championship on points when he finished third in Brazil. At 24 years and 59 days old, Alonso was 18 months younger than the previous youngest Formula One champion, Emerson Fittipaldi. By the end of the season, the young Spaniard helped Renault to win the Constructors'

Giovanna Amati

Championship for the first time.

Alonso went on to win the Championship again in 2006, thus becoming the youngest double champion in Formula One history. A move to McLaren for 2007 saw Alonso teamed with Lewis Hamilton, which proved to be an unhappy partnership and his relationship within the team also deteriorated. Towards the end of the season Alonso made it clear that he would not stay with McLaren for 2008, despite being contracted to do so.

Giovanna AMATI
Nationality: Italian
Born: 20th July 1962
Seasons: 1992
Team/manufacturer(s): Brabham
Grands Prix: 3
Race wins: 0
Championship wins: 0

Born in Rome to wealthy parents, Giovanna Amati was

Fernando Alonso

kidnapped as a child, and went on to buy a motorcycle at the age of 15 and hide it from her parents for two years.

After attending a motor racing school, Amati raced in Formula Abarth and Italian Formula 3 and 3000. From 1987 she moved from team to team but had little success as a driver.

Her money was reputed to have helped her secure a season with Brabham in 1992. Not to mention the fact that, being one of just five women to have competed in Formula One, was a good publicity stunt for the team. After a poor performance, failing to qualify in three Grands Prix, Brabham replaced her with Damon Hill. Amati went on to race sports cars, and has worked in magazines and television, writing and commentating on motorsport.

Christopher Arthur (Chris) AMON

Nationality: New Zealander
Born: 20th July 1943
Seasons: 1963-1976
Team/manufacturer(s): Parnell, Raby, Cooper, Amon, Ferrari, March, Matra, Tecno, Tyrrell, BRM, Ensign, Wolf
Grands Prix: 108
Race wins: 0
Championship wins: 0

It has been joked that Chris Amon was the best Formula One driver never to win a race, although he did manage 11 podium finishes.

After competing in local races in New Zealand, beginning with an Austin A40 Special, Amon moved to the UK to race for the Parnell Formula One team in 1963.

Over the years, he competed with various teams, including some very small ones, one of which was under his own name – Chris Amon Racing. His most successful season was 1967, when he took three third places and finished fourth in the championship.

Mario Andretti

Amon also took part in a number of other events, including Le Mans 24 Hours, Daytona 24 Hours and Monza 1000, and a number of Formula 2 series.

Amon retired from Formula One in 1976 and returned to run the family farm in New Zealand and present television programmes.

Robert (Bob) ANDERSON

Nationality: British
Born: 19th May 1931
Died: 14th August 1967
Seasons: 1963-1967
Team/manufacturer(s): Reg Parnell Racing, DW Racing Enterprises
Grands Prix: 29
Race wins: 0
Championship wins: 0

Born in London, Bob Anderson began racing motorcycles before switching to competing in cars in 1961, when he drove a Lola in Formula Junior.

In 1963 he bought a second-hand Lola Formula One car and entered it as a privateer, in a team that consisted of not much more than Bob, his wife and a small number of mechanics. The following year he upgraded to a Brabham and managed a third-place finish at The Austrian Grand Prix, partly because a number of competitors retired with mechanical problems caused by the bumpy surface.

He was planning to retire at the end of the 1967 season, but tragedy struck. He was testing at Silverstone when his car left the track in very wet conditions and collided with a marshal's post. He suffered serious chest and neck injuries and died soon after.

Conny ANDERSSON

Nationality: Swedish
Born: 28th December 1939
Seasons: 1976-1977
Team/manufacturer(s): Surtees, BRM
Grands Prix: 5
Race wins: 0
Championship wins: 0

Conny Andersson was a successful motocross rider in his native Sweden, but juggled his racing with bringing up a family and helping to run his father's garage business.

After a session at a racing school, he got hooked on car racing and, by buying and selling second-hand cars, he raised enough money to buy a second-hand Brabham BT21 and start racing, at the age of 29.

From 1970 to 1976 Andersson raced in Formula 3 and made a good name for himself. However, he didn't have the money to break into Formula One.

In 1976, he was offered a one-off drive in a Surtees at the Dutch Grand Prix and, a year later, drove for BRM before giving up Formula One after the French Grand Prix.

Chris Amon

Mario Gabriele ANDRETTI

Nationality: American
Born: 28th February 1940
Seasons: 1968-1972, 1974-1982
Team/manufacturer(s): Lotus, STP Corporation, Ferrari, Parnelli, Alfa Romeo, Williams
Grands Prix: 131
Race wins: 12
Championship wins: 1

Mario Andretti is the only person to have won the Formula One World Championship, the Indianapolis 500 and the Daytona 500.

Michael Andretti

René Arnoux

Born in Italy, his family emigrated to the USA and settled in Pennsylvania. There, he and his twin brother, Aldo, took to racing an old Hudson around dirt tracks. Mario went on to compete in USAC sprint car and Indy car racing. In 1965 he entered the Indianapolis 500 and came third, taking the Rookie of the Year award (he went on to win the event in 1969; the first of four times).

Lotus team owner, Colin Chapman, had spotted Andretti's talents and had promised him a drive in one of his cars so, in 1968, Andretti entered his first Grand Prix, at Watkins Glen. Driving a Lotus 49B, he took pole position but had to retire from the race due to mechanical problems.

Andretti raced sporadically in Formula One for the next few years, winning his first race with a Ferrari in 1971 and also racing for the Parnelli team. However, he was continuing to compete in USAC events, and travelling back and forth on Concorde, so he was unable to devote himself fully to Formula One until 1976. Now back with Lotus in 1978 he claimed the World Championship.

Andretti and the Lotus team were unable to repeat their success and he had little luck over the next three seasons. He raced with Alfa Romeo in 1981 but returned to Ferrari at the end of the 1982 season, after which he retired from Formula One. He continued to race in Champ Car racing and competed many times at Le Mans.

Michael Mario ANDRETTI

Nationality: American
Born: 5th October 1962
Seasons: 1993
Team/manufacturer(s): McLaren
Grands Prix: 13
Race wins: 0
Championship wins: 0

The son of Mario Andretti, the famous American driver, Michael Andretti began racing in Super Vee in the early 1980s and soon became a force to be reckoned with, winning the championship in 1982 before going on to take the Formula Atlantic championship the following season.

Andretti went on to have some success in CART and at the Indianapolis 500, although he never won the latter.

In 1993, he spent a season with the McLaren Formula One team, driving alongside Ayrton Senna. Sadly, he struggled to cope with the more sophisticated cars and also commuted back and forth from the USA to Europe, rather than relocating. It wasn't a successful season, with Andretti retiring from seven of the 13 races he entered. That said, he did have some success, most notably at third place finish in Italy and he picked up seven Championship points in total that year.

After that, Andretti returned to CART until his retirement in 2007. He also continued to enter the Indy 500 but victory eluded him.

Marco APICELLA

Nationality: Italian
Born: 7th October 1965
Seasons: 1993
Team/manufacturer(s): Jordan
Grands Prix: 1
Race wins: 0
Championship wins: 0

Marco Apicella has the dubious distinction of having the shortest Formula One career ever, in terms of distance raced. He competed in the Italian Grand Prix at Monza, but was involved in a multiple car pile-up at the first chicane and was out of the race.

Before that, he was a successful Formula 3 and Formula 3000 driver. Indeed, after his crash at Monza, it was Formula 3000 commitments that stopped him from returning to Formula One.

Apicella continued in Formula 3000 and also competed at Le Mans and became involved in sports car racing. He is also a driving instructor at an Italian racing school.

Mário (Nicha) DE ARAÚJO CABRAL

Nationality: Portuguese
Born: 15th January 1934
Seasons: 1959-1960, 1963-1964
Team/manufacturer(s): Scuderia Centro Sud, Derrington Francis-ATS
Grands Prix: 4
Race wins: 0
Championship wins: 0

The first Portuguese Formula One driver, Mário de Araújo Cabral was more commonly known as Nicha Cabral.

He made his debut at the 1959 Portuguese Grand Prix at Monsanto Park, Lisbon. Cabral started near the back of the grid of 16 cars and was making his way forward when Jack Brabham tried to pass him but was forced off the track by the local man, almost putting Brabham out of the running for the championship that year. Cabral, meanwhile, finished in 10th place.

Cabral retired from Formula One after the 1964 season, but continued to enjoy racing in other events before retiring to his hometown of Lisbon.

René Alexandre ARNOUX

Nationality: French
Born: 4th July 1948
Seasons: 1978-1989
Team/manufacturer(s): Martini, Surtees, Renault, Ferrari, Ligier
Grands Prix: 165
Race wins: 7
Championship wins: 0

René Arnoux was born in Grenoble, in France and started off his career racing karts in Italy. He moved on to the Volant Shell championship and then Formula Renault, which he won in 1973. In 1975 he went on to take the European Super Renault title before moving into Formula 2 the following year. He won that championship in 1977 for Martini.

When Martini moved into Formula One, Arnoux went with them but had little success with uncompetitive cars, so he moved to Renault for 1979 and went on to finish sixth in the championship the following year.

Arnoux's best year was 1983 when, driving for Ferrari, he won the Canadian, German and Dutch Grands Prix and took third place in the championship.

After an unsuccessful time with Ligier, Arnoux retired from racing in 1989. He went on to be a partner in a Formula 3000 team, and has competed in the GP Masters series.

Peter ARUNDELL

Nationality: English
Born: 8th November 1933
Seasons: 1963-1964, 1966
Team/manufacturer(s): Lotus
Grands Prix: 13
Race wins: 0
Championship wins: 0

Peter Arundell hailed from Essex and started his career racing MGs. After a spell in the RAF after the war, he became a professional racing driver and, in 1962, he won the British Formula Junior championship in a Lotus 22. Indeed, he did so well that he was accused of using an illegally tuned engine.

Arundell's Formula One career began in 1963 when he started to drive for Lotus. However, he also raced in Formula 2 and a bad crash at Reims meant that he missed most of the 1965 season.

He returned to Formula One briefly in 1966, but retired from the championship at the end of the season. He then retired from racing completely in 1969 and later moved to Florida, where he set up a software company.

Alberto ASCARI

Nationality: Italian
Born: 13th July 1918
Died: 26th May 1955
Seasons: 1950-1955
Team/manufacturer(s): Ferrari, Maserati, Lancia
Grands Prix: 32
Race wins: 13
Championship wins: 2

Alberto Ascari was seven when his Grand Prix driver father was killed, but was determined to follow in his footsteps.

After racing motorcycles, Ascari's first car race was the 1940 Mille Miglia, driving a Ferrari and after the war he bought a 3CLT Maserati and won the 1948 San Remo Grand Prix.

He then drove for Ferrari in the first Formula One season in 1950 and ended the season in fifth place in the championship. In 1952, Ascari became the only European driver to race in the Indy 500 in the circuit's 11 years as a Formula One host. He failed to finish that race but it was the only Grand Prix which he didn't win that season! He walked away with the Drivers' Championship, and did so again in 1953 Ascari had less success in 1954, when he failed to finish a Formula One race. The 1955 season began in a similar vein, with Ascari retiring from the first two races, the second after

he spectacularly crashed into Monaco harbour after missing a chicane. The car sank into the bubbling water and, after a few tense seconds, the crowd saw Ascari's pale-blue helmet bob to the surface and he was hauled into a nearby boat.

A week later, on 26th May, Ascari was at Monza and decided to do a few fun laps in a friend's Sports Ferrari. Dressed in his ordinary clothes, he roared off. On the third lap, for reasons that have never been explained, the car skidded coming out of a bend, turned on its nose and somersaulted twice. Ascari was thrown onto the track and died of multiple injuries a few minutes later.

Peter ASHDOWN

Nationality: British
Born: 16th October 1934
Seasons: 1959
Team/manufacturer(s): non-works Cooper
Grands Prix: 1
Race wins: 0
Championship wins: 0

Essex-born Peter Ashdown made a name for himself in the British Formula Junior championship in the 1950s. However, he was involved in a bad accident at Rouen in 1958, when he broke his collarbone, which hampered his career.

In 1959, he raced a Formula 2 Cooper-Climax, entered by Alan Brown, at the British Grand Prix, which took place at Aintree that year. This was the only Formula One race in which he participated.

Ashdown then returned to Formula Junior, driving a Lola, before retiring from the sport in 1962. He went on to run Candy Apple, a race-orientated garage and had other business concerns. He retired to the South of France.

Ian ASHLEY

Nationality: British
Born: 26th October 1947
Seasons: 1974-1977
Team/manufacturer(s): Token, Williams, BRM, Hesketh
Grands Prix: 11
Race wins: 0
Championship wins: 0

Ian Ashley was born in Germany and began his racing career by taking a course at the Jim Russell Racing School in 1966. By 1972 he had entered Formula 5000 and won the championship the following year.

He began racing in Formula One in 1974 with the Token team, and had a brief spell with Williams the following year. Unfortunately, his fast but erratic driving led to some spectacular accidents and earned him the nickname 'Crashley'. A bad crash in 1975 led to him retiring from Formula One and becoming an airline pilot.

However, he continued racing in British Touring Cars and, later, the TVR Tuscan series, not to mention motorcycle sidecars. He is still involved in motorsport today.

Gerald (Gerry) ASHMORE

Nationality: British
Born: 25th July 1936
Seasons: 1961-1962
Team/manufacturer(s): Lotus
Grands Prix: 4
Race wins: 0
Championship wins: 0

Gerry Ashmore was born in Staffordshire and raced in Formula Junior alongside his brother, Chris, in 1960.

He graduated to Formula One, driving for Lotus, in 1961. That season he competed at the British, German and Italian Grands Prix, but he only completed the German event, taking 13th place. The following year he remained with Lotus but only competed in one Grand Prix that season; the Italian one. Sadly, though, he was disqualified from the race.

Ashmore continued to race in non-Formula One events before retiring to France.

He continued to take a keen interest in the sport, regularly attending historic events.

William (Bill) ASTON

Nationality: British
Born: 29th March 1900
Died: 4th March 1974
Seasons: 1952
Team/manufacturer(s): Aston Butterworth
Grands Prix: 3
Race wins: 0
Championship wins: 0

Bill Aston served in the First World War and went on to be a test pilot and motorcycle racer. In the 1940s he moved into racing cars, first in Formula Junior and then Formula 2.

However, racing remained a hobby, and Aston made his money as a civil engineer and a fruit farmer. Working with Archie Butterworth, he built his own Formula 2 cars in which he competed under his own team name.

He entered one of his cars in the 1952 Formula One series and attempted to race it at the British Grand Prix but failed to start because of mechanical failure.

In Germany that year the car packed up on the second lap, and Aston failed to qualify in Italy. Aston then went on to enjoy club racing, in cars such as a D-type Jaguar, Aston Martin DBR1, Mini and Jaguar 3.8 saloon.

Richard (Dickie) ATTWOOD

Nationality: British
Born: 4th April 1940
Seasons: 1964-1965, 1967-1969
Team/manufacturer(s): BRM, Reg Parnell, Cooper, Lotus
Grands Prix: 17
Race wins: 0
Championship wins: 0

The son of a motor trader, Richard Attwood started off his racing career in 1960 with a Triumph TR3 and then moved on to Formula Junior in 1963 and won at Monaco driving a Lola, for which he won £500 and gained valuable publicity.

He then moved on to Formula 2 and also began to compete in Formula One for BRM. He raced sporadically in Formula One over the years, and his high point was at Monaco in 1968, when he put in a stunning performance for BRM, chasing Graham Hill to finish in second place.

Sadly, he was unable to match this the following season and, after a number of disappointing finishes, he retired from Formula One to compete in sports car racing.

His greatest moment was in 1970, when he drove a Porsche 917 to victory at Le Mans, along with Hans Herrmann. Attwood retired from full time racing the following year, but has continued to race in historic events.

Alberto Ascari

B

Jenson Button

BADOER, Luca	BELL, Derek	BLEEKEMOLEN, Michael	BRANDON, Eric
BAGHETTI, Giancarlo	BELLOF, Stefan	BLOKDYK, Trevor	BRIDGER, Tom
BAILEY, Julian	BELMONDO, Paul	BLUNDELL, Mark	BRISE, Tony
BALDI, Mauro	BELSO, Tom	BOESEL, Raul	BRISTOW, Chris
BALSA, Marcel	BELTOISE, Jean Pierre	BONDURANT, Bob	BROEKER, Peter
BANDINI, Lorenzo	BERETTA, Olivier	BONETTO, Felice	BROOKS, Tony
BARBAZZA, Fabrizio	BERG, Allen	BONNIER, Jo	BROWN, Alan
BARBER, John	BERGER, Georges	BONOMI, Roberto	BROWN, Warwick
BARBER, Skip	BERGER, Gerhard	BORDEU, Juan Manuel	BRUDES, Adolf
BARILLA, Paolo	BERNARD, Eric	BORGUDD, Slim	BRUNDLE, Martin
BARRICHELLO, Rubens	BERNOLDI, Enrique	BOTHA, Luki	BRUNI, Gianmaria
BARTELS, Michael	BERTAGGIA, Enrico	BOULLION, Jean Christophe	BUCCI, Clemar
BARTH, Edgar	BEUTTLER, Mike	BOUTSEN, Thierry	BUCKNUM, Ronnie
BASSI, Giorgio	BHANUBANDH, Birabongse	BRABHAM, David	BUEB, Ivor
BAUER, Erwin	BIANCHI, Lucien	BRABHAM, Gary	BUENO, Luiz
BAUMGARTNER, Zsolt	BIANCO, Gino	BRABHAM, Jack	BURGESS, Ian
BAYOL, Elie	BINDER, Hans	BRACK, Bill	BURTI, Luciano
BEAUMAN, Don	BIONDETTI, Clemente	BRAMBILLA, Ernesto	BUSSSINELLO, Roberto
BECHEM, Karl Gunther	BIRGER, Pablo	BRAMBILLA, Vittorio	BUTTON, Jenson
BEHRA, Jean	BLANCHARD, Harry	BRANCATELLI, Gianfranco	BYRNE, Tommy

Giancarlo Baghetti

Luca Badoer

Luca BADOER

Nationality: Italian
Born: 25th January 1971
Seasons: 1993, 1995-1996, 1999
Team/manufacturer(s): BMS Scuderia Italia, Minardi, Forti Corse
Grands Prix: 56
Race wins: 0
Championship wins: 0

Italian Luca Badoer started his career in karts and became Italian champion before progressing to Formula 3 and then Formula 3000, of which he was champion in 1992.

Badoer entered Formula One in 1993, driving for Scuderia Italia, which was later taken over by Minardi. Badoer then worked as a test driver, but did some races in 1995.

After an unsuccessful spell with Forti Corse in 1996, Badoer worked as a test driver for Ferrari, briefly returning to Formula One in 1999, again with Minardi.

By 2000, Badoer was the driver who had competed in the most Grands Prix without scoring a point. At this time he decided to retire from racing and became a test-driver for Ferrari again.

His moment of fame came in 2006, when he doughnut-ted a Ferrari Formula One car at the opening ceremony of the 2006 Winter Olympics in Italy; a dramatic stunt seen by millions around the world.

Giancarlo BAGHETTI

Nationality: Italian
Born: 25th December 1934
Died: 27th November 1995
Seasons: 1961-1967
Team/manufacturer(s): Ferrari, ATS (Ita), Scuderia Centro Sud, Brabham, Reg Parnell, Lotus
Grands Prix: 21
Race wins: 1
Championship wins: 0

Giancarlo Baghetti began racing in production cars in 1955, and moved to Formula Junior in 1958. He was then picked to drive a Ferrari Formula 2 car in non-championship races in 1961.

Baghetti's claim to fame is that he won his first ever Formula One race – the 1961 French Grand Prix. Sadly, though, he was never to achieve another win during his Grand Prix career. He moved to the ATS team in 1963 but

failed to finish a race that season. From there, Baghetti drove for Scuderia Centro Sud the following year, and then competed in just one race a season for the next three years.

Baghetti later raced in touring cars and Formula 2, but retired after a bad accident in 1968. He then became a motorsport and fashion journalist and photographer, before dying of cancer in 1995.

Julian BAILEY

Nationality: British
Born: 9th October 1961
Seasons: 1988, 1991
Team/manufacturer(s): Tyrrell, Lotus
Grands Prix: 20
Race wins: 0
Championship wins: 0

After being born in London, Julian Bailey was brought up in Spain. However, he returned to the UK to race in Formula Ford. In 1986 he moved to Formula 3000 and became the first British driver to win a race in this formula.

The following year he was contracted to drive for Tyrrell, alongside Jonathan Palmer. However, Bailey failed to win any points and changed to sports car racing the following year.

In 1991, Bailey returned to Formula One, this time driving for Lotus, but didn't complete the season.

Bailey later moved into British Touring Cars and then sports cars, winning the FIA GT Championship in 2000.

Mauro BALDI

Nationality: Italian
Born: 31st January 1954
Seasons: 1982-1985
Team/manufacturer(s): Arrows, Alfa Romeo, Spirit
Grands Prix: 41
Race wins: 0
Championship wins: 0

Julian Bailey

Italian Mauro Baldi is unusual in that he started his race career in rallying, in 1972, moving on to track driving in 1975 when he competed in the Italian Renault 5 Cup series.

However, Baldi's career really took off in 1981, when he won the European Formula 3 Championship. This got the attention of the Arrows Formula One team, which signed him for the 1982 season.

Baldi went on to drive for Alfa Romeo the following year and then Spirit in 1984. However, after 1985 he switched to sports car racing and, in 1990, won the World Sportscar Championship, driving for Sauber-Mercedes.

He also won the Le Mans 24 Hour race in 1994 and, in 1998, he won both the 24 Hours of Daytona and the 12 Hours of Sebring events.

Marcel Lucien BALSA

Nationality: French
Born: 1st January 1901
Died: 11th August 1984
Seasons: 1952
Team/manufacturer(s): Balsa
Grands Prix: 1
Race wins: 0
Championship wins: 0

Marcel Balsa was born in Creuse, in the Limousin district, and began racing in earnest after the Second World War.

He was an enthusiastic amateur and bought a Bugatti Type 51 which he had some success racing in French national events. However, he realised that he needed something more competitive and so built a BMW-engined Formula 2 special. He raced this and a Jicey-BMW in pre-Formula One Grands Prix.

In 1952 he competed in his only Formula One Grand Prix, at the Nürburgring in Germany, but retired after six laps.

Lorenzo BANDINI

Nationality: Italian
Born: 21st December 1935
Died: 10th May 1967
Seasons: 1961-1967
Team/manufacturer(s): Scuderia Centro Sud, Ferrari
Grands Prix: 42
Race wins: 1
Championship wins: 0

Italian Lorenzo Bandini was born in North Africa, where his family had fled to escape Mussolini. However, he went back to his homeland when war broke out and his father was murdered.

After a difficult childhood, he did some racing in a Fiat 1100 and then competed in the 1959 Mille Miglia, driving a Lancia, in which he won his class.

He then competed in Formula Junior before joining the Scuderia Centro Sud Formula One team in 1961, in which year he raced in four World Championship events.

Bandini moved to Ferrari in 1962, racing mainly sports cars, although he participated in three Grands Prix that season. After winning at Le Mans in 1963, he returned to Scuderia Centro Sud and competed in some Formula One events, as well as sports car races.

He won the first-ever Austrian Grand Prix in 1964 but, on the whole, had more success in sport cars – he won the 1965 Targa Florio and 1967 Daytona 24 Hours.

At the 1967 Monaco Grand Prix, Bandini was back with Ferrari under pressure to win. He was chasing for first place

when his car rolled and caught fire. He died of his burns three days later.

Fabrizio BARBAZZA

Nationality: Italian
Born: 2nd April 1963
Seasons: 1991, 1993
Team/manufacturer(s): AGS, Minardi
Grands Prix: 20
Race wins: 0
Championship wins: 0

Fabrizio Barbazza hails from Monza and was a motocross rider in his teens. In 1982 he began competing in Formula Monza and then, a year later, he moved to Italian Formula 3. By 1985 he finished a respectable third in the championship.

From there Barbazza went across the Atlantic to compete in the American Racing Series, where he took the title in his first season. In 1987, he was CART's Rookie of the Year, and then moved to Formula 3000 for 1990.

Just a year after that, in 1991, he joined the AGS Formula One team but failed to qualify for any races that season. Barbazza moved to Minardi in 1993, where he had more success.

In 1995, he crashed a Ferrari in which he was racing and was badly injured. Once recovered, he decided to retire from racing. He returned to Monza to run a kart track and did some design work on crash-barriers. Barbazza later moved to Cuba to run a fishing resort.

John BARBER

Nationality: English
Born: 22nd July 1929
Seasons: 1953
Team/manufacturer(s): Cooper
Grands Prix: 1
Race wins: 0
Championship wins: 0

John Barber was born in Buckinghamshire in 1929 and, as an adult, worked as a fish merchant at London's

Lorenzo Bandini

Paolo Barilla

Billingsgate Market.

He first raced a Cooper-JAP and then bought a Formula 2 Cooper-Bristol Mk1 which he raced during 1952. Despite winning a minor race at Snetterton, he had little success and finally crashed the car badly towards the end of the season.

At the start of 1953, Barber travelled to Argentina to compete in the Grand Prix there, in which he came a worthy eighth. He also competed in the Buenos Aires Libre race and finished 12th.

Back in England, he raced a Golding-Cooper, which may have been built from the remains of his crashed Mk1. While racing this car, he was involved in an accident which killed another driver, James Neilson. Barber sold the car soon after. He next raced in 1955, driving a Jaguar C-type.

It is believed that Barber retired to live on a boat in the Mediterranean.

John (Skip) BARBER III

Nationality: American
Born: 16th November 1936
Seasons: 1971-1972
Team/manufacturer(s): Gene Mason Racing/March
Grands Prix: 6
Race wins: 0
Championship wins: 0

John Barber III was born in Philadelphia, USA, and is more commonly known as 'Skip' Barber.

He began his racing days in Formula Ford in 1969. In 1971, though, he bought a March 711 race car in Europe which he planned to take back to the USA and use for racing in the Formula 5000 competition.

Before that, however, Barber raced it in the Monaco and Dutch Grands Prix that season, as a privateer. He also competed in the US and Canadian Grands Prix that year and the following.

Barber went on to race GT cars and then retired from racing to start the Skip Barber Racing School, which has grown to have branches around the USA. He later sold this and became part-owner of the Lime Rock racing circuit.

Paolo BARILLA

Nationality: Italian
Born: 20th April 1961
Seasons: 1989-1990
Team/manufacturer(s): Minardi
Grands Prix: 15
Race wins: 0
Championship wins: 0

Milan-born Paolo Barilla came from the wealthy Barilla family, which made its money from pasta. He started racing karts in 1975 and, the following year, won the Italian 100cc kart championship.

In 1980 he moved up to Formula Fiat Abarth and then Formula 3 in 1981, where he finished a respectable third in the Italian championship. This led to a move to Formula 2, driving for Minardi, in 1982.

Unusually, Barilla then moved to sports car racing between 1983 and 1988, and did very well, even winning the Le Mans 24 Hours in 1985.

In 1987, Barilla returned to single-seat racing and competed in the Japanese Formula 3000 Championship. By 1989, he was back with Minardi, this time racing in Formula One. Unfortunately, though, he failed to qualify for many races and left the team before the end of the 1990 season.

Barilla then retired from racing and went to help run his family business, which sponsored disabled racing driver, Alex Zanardi.

Rubens Gonçalves BARRICHELLO

Nationality: Brazilian
Born: 23rd May 1972
Seasons: 1993-
Team/manufacturer(s): Jordan, Stewart, Ferrari, Honda
Grands Prix: 253
Race wins: 9
Championship wins: 0

As a youngster, Rubens Barrichello won five karting championships in Brazil. He then moved to Europe in 1990 to compete in Formula Lotus where he won the championship. He did the same a year later in British Formula 3.

After a short spell in Formula 3000, Barrichello joined the Jordan Formula One team for 1993, where he soon gained a reputation for being an impressive driver.

A crash during practice at San Marino the following year almost killed him, but he recovered enough to finish sixth in the championship at the end of the season.

Barrichello spent an unfulfilled time with Stewart Grand Prix from 1997 to 1999, although he did finish seventh in the championship that last year. After that, he was poached by Ferrari, where he stayed until the end of 2005.

The problem he had at Ferrari was that he was always second fiddle to Michael Schumacher and had to follow team orders to ensure that the German finished before him at a number of races. By the end of the 2005 season, Barrichello had had enough and so moved to Honda, driving with Jenson Button during 2006 and 2007.

Rubens Barrichello

Michael BARTELS

Nationality: German
Born: 8th March 1968
Seasons: 1991
Team/manufacturer(s): Lotus
Grands Prix: 4
Race wins: 0
Championship wins: 0

Born in Plettenberg, Michael Bartels made a name for himself as a teenager when, in 1985, he became the German karting champion. Just a year later, he rose to the top of his country's Formula 3 championship.

Sadly, his one season with the Lotus Formula One team was less successful. He failed to qualify in any of the four Grands Prix he entered.

Bartels went on to race in the FIA GT championship with some success. His other claim to fame is that he went out with tennis player Steffi Graf for seven years.

Edgar BARTH

Nationality: German
Born: 26th January 1917
Died: 20th May 1965
Seasons: 1953, 1958, 1960, 1964
Team/manufacturer(s): EMW, Porsche, Cooper
Grands Prix: 5
Race wins: 0
Championship wins: 0

Edgar Barth started off racing motorcycles in Eastern Germany before switching to BMW sportscars. In 1957, he moved to West Germany and drove for Porsche, winning the 1959 Targa Florio for the company.

Barth also competed for a number of years in the Le Mans 24 Hour race, driving Porsches.

His Formula One appearances were all at the German Grand Prix. The first, he was driving for EMW (what was BMW in Eastern Europe before the war), then twice for Porsche and, finally, for Cooper. He died of cancer less than a year later.

Edgar's famous son, Jürgen Barth, was also closely involved with Porsche, becoming an engineer and then a driver, winning Le Mans in 1977.

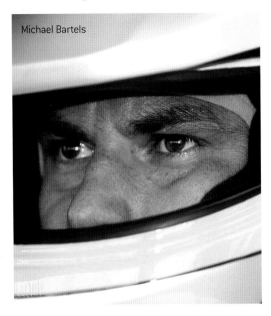

Michael Bartels

Zsolt Baumgartner

Giorgio BASSI

Nationality: Italian
Born: 20th January 1934
Seasons: 1965
Team/manufacturer(s): Scuderia Centro Sud
Grands Prix: 1
Race wins: 0
Championship wins: 0

Giorgio Bassi hailed from Milan and was a regular Formula 3 driver in the early 1960s, driving a De Tomaso Ford. His best result was a third place finish at Monza in 1964. However, the following year he managed to win his class at the Targa Florio, driving a 1000cc ASA prototype.

Bassi's one and only Formula One appearance was driving a Scuderia Centro Sud BRM at the 1965 Italian Grand Prix at his home town of Monza. Sadly, he retired after just eight laps.

Erwin BAUER

Nationality: German
Born: 17th July 1912
Died: 3rd June 1958
Seasons: 1953
Team/manufacturer(s): Veritas
Grands Prix: 1
Race wins: 0
Championship wins: 0

Erwin Bauer was a keen amateur driver who made a name for himself in 1954 when, against all odds, he drove an underpowered Lotus to fourth place at the Nürburgring 1000km event that year. It was one of Lotus's best continental results to date. Bauer's one Formula One appearance was a year earlier at the German Grand Prix, held at the Nürburgring. There he drove a German Veritas RS for just one lap before retiring. The Nürburgring was to be the place where Bauer met his end. Driving a 2-litre Ferrari in the 1958 1000km event, he failed to realise that the race had, in fact, come to an end, and carried on competing during the slowing down lap, and crashed.

Zsolt BAUMGARTNER

Nationality: Hungarian
Born: 1st January 1981
Seasons: 2003-2004
Team/manufacturer(s): Jordan, Minardi
Grands Prix: 20
Race wins: 0
Championship wins: 0

At the age of 13, Zsolt Baumgartner began racing cars in Hungary. By 1997, he was competing in the German Formula Renault Championship, followed by spells in Formula 3 and Formula 3000.

In August 2003, he bought himself a place as Jordan's test driver and, after teammate Ralph Firman was injured in a crash, Baumgartner made his debut at the Hungarian Grand Prix. It was particularly apt that this was on his home territory because he was the first ever Hungarian Formula One driver. Baumgartner also took Firman's place in Italy that season.

The following year, Baumgartner drove full-time for

Minardi and managed to gain the team its first point in two years when he came eighth in the US Grand Prix. Other than that, though, he failed to shine.

Élie Marcel BAYOL

Nationality: French
Born: 28th February 1914
Died: 25th May 1995
Seasons: 1952-1956
Team/manufacturer(s): OSCA, Gordini
Grands Prix: 8
Race wins: 0
Championship wins: 0

Élie Bayol was born in Marseilles and enjoyed racing DB-Panhards in Formula 2 and hillclimbs in his native France, during the early 1950s. His best result during this period was a fourth place at the Circuit de Cadours in 1951.

Bayol was an occasional Formula One driver, entering eight races over five seasons. For the first two of these years, he drove for the Italian OSCA team, which was formed by members of the Maserati family. He then moved to Gordini in 1954.

The only Formula One points Bayol gained were two points after finishing fifth at the Argentina Grand Prix in 1955. He made just one appearance in the 1956 season, at Monaco, and then faded away from the racing scene.

Donald (Don) BEAUMAN

Nationality: English
Born: 28th July 1928
Died: 9th July 1955
Seasons: 1954
Team/manufacturer(s): Connaught
Grands Prix: 1
Race wins: 0
Championship wins: 0

Born in Farnborough, Don Beauman was a friend of driver, Mike Hawthorn, and started off racing sportscars, where he proved himself as a good driver.

In 1954, Beauman joined the British Connaught team and began competing in Formula One and Formula 2. The one and only Grand Prix he raced in was the British event at Silverstone that year, when he finished a respectable seventh place.

Beauman continued to impress in non-championship races throughout the season and into the next. Tragically, though, he was killed the weekend before the British Grand Prix, when he crashed his ex-Hawthorn Riley at the Leinster Trophy race.

Karl-Günther BECHEM (Bernhard Nacke)

Nationality: German
Born: 21st December 1921
Seasons: 1952-1953
Team/manufacturer(s): BMW, AFM
Grands Prix: 2
Race wins: 0
Championship wins: 0

Amateur driver Günther Bechem began racing BMWs in the 1950s, but his family disapproved. So when he started competing in Formula One, at the 1952 German Grand Prix, he adopted the name 'Bernhard Nacke'; a name that stuck with him throughout his career.

He was driving a BMW at this Nürburgring race but retired after just five laps. Bechem had another attempt at the same race the following year, driving for AFM but, this time, he managed just two laps of the demanding circuit.

In 1954, Bechem entered the Carrera Panamericana driving a Rennsports car. At one point he was leading the gruelling race but then, at the end of the fourth leg of the 2000-mile race, he suffered a bad crash. Bechem recovered from his injuries but never raced again.

Jean Marie BEHRA

Nationality: French
Born: 16th February 1921
Died: 1st August 1959
Seasons: 1952-1959
Team/manufacturer(s): Gordini, Maserati, BRM, Ferrari, Porsche
Grands Prix: 58
Race wins: 0
Championship wins: 0

Jean Behra was a successful motorbike racer both before and after the Second World War. Indeed, racing for Moto Guzzi, he won four French national titles between 1948 and 1951.

In 1949, though, he tried racing a Maserati and was hooked. Before long he was competing in the Monte Carlo rally and at Le Mans.

He was soon signed by Gordini, despite being older than average for a Grand Prix driver. Behra then shot to fame by winning the non-championship Reims Grand Prix in 1952. Unfortunately, this became typical throughout his Formula One days – he had plenty of successes but not in championship Grands Prix.

Outside Formula One, Behra also had more luck, including winning the Sebring 12 Hours race with Fangio in 1957.

While driving in a sportscar event in Berlin in 1959, Behra lost control of his Porsche RSK on the wet track and crashed at high speed. He was killed instantly.

Derek Reginald BELL MBE

Nationality: English
Born: 31st October 1941
Seasons: 1968-1972, 1974
Team/manufacturer(s): Ferrari, McLaren, Brabham, Surtees, Tecno
Grands Prix: 16
Race wins: 0
Championship wins: 0

Derek Bell first raced in a Lotus Seven, back in 1964. He then moved swiftly into Formula 3 with a Lotus 31 and, by 1967, had won seven races in that series.

Next up was Formula 2, racing a Brabham run by his

Derek Bell

Paul Belmondo

step-father's team, Church Farm Racing. Before long, his sparkling performances were spotted by Ferrari, who signed him for the 1968 season. He continued to sporadically compete in Formula One but had little real success.

Where Bell really shone, however, was in sportscar racing. He won two World Sportscar Championships, three Daytona 24 Hour races and – most significantly – won the Le Mans 24 Hour no less than five times.

Bell went on to do consultancy work for Bentley, among others, and commentates on Formula One races. His son, Justin, is also a well-known race driver.

Stefan BELLOF

Nationality: German
Born: 20th November 1957
Died: 1st September 1985
Seasons: 1984-1985
Team/manufacturer(s): Tyrrell
Grands Prix: 22
Race wins: 0
Championship wins: 0

Stefan Bellof quickly rose to prominence in German racing, and became known outside his own country when, in 1982, he unexpectedly won Formula 2 races in Britain and Germany. This drew the attention of the big players

and, that year, he was signed by the Rothmans Porsche team to drive in the World Endurance Championship.

However, Formula One teams were keen to sign him, too, and so, in 1984, he began driving for Tyrrell, while still involved in sportscar racing, winning the World Endurance Championship that year.

He soon made his mark in Formula One, though, finishing sixth in Belgium and fifth at Imola. He also put in a stunning performance at Monaco, catching Prost and Senna, before rain stopped the race.

Bellof was tipped to be a future World Champion, but it was not to be. He was killed at the 1985 Spa 1000km race, after his Porsche 956 crashed. Michael Schumacher says that Bellof was his childhood idol.

Paul BELMONDO

Nationality: French
Born: 23rd April 1963
Seasons: 1992, 1994
Team/manufacturer(s): March, Pacific
Grands Prix: 27
Race wins: 0
Championship wins: 0

The son of famous French actor, Jean-Paul Belmondo, Paul Belmondo worked his way through Formula 3 and

Formula 3000. He joined the March Formula One team as a pay driver in 1992, driving at a number of Grands Prix and even managing to finish a respectable ninth place at Hungary that year. Lack of money stopped him from continuing with March.

Two years later Belmondo joined the Pacific team, but he only qualified for two races. That was the end of his Formula One career, and he went on to compete in GT racing, starting his own team, Paul Belmondo Racing.

Belmondo is also known for having dating Princess Stéphanie of Monaco when the two were teenagers.

Tom BELSØ

Nationality: Danish
Born: 27th August 1942
Seasons: 1973-1974
Team/manufacturer(s): Williams
Grands Prix: 5
Race wins: 0
Championship wins: 0

Tom Belsø was born in Copenhagen and started his career racing Touring Cars. He moved to Formula 2 in 1972 and then Formula 5000 a year later, when he took part in the Race of Champions and the International Trophy where he finished seventh and eighth respectively.

Belsø drove for Williams in 1973 and qualified for the Swedish Grand Prix, but was unable to race because of a problem with sponsorship money.

The following year, he also drove for Williams, but only got past qualifying in South Africa and Sweden. At the latter he finished a respectable eighth place.

Living in England, Belsø formed Belsø Foods in 1977, selling the sort of healthy cereals that he ate as a sportsman. He still races occasionally in historic events.

Jean-Pierre Maurice Georges BELTOISE

Nationality: French
Born: 26th April 1937
Seasons: 1967-1974
Team/manufacturer(s): Matra, Tyrrell, BRM
Grands Prix: 87
Race wins: 1
Championship wins: 0

Frenchman Jean-Pierre Beltoise was a successful motorcycle racer, winning 11 national titles in just three years.

He then moved to competing in cars, but his career was almost cut short when he was involved in a massive crash at Reims in 1963. Luckily, though, he walked away with just a broken arm.

After a season in Formula 3, Beltoise moved to Formula 2 in 1966 and had a couple of good seasons. This led to him entering Formula One, driving a V12 Matra. In 1968 he had managed to finish an incredible second place at the Dutch Grand Prix and, the following year, he was recruited by Tyrrell to drive full time in Formula One, alongside Jackie Stewart. That year, he finished second at the French Grand Prix.

In 1972, Beltoise moved to BRM and had his one and only Formula One win at Monaco in heavy rain.

Tom Belso

Jean-Pierre Beltoise

Olivier Beretta

After retiring from Formula One at the end of 1974, Beltoise got involved in touring cars, winning the French title twice. He also ran a kart track in Paris and his two sons are keen racing drivers.

Olivier BERETTA

Nationality: Monegasque
Born: 23rd November 1969
Seasons: 1994
Team/manufacturer(s): Larrousse
Grands Prix: 10
Race wins: 0
Championship wins: 0

Hailing from Monaco, Olivier Beretta surely was destined to become a racing driver. After some success in karts, he moved to Formula 3, in France and Britain, and had reasonable results.

A move to Formula 3000 in 1992 led to a slow start followed by a dramatic win at Donington the following year. He finished the series in sixth place and was already getting a taste for Formula One, having tested for Lotus.

In 1994, Beretta drove for the Larrousse Formula One team, but bad luck and mechanical problems hampered his season. The highpoint came in Germany that year, when he came from the back of the grid to finish seventh.

Beretta then retired from Formula One and went on to be a great success in sportscar racing. He still lives in Monaco.

Allen BERG

Nationality: Canadian
Born: 1st August 1961
Seasons: 1986
Team/manufacturer(s): Osella
Grands Prix: 9
Race wins: 0
Championship wins: 0

Allen Berg began racing karts in Alberta and, at the age of 19, moved to Canadian Formula Ford, where he finished second in 1981. Next came a year with Formula Atlantic, in which he won Rookie of the Year.

He then left Canada to race in the Australian Formula Pacific Tasman Championship, which he won and so was then offered a place in British Formula 3 for 1983.

Despite a successful couple of seasons, Berg was unable to continue to find backing and ended up returning home to Canada to earn some money. However, by 1986 he'd saved enough to get in with Osella as a pay driver that season. He qualified for nine races but made no real impression.

Berg finally returned to Canada yet again and continued to race whenever possible. He later set up his own Formula Junior team.

Georges BERGER

Nationality: Belgian
Born: 14th September 1918
Died: 23rd August 1967
Seasons: 1953-1954
Team/manufacturer(s): Simca-Gordini
Grands Prix: 2
Race wins: 0
Championship wins: 0

Georges Berger was an amateur racing driver who began competing in a number of race series, including Formula 2, during the 1950s. His greatest success at that time was a third place at the 1950 Grand Prix des Frontieres at Chimay.

He began racing in a Simca-Gordini car in 1953 and entered the Belgian Grand Prix that year, but retired with engine failure after just three laps. The following year, Berger attempted the French Grand Prix at Reims but, once again, he had to retire because of mechanical problems.

Berger then moved away from single-seat racing and moved to sportscars. The high point of his career was driving a Ferrari to victory at the 1960 Tour de France. He was killed when his Porsche 911 crashed during a race at the Nürburgring in 1967.

Gerhard BERGER

Nationality: Austrian
Born: 27th August 1959
Seasons: 1984-1997
Team/manufacturer(s): ATS, Arrows, Benetton, Ferrari, McLaren
Grands Prix: 210
Race wins: 10
Championship wins: 0

Gerhard Berger began racing Alfa Suds then moved quickly up to Formula 3, where he soon proved himself to be a useful driver. By 1984, he'd caught the attention of the Formula One world and was offered the chance to drive for ATS at the Austrian Grand Prix.

The following season he was signed for Arrows but his career really took off in 1986, when he drove for Benetton and won his first Grand Prix in Mexico. This led to him being signed by Ferrari, where he did well, most noticeably winning the Italian Grand Prix just weeks after the death of Enzo Ferrari.

Between 1990 and 1992, Berger drove for McLaren and became good friends with his teammate, Ayrton Senna, as well as continuing to perform superbly.

By 1993, Ferrari was struggling and brought Berger back to help turn around its fortunes. The Austrian delivered by winning at Hockenheim; the team's first victory for three years. After 1995, Berger felt he would become overshadowed by Michael Schumacher and so moved to Benetton. There, he won again at Hockenheim in 1997.

After retiring from racing at the end of 1997, Berger

Gerhard Berger

became Competitions Director for BMW and, later, took a stake in the Scuderia Toro Rosso team.

Éric BERNARD

Nationality: French
Born: 24th August 1964
Seasons: 1989-1991, 1994
Team/manufacturer(s): Larrousse, Ligier, Lotus
Grands Prix: 47
Race wins: 0
Championship wins: 0

After earning his stripes karting, Éric Bernard won himself a sponsored drive in Formula Renault for 1984. A year later, he won the series and entered French Formula 3 in 1986, winning that series the following year.

After a season in Formula 3000, Bernard drove for Larrousse in the 1989 French Grand Prix and put in a good show, running in seventh place when his engine blew up. After driving at the British Grand Prix that year, Bernard was given a full-time place on the Larrousse team for 1990. In that first year, he gained a sixth place at Monaco and a fourth in Britain.

After a break from Formula One, Bernard moved to Ligier as a test driver in 1993 and was soon promoted to team driver, alongside Olivier Panis. That year, he managed to take third place at the German Grand Prix before being dropped by the team.

Bernard then had a one-off drive with Lotus at the

Éric Bernard

Enrique Bernoldi

European Grand Prix. He then moved onto a successful career racing sportscars before running the KTM Gauloises team.

Enrique Antônio Langue e Silvério de BERNOLDI

Nationality: Brazilian
Born: 19th October 1978
Seasons: 2001-2002
Team/manufacturer(s): Arrows
Grands Prix: 29
Race wins: 0
Championship wins: 0

After starting out racing karts in Brazil at the age of 9, Enrique Bernoldi moved to Europe as a teenager to race Formula Alfa Boxer in Italy, and came fourth in his first race. He moved to Formula Renault, and won the championship in his second season.

After a successful spell in British Formula 3 and Formula 3000, Bernoldi tested for the Sauber in 1999 but failed to get a place. However, Arrows went on to offer him a drive in 2001 and he had a successful season,

despite getting bad publicity after he blocked David Coulthard from winning the Monaco Grand Prix. He remained with Arrows for part of the following year and then left Formula One.

Bernoldi went on to race in the Nissan World Series and, in 2004, was a test driver for BAR.

Enrico BERTAGGIA

Nationality: Italian
Born: 19th September 1964
Seasons: 1989, 1992
Team/manufacturer(s): Coloni, Andrea Moda
Grands Prix: 8
Race wins: 0
Championship wins: 0

Enrico Bertaggia was the son of a Venice hotel owner and raced karts as a boy. In 1985, he took a major step into Formula 3 and, two years later, he won the Italian championship.

A move to Formula 3000 in 1988 was not a success, so Bertaggia went back to Formula 3 the next year. Also in 1989, he was offered a drive with the Coloni Formula One team, but was the slowest entrant in all six Grands Prix he entered, failing to qualify in any of them.

In 1992, he entered two more Grands Prix, this time with the Andrea Moda team but, once again, had no success.

Bertaggia later moved to England where he became Maserati's chief driving instructor.

Michael (Mike) BEUTTLER

Nationality: British
Born: 13th April 1940
Died: 29th December 1988
Seasons: 1971-1973
Team/manufacturer(s): Non-works March
Grands Prix: 29
Race wins: 0
Championship wins: 0

Mike Beuttler was British but born in Cairo, Egypt. He proved himself as a talented driver in Formula 3 during the 1960s and worked his way up through Formula 2 and onto Formula One.

His private team was funded by a group of wealthy stockbroker friends and he began his first season by driving a rented March 711 car. For his following seasons, though, he graduated to a newer March 721.

Beuttler had mixed results in Formula One, his best finish being a seventh place at the 1973 Spanish Grand Prix. He then retired from racing at the end of that season.

He later moved to the United States where, in 1988, he died of an AIDs-related illness.

Birabongse Bhanutej BHANUBANDH (Prince Bira)

Nationality: Thai
Born: 15th July 1914
Died: 23rd December 1985
Seasons: 1935-1939, 1950-1954
Team/manufacturer(s): HWM, Simca-Gordini, Connaught, Milano
Grands Prix: 19
Race wins: 0
Championship wins: 0

Prince Birabongse Bhanutej Bhanubandh was part of the Siam royal family and grandson of King Mongkut, who was

Éric Bernard

immortalised in the musical 'The King and I'. Commonly known as Prince Bira, he was educated at Eton and Cambridge and settled in the UK.

Bira's cousin ran White Mouse Racing and, in 1936, Bira began driving an ERA for the team, winning a race at Monte Carlo and being generally successful.

After the war, Bira tried unsuccessfully to resurrect White Mouse before going on to race a Maserati privately. He then raced for other teams but, in 1953, he was back to his own Maserati, which was painted in the blue and yellow Thai racing colours. His best Grand Prix victory was a fourth place at Reims in 1954.

After the 1954 season, Bira retired from racing and went to live in Thailand. He died of a heart attack on the London Underground in 1985.

Luciano (Lucien) BIANCHI
Nationality: Belgian
Born: 10th November 1934
Died: 30th March 1969
Seasons: 1959-1963, 1965, 1968
Team/manufacturer(s): Cooper, Emeryson, Lotus, ENB, Lola, BRM
Grands Prix: 19
Race wins: 0
Championship wins: 0

Lucien Bianchi was born in Italy but brought up in Belgium, where his race-mechanic father was working. Bianchi was soon hooked on racing himself and, aged just 17, he entered the Alpine Rally in 1951. He worked hard to earn money to race and won the Tour de France Automobile in 1957, 1958 and 1959.

Bianchi first attempted Formula One in 1959, driving an old Cooper at Monaco, but was disqualified. He continued to enter Formula One races through the years, but had more success in other events; most notably winning Le Mans in 1968, driving a Ford GT40 with Pedro Rodriguez.

He rejoined Formula One in 1968 and was planning to continue, but was killed when the Alfa Romeo T33 he was testing at Le Mans went out of control and hit a telegraph pole.

Luigi Emilio Rodolfo (Gino) Bertetti BIANCO
Nationality: Brazilian
Born: 22nd July 1916
Died: 8th May 1984
Seasons: 1952
Team/manufacturer(s): Maserati
Grands Prix: 4
Race wins: 0
Championship wins: 0

Gino Bianco's full name was Luigi Emilio Rodolfo Bertetti Bianco. Although born in Turin, Italy, he was brought up in Brazil, after his family emigrated there when he was 12 years old. He started out as a mechanic, but soon began competing in hillclimb events. In 1952 he joined Eitel Cantoni's Escuderia Bandeirantes, driving a Maserati A6GCM in both Brazil and Europe, but with little noteworthy success.

In 1954, he raced for the Maserati Formula One team, competing in a total of four races. His best finish was 18th place at the British Grand Prix that year.

Hans BINDER
Nationality: Austrian
Born: 12th June 1948
Seasons: 1976-1978
Team/manufacturer(s): Ensign, Wolf, Surtees, ATS
Grands Prix: 15
Race wins: 0
Championship wins: 0

Born in Innsbruck, Austria, Hans Binder made a promising start to his career when he won the European Formula Ford Championship in 1972.

In 1976, he moved up to Formula Two and, in the same year, he raced for the Ensign Formula One team, at the Austrian and Japanese Grands Prix, but failed to finish either race.

Mark Blundell

The following year, he raised the sponsorship necessary to buy a place in the Surtees team for part of the season, although he also raced three times for ATS that year. His best result that year was eighth place at the Dutch Grand Prix at Zandvoort.

In 1978, Binder failed to qualify for the Austrian Grand Prix, driving with ATS again. He then retired from Formula One and went on to run the family sawmill in Austria.

Clemente BIONDETTI

Nationality: Italian
Born: 18th August 1898
Died: 24th February 1955
Seasons: 1950
Team/manufacturer(s): Ferrari
Grands Prix: 1
Race wins: 0
Championship wins: 0

Clemente Biondetti grew up in rural Sardinia and did not begin racing until his family moved to Florence in the 1920s. There, he got involved in motorcycle racing, followed by cycle cars in which he won his class in the national championship in 1923.

By 1931, he raced in the Tripoli Grand Prix, in the light-car category. Biondetti then became a factory driver for Maserati and finished third in the French and Rome Grands Prix. In other events, he won the Mille Miglia in 1938, 1947, 1948 and 1949; more times than any other driver. In the last two of those years, he also won the Targa Florio.

By 1950, Biondetti was driving for the Jaguar sportscar team and suggested that the team's engine was good enough to compete in the new Formula One championship. Jaguar wasn't interested, so he went away and fitted a Jag engine in the back of a Ferrari 166. He drove this in his one and only Formula One race, the Italian Grand Prix, but had to retire with engine problems.

Mark Blundell

He continued to race in other events, despite suffering from cancer for many years. The illness forced him to retire in 1957 and he died early the following year.

Pablo BIRGER

Nationality: Argentinean
Born: 7th January 1924
Died: 9th March 1966
Seasons: 1953, 1955
Team/manufacturer(s): Ferrari
Grands Prix: 2
Race wins: 0
Championship wins: 0

Pablo Birger came from Buenos Aires in Argentina. There, he raced in the Mecánica Nacional series, as well as other local events.

In 1953, he entered the Argentinean Grand Prix, driving a rented Simca-Gordini. Sadly, he had to retire after just 21 laps. In 1955, he had another attempt, again in a Simca-Gordini which he'd hired for the occasion. This time, he did well in qualifying but spun his car on the first lap and was out of the race.

Birger never entered another Grand Prix, but remained involved in motorsport until his untimely death in a traffic accident, when he was just 42 years old.

Harry BLANCHARD

Nationality: American
Born: 13th June 1929
Died: 31st January 1960
Seasons: 1959
Team/manufacturer(s): Porsche
Grands Prix: 1
Race wins: 0
Championship wins: 0

Harry Blanchard ran a car dealership in Connecticut, which specialised in British sports cars. He was also a keen racing and rally driver in his spare time.

Blanchard owned a 1958 Porsche 550A Spyder which had previously been driven by Herbert Kaes, Ferdinand Porsche's nephew. He was invited to race his car in the inaugural US Grand Prix at Sebring in 1959, simply to make up the numbers. He finished seventh and last, a whole four laps behind the winner, Bruce McLaren.

The following year, Blanchard travelled to South America to compete in the Buenos Aires 1000km race, driving a Porsche 718 RSK. Tragically, though, he crashed on the first lap, the car somersaulting several times. He was killed on the spot.

Michael BLEEKEMOLEN

Nationality: Dutch
Born: 2nd October 1949
Seasons: 1977-1978
Team/manufacturer(s): RAM, ATS
Grands Prix: 5
Race wins: 0
Championship wins: 0

Born in Amsterdam, Michael Bleekemolen graduated from Formula Super Vee and attempted his first Formula One Grand Prix in his home country in 1977, driving for RAM Racing. Sadly, he failed to qualify.

Not deterred, though, he had another attempt in 1978, this time with ATS. However, out of four Grands Prix, he only

qualified for the USA one, and then had to retire from the race itself.

Bleekemolen then raced in Formula 3 for three years, and finished second in the European Championship. He then went onto Renault racing.

Later, Bleekemolen became successful in business, as owner of Race Planet, a Dutch karting venue and race school. He also formed his own Porsche Supercup team, in which he competed. His two sons are also race drivers.

John Trevor BLOKDYK

Nationality: South African
Born: 30th November 1935
Died: 19th March 1995
Seasons: 1963, 1965
Team/manufacturer(s): Cooper
Grands Prix: 2
Race wins: 0
Championship wins: 0

Trevor Blokdyk hailed from a small farming community near Johannesburg and became a successful speedway rider, winning the South African Championship.

In the late 1950s, he moved to England to pursue a career racing cars. Once he'd learnt the trade, he returned to his home country and, in 1963, he competed in the South African Grand Prix at East London. He finished in 12th place, despite driving an outdated 1959 Scuderia Lupino Cooper-Maserati.

The following year, Blokdyk returned to Europe to race in Formula Junior, but had another stab at the South African Grand Prix in 1965, again in an old Cooper. This time, he failed to qualify.

Blokdyk then raced in Formula 2 in Europe in 1966, and in Formula 3 the following two years. After that, he decided he'd never make it in racing, so he returned to South Africa to take up farming. He died of a heart attack in 1995, aged 55.

Mark BLUNDELL

Nationality: British
Born: 8th April 1966
Seasons: 1991, 1993-1995
Team/manufacturer(s): Brabham, Ligier, Tyrrell and McLaren
Grands Prix: 63
Race wins: 0
Championship wins: 0

Mark Blundell was born in Hertfordshire and began racing at the age of 14, riding motocross bikes. Within a couple of years, he was one of the country's top riders.

At the age of 17 he switched to Formula Ford and, in his first season, he came second in the British Junior Formula Ford Championships. The next year, he won both the Esso British and Snetterton FF1600 championships. And, a year after that, he won the BBC Grandstand series in FF2000. In 1986, he won the FF2000 European Championship.

After this, Blundell spent time in Formula 3000 and showed plenty of talent and, in 1990, was offered a test-drive Williams in Formula One. However, at this point he was concentrating on sportscar racing, becoming the youngest ever driver to gain pole position at Le Mans.

He finally made it to Formula One in 1991 but just for the one season. Also he continued testing for Formula

One in 1992, his big success was winning at Le Mans for Peugeot. Blundell returned to Formula One for 1992 where he stayed until 1995. After that, he went to the USA to race in the CART championship and he also continued sportscar racing.

Blundell has also commentated on Formula One for the ITV television channel and formed a sports management company with Martin Brundle.

Raul de Mesquita BOESEL

Nationality: Brazilian
Born: 4th December 1957
Seasons: 1982-1983
Team/manufacturer(s): March, Ligier
Grands Prix: 30
Race wins: 0
Championship wins: 0

Born into a wealthy Brazilian family Raul Boesel planned to follow in his brothers' footsteps and be a horse show jumper; a sport he'd proved to be very skilled at. However, part-way through an engineering degree, Boesel decided that he wanted to be a racing driver. He moved to the UK in 1980 to race in Formula Ford 1600. The next year he finished third in the Formula 3 championship.

Raul Boesel

This gained him a test with McLaren but, in 1982, he joined the Rothmans March team, although he had little success. The following year he drove for Ligier but, again, failed to shine, partly because the team was under-funded.

Boesel then went to the USA to compete in the CART series. In 1987 he switched to the World Sportscar Championship and won the title, driving for Jaguar. He continued to race in CART up until 1998 and then he competed in the Indy Racing League in the USA.

Boesel later returned to Brazil where he continued to race in the local Touring Car Championship.

Robert (Bob) BONDURANT

Nationality: American
Born: 27th April 1933
Seasons: 1965-1966
Team/manufacturer(s): Ferrari, Lotus, BRM and Eagle
Grands Prix: 9
Race wins: 0
Championship wins: 0

Bob Bondurant was born in Illinois but grew up in Los Angeles, where he spent his teenage years racing motorcycles on dirt tracks. In 1956 he moved on to racing a Morgan and then, in 1959, he won the West Coast B Production Championship in a Chevrolet Corvette.

In 1963 he travelled to Europe as part of the Ford Cobra team and won the GT class at Le Mans. His first Formula One drive was in a Ferrari at Watkins Glen in 1965, where he finished ninth. Later that year, he drove a Lotus at the Mexican Grand Prix but failed to finish.

Several Grand Prix entries followed in 1966, with his best result being a fourth place at Monaco, driving a BRM.

After that, Bondurant raced in the CanAm series until he was injured in a bad accident. He then went on to set up a successful racing school in Phoenix, USA and wrote books on racing. He has also done some television commentary.

Felice BONETTO

Nationality: Italian
Born: 27th April 1933
Died: 21st November 1953
Seasons: 1950-1953
Team/manufacturer(s): Maserati, Milano and Alfa Romeo
Grands Prix: 16
Race wins: 0
Championship wins: 0

Italian-born Felice Bonetto raced Alfa Romeos before the Second World War. After, his career moved fast, as he drove for Cisitalia and Ferrari in pre-Formula One events.

He began the first Formula One season of 1950 driving for Maserati and then Milano, but drove in just three Grands Prix that year, with no great success. The following year, driving for Alfa Romeo, he achieved a fourth place at Silverstone, a third at Monza and a fifth at Pedralbes in Spain.

Bonetto returned to Maserati for 1952 and 1953 and often finished in the top ten, his best result being a third place at the 1953 Dutch Grand Prix.

He also raced in sportscars and won the 1952 Targa Florio. He was killed in 1953 in an accident while driving a Lancia in the Carrera Panamericana.

Joakim (Jo) BONNIER

Nationality: Swedish
Born: 31st January 1930
Died: 11th June 1972
Seasons: 1956-1971
Team/manufacturer(s): Maserati, Scuderia Centro Sud, Joakim Bonnier Racing Team, BRM, Porsche, Rob Walker Racing Team, Lotus, Brabham, Anglo-Suisse Racing/Ecurie Bonnier and Honda
Grands Prix: 104
Race wins: 1
Championship wins: 0

Jo Bonnier came from a wealthy Swedish family and lived much of his life in Switzerland. His first Formula One event was driving a Maserati at the 1956 Italian Grand Prix. However, he really made a name for himself when he won the 1959 Dutch Grand Prix for BRM.

Despite this victory, though, Bonnier did not drive as a regular for many works teams, but more often drove as a one-off replacement when a regular driver wasn't available. He also had his own team, both early on in his Formula One career and again later.

Bonnier's last full season in Formula One was 1968, when he drove his own, outdated, McLaren M5A. However, he continued to make occasional appearances until 1971.

As well as Formula One, Bonnier was also a successful

Jo Bonnier

sportscar racer, winning the 1960 and 1963 Targa Florio events and the 1962 12 Hours of Sebring.

In 1971, Bonnier was killed at Le Mans when his Lola-Cosworth T280 collided with a Ferrari Daytona and was catapulted into some trees.

Roberto Wenceslao BONOMI

Nationality: Argentinean
Born: 30th September 1919
Died: 10th January 1992
Seasons: 1960
Team/manufacturer(s): Scuderia Centro Sud
Grands Prix: 1
Race wins: 0
Championship wins: 0

Born Roberto Wenceslao Bonomi Oliva in Buenos Aires, Roberto Bonomi was a wealthy land-owner and local politician who was able to finance his passion for motor-racing.

He was, though, also a talented driver and competed for the Ferrari and the Maserati works teams in the Buenos Aires 1000km race for a number of years. In 1958, Bonomi bought a Maserati 300S and raced it in a number of local events.

Bonomi had just one foray into Formula One, which was

at the 1960 Argentinean Grand Prix. He was driving a rented Centro-Sud Cooper-Maserati in which he finished a respectable 11th place, after starting 17th on the grid.

Juan Manuel BORDEU

Nationality: Argentinean
Born: 28th January 1934
Died: 24th September 1990
Seasons: 1961
Team/manufacturer(s): Lotus
Grands Prix: 1
Race wins: 0
Championship wins: 0

Juan Manuel Bordeu was born in Buenos Aires and became a good friend and protégé of the legendary driver, Juan Manuel Fangio. He was a successful racer in Formula Junior and later raced in the Argentinean Temporada series.

Bordeu's single foray into Formula One was at the 1961 French Grand Prix, in a Lotus run by the UDT Laystall team. A bad accident later put paid to his Formula One ambitions.

He continued to race until his retirement in 1973. During this time he represented Argentina as FISA member and held a place on the World Motorsport Council. Bordeu died of leukaemia in 1990.

Thierry Boutsen

Karl Edward Tommy (Slim) BORGUDD

Nationality: Swedish
Born: 25th November 1946
Seasons: 1981-1982
Team/manufacturer(s): ATS, Tyrrell
Grands Prix: 0
Race wins: 0
Championship wins: 0

Born Karl Edward Tommy Borgudd, but better known as Tommy or Slim Borgudd, this Swedish driver actually started off playing drums, mainly in jazz-rock bands, but he also played for ABBA on a number of tracks.

He began racing as a hobby in the mid-1960s but became serious in 1972 when he managed no less than five wins in sportscar events. A year later, he won the Scandinavian Formula Ford series.

From 1976, Borgudd raced in Formula 3 before making his Formula One debut in 1981 at the San Marino Grand Prix, driving an ATS car complete with 'ABBA' logos. It was a disappointing season, though, with the exception of a sixth place at Silverstone.

Next year he was hired by Tyrrell, but was dismissed after just three races because of a lack of sponsorship.

From then, Borgudd competed in sportscar events and then got involved in truck racing, with some success, winning the European Championship in 1995. He later retired from racing and settled down to live in Coventry, England.

Lukas (Luki) BOTHA

Nationality: South African
Born: 16th January 1930
Seasons: 1967
Team/manufacturer(s): Brabham
Grands Prix: 1
Race wins: 0
Championship wins: 0

Luki Botha began racing in the South African Formula One series in 1966 and showed great promise. At his first race, the Rhodesian Grand Prix, he finished in second place in his Brabham BT11.

The following year he continued racing the same car, albeit with a more powerful Repco engine, in local Grand Prix events. However, he also entered the international South African Grand Prix, but did not finish the race.

Sadly, in 1968, Botha crashed his car during a race in Mozambique, killing eight spectators. He never raced again after that and is believed to have gone to live in Pretoria.

Jean-Christophe BOULLION

Nationality: French
Born: 27th December 1969
Seasons: 1995
Team/manufacturer(s): Sauber
Grands Prix: 11
Race wins: 0
Championship wins: 0

A quiet Frenchman, Jean-Christophe Boullion, began racing karts in 1982 and then, in 1988, he attended a racing school near Paris. After this he raced in Formula Ford 1600, winning the French title in 1990.

This led to a move to Formula 3 in 1993 and then to Formula 3000 the following year, when he won the European Championship.

In 1995, Boullion was signed to test for Williams but, instead, was loaned to Sauber to replace Karl Wendlinger. He drove in 11 Grands Prix that year, with his best result

being fifth place in Germany. The next year, Boullion returned to Williams and later also tested for Tyrrell.

By 1996, he was also racing in the Renault Spider Eurocup and then he moved to Touring Cars. Since 2000, Boullion has raced sports cars, including several appearances at Le Mans, where he finished second in 2005.

Thierry BOUTSEN
Nationality: Belgian
Born: 13th July 1957
Seasons: 1983-1993
Team/manufacturer(s): Arrows, Benetton, Williams, Ligier and Jordan
Grands Prix: 164
Race wins: 3
Championship wins: 0

Thierry Boutsen made a name for himself in 1978 when he took the Formula Ford 1600 Championship by winning no less than 15 out of the 18 races. The next year he moved to Formula 3 and came second in the championship in 1980.

Boutsen then came second in the Formula 2 Championship in 1981. However, despite all this success,

Karl Borgudd

he had to buy his way into Formula One, paying $500,000 for a drive with the Arrows team in 1983. It wasn't long, though, before his talents became apparent and he moved to Benetton in 1987 and then Williams two years later.

It was in his first year with Williams that he won both the Canadian and the Australian Grands Prix. The next year, 1990, he won the Hungarian Grand Prix.

Boutsen went on to race for Ligier and then Jordan before retiring from Formula One at the end of 1993. He then raced sportscars until a bad crash at Le Mans in 1999 made him retire from the sport. He then formed his own aviation company and a motorsports team.

David BRABHAM
Nationality: Australian
Born: 5th September 1965
Seasons: 1980, 1994
Team/manufacturer(s): Brabham, Simtek
Grands Prix: 30
Race wins: 0
Championship wins: 0

The youngest son of famous driver, Sir Jack Brabham, David Brabham was born in London but was brought up in Australia. There, he showed little interest in motor racing until after he left school, preferring to play football.

However, once he tried karting at the age of 17, the youngster was hooked and raced them for two years before moving to Formula Ford 1600 in 1986. By 1989, he was living in Europe winning the British Formula 3 Championship.

Sadly, Brabham's Formula One career, beginning with his father's team, was less successful, with him only qualifying six out of 14 races in 1990. This, though, was in part down to an uncompetitive car.

A move to sportscar racing in 1991 was better, with him winning the Spa 24 Hours and, a year later, the 24 Hours of Daytona.

Brabham had another foray into Formula One in 1994, driving for Simtek. Once again, though, he struggled with uncompetitive cars. The next year he returned to sportscars and has had continued success in this sector.

Gary BRABHAM
Nationality: Australian
Born: 29th March 1961
Seasons: 1990
Team/manufacturer(s): Life
Grands Prix: 2
Race wins: 0
Championship wins: 0

London-born Gary Brabham is the son of Sir Jack Brabham and, early on, had no desire to be a racing driver, and was looking forward to a life of farming in rural New South Wales. However, by 1982 he had caught the racing bug and was competing in Formula Ford in Australia.

A move to Europe saw Brabham competing in Formula Ford 2000 in 1983, followed by British Formula 3, in which he came second in the championship in 1988. During this time, he also raced in other categories, including sportscars.

In 1990, Brabham joined the Italian Life Formula One team, which had an unusual – and troublesome – W12 engine. He entered the USA and Brazilian Grands Prix, but failed to qualify in either, after which he quit the team.

Brabham continued to race in sportscars and CART but with limited success. In 1995, he retired from racing and went to live in Brisbane, where he taught advanced driving skills.

Sir John Arthur (Jack) BRABHAM OBE
Nationality: Australian
Born: 2nd April 1926
Seasons: 1955-1970
Team/manufacturer(s): Cooper, Rob Walker, Brabham
Grands Prix: 128
Race wins: 14
Championship wins: 3

Australian Jack Brabham's father was a keen motorist and taught Jack to drive a car when he was 12 years old. He left school at the age of 15 and got a job at a garage, helping repair cars. Keen to get ahead in his chosen profession, the teenager spent his evenings studying engineering at college.

Jack Brabham

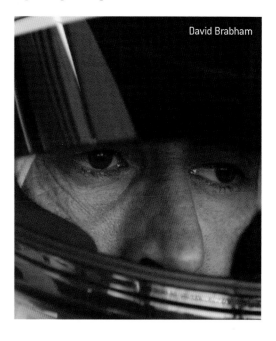
David Brabham

Anthony Brise

After serving in the airforce during the war, Brabham returned home and started his own car repair business. One of his customers was an American, Johnny Schonberg, who raced midgets. Brabham helped to prepare his car for him but Schonberg's wife persuaded her husband to give up racing, and Brabham found himself with a car. So he decided to try his hand at racing.

Amazingly, despite being inexperienced, Brabham won the New South Wales Championship in his first season! Significantly, at this time he met up with engineer Ron Tauranac, who was to become a long-term friend and colleague.

Brabham moved to England in 1955 and made his Grand Prix debut at Aintree, driving his own Maserati 250F. Before long, he joined the Cooper team. Brabham proved himself as a staggeringly competent driver, winning the Drivers' Championship in 1959 and 1960.

As good as the Coopers were, Brabham decided to strike out on his own and, in 1961, he teamed up with Ron Tauranac to found the Brabham Racing Organisation. Unfortunately, Formula One had introduced a 1500cc limit on engine size at this time, which did not suit Brabham's aggressive driving style, and he failed to win any races with the less powerful cars. However, teammate Dan Gurney gave the Brabham team its first victory at Rouen in 1964.

Brabham's luck changed in 1966, when the allowed engine size of Formula One cars increased to 3000cc. He sourced an engine from Repco and, in its first year, the new car took Brabham to victory at the French, British, Dutch and German Grands Prix, allowing him to claim the Drivers' Championship with ease. He was the first Formula One driver to win the championship in a car bearing his own name.

Brabham planned to retire from racing in 1970, but he couldn't sign a suitable driver to take his place, so he took it on himself to pilot a Brabham car once again. He started the season well with a win at the opening South African Grand Prix and announced his retirement after the Mexican Grand Prix.

He then returned to Australia, where he continued to run his garage business and made appearances at historical motorsport events. He was knighted in 1979 and all three of his sons have been involved in motorsport.

William (Bill) BRACK

Nationality: Canadian
Born: 26th December 1935
Seasons: 1968-1969, 1972
Team/manufacturer(s): Lotus, BRM
Grands Prix: 3
Race wins: 0
Championship wins: 0

Born William Brack, this Canadian had an unusual introduction into motorsport, in that he raced Minis on ice in Ontario during the 1960s. He went on to more conventional Mini racing, too.

However, racing was strictly a hobby and Brack earned his money from his own car sales company, which became the Canadian distributor for Lotus. It was this connection that led to him racing a Lotus 47, in which he won the Formula B Championship in 1967 and 1968. Also in 1968, Brack entered his first Grand Prix, driving a Lotus in the Canadian event, but retired with mechanical failure.

The following year, he also entered the Canadian Grand Prix, this time in a BRM. Brack returned to Formula One, again with BRM, in 1972 when he raced in the Canadian Grand Prix once more.

Brack went on to be successful in Formula Atlantic, winning the Canadian Championship three times in the early 1970s. He later retired to run a car dealership in Toronto but continued to race in historic events.

Ernesto (Tino) BRAMBILLA

Nationality: Italian
Born: 31 January 1934
Seasons: 1963, 1969
Team/manufacturer(s): Cooper, Ferrari
Grands Prix: 2
Race wins: 0
Championship wins: 0

Born in Monza, Ernesto Brambilla was the older brother of the more famous driver, Vittorio Brambilla.

His first Formula One event was long before his brother's – the 1963 Italian Grand Prix, driving a Cooper. However, he failed to qualify. Brambilla had another go at the Italian Grand Prix in 1969, this time in a Ferrari. In the event, though, his place was taken by Pedro Rodriguez.

Brambilla went on to run a racing workshop in Monza,

Vittorio Brambilla

alongside his brother Vittorio and, ultimately, their sons. He continued this company after Vittorio's death.

Vittorio BRAMBILLA

Nationality: Italian
Born: 11th November 1937
Died: 26th May 2001
Seasons: 1974-1980
Team/manufacturer(s): March, Surtees, Alfa Romeo
Grands Prix: 79
Race wins: 1
Championship wins: 0

Known as the 'Monza Gorilla', Vittorio Brambilla started his career racing motorcycles in the 1950s, and won the Italian 175cc championship in 1958. After a spell as a mechanic, he returned to racing in 1968, this time in Formula 3; a championship he won five years later.

At this time, he was also competing in Formula 2 and, in 1974, bought a drive with the March Formula One team. In his second season Brambilla won the Austrian Grand Prix, under very wet conditions. However, the highlight of the race was when he spun his car just after crossing the finishing line, smashing the front end!

While driving for Surtees in 1978, Brambilla was involved in a multiple pile-up and was badly injured. However, he recovered and drove for Alfa Romeo in 1979 and 1980, before retiring from racing. He then returned to Monza to run his racing workshop with his brother Ernesto. Brambilla died of a heart attack in his garden in 2001.

Gianfranco BRANCATELLI

Nationality: Italian
Born: 18th January 1950
Seasons: 1979
Team/manufacturer(s): Kauhsen and Merzario
Grands Prix: 3
Race wins: 0
Championship wins: 0

Gianfranco Brancatelli was born in Turin and began his career in Formula Abarth and was national champion in 1974. The following year he finished second in the Italian Formula 3 Championship.

By 1977, he had moved to Formula 2 but had little success. In 1979, things would get worse when he signed for the Kauhsen Formula One team. He entered three races but failed to qualify in any, struggling with a very uncompetitive car. Disillusioned, Brancatelli moved to Merzario later in the season and entered the Monaco Grand Prix, but failed to qualify. In later life, he became a successful touring car driver and won various championships.

Eric BRANDON

Nationality: British
Born: 18th July 1920
Died: 8th August 1982
Seasons: 1952, 1954
Team/manufacturer(s): Cooper
Grands Prix: 5
Race wins: 0
Championship wins: 0

Born in the East Ham area of London, Eric Brandon earned his living as an electrical goods wholesaler, and raced cars in his spare time. Friends with John Cooper from childhood, Brandon bought one of the first Cooper 500cc cars in 1946 and raced it

Eric Brandon

in hillclimbs and sprints. In 1947 he won the UK's first 500cc race, at Gransden Lodge airfield.

That series was renamed Formula 3 in 1950 and Brandon won it in 1951. He used the same car to compete in a number of Grand Prix races in 1952, and the British Grand Prix in 1954.

After that, Brandon turned his attention to hydroplane racing on England's south coast. He died in Gosport in 1982.

Thomas (Tom or Tommy) BRIDGER

Nationality: British
Born: 24th June 1934
Died: 30th July 1991
Seasons: 1958
Team/manufacturer(s): Cooper
Grands Prix: 1
Race wins: 0
Championship wins: 0

Born in Hertfordshire, Tom Bridger began racing with a Cooper-JPA in the 500cc Formula 3 category in 1953. By 1958, he was competing in Formula 2 as well as Formula 3 and was doing reasonably well.

It was in 1958 that Bridger made his one and only Formula One appearance, driving a Cooper-Climax T4 at the Moroccan Grand Prix. However, on the 29th lap he was involved in a major crash with two other cars, because of oil on the track. Bridger was uninjured but out of the race.

Bridger later returned to Formula 3 racing and, later, Formula Junior.

Anthony William (Tony) BRISE

Nationality: British
Born: 28th March 1952
Died: 29th November 1975
Seasons: 1975
Team/manufacturer(s): Williams, Hill
Grands Prix: 10
Race wins: 0
Championship wins: 0

The son of John Brise, a Formula 3 racing driver, Tony Brise began racing karts at a young age and, by the time he was 17 in 1969, he was British Champion. From there, he moved into Formula Ford the following year and, in 1972, to Formula 3. In 1973, he was John Player Champion and joint Lombard Champion.

Money problems, though, meant he was unable to graduate to Formula 2 and, instead, he spent 1974 competing in Formula Atlantic.

Brise's Formula One debut came in 1975, when he got a drive with Williams and he finished a respectable seventh at his first event, the Spanish Grand Prix.

Later in the season, Brise switched to the new Hill team, after team founder Graham Hill decided to retire from driving. Brise made a good impression and he was signed to continue with Hill in 1976. It was not to be, though, because he was killed in the light-plane crash that also claimed the life of Graham Hill, in November 1976. Brise was just 23 years old.

Christopher (Chris) BRISTOW

Nationality: British
Born: 2nd December 1937
Died: 19th June 1960
Seasons: 1959-1960
Team/manufacturer(s): Cooper
Grands Prix: 4
Race wins: 0
Championship wins: 0

Chris Bristow was the son of a London car hire operator and began racing in an MG in the mid-1950s. However, he first made an impact on the sport at a Formula 2 race in 1959, when his driving skills were spotted by Cooper's Ken Gregory.

Before long, Bristow was signed to drive for Cooper and came tenth in the 1959 British Grand Prix, the only Formula One race he competed in that year. He did drive in other events that year, and managed to write off a Porsche at Goodwood during a TT race.

In 1960, Bristow stayed with Cooper and travelled to Spa to compete in the Belgian Grand Prix there. From ninth on the grid he pushed his way up and was battling for sixth place when he misjudged a corner and rolled his car several times. Bristow was decapitated in the accident and a promising career was cut short.

Martin Brundle

Peter BROEKER

Nationality: Canadian
Born: 15th May 1929
Died: 1980
Seasons: 1963
Team/manufacturer(s): Stebro
Grands Prix: 1
Race wins: 0
Championship wins: 0

Peter Broeker's childhood was spent in a number of countries around the world because of the nature of his father's work. As an adult, he co-founded Stebro Systems in 1956, a Canadian company that supplied replacement parts for high-performance and imported cars.

As a way to promote itself, the company sponsored the Formula Junior series in Canada by paying for the cars' chassis. In 1963, Stebro entered two Ford-engined Stebro-chassised cars into the US Grand Prix at Watkins Glen. In the event, though, just one car raced, and this was driven by Broeker himself. Amazingly, he finished in seventh place.

In 1973, Broeker published a book on Olympic coins – he was a keen coin collector.

Charles Anthony Stanford (Tony) BROOKS

Nationality: British
Born: 25th February 1932
Seasons: 1956-1961
Team/manufacturer(s): BRM, Vanwall, Ferrari, Cooper
Grands Prix: 39
Race wins: 5
Championship wins: 0

Born Charles Anthony Stanford Brooks in Cheshire, Tony Brooks was the son of a dentist. While studying to follow in his father's footsteps, he started racing a Healey in club events from 1952.

In 1955, Brooks drove a Formula 2 car at Crystal Palace and managed to beat three Formula One cars, finishing in fourth place. That same year, he travelled to Sicily to take part in a non-championship Grand Prix, driving a Connaught. He won the event and became the first British driver since 1924 to win a continental race in a British car.

Brooks then drove for BRM in 1956 but crashed during his debut race at Silverstone when his car's throttle stuck. By 1958 he was with Vanwall, achieving excellent results, with wins in Belgium, German and Italy that year, leading to him being third in the championship.

A move to Ferrari in 1959 brought wins in France and Germany, and Brooks finished second that season. He continued racing in Formula One until 1961 but was devoting more and more time to his garage business in Weybridge. He went on to run this full time after he retired from racing but continued to appear in historic festivals.

Tony Brooks

Alan Everest BROWN

Nationality: British
Born: 20th November 1919
Died: 20th January 2004
Seasons: 1952-1954
Team/manufacturer(s): Cooper
Grands Prix: 9
Race wins: 0
Championship wins: 0

Yorkshireman Alan Brown worked as a truck sales representative in Guildford and made a name for himself as a 500cc Formula 3 driver after the Second World War, winning the 1951 Luxembourg Grand Prix.

In 1952 he moved to Formula 2, driving a Cooper-Bristol alongside Eric Brandon. He got off to a good start and, that year, also entered four Formula One events, his best results being fifth in Switzerland and sixth in Belgium. He also entered some Grand Prix events in 1953 and 1954 but, by this time, his car was slow compared to some of the competition and he had little success

Brown retired from racing in 1956 but continued to manage race teams before becoming a car dealer. He retired to Spain for many years, but died of a heart attack in 2004 during a stay in England.

Warwick BROWN

Nationality: Australian
Born: 24th December 1949
Seasons: 1976
Team/manufacturer(s): Wolf
Grands Prix: 1
Race wins: 0
Championship wins: 0

Warwick Brown was born in Sydney and started motor racing in 1972, driving an elderly McLaren. After an encouraging first year, he went on to buy a Lola T300 with which to compete in the 1973 Tasman series. However, a bad crash at Surfers Paradise led to him being confined to hospital for three months with two broken legs.

Recovered for the following season, Brown again entered the Tasman series and won the race at Adelaide. He also travelled to the USA to compete in Formula 5000 that year. In 1975, he won the Tasman title.

Brown's one Formula One race was the 1976 USA Grand Prix at Watkins Glen where he finished in 14th place driving for Wolf. He stayed in the US to compete in Formula 5000 and Can-Am until 1979. He then returned to Sydney and set up a flying business.

Adolf BRUDES VON BRESLAU

Nationality: German
Born: 15th October 1899
Died: 5th November 1986
Seasons: 1952
Team/manufacturer(s): Veritas
Grands Prix: 1
Race wins: 0
Championship wins: 0

Often known simply as Adolf Brudes, he was born in Poland at the end of the 19th century. Before the Second World War he first competed in motorcycle races but turned to four wheels in 1940, when he came third in the Coppa Brescia driving a BMW.

Brudes continued racing after the war, mainly in a Borgward in a range of events, including the Buenos Aires 1000km, the Le Mans 24 Hour and the Carrera Panamericana. However, he also drove a Veritas RS-BMW from time to time, which was what he was in for his single Formula One appearance, at the 1952 German Grand Prix at the Nürburgring. He retired from the race with engine trouble.

Martin BRUNDLE

Nationality: British
Born: 1st June 1959
Seasons: 1984-1989, 1991-1996
Team/manufacturer(s): Tyrrell, Zakspeed, Williams, Brabham, Benetton, Ligier, McLaren, Jordan
Grands Prix: 161
Race wins: 0
Championship wins: 0

Martin Brundle was born in Norfolk and first hit headlines when he went head to head with Ayrton Senna in the British Formula 2 Championship in 1983, making it an exciting season.

It was enough to promote both drivers to Formula One the following year, with Brundle driving for Tyrrell. In his first race, in Brazil, he finished in fifth place, while at Detroit later that year he came second, behind Nelson Piquet.

Over the following years, Brundle raced with a number of teams but bad luck and, at times, underdeveloped cars, stopped him from achieving any wins in Formula One and he retired from the championship at the end of 1996.

At the same time as he was racing in Formula One, Brundle also competed in sportscars, becoming World Sportscar Champion in 1988 and, in 1990, he won at Le Mans, driving for Jaguar.

He largely retired from racing after 2001 and went on to make a name for himself as a Formula One commentator for ITV, and he also acted as David Coulthard's manager.

Gianmaria Bruni

Gianmaria (Gimmi) BRUNI

Nationality: Italian
Born: 30th May 1981
Seasons: 2004
Team/manufacturer(s): Minardi
Grands Prix: 18
Race wins: 0
Championship wins: 0

Nicknamed Gimmi, Gianmaria Bruni began karting at the age of 10, even though he was meant to be 12 to compete. He drove a borrowed kart and his skills and determination soon showed through. By 1997 he was racing in Italian Formula Renault and won the championship the following year.

In 1999 Bruni won the European Formula Renault title before competing in British Formula 3 in 2000. He finished in fifth place that season and fourth the following.

He tested for Minari during 2003 and was offered a drive for 2004, but struggled to raise enough sponsorship. He did, though, but had a very disappointing season with an uncompetitive car. He was one of only two drivers not to score any points that year.

Bruni was unable to continue in Formula One for 2005, so he competed in the GP2 Series, which has close links with Formula One. He proved himself a good driver throughout the season and stayed with GP2 for 2006.

Clemar BUCCI

Nationality: Argentinean
Born: 4th September 1920
Seasons: 1954-1955
Team/manufacturer(s): Gordini and Maserati
Grands Prix: 5
Race wins: 0
Championship wins: 0

Often described as a 'dour pipe-smoker', Clemar Bucci made his reputation racing a 4.5-litre Alfa Romeo in his native Argentina, finishing third in the 1950 Eva Peron Cup race.

While competing in his Alfa, Bucci was also involved with the innovative Porsche-designed Cisitalia Formula One car, and he broke the South American land-speed record in this. However, when it came to racing the car proved uncompetitive.

Bucci came to Europe in 1954 to drive for Gordini in Formula One, but with no success. The following year saw him race for Maserati in the Argentinean Grand Prix but, again, he didn't have much success.

He later retired from racing but continued to appear at historic events and built up an impressive collection of classic cars at his home in Buenos Aires.

Ronald (Ronnie) BUCKNUM

Nationality: American
Born: 5th April 1936
Died: 23rd April 1992
Seasons: 1964-1966
Team/manufacturer(s): Honda
Grands Prix: 11
Race wins: 0
Championship wins: 0

Ronnie Bucknum originated from California and began motor racing in 1956. He soon proved himself a competent driver by winning the Sports Car Club of America titles four times between 1959 and 1964, winning 44 out of 48 races.

He was picked as a Formula One driver by the new Honda team, after he was spotted racing a Porsche 904 at Sebring. Apparently, the Japanese company thought that, because they had no experience in Formula One, it would make sense to have a driver in the same situation!

Bucknum entered 11 Grands Prix over two seasons and scored a total of just two points. His best result was a fifth place in Mexico in 1965.

He went on to compete in a Carroll Shelby GT40 at Le Mans in 1966 and finished in third place. He also competed in Indycar events. Sadly, Buckham died at the age of just 56 from a diabetes-related illness.

Ivor Léon John BUEB

Nationality: British
Born: 6th June 1923
Died: 1st August 1959
Seasons: 1957-1959
Team/manufacturer(s): Connaught, Maserati, Lotus, Cooper
Grands Prix: 6
Race wins: 0
Championship wins: 0

London-born Ivor Bueb was nicknamed 'Ivor the Driver' and ran a garage business in Cheltenham. He began his race career in a 500cc Formula 3 Cooper in 1953. Being some 15 stone in weight, he drove a specially lightened car and did surprisingly well.

In 1955, Bueb had his greatest moment, when he won Le Mans, driving with Mike Hawthorn. The following year, he won the Reims 12 Hours for Jaguar and, in 1957, he again triumphed at Le Mans.

Bueb's Formula One debut came in 1957, when he drove for Connaught, then managed by Bernie Ecclestone. In the same season he also raced a private Maserati. For 1958, he competed in his own Lotus and also drove a Cooper-Borgward. It was in this car that he was killed when it crashed at Clermont Ferrand in August 1959.

Luiz Pereira BUENO

Nationality: Brazilian
Born: 16th January 1937
Seasons: 1973
Team/manufacturer(s): Surtees
Grands Prix: 1
Race wins: 0
Championship wins: 0

A Brazilian government scheme paid for Luiz Bueno to come to England in 1969 to race in Formula Ford. He won five races but did not have the money to continue so he returned home. There, he competed in various events and was offered another drive in Europe but, again, lacked the necessary finances.

In 1971, the European Formula 2 teams visited South America and Bueno had the chance to race a March car in which he performed well. He also drove a March 711 in the non-championship Brazilian Grand Prix in 1972.

For 1973, Bueno rented an old Surtees for his one and only Formula One appearance, at the Brazilian Grand Prix, where he qualified last and finished last.

Bueno went on to have more success in touring cars, where he was twice Brazilian champion. After retiring from racing, he became a motorsport team management consultant in his home country.

Ian BURGESS

Nationality: British
Born: 6th June 1930
Seasons: 1958-1963
Team/manufacturer(s): Cooper, Lotus, Scirocco
Grands Prix: 20
Race wins: 0
Championship wins: 0

Ian Burgess first made a name for himself in 1951, when he won the Eifelrennen 500cc race at the Nürburgring, in pouring rain and ahead of other, more experienced drivers.

That, however, turned out to be a one-off and he spent the next few years unable to match his success. He then got a job at the Cooper factory, helping to manage both the office and the race driver school. This led to him competing in the company's Formula 2 cars, with reasonable success.

In 1958, Burgess drove Coopers in the British and German Grands Prix; he retired from the first with mechanical problems and finished a respectable sixth in the second. From then on, he continued to compete in Formula One races, for Cooper and Lotus. And then, in 1963, he signed for the Scirocco team, which had the backing of a wealthy American businessman. Sadly it was not a successful project and Burgess only competed in two Grands Prix; again, the British and German ones, retiring each time.

In later life, Burgess spent time in jail for alleged drug dealing. After living in various parts of the world he finally settled in London.

Luciano Pucci BURTI

Nationality: Brazilian
Born: 5th March 1975
Seasons: 2000-2001
Team/manufacturer(s): Jaguar, Prost
Grands Prix: 15
Race wins: 0
Championship wins: 0

Brazilian Luciano Burti began racing karts in his homeland at the age of 16 before heading for Europe. There, he competed in Formula Vauxhall Junior and finished third in the 1996 series, with four wins. The following year he won the Formula Vauxhall Championship before switching to British Formula 3 in 1998. He came third in his first season, then second the following year.

This led to a job as a test driver for Jaguar in 2000, and he made his Formula One debut in Austria that year, replacing Eddie Irvine. The next year he had a full-time place with the team but only ran in four races before leaving.

Burti then joined Prost for the rest of the 2001 season and his best result was eighth place in Canada. Unfortunately, he suffered a nasty accident during the Belgian Grand Prix and was unable to complete the season.

He later returned to Brazil where he pursued a career in stockcar racing.

Roberto BUSSINELLO

Nationality: Italian
Born: 4th October 1927
Died: 24th August 1999
Seasons: 1961, 1965
Team/manufacturer(s): De Tomaso, BRM
Grands Prix: 3
Race wins: 0
Championship wins: 0

Jenson Button

BUTTON

Luciano Burti

Italian Roberto Bussinello graduated as an engineer and worked as a development engineer and test driver for the De Tomaso race team. He also raced the team's cars on occasion, mainly in Italy.

His Formula One debut came in 1961, when he drove a four-cylinder Alfa Romeo-engined De Tomaso at the Italian Grand Prix, but he had to retire with engine failure.

In 1963, Bussinello moved to Alfa Romeo; again as a development engineer but, once more, he found himself racing, this time in a Giulietti GT. He came third in the 1964 Targa Florio.

In 1965, Bussinello once more found himself driving in Formula One. This time he was in an aging BRM at the German and Italian Grands Prix. However, he failed to qualify for the first race and retired from the second.

In later life, Bussinello continued his career as an engineer before retiring.

Jenson Alexander Lyons BUTTON

Nationality: British
Born: 19th January 1980
Seasons: 2000-
Team/manufacturer(s): Williams, Benetton/Renault, BAR, Honda
Grands Prix: 137
Race wins: 1
Championship wins: 0

Jenson Button began karting at the age of eight and was soon hooked. With the support of his father, John (a rallycross driver), the youngster excelled at the 1991 British Cadet Kart Championship, when he won all 34 races to take the championship.

He went onto be three-times British Open Kart Champion and, in 1995, he won the Italian ICA Senior title. Two years later, he became the youngest ever winner of

the European Supercup A and also won the Ayrton Senna Memorial Cup in Japan.

In 1998, Button moved to Formula Ford. He took the British Championship with nine wins, was runner-up in the European Championship and won the Formula Ford Festival. The following year saw Button move up to Formula 3 where, once again, he made an instant impression. Indeed, he took pole position for the very first race of the year. He finished the season third in the championship; achievements that earned him the Formula 3 Avon Rookie of the Year award.

In 1999 Button tested for Prost and outpaced Jean Alesi! Williams quickly signed him for the following season, to drive alongside Ralf Schumacher.

Button's first year in Formula One was a success, with him winning a point at his second Grand Prix, in Brazil, where he was the youngest ever British driver to score a championship point. He went on to finish the season in eighth place. In 2001, Button moved to Benetton, where he struggled with an innovative new car. However, the following season, with the team renamed Renault F1, things improved and he finished the championship in seventh place.

Button went on to drive for BAR Honda in 2003, alongside Jacques Villeneuve, with whom Button fell out in the first race of the season. Villeneuve spoilt a points-finish by coming into the pits when it was Button's turn. Even so, Button still finished ninth in the championship.

In 2004, his second year with BAR Honda, despite not winning a race, Button managed to finish third in the Championship by consistent point scoring, including four second places and six third places.

Sadly, he did less well in 2005, finishing ninth in the championship. This was due in part to a disqualification at San Marino, which led to a three-race ban.

For 2006, Button signed to drive for Williams, but

backed out when he found that BMW would not be supplying engines. Therefore, he remained with BAR Honda. Ironically, though, Button had tried to return to Williams for 2005, but BAR Honda refused to let him go.

He remained with Honda for 2007 and 2008.

Thomas (Tommy) BYRNE

Nationality: Irish
Born: 6th May 1958
Seasons: 1982
Team/manufacturer(s): Theodore
Grands Prix: 5
Race wins: 0
Championship wins: 0

Irishman Tommy Byrne started off rallying a Mini in the mid-1970s but stopped after a crash. However, his interest was soon rekindled and, in 1977, he bought a Formula Ford car and entered a number of races but without any success.

The following year, his luck changed when he drove a PRS car in Formula Ford where he won his first race. This led to a works drive with PRS in 1979 but he lost control of his car too many times.

In 1981, Byrne switched to Formula 2000 and won the British and European titles. This changed his fortunes and he drove in British Formula 3 the next year, winning the Marlboro title. That same year he was offered the chance to test for McLaren but turned it down in favour of a drive with the Theodore team. Sadly, though, his one season was not a success and he failed to complete any of the five Grands Prix he entered.

Byrne then returned to Formula 3 until 1985 when he moved to the USA to drive in the American Racing Series and other events. After retiring from racing he settled in Ohio and worked as a race instructor and commentator.

C

CABIANCA, Giulio
CADE, Phil
CAFFI, Alex
CAMPBELL JONES, John
CAMPOS, Adrian
CANNON, John
CANTONI, Eitel
CAPELLI, Ivan
CARINI, Piero
CASTELLOTTI, Eugenio
CECOTTO, Johnny
CERVERT, Francois
CHABOUND, Eugene
CHAMBERLAIN, Jay
CHAPMAN, Colin
CHARLTON, Dave
CHAVES, Pedro
CHEEVER, Eddie
CHIESA, Andrea
CHIMERI, Ettori

CHIRON, Louis
CLAES, Johnny
CLARK, Jim
COGAN, Kevin
COLLINS, Peter
COLLOMB, Bernard
COLOMBO, Alberto
COMAS, Erik
COMOTTI, Franco
CONSTANTINE, George
CORDTS, John
COULTHARD, David
COURAGE, Piers
CRAFT, Chris
CRAWFORD, Jim
CRESPO, Alberto
CREUS, Antonio
CROOK, Tony
CROSSLEY, Geoff

Adrian Campos

Giulio Cabianca

Giulio CABIANCA

Nationality: Italian
Born: 17th February 1923
Died: 15th June 1961
Seasons: 1958-1960
Team/manufacturer(s): OSCA, Maserati, Cooper
Grands Prix: 4
Race wins: 0
Championship wins: 0

Giulio Cabianca was born to a respected family in Verona, Italy and began racing in his twenties. He first made a name for himself as a sportscar driver in the 1950s when he was driving for OSCA. In 1951 he was Italian 1100cc Champion and also won the Italian Grand Prix class. The following year, he was Italian 1500cc champion.

By 1955, Cabianca won his class in the Targa Florio and finished seventh overall.

In 1958, Cabianca was the Italian GT Champion and also made his first Formula One appearances at the Monaco and Italian Grands Prix, driving for first OSCA then Maserati.

The following year, he again entered the Italian Grand Prix in a Maserati and, in 1960, he drove a Cooper-Ferrari in the same event and finished fourth.

Cabianca was racing the same car at Modena in 1961 when the throttle appeared to stick. The car flew out through the entrance and collided with a taxi on a public road. He was killed, along with three people in the taxi.

Philip (Phil) CADE

Nationality: American
Born: 12th June 1916
Died: 28th August 2001
Seasons: 1959
Team/manufacturer(s): Maserati
Grands Prix: 1
Race wins: 0
Championship wins: 0

Iowa-born Philip Cade was a keen amateur driver who was best known for racing his highly modified prewar Maserati single-seater at various SCCA events around the USA. This unique car had a V8 Chrysler engine in place of the usual Maserati V8 and became a regular sight at races and hillclimbs.

In 1959, Cade entered the car into the US Grand Prix, which was held at Sebring. Unfortunately, it suffered from engine problems and he was unable to start the race.

Cade later bought another Maserati, a 250F, and contin-ued to race through the 1960s. His original car is still in existence, although Cade died in 2001.

Alessandro (Alex) CAFFI

Nationality: Italian
Born: 18th March 1964
Seasons: 1986-1991
Team/manufacturer(s): Footwork (Arrows), Dallara, Osella
Grands Prix: 75
Race wins: 0
Championship wins: 0

Alex Caffi was born to race because his father was one of five brothers who enjoyed racing cars and bikes. Alex himself began racing motorbikes when he was just 11 years old. Five years later, he switched to competing in cars and, a year after that, he progressed to single-seaters.

By 1983, Caffi was doing well in Formula 3, coming second in the Italian championship in 1984 and 1985. This led to his Formula One debut in 1987, driving for Osella, but with little success. A move to Scuderia Italia Dallara the following year helped and, in 1989, his best result was a fourth place at Monaco.

After a string of unlucky seasons, which were more down to the cars than him, Caffi quit Formula One to concentrate on touring cars and later, sportscars. He has also spent time as an instructor in Italy and has also acted as the Grand Prix Masters' safety car and test driver.

Michael John CAMPBELL-JONES

Nationality: British
Born: 21st January 1930
Seasons: 1962-1963
Team/manufacturer(s): Lotus, Lola
Grands Prix: 2
Race wins: 0
Championship wins: 0

Born in Leatherhead, John Campbell-Jones, as he was known, earned his money as a car dealer and had some success racing sportscars in the 1950s. Then, towards the end of the decade he bought a Formula 2 Cooper which he raced in England and abroad.

His first Formula One race was the 1962 Belgian Grand Prix, in which he finished in 11th place, driving a Lotus-

Adrian Campos

Climax. The following year he raced a Lola-Climax at the British Grand Prix and came 13th.

Campbell-Jones then slowly dropped out of racing to concentrate on his car dealership and he also owned a restaurant. He retired to Ramsgate in Kent.

Adrián CAMPOS SUÑER

Nationality: Spanish
Born: 17th June 1960
Seasons: 1987-1988
Team/manufacturer(s): Minardi
Grands Prix: 21
Race wins: 0
Championship wins: 0

Born Adrián Campos Suñer to a very wealthy family, as a child he raced radio-controlled cars and was the 1980 Spanish National Champion. The next year he was kid-

Alex Caffi

Ivan Capelli

Piero Carini

napped by Basque separatists and held hostage for three months. After that, he decided to race real cars but his family insisted he was accompanied by an armed bodyguard.

Campos began in European Formula 3 but had little success with his own car. By 1985, though, he had finished third in the German Formula 3 Championship. The following year he competed in Formula 3000 and did some testing for Tyrrell.

By 1987, he got some financial backing and was able to buy a drive with Minardi for that season and part of the following. However, he failed to shine in Formula One.

Campos later turned his attention to business, but continued to race as well, winning the Spanish Touring Car Championship in 1994. He then retired and formed Adrián Campos Motorsport which ran cars in the Open Fortuna serie and, later, GP2 and Spanish Formula 3.

John CANNON

Nationality: Canadian
Born: 23rd June 1937
Died: 18th October 1999
Seasons: 1971
Team/manufacturer(s): BRM
Grands Prix: 1
Race wins: 0
Championship wins: 0

A Canadian born in England, John Cannon began his racing career in California, driving an Elva Courier in 1960. He later moved on to Can-Am where he performed well, including a dramatic win in the wet at Laguna Seca in 1968.

Cannon was then able to move to single-seaters and drove in Formula A for the 1969 season, finishing fourth in the championship and winning it the following year.

In 1971, Cannon drove a BRM in the US Grand Prix, his only Formula One appearance where he finished in 14th place. After that, he raced in Formula 5000 and also did some USAC and Can-Am races.

Cannon was killed in 1991 when the light aircraft he was in crash-landed in a cornfield in New Mexico.

Eitel Danilo CANTONI

Nationality: Uruguayan
Born: 4th October 1906
Died: 6th June 1997
Seasons: 1952
Team/manufacturer(s): Maserati
Grands Prix: 3
Race wins: 0
Championship wins: 0

Eitel Cantoni was born in Montevideo and came to Europe in the late 1940s, along with other South American drivers, to compete in motor racing.

In 1952, he competed in three Formula One races, driving a Maserati. These were the British, German and Italian Grands Prix. Unfortunately, the only race he finished was the latter one, where he came 11th.

While in Europe, Cantoni also took part in some non-championship races. He later returned to South America where he died in 1997.

Ivan Franco CAPELLI

Nationality: Italian
Born: 24th May 1963
Seasons: 1985-1993
Team/manufacturer(s): Tyrrell, AGS, March, Leyton House, Ferrari, Jordan
Grands Prix: 98
Race wins: 0
Championship wins: 0

Italian Ivan Capelli went via the usual karting route straight to Formula 3 and won the Italian series in his second season, 1983. A year later, he'd won the European Formula 3 Championship.

The next season, 1985, saw Capelli make a detour into Formula 3000 and he impressed enough to find himself racing in Formula One for Tyrrell that same season. Despite finishing fourth at the Australian Grand Prix that year, he

was unable to secure a drive for 1986, so Capelli returned to Formula 3000 and ended up winning the championship.

This led to renewed interest from the top and the offer of a drive with March in 1987. However, he was struggling with second-rate cars that year and did much better in 1988, with a second place at the French Grand Prix.

Sadly, though, that was the height of his Formula One success and Capelli made little progress in the seasons that followed. After just two races with Jordan in 1993, he was dismissed from the team and went on to compete in sportscar and touring car events. He also worked as a commentator for Italian television.

Piero CARINI

Nationality: Italian
Born: 6th March 1921
Died: 30th May 1957
Seasons: 1952-1953
Team/manufacturer(s): Ferrari
Grands Prix: 3
Race wins: 0
Championship wins: 0

Born in Genova, Italy, Piero Carini first made a name for himself in 1950 when he finished third in the Formula 2 Modena Grand Prix, driving an OSCA. This led him to drive a Ferrari for the 1952 season and he competed in the French and German Grands Prix but failed to finish.

The following season he became a works driver for Ferrari but only drove in one Formula One event, the Italian Grand Prix. Again, though, he had to retire with mechanical problems.

Carini continued racing and achieved a class win in the 1955 Targa Florio, driving an OSCA. Two years later, he was competing in a 1500cc sportscar race near St Etienne, when his Ferrari Testarossa ploughed through the central barrier and hit another car. Both Carini and the other driver were killed on the spot.

Eugenio CASTELLOTTI

Nationality: Italian
Born: 10th October 1930
Died: 14th March 1957
Seasons: 1955-1957
Team/manufacturer(s): Lancia, Ferrari
Grands Prix: 14
Race wins: 0
Championship wins: 0

Italian Eugenio Castellotti came from a wealthy background and used his money to help work his way up to the top of the racing scene in the 1950s.

By 1955, he was ready for his Formula One debut, driving a Lancia at the Argentinean Grand Prix. Soon after, he finished in second place at the Monaco Grand Prix that year. And, at the end of the season he finished the championship in a very respectable third place.

The following year, Castellotti didn't do quite as well in Formula One, coming sixth in the championship. He did, however, make up for it in other disciplines, by winning the Mille Miglia and the Sebring 12 Hours.

In 1957, Castellotti's promising career came to a tragic end when he was killed at Modena while testing a Ferrari. He was only 27 years old.

Alberto (Johnny) CECOTTO

Nationality: Venezuelan
Born: 25th January 1956
Seasons: 1983-1984
Team/manufacturer(s): Theodore, Toleman
Grands Prix: 23
Race wins: 0
Championship wins: 0

Venezuela-born Johnny Cecotto made a name for himself in motorcycle racing, when he became the youngest ever 350cc World Champion in 1975, at the age of just 19. He repeated the success the following year and then, in 1978, won the 750cc World Championship.

In 1980, he decided to transfer his skills to four wheels, driving in Formula 2. Just two years later, he finished second in the championship. Formula One followed just a year later, driving for the little known Theodore team, run by multimillionaire, Teddy Yip. Cecotto got off to a good start, finishing sixth at Long Beach, his second Grand Prix. Sadly, though, the rest of his season was less successful.

A move to Toleman in 1984 was cut short when he crashed at Brands Hatch and ended up breaking his leg badly. The injury meant that Cecotto had to stop competing in single-seater cars and, the next year, he switched to touring cars; a discipline in which he excelled.

Albert François CERVERT (François Cervert)

Nationality: French
Born: 25th February 1944
Died: 6th October 1973
Seasons: 1970-1973
Team/manufacturer(s): March, Tyrrell
Grands Prix: 47
Race wins: 1
Championship wins: 0

This talented Frenchman started off on a very different career path – he wanted to become a concert pianist. However, a Volant Elf scholarship win in 1966 kick-started

François Cervert

Dave Charlton

a life as a racing driver.

Cervert's first year of racing proper was in Formula 3, and he won the French Championship in his second season in 1968. A year after this, he found himself racing in Formula 2 and finished second in the French championship.

That same year, Cervert made his Formula One debut, driving his Formula 2 Tecno at the Nürburgring. In 1970, he was signed up with Tyrrell for a full season in Formula One. He drove very well that year and the next, finishing in second place at the French and German Grands Prix in 1971, before winning at Watkins Glen in the USA.

In 1972 Cervert continued to race in Formula One and in other disciplines (he came second at Le Mans) and looked set to be a great success. In 1973, though, he was qualifying at Watkins Glen, the circuit where he'd won just two years before, when his Tyrrell crashed and he died of his injuries.

Marius Eugène CHABOUND

Nationality: French
Born: 12th April 1907
Died: 28th December 1983
Seasons: 1950-1951
Team/manufacturer(s): Talbot-Lago
Grands Prix: 3
Race wins: 0
Championship wins: 0

Eugène Chabound was born in Lyons, the son of a wealthy businessman. As a teenager, he was a successful athlete but moved into racing in 1936, driving a Delahaye. Just a year later, he entered the Le Mans 24 Hour race and, the year after that, he won the same event, driving with Jean Tremoulet.

After the Second World War, Chabound continued his racing career and, in 1946, he won the Belgian Grand Prix and also did well in a number of French races, still driving a Delahaye. A year later, he was French Champion with Ecurie France.

By the end of the 1940s, the Delahayes were no longer competitive so Chabound cut back on his racing to build a second-hand car dealership. Before long, though, he was back racing at Le Mans and the Monte Carlo Rally, among other events. In 1950 and 1951 he took part in three Formula One Grands Prix, driving Talbot Lagoes, his best result being a fifth place at Reims.

Chabound was involved in a bad accident at the 1951 Le Mans 24 Hour and got trapped under his car. After that, he decided to retire from racing, although he competed in rallying until 1953. He then concentrated on his car-sales business.

Jay CHAMBERLAIN

Nationality: American
Born: 29th December 1925
Died: 1st August 2001
Seasons: 1962
Team/manufacturer(s): Lotus
Grands Prix: 3
Race wins: 1
Championship wins: 0

Born in Los Angeles, Jay Chamberlain was a keen Lotus fan, to the extent that he was the first US distributor for the marque, back in the 1950s. He also enjoyed racing the little British sportscars in SCCA events.

In 1957, Chamberlain came to Europe to race at Le Mans in a Lotus, coming ninth overall and winning the 750cc class. He also raced at Rouen that year but was badly injured in a crash in practice for the Reims 12 Hour event. The next year, fully recovered, he returned to Le Mans with a Lotus, but crashed at Musanne.

Thankfully, he was uninjured this time.

Back in the USA, Chamberlain turned his hand to racing a Formula Junior Lotus and then, in 1962, he came to

Colin Chapman

Europe again to compete with a Lotus 18. That year, he raced the car in three Formula One events: the British, German and Italian Grands Prix. His best result was 15th at the British event at Aintree.

After retiring from racing, Jay Chamberlain remained actively involved with Lotus and with other historic cars. He died in 2001, soon after retiring.

Anthony Colin Bruce CHAPMAN

Nationality: British
Born: 19th May 1928
Died: 16th December 1982
Seasons: 1956
Team/manufacturer(s): Lotus
Grands Prix: 1
Race wins: 1
Championship wins: 0

Full name, Anthony Colin Bruce Chapman, this talented engineer car builder actually entered one Formula One race. Born in London, Chapman studied structural engi-

neering and, in 1948, he modified an Austin 7 for use in local races. This was the Lotus Mk1. This, in turn, led to other cars and, in 1957, came the Mk7 – the legendary Lotus 7.

Chapman's engineering skills revolutionised Formula One, with his lightweight, mid-engined cars, often driven by Jim Clark. By 1963, Team Lotus had won its first World Championship in Formula One.

Although by this time Chapman didn't usually race, he was an accomplished driver and, in 1956, he entered the French Grand Prix. However, he crashed into the back of teammate Mike Hawthorn's car and Chapman's car was too damaged to continue to race with. That, then, was the extent of his Formula One race career.

However, Chapman's influence on the sport was immense. As well as his engineering innovations, he also introduced major advertising sponsorship into racing.

Chapman died of a heart attack in 1982, but Lotus cars continue to be made, and his influence remains to be seen in Formula One and other types of motorsport.

David (Dave) CHARLTON

Nationality: South African
Born: 27th October 1936
Seasons: 1965, 1967-1968, 1970-1975
Team/manufacturer(s): Lotus, Brabham, McLaren
Grands Prix: 13
Race wins: 0
Championship wins: 0

Although brought up in South Africa, Dave Charlton was born in Yorkshire, England. He began racing in club events, and then progressed to the South African national series in 1965, first in a Lotus 20, then a more powerful Brabham BT11 and, by 1974, a McLaren M23.

This meant that he competed in the South African Grand Prix every year between 1965 and 1975. He also travelled to Europe to race in the 1971 British Grand Prix and, the next year, the French, British and German events.

Although Charlton was successful in his own country, winning the national series in 1972, 1974 and 1975, after that he had less success and moved into saloon car racing,

Eddie Cheever

in which he continued to compete until the early 1980s. After retiring, he continued to race in historic events and hillclimbs in South Africa and England.

Pedro Matos CHAVES

Nationality: Portuguese
Born: 27th February 1965
Seasons: 1991
Team/manufacturer(s): Coloni
Grands Prix: 13
Race wins: 0
Championship wins: 0

Pedro Chaves, was born in Bonfirm in Portugal and worked his way up through karting to Formula Ford, in which series he won the local championship in 1985.

He then became the first Portuguese driver to go international. He moved to the UK in 1987 to race in British Formula Ford. By 1990, he had progressed to, and won, the British Formula 3000 Championship.

The following year, Chaves moved to Formula One, driving a Cosworth C4 for the Coloni team. Sadly, though, it was not a successful season, with him failing to pre-qualify for any of the 13 Grands Prix he entered. After the Portuguese Grand Prix, he quit the team and finished his Formula One career.

Chaves returned to Formula 3000 in 1992 before going to the USA to compete in the Indy Lights series. He has also rallied, twice winning the Portuguese Rally Championship, and has raced at Le Mans and the FIA GT Championship.

Edward McKay (Eddie) CHEEVER

Nationality: American
Born: 10th January 1958
Seasons: 1978, 1980-1089
Team/manufacturer(s): Theodore, Hesketh, Osella, Tyrrell, Ligier, Renault, Alfa Romeo, Haas Lola, Arrows
Grands Prix: 143
Race wins: 0
Championship wins: 0

Although born in Arizona, American Eddie Cheever grew up in Rome. There, he began racing karts at an early age and, at the age of 15, he won both the Italian and the European championships.

Just two years later, he was making a name for himself in Formula 3 at just 17 years old. The next season he was driving in Formula 2 and was hoping to break into Formula One by the time he was 19. His first choice of team was Ferrari, but the place was taken by Gilles Villeneuve, so Cheever had to make do with the less promising Theodore team.

By the time he was 20, in 1978, Cheever was at his first Grand Prix, in Argentina, but failed to qualify. Over the next couple of seasons, he switched from one team to the next to progress his career. In 1981 he gained five points with Tyrrell and, the next year, three podium finishes with Ligier.

However, the peak of his Formula One career was in 1983. Driving for Renault, alongside Alain Prost, he achieved four podium finishes and 22 points. From then on, he had little success in Formula One and retired from it in 1989. Cheever then raced in the American CART series and also competed in the Indy 500 – winning the event in 1998, with his own team, Cheever Racing. He continued to race part-time, including Indy 500 and the GP Masters series, which he won at Silverstone in 2006.

Pedro Chaves

Andrea CHIESA

Nationality: Swiss
Born: 6th May 1964
Seasons: 1992
Team/manufacturer(s): Fondmetal
Grands Prix: 10
Race wins: 0
Championship wins: 0

Andrea Chiesa was actually born in Milan, Italy but with Swiss nationality. He began racing in karts and moved on to Italian Formula 3 in 1986, showing great promise.

A switch to Formula 3000 in 1988 led to a slow start for Chiesa but, the next year, he finished the championship in sixth place. This was followed by a seventh place in 1990, while he didn't perform well in 1991.

Despite that, Chiesa was signed for Fondmetal's Formula One team for the next season. However, it was not a success and he only qualified for three out of ten Grands Prix and failed to finish those. He left the team before the end of the season.

In 1993, Chiesa made a short incursion into Indycar before having a break from the sport for a couple of years. By 1996, he was back in the driving seat, competing in the FIA GT Championship. He's since appeared in various sportscar races with some successful results. He has also done some media work and driving instruction.

Ettore Muro CHIMERI

Nationality: Venezuelan
Born: 4th June 1924
Died: 27th February 1960
Seasons: 1960
Team/manufacturer(s): Maserati
Grands Prix: 1
Race wins: 0
Championship wins: 0

Ettore Chimeri was born in Milan to Italian parents, but his family moved to Venezuela when he was just two years old. As an adult, he built up a successful construction business which gave him the money to indulge in his hobby of motor racing.

In the 1950s, he won several local events in his Ferrari 250GT. In 1959, he competed in a Maserati at Sebring and, apparently, he stopped off during qualifying to buy a hot-dog from a stand and then continued to race, still finishing well. Sadly, though, he was disqualified for his diversion.

Chimeri's one Formula One outing was in a tatty Maserati 250F at the Argentinean Grand Prix in 1960. However, he ran into the back of a stalled car and so was unable to finish the race.

Chimeri was killed later that same year when his Ferrari 250 crashed during practice for the Gran Premio Libertad sportscar race near Havana.

Louis Alexandre CHIRON

Nationality: Monegasque
Born: 3rd August 1899
Died: 22nd June 1979
Seasons: 1950-1951, 1953, 1955-1956, 1958
Team/manufacturer(s): Maserati, Talbot-Lago, OSCA, Lancia
Grands Prix: 19
Race wins: 0
Championship wins: 0

Louis Chiron was born in Monte Carlo and was passionate about cars and motorsport from a young age. During the First World War he served as a chauffeur in the army. After the war he worked for a time as a professional dancer but soon began racing in Grand Prix events.

Before long, he was winning races across Europe, including the 1933 Spa 24 Hours event.

Chiron retired from racing just before the outbreak of the Second World War but soon made a comeback after the end of hostilities and drove a Talbot-Lago to victory in two French Grands Prix.

After the 1949 Monte Carlo Rally, Chiron made the news

Louis Chiron

Jim Clark

when he publicly announced, at the post-event party, that one of the female drivers, Hellé Nice, had been a Gestapo agent. Although he couldn't substantiate this claim, it destroyed the woman's career.

Despite his age, Chiron continued racing during the 1950s, winning the 1954 Monte Carlo Rally. He also competed in the new Formula One series and, in 1965 at the age of 56, he became the oldest driver to compete in a Formula One race. To great applause, he drove a Lancia D50 to finish sixth at the Monaco Grand Prix.

After retiring, Chiron became involved in the organisation of the Monaco Grand Prix. He was later honoured with a statue alongside the circuit and one of the corners was named after him. More recently, Bugatti named a concept car after him.

Jonathan (Johnny) CLAES

Nationality: Belgian
Born: 11th August 1916
Died: 3rd February 1956
Seasons: 1950-1953, 1955
Team/manufacturer(s): Ecurie Belge, Gordini, HWM, Maserati, Ecurie Nationale Belge
Grands Prix: 25
Race wins: 0
Championship wins: 0

Johnny Claes was brought up in Belgium but was born in London to a Scottish mother and Belgian father. He began his career as a jazz musician but fell in love with racing in his early twenties, when he went to the 1947 French Grand Prix.

His wealthy father promptly bought his son a Talbot and set him on the road to becoming a racing driver. The young man made good use of his new car, competing in various events. These included a number of Grand Prix entries, starting in 1950.

Later, he drove with various teams in 1952 and 1953, but with little success. He faired better outside Formula One, when he won the 1953 Liège-Rome-Liège Rally, after driving single-handed for 52 hours.

Illness meant that Claes raced little in 1954, but he did more in 1955, including finishing in third place at Le Mans. His last Grand Prix was in Holland that year, when he finished 11th. Sadly, his health continued to deteriorate and he died of tuberculosis in February 1956, at the age of just 39.

James (Jim) CLARK

Nationality: British
Born: 4th March 1936
Died: 7th April 1968
Seasons: 1960-1968
Team/manufacturer(s): Lotus
Grands Prix: 73
Race wins: 25
Championship wins: 2

Clark grew up on a farm in Scotland and enjoyed racing bicycles and, later, cars from an early age. His first competition driving was in rallying and local racing. He initially raced in his own Sunbeam Talbot, but scored his first big win in 1957 in a Porsche 356 1600 Super, when he took the Border Motor Racing Club Trophy. Before long, he was driving a Jaguar D-Tyre for the Borders Reivers Team.

In 1959, Clark tested a Lotus Formula Two car and

Jim Clark

Lotus on 7th April. The track was damp and, during testing, his car went off the track and hit some trees at high speed. Clark was killed instantly. It was claimed that the accident was due to a flat tyre, not driver error.

Kevin COGAN

Nationality: American
Born: 31st March 1956
Seasons: 1980-1981
Team/manufacturer(s): RAM, Tyrrell
Grands Prix: 2
Race wins: 0
Championship wins: 0

American driver Kevin Cogan was born in California and shot to prominence in the Formula Atlantic Championship. Indeed, his performance was such that he got a drive with a private Williams for the 1980 Canadian Grand Prix, but he failed to qualify. The following year he had a works drive with Tyrrell at the US Grand Prix West but again, he failed to qualify and the team let him go. And that was the end of his Formula One career.

In 1981, Cogan moved to Indy cars but got off to a bad start at the 1982 Indy 500 event. During warm-up, his car span out of control and crashed into Mario Andretti's car. The famous driver yelled furiously "This is what happens when children do a man's job!" However, four years later

Cogan proved himself by finishing the race in second place.

Unfortunately, Cogan had more of his fair share of accidents, including a very bad one during the 1989 Indy 500, when his car exploded into hundreds of pieces. In 1993 he retired from racing and became a successful businessman.

Peter John COLLINS

Nationality: British
Born: 6th November 1931
Died: 3rd August 1958
Seasons: 1952-1958
Team/manufacturer(s): HWM, Vanwall, Maserati, Ferrari
Grands Prix: 35
Race wins: 0
Championship wins: 0

Peter Collins' father worked in the motor trade and his son served an apprenticeship at Ford's Dagenham plant. He also raced successfully in 500cc Formula 3, where he made an impression.

The young Peter Collins switched to Formula 2 in 1952, sharing a drive with Stirling Moss for HWM, and the pair raced successfully in Britain and Europe. He also competed in five Formula One races that season and three the next, but had no success so he left the team.

After spells with Vanwall and Maserati, Collins signed with Ferrari for 1956 and really started to get results. He

returned times comparable to the team's Formula One driver, Graham Hill, despite not having had any experience with single-seaters.

Lotus signed Clark to drive in its Formula Two team but, within months, he'd been switched to Formula One, Graham Hill having moved to BRM. Clark soon began to make a name for himself, scoring points at his second Grand Prix, at Spa, by finishing fifth. Sadly, this success was marred by a crash that claimed the life of his teammate, Alan Stacey.

The 1961 season was a difficult one for Clark. A collision with a Ferrari driven by Wolfgang von Trip at the Italian Grand Prix led to the Ferrari careering into the crowd, killing the driver and 14 spectators. Although Clark knew the accident wasn't his fault, he still had to be involved in a lengthy enquiry.

The following year was better, with Clark finishing second in the championship. In 1963, though, he took the World Championship with 54 points.

In 1965, Clark again won the World Championship, despite missing the Monte Carlo Grand Prix to travel to the US to compete in the Indy 500. Here, he was the first driver to win the race in a mid-engined car, and the only driver ever to win both events in the same year.

Sadly, the following year was less successful, with Lotus struggling to compete with new 3.0-litre regulations. With an underpowered car, Clark finished the championship in sixth place.

For 1967, though, the combination of the Lotus 49 car and Cosworth 3.0-litre V8 was destined to be a success, and Clark took third place in the championship.

The next year began with Clark winning his 25th Formula One race and it looked as if victory would be in his grasp. However, it was not to be. Against his wishes, Clark travelled to Hockenheim to compete in a Formula Two race for

Peter Collins

Erik Comas

finished second at Monaco and won at Belgium and France. He could have been World Champion that year but, during the Italian Grand Prix, he passed his car to team leader, Fangio, to let him go on and take the title.

Collins' last Formula One win was at the 1957 British Grand Prix. Later that year, though, he crashed at the German Grand Prix and died of head injuries later the same day

Niçois Bernard COLLOMB-CLERC (Bernard Collomb)

Nationality: French
Born: 7th October 1930
Seasons: 1961-1964
Team/manufacturer(s): Cooper, Lotus
Grands Prix: 6
Race wins: 0
Championship wins: 0

Bernard Collomb came from Nice, where he ran a garage and raced motorcycles. In 1960 he bought a Formula 2 car and began to race it, albeit without success.

The next year, he took his racing more seriously, entering Formula One events in a Lotus 24-Climax V8. His first champi-

onship race was at Reims. From then to 1964, he competed intermittently but had little success and gave up Formula One at the end of that season and went back to Formula 2.

By the end of 1968, he'd given up with single-seater racing and competed occasionally in GT racing, while continuing with his garage business.

Alberto COLOMBO

Nationality: Italian
Born: 23rd February 1946
Seasons: 1978
Team/manufacturer(s): ATS, Merzario
Grands Prix: 3
Race wins: 0
Championship wins: 0

Italian Alberto Colombo's first success was winning the Italian Formula 3 Championship in 1974. The following year saw him move into Formula 2, a series he stayed with, with mixed success until, in 1978, he had a chance of a Formula One drive.He was drafted in by ATS to drive at the Belgian Grand Prix, after the team's own driver quit. Colombo drove well but, in the face of more experienced

competition, he failed to qualify for the race proper. The same happened at the Spanish Grand Prix and ATS let him go after that.

Colombo had one more chance at Formula One that year, when he drove for Merazio at the Italian Grand Prix. This time, though, he failed to pre-qualify and that was the end of his Formula One adventure.

He then returned to Formula 2 for the next two seasons, where he drove reasonably well with some top five finishes. After that, he retired from racing to manage the Sanremo team.

Érik COMAS

Nationality: French
Born: 28th September 1963
Seasons: 1991-1994
Team/manufacturer(s): Ligier, Larrousse
Grands Prix: 63
Race wins: 0
Championship wins: 0

Érik Comas had a short spell in karts in his late teens but soon switched to racing a Renault 5 (which he bought from

Jean Alesi). In 1983, he won the Volant Elf competition and, the following year, competed in Formula Renault and finished fourth in the championship. In 1985, he won the championship with no less than eight wings.

By 1988, Comas had won the French Formula 3 title and, two years after, won the Formula 3000 title. This led to the offer of a Formula One drive with Ligier but the cars weren't up to his talent and he had a disappointing two seasons. Next came a move to the Larrousse team in 1993, where he had a little more success, regularly finishing in the top ten.

In 1994, Comas witnessed the accident which claimed the life of Ayrton Senna at Imola, and that put him off Formula One. He retired at the end of the season. He went on to compete in Japanese sportscars and rallying, and also managed other drivers.

Gianfranco (Franco) COMOTTI

Nationality: Italian
Born: 24th July 1906
Died: 10th May 1963
Seasons: 1950, 1952
Team/manufacturer(s): Maserati, Ferrari
Grands Prix: 2
Race wins: 0
Championship wins: 0

Born Gianfranco Comotti in Brescia, northern Italy, this Italian driver had a successful racing career between the wars, when he raced an Alfa Romeo to victory in the 1933 Naples Grand Prix, and performed well in countless other events.

After the Second World War, Comotti moved to France to compete in Lago-Talbot cars, in which he performed well; most notably coming fourth in the 1948 French Grand Prix.

Returning to Italy, he raced a Maserati in the first Italian Formula One Grand Prix, at Monza. Unfortunately, the car wasn't up to the job, and he finished second to last.

Comotti had another attempt at a Formula One race in 1952, when he drove a Ferrari at the French Grand Prix. This time he finished 12th. It wasn't enough to persuade him to continue, though, and he retired from racing soon after.

In later life, Comotti worked for BP around the Mediterranean.

George CONSTANTINE

Nationality: American
Born: 22nd February 1918
Died: 7th January 1968
Seasons: 1959
Team/manufacturer(s): Cooper
Grands Prix: 1
Race wins: 0
Championship wins: 0

George Constantine was born in Massachusetts in 1918. In the 1950s, he made a name for himself driving, usually, a Jaguar XK120 in SCCA events in North America. In 1956, he won the Watkins Glen Grand Prix, driving a Jaguar D-type.

He had a good season in 1959, driving an Aston Martin DBR2 to victory on a number of occasions, including the Nassau Trophy, and earned the USSC Driver of the Year award. Also in 1959, he made his one and only Formula One entry, in the inaugural US Grand Prix at Sebring, driving a Cooper-Climax T45. However, he had to retire because of an overheating engine.

Constantine continued to race into the 1960s, but died in 1968 after fighting a long illness.

John CORDTS

Nationality: Canadian
Born: 23rd July 1935
Seasons: 1969
Team/manufacturer(s): Brabham
Grands Prix: 1
Race wins: 0
Championship wins: 0

Although a Canadian, John Cordts was born in Sweden but he grew up in Ontario. There, he raced sportscars during the 1960s and made enough of an impression to be crowned Canadian Driver of the Year in 1965.

He competed in the USRRC Championship in a McLaren

M2B. Later, he got a taste for Can-Am and became a regular competitor between 1969 and 1974, driving a variety of McLaren cars. His best result was second place in the Road America round at Elkhart Lake in 1974.

Cordts' single Formula One appearance was at the Canadian Grand Prix of 1969, when he drove a Brabham but had to retire because of an oil leak.

He retired to Vancouver Island where he became known as a talented woodcarver.

David Marshall COULTHARD

Nationality: British
Born: 27th March 1971
Seasons: 1994-
Team/manufacturer(s): Williams, McLaren, Red Bull
Grands Prix: 229
Race wins: 13
Championship wins: 0

David Coulthard was brought up in the southwest of Scotland, where his father ran the family haulage company and was a keen karter; the young lad took up the same interest at an early age. At the age of just 12, he was the Scottish Junior Kart Champion, and he was to take this title again for the next five years running. What's more, in 1986 and 1987, he was also British Super Kart 1 Champion.

At the age of 18, he was racing in Formula Ford, where he won both the Dunlop/Autosport and P&O Ferries Junior Championships in his first year, which led to him receiving the McLaren/Autosport Young Driver of the Year Award.

The following season, Coulthard competed in Formula Vauxhall Lotus and the GM Lotus Euroseries. He came fourth and fifth, respectively, in the championships.

Coulthard progressed to British Formula 3 in 1991, and finished the season second in the championship. In 1992 and 1993 he raced in Formula 3000, and came ninth and then third at the end of the seasons. In 1992, Coulthard also won the GT class at Le Mans. While competing in Formula 3000, Coulthard tested for Benetton and Williams and became Williams' test driver for the 1994 season. He was meant to continue in Formula 3000 that year but a tragic event intervened; Williams' driver Ayrton Senna was killed at the San Marino Grand Prix. Coulthard was called in to take Senna's place, alongside Damon Hill, and his Formula One career began.

Coulthard spent his first season in the shadow of Hill and, on four occasions, had to step aside to let ex-champion Nigel Mansell drive. Even so, the Scot drove well and took second place at Estoril, and finished eighth in the championship. This gained him a full place on the Williams team in 1995, albeit still second to Damon Hill. Coulthard put in mixed performances, with a win at Portugal tainted by some mistakes in other races. He took third place in the championship.

In 1996, Coulthard moved to McLaren and took seventh place in the championship. However, the following year he won two Grands Prix and finished the season in third place.

Coulthard stayed with McLaren and, in 1998, the team had the fastest cars on the track, but the Scot had to give way to his teammate Häkkinen, who went on to win the championship. Coulthard made do with fourth place; a position he matched in 1999. In 2001, Coulthard managed to finish the season in second place, beaten by Michael Schumacher. After that, though, his performances were less successful and he left McLaren at the end of 2004. His next team was the new Red Bull Racing, which he joined

David Coulthard

David Coulthard

in 2005 because they were keen to have a big-name driver on their books. He remained with the team through to 2008.

Piers Raymond COURAGE

Nationality: British
Born: 27th May 1942
Died: 21st June 1970
Seasons: 1967-1970
Team/manufacturer(s): Lotus, BRM, Brabham, De Tomaso
Grands Prix: 29
Race wins: 0
Championship wins: 0

Piers Courage's family ran the famous brewery company of the same name. He was born in Colchester and went to Eton College, the plan being that he'd go into the family business.

Instead, though, he got hooked on racing after his father bought him a Lotus Seven. From there, he got a Lotus 22 and travelled around Europe competing in various events, by now with little financial support from his family.

In 1967, Courage competed in three Formula One events in a Lotus, but didn't perform well. He had a full season racing a BRM in 1968; his best result was fourth place in Italy, plus a handful of top-ten finishes.

In 1969, he moved to Brabham for another full quota of Formula One entries, during which he came second at Monaco and USA.

Courage then moved to De Tomaso-Ford for 1970, driving an underdeveloped car. It was in this car that he crashed during the Dutch Grand Prix at Zandvoort. The car skidded, ran up a bank and rolled over, bursting into flames. Courage was killed instantly.

Piers Courage

Christopher (Chris) CRAFT

Nationality: British
Born: 17th November 1939
Seasons: 1971
Team/manufacturer(s): non-works Brabham
Grands Prix: 2
Race wins: 0
Championship wins: 0

Cornish-born and Essex-bred, Chris Craft began his working life buying women's underwear before he got involved with motor racing, thanks to his brother, who did body repairs. In 1962, he started racing a Ford Anglia and became a successful saloon car and touring car driver.

His single-seater debut was in Formula 3 and he spent some time in this series before driving a Porsche 908 for Alain de Cadenet. This led to a couple of Formula One drives, in De Cadenet's Brabham BT33. However, he failed to qualify for his first event, the Canadian Grand Prix, and retired from the US Grand Prix with suspension problems.

Craft then went on to race sportscars and F5000 cars in the 1970s, before getting back into saloon-car racing.

Later, he teamed up with designer Gordon Murray to develop the Rocket Roadster sports car.

James (Jim) CRAWFORD

Nationality: British
Born: 13th February 1948
Died: 6th August 2002
Seasons: 1975
Team/manufacturer(s): Lotus
Grands Prix: 2
Race wins: 0
Championship wins: 0

Scotsman Jim Crawford was born in Dunfermline and raced in Formula Ford there, while working as a mechanic. He later moved to northern England as a mechanic for racing teams, and built himself a March 73B Formula Atlantic car from spare parts. He drove this to victory in the Southern Organs championship in 1974.

This led to a drive in Formula Atlantic in 1975 and he finished second in the championship. Also in the same year, he was asked to drive for Lotus in the British Grand Prix. However, his lack of experience let him down and he retired after an accident. A second attempt in Italy put him in 13th place, after which he was dropped from the team. Crawford went on to race in various championships in Europe and the USA, including a number of Indy 500 entries. He then retired from racing and moved to Florida where he became captain of a fishing boat. He died of ill health in 2002, at the age of just 54.

Alberto Augusto CRESPO

Nationality: Argentinean
Born: 16th January 1920
Died: 14th August 1991
Seasons: 1952
Team/manufacturer(s): Maserati
Grands Prix: 1
Race wins: 0
Championship wins: 0

Alberto Crespo was born in Buenos Aires in 1920. Very little is known about him, but he was a racing driver for most of his life. In 1952, Crespo was entered into the Italian Grand Prix, driving a Maserati 4CLT-48 run by Erico Plate, however he narrowly missed qualifying for the race.

He later returned to his home country where he became involved with motorsport administration there until his death in Buenos Aires in 1991.

Antonio CREUS

Nationality: Spanish
Born: 28th October 1924
Died: 19th February 1996
Seasons: 1960
Team/manufacturer(s): Maserati
Grands Prix: 1
Race wins: 0
Championship wins: 0

Spanish driver Antonio Creus was born in Madrid in 1924 and was a keen motorcycle racer, as well as competing in cars.

In 1960, Creus entered just one World Championship event, the Argentinean Grand Prix at the start of the season. Driving a Maserati 250F, he qualified in 22nd place but retired from the race after just 16 laps (the winner, Bruce McLaren, completed 80). Afterwards, he explained that the problem was the extreme heat of the day and the fact he was breathing in exhaust fumes from the cars in front – the leaders didn't have this problem. Creus had to go to hospital

where he was treated with oxygen.

Creus then disappeared from top level racing.

Anthony (Tony) CROOK

Nationality: British
Born: 16th February 1920
Seasons: 1952-1953
Team/manufacturer(s): Frazer Nash, Cooper
Grands Prix: 2
Race wins: 0
Championship wins: 0

Born Anthony Crook in Manchester, he was very active in single-seater and sportscar racing in the late 1940 and early 1960s, competing successfully in a Fraser Nash and, less often, an Alfa Romeo. In 1951, he finished the Goodwood season second, behind Mike Hawthorn.

It was in his Frazer Nash that Crook competed in his First Formula One event, the 1952 British Grand Prix at Silverstone, in which he finished in 21st place. He entered the same event the following year, this time in a Cooper-Bristol MkII but had to retire with fuelling problems.

Crook continued to race his Cooper-Bristol in countless events, mostly in the UK, but never another Grand Prix. After a bad accident in the Goodwood 12 Hours race, he

was in hospital for two weeks and decided it was time to retire from the sport. He went on to run Bristol cars and remained chairman after his retirement.

Geoffrey (Geoff) CROSSLEY

Nationality: British
Born: 11th May 1921
Died: 7th January 2002
Seasons: 1950
Team/manufacturer(s): Alta
Grands Prix: 2
Race wins: 0
Championship wins: 0

Derbyshire-born Geoff Crossley raced a Riley before the Second World War. After, though, he bought a brand new Alta racecar and promptly took it to the 1949 Belgium Grand Prix, where he finished in seventh place. Crossley was a keen amateur driver and continued to compete in his car in various events around the UK and, occasionally, abroad. These included two Formula One Grands Prix in 1950. In the British event at Silverstone he finished 17th, while in Belgium he came ninth. Soon after, though, he found the cost of racing prohibitive, and so gave up the sport. He worked as a furniture manufacturer until his retirement.

Anthony Crook

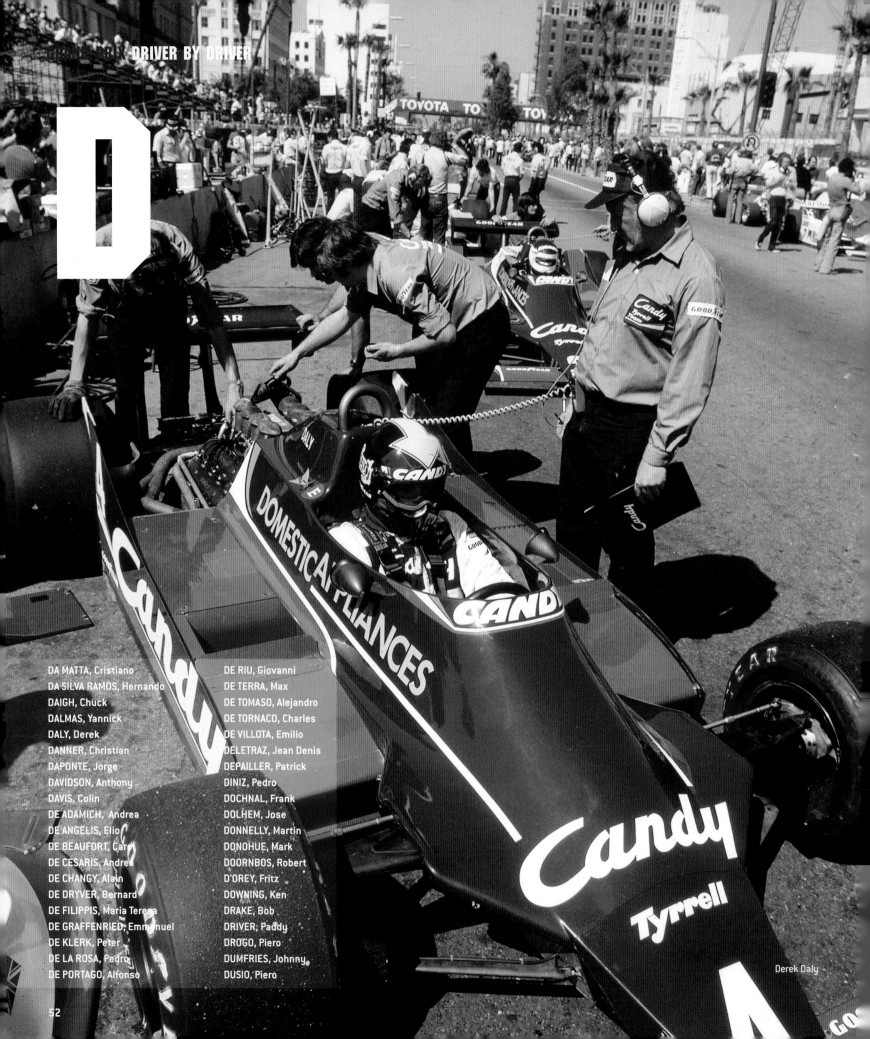

D

Derek Daly

52

Yannick Dalmas

Cristiano Da Matta

Cristiano DA MATTA

Nationality: Brazilian
Born: 19th September 1973
Seasons: 2003-2004
Team/manufacturer(s): Toyota
Grands Prix: 28
Race wins: 0
Championship wins: 0

Cristiano da Matta followed in his father's footsteps – he was Brazilian Touring Car Champion no less than 14 times. Even so, it was not until he was 11 years old that he began racing karts. Before long, though, he was making an impression and soon moved to Formula Ford, winning the Brazilian Championship in 1993, and then the Formula 3 Championship the following year.

After a brief spell racing in the UK, Da Matta moved to the USA to race in Indy Lights, winning the championship in 1998.

He then went on to win the CART Championship in 2001.

By 2003, Da Matta was racing in Formula One, driving for Toyota. He had a good first year, scoring 10 points despite unreliable cars. The next year, though, the car got the better of him and Da Matta didn't do as well.

After that, Da Matta gave up with Formula One, saying there was too much emphasis on car performance and not enough on driver skill. Instead, he raced in the US Champ Car World Series. In 2006, Da Matta's Champ Car collided with a deer during testing and he was very badly injured.

Hernando (Nano) DA SILVA RAMOS

Nationality: Brazilian
Born: 7th December 1925
Seasons: 1955-1956
Team/manufacturer(s): Gordini
Grands Prix: 7
Race wins: 0
Championship wins: 0

Although born in Paris, Hernando da Silva Ramos – nicknamed 'Nano' – was brought up in Brazil. It was there that his racing career began, in an MG. However, for whatever reason, he didn't really take to the sport at that time.

Later, though, he returned to France and bought an Aston Martin DB2, with which he won the 1953 Rallye de Sable, among other events.

By 1955, he was racing with the Gordini team and competed in three Grands Prix that year, his best result being eighth place at his first race, the Dutch Grand Prix. He faired better the following year, with a fifth at Monaco.

Da Silva Ramos then left Gordini but continued to race in other cars, including Coopers and Maseratis. He remained in France after his retirement.

Charles (Chuck) DAIGH

Nationality: American
Born: 29th November 1923
Seasons: 1960
Team/manufacturer(s): Scarab, Cooper
Grands Prix: 7
Race wins: 0
Championship wins: 0

Californian Chuck Daigh raced a Mercury-Kurtis car during the 1950s. He then became involved in a project to build a new sportscar, the Scarab. In this he won various races and the company was spurred on to produce a Formula One car.

Unfortunately, by the time it was built, the front-engined car was dated against the agile new mid-engined single-seaters from the likes of Cooper. Even so, Daigh drove the car for much of the 1960 Formula One season, albeit without much success. That year he drove a Cooper, instead of the Scarab, at the British Grand Prix.

Daigh continued to race the Scarab in 1961, until he crashed it and broke his pelvis. After that, he continued racing in other cars before retiring from the sport and concentrating on engineering.

Yannick DALMAS

Nationality: French
Born: 28th July 1961
Seasons: 1987-1990, 1994
Team/manufacturer(s): Larrousse, AGS
Grands Prix: 49
Race wins: 0
Championship wins: 0

Yannick Dalmas began competing in motocross as a youngster but soon switched to cars after he injured his leg. He then won a prize to race in French Formula Renault, where he came third in his first year, and won the championship the next.

From there, he spent 1987 in Formula 3000 and, that same year, he made his Formula One debut, driving a Larrousse-Calmels Lola in the Mexican Grand Prix, where he came fifth.

That led to a full-time drive with Larrousse in 1988, but it was not a good year for Dalmas; not only did he not drive his best, he also came down with Legionnaire's disease. The next year was not much better and he left the team mid-season, after failing to qualify for a number of races. He moved to AGS but, again, he failed to perform well.

Chuck Daigh

Derek Daly

Dalmas then turned his hand to sportscar racing with great success, winning Le Mans no less than four times during the 1990s.

Derek DALY

Nationality: Irish
Born: 11th March 1953
Seasons: 1978-1982
Team/manufacturer(s): Hesketh, Ensign, Tyrrell, March, Theodore, Williams
Grands Prix: 64
Race wins: 0
Championship wins: 0

Irishman Derek Daly hailed from Dublin and started off by racing stockcars. From there, he moved to Formula Ford in 1975, after spending time working in an Australian tin mine to fund the season. It paid off, because he won the Irish championship.

He went to England to race in Formula Ford the next year, followed by Formula 3 in 1977, and he won the championship that year. That led to a drive with the Formula One Hesketh team, but he left after three races and moved to Ensign and then, in 1980, Tyrrell.

The next year he drove for March and then Theodore, but with mixed results. Finally, he spent 1982 with Williams but left at the end of the season.

Daly then moved to the USA to race Indy cars followed by endurance racing. He then retired from racing in 1992. Remaining in the US, he worked as a television commentator and ran his own racing school.

Christian DANNER

Nationality: German
Born: 4th April 1958
Seasons: 1985-1987, 1989
Team/manufacturer(s): Zakspeed, Osella, Arrows, Rial
Grands Prix: 47
Race wins: 0
Championship wins: 0

The son of a car safety expert, Christian Danner began racing in the Renault 5 Cup, followed by a spell in the German G4 championship. This led to a drive in Formula 2, when he broke the lap record for a Formula 2 car on the Nürburgring.

After winning the inaugural Formula 3000 championship in 1985, Danner made his Formula One debut that same year, at the Belgium Grand Prix. The following year, he did a whole season of Formula One, starting with Zakspeed, then Osella and finally Arrows.

In 1989, Danner had his final year in Formula One, driving for Rial. His best result was fourth in the USA, but he

Christian Danner

failed to qualify for many other races.

From then, Danner competed in various championships around the world and ran his own CART team. He has also been a commentator on German television.

Jorge DAPONTE

Nationality: Argentinean
Born: 5th June 1923
Died: 1st March 1963
Seasons: 1954
Team/manufacturer(s): Maserati
Grands Prix: 2
Race wins: 0
Championship wins: 0

Jorge Daponte was born in Buenos Aires, Argentina and in 1954 he entered two Formula One Grands Prix. Both times, he drove his own car, a Maserati A6GCM/250F. This was a works car, from the previous year, that been converted by the factory for use by Daponte.

The first was on his home turf right at the start of the season, but he had to retire with gearbox problems. His second race was towards the end of the season in Monza, Italy. This time he finished in 11th place. That same year, he competed in other events in Europe.

That was the extent of Daponte's Formula One career and he returned to South America as a businessman. He died suddenly in 1963, at the age of just 39 years.

Anthony Denis (Ant) DAVIDSON

Nationality: British
Born: 18th April 1979
Seasons: 2002, 2005, 2007
Team/manufacturer(s): Minardi, BAR/Honda, Super Aguri
Grands Prix: 20
Race wins: 0
Championship wins: 0

Anthony Davidson

Elio De Angelis

Born in Hemel Hempstead, Anthony Davidson, nicknamed 'Ant', began racing karts at the age of just eight. By the time he was 20, he was competing in Formula Ford and won the Young Driver of the Year award in 2000.

A year later, he won the European Formula 3 championship and came second in the British championship. He also started testing for BAR. A year later, he raced in two Grands Prix for Minardi and performed well, despite having to retire from each.

Contractual problems blocked a move to Williams in 2005, so he stayed with BAR and raced at the Malaysian Grand Prix, but had to retire when his car caught fire.

Davidson remained with the same team, renamed Honda, as a test driver in 2006. He has also worked as a television and radio commentator. For the 2007 season, he drove for the Super Aguri team.

Colin Charles Houghton DAVIS

Nationality: British
Born: 29th July 1932
Seasons: 1959
Team/manufacturer(s): Cooper-Maserati
Grands Prix: 2
Race wins: 0
Championship wins: 0

Colin Davis was the son of SCH 'Sammy' Davis who was a well-known motoring journalist and one of the 'Bentley Boys' who raced Bentleys in the 1920s, winning at Le Mans. No wonder, then, that Davis Junior followed the same route and began competing in Formula 3 when he was in his early twenties.

He later moved to Italy to race there, and in 1959 he entered two Formula One Grands Prix, driving a Cooper-Maserati. The first was the French event at Reims where he had to drop out of the race because of an oil leak. Next, though, he raced at the Italian Grand Prix at Monza and finished 11th.

Davis went on to win the 1964 Targa Florio, driving a Porsche 904GT. After that, he continued to compete in sportscar events with some success. He later retired to South America.

Andrea DE ADAMICH

Nationality: Italian
Born: 3rd October 1941
Seasons: 1968, 1970-1973
Team/manufacturer(s): Ferrari, McLaren, March, Surtees, Brabham
Grands Prix: 36
Race wins: 0
Championship wins: 0

Andrea de Adamich competed successfully both in Italian Formula 3 and European Touring Cars in the mid-1960s, which led to a non-championship drive for Ferrari in 1967.

The following year, he was signed with Ferrari but only competed in the first Grand Prix of the year, in South Africa. There, he spun on oil and was out of the race early on. Soon after, he crashed his car during a practice session at Brands Hatch, and neck injuries meant that he was unable to race for the rest of that season.

The next year, he raced a McLaren but only finished one race that season. A switch to March for 1971 gave him no better luck, either.

However, in 1972 he fared better driving for Surtees and finished a worthwhile fourth in the Spanish Grand Prix that year. The next year saw him also achieve a fourth place finish, this time in Belgium, driving a Brabham.

Later in 1973 De Adamich crashed badly at the British Grand Prix and retired from racing soon after. He went on to become a motorsport journalist and television presenter, and ran a company preparing racecars for Alfa Romeo.

Elio DE ANGELIS

Nationality: Italian
Born: 26th March 1958
Died: 15th May 1986
Seasons: 1979-1986
Team/manufacturer(s): Shadow, Lotus, Brabham
Grands Prix: 109
Race wins: 2
Championship wins: 0

Elio de Angelis came from a wealthy Italian family and so had the resources to work his way from karting to Formula

3 in 1977. That said, he also had talent and won his third race and went on to take the Italian Championship that same year.

After a brief spell in Formula 2, the 20-year-old De Angelis made the brave move of driving for the underfunded Shadow team in 1979 and surprised everyone by performing well for most of the season, with his best result being fourth place in the US Grand Prix.

His performance led to him being signed to Lotus, where he remained until 1985. Throughout this time, he regularly finished in the top ten, consistently scoring points for the team. His two wins were in Austria in 1982 and San Marino in 1985.

After a move to Brabham in 1986, De Angelis was testing at the Paul Ricard circuit in France when the car's rear wing came off, causing the car to cartwheel and catch fire. Tragically, De Angelis, although not seriously injured, was unable to get out of the car and he died of asphyxiation after inhaling the smoke.

Count Carel Godin DE BEAUFORT

Nationality: Dutch
Born: 10th April 1934
Died: 2nd August 1964
Seasons: 1957-1964
Team/manufacturer(s): Porsche, Maserati, Cooper
Grands Prix: 31
Race wins: 0
Championship wins: 0

Count Carel Godin de Beaufort came from a wealthy Dutch family and raced on a purely amateur basis. In the mid 1950s, he drove a Porsche RSK and it was in this that he competed in his first Grand Prix in Holland in 1958, where he finished 11th. He retired from his second Grand Prix that year, at the Nürburgring.

In 1960, De Beaufort made a single appearance in a Formula One event, at the Dutch Grand Prix, driving a Cooper-Climax to an eighth place finish. For the next season, he bought a Porsche 718 with which he competed extensively over the next few years, including a number of Grands Prix.

It was this car that led to De Beaufort's death in 1964. He was in practice for the German Grand Prix at the Nürburgring when he crashed, sustaining serious injuries. He died three days later in hospital and is remembered as the last true amateur driver to compete in Formula One.

Andrea DE CESARIS

Nationality: Italian
Born: 31st May 1959
Seasons: 1980-1994
Team/manufacturer(s): Porsche, Maserati, Cooper
Grands Prix: 214
Race wins: 0
Championship wins: 0

Andrea de Cesaris was born in Rome and his karting career culminated in him becoming World Champion. This led to a drive in British Formula 3 at the age of 18.

De Cesaris drove for Alfa Romeo in two Grands Prix at the end of the 1980 season, but failed to finish either the Canadian or USA event (he crashed in the latter). In 1984, he was driving for McLaren but managed to crash or spin out of six of his 14 races. It was around this time that he gained the nickname 'De Crasheris'.

However, as time went on, he matured and proved to be a competent driver, although he still lost it at times; most memorably at the 1985 Austrian Grand Prix, when he drove into a grass bank, destroying his Ligier car. He was later fired from the team.

De Cesaris then spent time with Minardi and Brabham before going to Rial in 1988, where he had a good season, taking fourth place at the US East Grand Prix. It was then on to a number of other teams until he retired from Formula One at the end of 1994, then with the Sauber team. True to form, he finished his career by spinning off during his last race, the Portuguese Grand Prix.

He retired to Monte Carlo, where he spent his time as a currency broker and as a keen windsurfer.

Alain DE CHANGY

Nationality: Belgian
Born: 5th February 1922
Died: 5th August 1994
Seasons: 1959
Team/manufacturer(s): Cooper
Grands Prix: 1
Race wins: 0
Championship wins: 0

Alain de Changy was born in Brussels and was mainly an endurance racer, the high point of his career being a sixth place finish at Le Mans in 1958, driving a Ferrari.

However, he also dabbled with single-seater racing, and in 1959 he entered the Monaco Grand Prix, driving a Cooper that was run by, of all things, the Belgian national football team. But with a large number of drivers competing for just 16 places, he failed to qualify. He went on to enter some non-championship events that year, but then retired from single-seater racing.

Bernard DE DRYVER

Nationality: Belgian
Born: 19th September 1952
Seasons: 1977-1978
Team/manufacturer(s): non-works March and Ensign
Grands Prix: 2
Race wins: 0
Championship wins: 0

During the 1970s, Belgian Bernard de Dryver raced in Formula 2 and Formula 3000. He also attempted his local Grand Prix twice, in 1977 and 1978. The first time was in a March but he failed to qualify. The second time he did not even get through pre-qualifying.

Later, he turned his attention to sportscar racing and was a regular competitor at Le Mans up until 2000. He has also competed in GT racing.

De Dryver reduced his racing activities and concentrated on restoring classic racecars and property development in Malta. His two sons became involved in kart racing.

Maria Teresa DE FILIPPIS

Nationality: Italian
Born: 11th November 1926
Seasons: 1958-1959
Team/manufacturer(s): Maserati, Behra-Porsche
Grands Prix: 5
Race wins: 0
Championship wins: 0

Maria Teresa de Filippis originated from Naples and made a

Andrea De Cesaris

Pedro de la Rosa

Toulo de Graffenried

career racing in national sportscar racing in her home country, driving an OSCA and later, a Maserati.

In 1958, she became the first ever woman to attempt a Formula One Grand Prix event, when she entered the Monaco Grand Prix that year. Sadly, she failed to qualify for that event, but she went on to finish 10th in Belgium that year, but then failed to finish at Portugal and Italy.

The following year she drove a Porsche at the Monaco Grand Prix but failed to qualify, and that was the end of her short, but historic, Formula One career.

De Filippis kept involved in motorsport throughout her life and worked for the Société de Ancients Pilotes.

Baron Emmanuel (Toulo) DE GRAFFENRIED

Nationality: Swiss
Born: 18th May 1918
Seasons: 1950-1954, 1956
Team/manufacturer(s): Maserati, Alfa Romeo
Grands Prix: 23
Race wins: 0
Championship wins: 0

Baron Emmanuel de Graffenried, or 'Toulo' as he was known, was born in Paris but had Swiss nationality. In 1949, a year before Formula One began, he won the British Grand Prix, driving a Maserati.

He continued to compete enthusiastically until 1956.

During that time, he entered a number of Grands Prix, mainly in Maseratis, although he did dabble with Alfa Romeos in three races during the 1951 season. His best result was fourth place at Spa in 1953.

In 1955, De Graffenried worked for the film industry, acting as a double for Kirk Douglas in the action scenes for the film, The Racers. From 1956, though, he began to cut back on his racing activities, but continued to be involved in the sport for many years after.

In 1984, the 84-year-old De Graffenried drove a lap of Silverstone as part of the circuit's 50th birthday celebrations.

Piet DE KLERK

Nationality: South African
Born: 16th March 1935
Seasons: 1963, 1965, 1969-1970
Team/manufacturer(s): Alfa Romeo, Brabham
Grands Prix: 4
Race wins: 0
Championship wins: 0

South African Piet de Klerk worked as a mechanic in South Africa and England, including a spell with Lotus, during which time he learnt much about racecars. Ultimately, though, he wanted to drive the cars, not just work on them.

In the early 1960s, he was involved in the building of an Alfa Romeo special in Johannesburg. By 1962 he was, at last, behind the wheel and realising his dream. The following year, he raced the car in the South African Grand Prix, but had to drop out with gearbox problems.

He continued to compete locally and, two years on, De Klerk again raced in his country's Grand Prix, this time finishing 10th. He then went on to compete in sportscars in Europe, including entering Le Mans in 1967.

By 1969, though, he was back in South Africa, this time driving a Brabham BT20. He raced in the local Grand Prix that year and the following, but with little success.

De Klerk then went back to sportscar racing and continued to compete into the 1980s. He went on to run a car dealership in Cape Town.

Pedro DE LA ROSA

Nationality: Spanish
Born: 24th February 1971
Seasons: 1999-2002, 2005-
Team/manufacturer(s): Arrows, Jaguar, McLaren
Grands Prix: 69
Race wins: 0
Championship wins: 0

Born in Barcelona in 1971, Pedro de la Rosa began his career with model cars, and was twice European Radio-controlled Car Off-road Champion in the 1980s. He then moved to karts and then, in 1989, became Spanish Formula Fiat Uno Champion.

A year later, he was Spanish Formula Ford Champion, then in 1992, he won the European and the British Formula Renault Championships. In 1995, he was Japanese Formula 3 Champion and in 1997 he won the Formula Nippon F3000 Championship and was the Japan

All GT Champion.

All this success led to a job testing for Jordan in 1998 and then on to Arrows as a driver in 1999 and 2000, when he had limited success. A move to Jaguar the following year was also disappointing and he left at the end of 2002.

The next two years were spent testing for McLaren and then, in 2005, he got a chance to race for the team at the Bahrain Grand Prix, where he finished an impressive fifth place. The next year saw De la Rosa compete in five Grands Prix, and he finished three of them – in seventh, fifth and – at Hungary – a fantastic second place, behind Jenson Button.

Alfonso DE PORTAGO

Nationality: Spanish
Born: 11th October 1928
Died: 12th May 1957
Seasons: 1956-1957
Team/manufacturer(s): Ferrari
Grands Prix: 5
Race wins: 0
Championship wins: 0

Spanish aristocrat, Alfonso de Portago, was a successful jockey, who twice raced in the Grand National, a champion swimmer and a bob sleigher. No wonder, then, that he was drawn to motor racing, beginning in 1954 when he began competing in a Ferrari and a Maserati.

He joined the Ferrari team the following year and raced in a number of non-championship events, as well as compet-

D
E
F

Alfonso de Portago

ing in sportscar events. In 1956, he made his Formula One debut, driving a Ferrari in four Grands Prix, beginning with the French one. Amazingly, he finished second at Silverstone, behind Fangio.

In 1957, De Portago competed in one more Grand Prix, the Argentinean, and came fifth. He was, then, a real talent. Sadly, though, he was killed in May of that year when he crashed at the Mille Miglia, a tragedy that also claimed the life of his co-driver and 10 spectators. The race was banned after this.

Giovanni DE RIU

Nationality: Italian
Born: 10th March 1925
Seasons: 1954
Team/manufacturer(s): Maserati
Grands Prix: 1
Race wins: 0
Championship wins: 0

Italian driver Giovanni de Riu worked as an engineer when he wasn't racing. He owned a Maserati A6GCM which he used for non-Championship races.

However, he also entered it into the 1954 Italian Grand Prix, but failed to qualify.

Later, De Riu was involved in Italian motorsport administration and was part of the investigation into the accident which claimed the life of Jochen Rindt.

Max DE TERRA

Nationality: Swiss
Born: 6th October 1918
Died: 29th December 1982
Seasons: 1952-1953
Team/manufacturer(s): Simca-Gordini, Ferrari
Grands Prix: 2
Race wins: 0
Championship wins: 0

Max de Terra was a wealthy Swiss driver who raced in the 1940s and 1950s, usually in minor local events. He was known for his steady, almost sedate style which suited his gentlemanly demeanour.

Occasionally, De Terra entered more major races, often just to make up the numbers. Most noticeably, he competed in the Swiss Grand Prix twice, in 1952 and 1953.

The first time, he drove a Simca but had to retire when his car suffered electrical problems. Not to be deterred, he returned the following year, this time in a Ferrari 166, and finished in eighth place. And that was the last time he appeared in a Formula One race.

Alejandro DE TOMASO

Nationality: Argentinean-Italian
Born: 10th July 1928
Died: 21st May 2003
Seasons: 1957, 1959
Team/manufacturer(s): Ferrari, Cooper
Grands Prix: 2
Race wins: 0
Championship wins: 0

Alejandro de Tomaso was born in Buenos Aires but spent much of his life in Italy, to the extent that his name is often spelt Alessandro. While in Argentina, he raced sportscars as well as single-seaters and made his Grand Prix debut there, driving a Ferrari in 1957 and finishing ninth.

After he moved to Italy in his early twenties, he raced for Maserati before founding De Tomaso Automobili in 1959 to build his own sports cars. Based in Modena, this company went on to become a famous supercar marque, with cars such as the Mangusta and Pantera.

Also in 1959, De Tomaso raced in his second and last Formula One event, the USA Grand Prix. Driving a Cooper, he retired with brake problems. After that, he largely retired from racing to concentrate on his business.

De Tomaso went on to build a business empire in Italy

Alejandro De Tomaso

during the 1960s and 1970s, as well as his car company. He retired after a stroke in 1993 and his son continued to run the business. De Tomaso died in 2003, but he will always be remembered for his supercars, rather more than his racing career.

Baron Charles DE TORNACO

Nationality: Belgian
Born: 7th June 1927
Died: 18th September 1953
Seasons: 1952
Team/manufacturer(s): Ferrari
Grands Prix: 3
Race wins: 0
Championship wins: 0

Baron Charles de Tornaco's father was a wealthy man who raced in the 1920s. The young man began racing in the late 1940s, and even took part in the Spa 24 Hours race in 1949 and 1950.

In 1952, he competed in the Belgium, Dutch and Italian Grands Prix, driving a Ferrari T500. However, he only completed the Belgian event, where he finished in seventh place. The following year, De Tornaco was practicing for the Modena Grand Prix when he rolled his Ferrari. He fractured his skull and broke his neck, but there were no medical professionals on hand and he died on his way to hospital, in the back of a car.

Emilio DE VILLOTA

Nationality: Spanish
Born: 26th July 1963
Seasons: 1976-1978, 1981-1982
Team/manufacturer(s): RAM, non-works McLaren, non-works Williams, March
Grands Prix: 15
Race wins: 0
Championship wins: 0

Emilio de Villota was born in Madrid and worked as a bank

Patrick Depailler

Pedro Diniz

manager to pay for his hobby of motor racing. In 1976, though, he gave up work to concentrate on racing full-time. He attempted the Spanish Grand Prix that year, driving a RAM, but failed to qualify.

In 1977, he drove a McLaren M23, using his banking contacts to raise sponsorship. He struggled against more experienced competition, though, and only qualified for two out of the seven Grands Prix he attended. The next year, he only entered the Spanish race but, again, failed to qualify.

De Villota had another attempt at the Spanish Grand Prix in 1981, and went on to try five events the next year, driving for March, but failed to qualify for any.

However, he had more success in the Aurora AFX series, winning the championship in 1980. Later in the 1980s, he turned to sportscars and, again, was successful; he won the Spanish Porsche Carrera Cup no less than three times in the 1990s. He also set up his own racing school.

Jean-Denis DÉLÉTRAZ

Nationality: Swiss
Born: 1st October 1963
Seasons: 1994-1995
Team/manufacturer(s): Larrousse, Pacific
Grands Prix: 3
Race wins: 0
Championship wins: 0

Jean-Denis Délétraz was born in Geneva and had the wealth to indulge his motor racing career. He began in French FF1600 in 1985, moving to Formula 3 thereafter.

His Formula One career was aided by his wealth. In 1994, he drove for Larrousse in the Australian Grand Prix but failed to finish because of gearbox problems. The following year, he went to Pacific and entered the Portuguese Grand Prix but had to retire. Next came the European Grand Prix, held at the Nürburgring, where he finished 15th.

Délétraz then went on to have more success in sportscar racing, where he competed at Le Mans and other events. He announced his retirement at the end of 2003, but changed his mind and continued to race.

Patrick André Eugène Joseph DEPAILLER

Nationality: French
Born: 9th August 1944
Died: 1st August 1980
Seasons: 1972, 1974-1980
Team/manufacturer(s): Tyrrell, Ligier, Alfa Romeo
Grands Prix: 95
Race wins: 2
Championship wins: 0

Frenchman Patrick Depailler planned to become a dental technician but soon got distracted by motorbike and car racing, for which he had an undeniable talent. He began racing in Lotus Sevens and then, later, moved to Formula 3, winning the French title in 1971.

A 1972 season in Formula 2 also saw Depailler's Grand Prix debut, driving a Tyrrell at the French event and then, more successfully, in the USA, where he came seventh.

After a brief return to Formula 2 in 1973, Depailler went on to drive for Tyrrell and became a consistent points scorer for the team up until 1978; his first win being at Monaco that year.

Depailler then moved to Ligier, where he had a good start to the season, winning in Spain, but a hang-gliding accident meant he couldn't finish the season. A move to Alfa Romeo for 1980 saw him struggling with less competitive cars. It was an Alfa that he was driving at a test session at Hockenheim when a suspension failure caused him to crash. He died of head injuries.

Pedro Paulo DINIZ

Nationality: Brazilian
Born: 22nd May 1970
Seasons: 1995-2000
Team/manufacturer(s): Forti, Ligier, Arrows, Sauber
Grands Prix: 99
Race wins: 0
Championship wins: 0

Pedro Diniz was born in São Paulo to a father who, not only was a keen driver himself, but also owned a supermarket

chain, so was reasonably wealthy.

After spending time in Formula 3 and Formula 3000, Diniz moved to Formula One in 1995, driving for Forti, with the help of sponsorship provided by contacts his father made.

He proved to be a competent driver but the cars were not competitive, so he moved to Ligier for the following season but fared little better. He did hit the news that year, though, when his car burst into flames at the Argentinean Grand Prix, and the Sun printed the witty headline, 'Diniz in the oven'.

From there, Diniz spent two years with Arrows and then two years with Sauber, with a mixed bag of results with both teams. A bad crash with Jean Alesi at Hockenheim in 2000, spelt the end of his Formula One career and he retired at the end of the season.

Diniz then invested in the Prost team, but that folded in 2002, so he returned to Brazil where he continued to race at a local level. After retiring, he ran the family business as well as the Brazilian Formula Renault series.

Frank J DOCHNAL

Nationality: American
Born: 8th October 1920
Seasons: 1963
Team/manufacturer(s): non-works Cooper
Grands Prix: 1
Race wins: 0
Championship wins: 0

Frank J Dochnal was born in St Louis, Missouri, and raced locally at a club level, usually in midgets and sportscars.

He made one appearance in Formula One, when he entered the 1963 Mexican Grand Prix, driving a Cooper-Climax T51. Unfortunately, he failed to qualify after crashing during practice.

Dochnal retired from racing soon after and went on to work as a mechanic in Indycar. He also worked for Howard Hughes as a development machinist, and then as an official for the USAC.

Martin Donnelly

José DOLHEM

Nationality: French
Born: 26th April 1944
Died: 16th April 1988
Seasons: 1974
Team/manufacturer(s): Surtees
Grands Prix: 3
Race wins: 0
Championship wins: 0

Frenchman José Dolhem began racing with a Lotus Seven while he was at university in the 1960s, but his education meant he was unable to devote too much time to what was then a hobby.

In the early 1970s, he dabbled with Formula 3 and then Formula 2, while also doing some sportscar racing, including entering Le Mans in 1973 and finishing in seventh place.

For the 1974 season, Dolhem signed with Surtees, driving in both Formula 2 and Formula One. It was not a good season, though, with him failing to qualify in his first two Grands Prix. At the third, an accident claimed the life of his teammate, Helmut Koinigg, and so the team withdrew from the race.

It was also the end of Dolhem's Formula One career. He went on to compete in Formula 2 and sportscars again, and managed to finish in fourth place at Le Mans in 1978, driving an Alpine A442. Dolhem was killed in 1988, when his private plane crashed in France.

Hugh Peter Martin (Martin) DONNELLY

Nationality: British
Born: 26th March 1964
Seasons: 1989-1990
Team/manufacturer(s): Arrows, Lotus
Grands Prix: 15
Race wins: 0
Championship wins: 0

Belfast-born Martin Donnelly began his career competing in Formula 2000, Formula 3 and then Formula 3000. He proved very competitive and was a contender for the Formula 3000 title in 1989.

It was also in 1989 that Donnelly made his Formula One debut, driving for Arrows in the French Grand Prix, where he finished 12th.

The following season saw him sign for Lotus, where he made a reasonable start to the season, with a car that wasn't particularly competitive.

And then disaster struck during qualifying for the Spanish Grand Prix. His car hit the barriers and broke into pieces. Donnelly was flung into the air, still strapped to his seat and was severely injured.

He survived, though, but was unable to return to racing. Instead, he set up Martin Donnelly Racing, a Vauxhall Junior team and has also worked with other race teams.

Mark Neary DONOHUE

Nationality: American
Born: 18th March 1937
Died: 19th August 1975
Seasons: 1971, 1974-1975
Team/manufacturer(s): Penske
Grands Prix: 15
Race wins: 0
Championship wins: 0

Mark Donohue raced a 1957 Corvette in the late 1950s and early 1960s, and proved to be very talented. Before long, he was competing in sportscar racing, beginning with the 1965 Sebring 12 Hours event.

He went on to drive a Ford GT40 at Le Mans in 1966 and 1967, plus numerous other events, mainly in the USA. In the late 1960s he became one of the leading Trans-Am drivers, winning three championships with Roger Penske Racing. At the same time, he competed in his first Indy 500 race, in 1969.

It was with Penske that Donohue competed in Formula One, beginning at the Canadian Grand Prix in 1971, when he finished in an impressive third place. He announced his retirement from racing in 1973, but returned the following year, when he entered the Canadian and USA Grands Prix, but without much success.

Then 1975 saw Donohue compete in practically a full season of Formula One, with a number of top-ten finishes. And then, at the Austrian Grand Prix that year, his car went out of control and hit the barriers, with debris killing a marshal. Donohue appeared to be uninjured at the time, but he had suffered a brain haemorrhage and died in hospital soon after.

Robert Michael DOORNBOS

Nationality: Dutch
Born: 23rd September 1981
Seasons: 2005
Team/manufacturer(s): Minardi/Red Bull
Grands Prix: 8
Race wins: 0
Championship wins: 0

Dutch driver Robert Doornbos actually began his sporting career as a semi-professional tennis player. However, after a visit to the 1998 Belgium Grand Prix he gave up tennis to concentrate on racing. The following year he competed in the Opel Lotus UK Winter series and finished second in the championship.

By 2001, Doornbos was racing in Formula 3, which he continued with until 2003, during which time he proved himself as a talented driver. That led to a move to Formula 3000, sponsored by Red Bull, where he finished third in the championship and won at Spa.

Also in 2004, Doornas worked as a test driver for Jordan,

which he continued doing for the start of the 2005 season. This then led to him driving for Minardi for the second part of the year, starting with the Dutch Grand Prix. He did eight races that year, but his best finish was 13th place.

The following year, he returned to testing for the team, which had been renamed Red Bull.

Fritz D'OREY

Nationality: Brazilian
Born: 25th March 1938
Seasons: 1959
Team/manufacturer(s): Maserati, Tec-Mec
Grands Prix: 3
Race wins: 0
Championship wins: 0

Fritzy d'Orey was born in San Paulo to Portuguese parents. His family imported Packard cars into Brazil, which probably gave the youngster a head start in motor racing.

He began competing in a Porsche and then moved on to a Ferrari, with which he competed in various events in South America.

A trip to Europe in 1959 then saw him compete in two Formula One events there. The first, the French Grand Prix, he finished in 10th place driving a Maserati; the second was the British event at Aintree where he crashed and wrote off the same car. Later that same year, D'Orey entered the USA Grand Prix with a Tec-Mec Maserati, but failed to finish.

D'Orey suffered a bad crash at Le Mans in 1961 and retired from the sport after that. He went on to work for the family businesses.

Kenneth Henry (Ken) DOWNING

Nationality: British
Born: 5th December 1917
Died: 3rd May 2004
Seasons: 1952
Team/manufacturer(s): Connaught
Grands Prix: 2
Race wins: 0
Championship wins: 0

Kenneth Downing was born in Staffordshire to wealthy par-

Robert Doornbos

Johnny Dumfries

Although born in Italy, Piero Drogo began racing in South America in the 1950s, in both single-seaters and sports-cars. The high point was winning his class in the Buenos Aires 1000km racing, driving a Ferrari Testa Rossa.

He then headed to Europe, beginning with a disastrous race at Le Mans, when he crashed. Living in Italy, he worked as a mechanic to pay his way.

Drogo then got a chance to compete in the 1960 Italian Grand Prix, but only because the British teams had boycotted the event and he was asked to help fill the grid. He finished in eighth place, driving a Cooper-Climax.

In 1972, Drogo was killed when he crashed his car into an unlit lorry in a dark tunnel.

John Colum CRICHTON-STUART, 7th Marquess of Bute (Johnny Dumfries)
Nationality: British
Born: 26th April 1958
Seasons: 1986
Team/manufacturer(s): Lotus
Grands Prix: 16
Race wins: 0
Championship wins: 0

John Colum Crichton-Stuart, 7th Marquess of Bute, was called the Earl of Dumfries before 1993, and prefers to be known as John Bute or, in racing circles, as Johnny Dumfries.

Coming from a very wealthy Scottish family, Dumfries shunned his background to work as a van driver for Williams, so he could get a foothold in the industry. Unusually, he didn't use his wealth to begin racing, but posed as a workman when he started to compete in Formula Ford 1600 and, later Formula 3. In 1984 he won the Formula 3 Championship in the UK and was runner-up in the European series.

After a year testing for Ferrari, Dumfries joined the Lotus Formula One team in 1986, alongside Ayrton Senna. In this, his only Formula One season, Dumfries had a reasonable stab at it, scoring three championship points.

Dumfries then turned to endurance racing with some success, winning at Le Mans in 1988, driving a TWR Jaguar. With a great personal wealth, he runs a historic motorsports festival each year.

Piero DUSIO
Nationality: Italian
Born: 13th October 1899
Died: 7th November 1975
Seasons: 1952
Team/manufacturer(s): Cisitalia
Grands Prix: 1
Race wins: 0
Championship wins: 0

Piero Dusio is best remembered as the founder of the famous Formula One constructor, Cisitalia, which began in 1946. The most famous of the company's cars was perhaps the overly complex Type 360 which was designed by Ferdinand Porsche.

Dusio entered just one Grand Prix, the 1952 Italian event, driving one of his own cars. The man was in his fifties at the time, but was very determined. Even so, he failed to qualify because of engine problems.

Cisitalia went into receivership and was sold in 1952, but Dusio remained involved in car construction for most of his life.

ents; his father ran a company making building materials. He also grew up to be a successful businessman and was able to indulge in his hobby of motor racing.

Downing began racing an MG Midget before moving on to owning a string of Connaughts, which he modified to suit his purposes and soon became a regular on the local racing circuits.

In 1951, he treated himself to a 2-litre Connaught Formula 2 car which, the following year, became eligible for Grand Prix racing, thanks to a rule change. At the 1952 British Grand Prix at Silverstone, Downing found himself second on the grid but, sadly, fell back to ninth place by the end of the race. A second Grand Prix entry in Holland later that year was less successful.

Downing gave up racing soon after that to spend more time with his business concerns. He moved to South Africa for a while and then retired to Monaco.

Robert (Bob) DRAKE
Nationality: American
Born: 14th December 1919
Died: 18th April 1990
Seasons: 1960
Team/manufacturer(s): Maserati, Tec-Mec
Grands Prix: 1
Race wins: 0
Championship wins: 0

Born in San Francisco, Robert Drake grew up to run a restaurant in Los Angeles and, in his spare time, he was a SCCA racing driver in the mid 1950s.

He gave up competing for three years until he made a comeback in 1960 to race in the USA Grand Prix. Although he only finished in 13th place, Drake's performance is remembered for being the last championship appearance for the revered Maserati 250F racing car.

Drake later went on to become a film stunt driver.

Paddy DRIVER
Nationality: South African
Born: 19th May 1934
Seasons: 1963, 1974
Team/manufacturer(s): Lotus
Grands Prix: 2
Race wins: 0
Championship wins: 0

South African Paddy Driver's main profession was as a

motorcycle racer, usually riding a Norton and he was very successful at both a local and international level.

In 1963, though, he had a try with four wheels, racing a Lotus 24. However, at the South African Grand Prix that year, he crashed badly in practice, and the car was destroyed.

Driver then returned to motorcycles until the end of the decade, when he began to concentrate more and more on single-seater and sportscar racing. He entered the South African Grand Prix for a second time in 1974, but had to retire when his Lotus 72 developed clutch problems.

He raced saloon cars into the 1980s before retiring and becoming a property developer in South Africa.

Piero DROGO
Nationality: Italian
Born: 8th August 1926
Died: 28th April 1973
Seasons: 1960
Team/manufacturer(s): Cooper
Grands Prix: 1
Race wins: 0
Championship wins: 0

Johnny Dumfries

E

ARMSTRONG

FERODO

Vic Elford

George Ross EATON

Nationality: Canadian
Born: 12th November 1945
Seasons: 1969-1971
Team/manufacturer(s): Cisitalia
Grands Prix: 13
Race wins: 0
Championship wins: 0

Born in Toronto to a wealthy family, George Eaton began racing in the 1960s, most notably in an AC Cobra, in the American Can-Am series.

He then bought himself a brand-new McLaren M12 in which to compete in Can-Am, and also a McLaren M10 for use in Formula A. He did well in both cars and was the highest ranking Canadian in Can-Am in 1969.

That same year Eaton was asked by BRM to compete in two Grands Prix, the US and Mexican events. He failed to finish either, because of mechanical problems. However, he remained with BRM for a full season in 1971, but he had a very poor year, the best result being 10th at his home Grand Prix. Eaton again drove at the Canadian Grand Prix in 1971, his only Formula One race that year.

Eaton then slowly cut down on his racing and began to concentrate more on running the family business, the Eaton department store.

Bernard Charles (Bernie) ECCLESTONE

Nationality: British
Born: 28th October 1930
Seasons: 1958
Team/manufacturer(s): Connaught-Alta
Grands Prix: 1
Race wins: 0
Championship wins: 0

The son of a trawler man, Bernard Charles Ecclestone was born in Suffolk but moved to London as a child. His first love was motorcycles and, after the Second World War, he set up

Bernard Ecclestone

a spare-parts business for bikes.

He also dabbled in racing, in the 500cc Formula 3 series, but gave up after a crash at Brands Hatch in 1951. From there, he began to make money in property and other business concerns. In 1957, he bought the Formula One Connaught team. The following year, he tried to drive one of the team's cars himself at Monaco but failed to qualify. That was his one and only attempt at racing in Formula One.

Ecclestone went on to manage various racing teams and drivers. In 1972 he formed the Formula One Constructors Association (FOCA), along with other team owners. By 1978 he was Chief Executive and negotiated television rights for Formula One.

He has remained very much in control of Formula One and, in 2003, was named the UK's third richest person, with an estimated fortune of £2400 million.

Guy Richard Goronwy EDWARDS

Nationality: British
Born: 30th December 1942
Seasons: 1974, 1976-1977
Team/manufacturer(s): Hill, Hesketh, BRM
Grands Prix: 17
Race wins: 0
Championship wins: 0

Guy Edwards came from Cheshire and worked his way up through sportscars and Formula 5000 to Formula One. This was partly down to his driving ability, but perhaps more because he had a happy knack of clinching sponsorship deals.

His first taste of Formula One was in 1974 when he drove for Hill, with his best result being seventh place in Sweden. The next year Edwards was with Hesketh and he rose to prominence for helping Niki Lauda from his burning car at the German Grand Prix, an act of bravery which earned him the Queen's Gallantry Medal. In 1977, he entered just one Grand Prix, the British one, but failed to pre-qualify.

Edwards then went back to what he did best and became a sponsorship consultant, which made his fortune. He later retired to the South of France.

Victor Henry (Vic) ELFORD

Nationality: British
Born: 10th June 1935
Seasons: 1968-1969, 1971
Team/manufacturer(s): Cooper, McLaren, BRM
Grands Prix: 13
Race wins: 0
Championship wins: 0

Born Victor Elford, in London, he is best known as a sportscar driver, but has turned his hand to a number of disciplines. After seeing the British Grand Prix at the age of 13, he decided that was what he wanted to do. He started to race a Mini in his early twenties and also rallied. Within a few years he was working for the Porsche factory team, racing and rallying 911s, and in the late 1960s Porsche and Elford were an unbeatable combination, with him winning the European GT Rally Championship and the Le Mans 24 Hour, to name but two victories.

In 1968, Elford made his Formula One debut, driving a Cooper at the French Grand Prix where he finished fourth, after starting at the back of the grid. He went on to compete in six more Grands Prix that year, and five the next. However, a crash with Mario Andretti at the German event pretty much ended his Formula One career.

Paul Emery

In 1971, Elford entered just the German Grand Prix, but by this time he was concentrating his efforts on sportscars and continued to be a great success, winning the 12 Hours of Sebring that year.

After retiring from racing, Elford retained close connections with Porsche, started his own driving school and wrote books on driving. He retired to Florida.

Paul EMERY

Nationality: British
Born: 12th November 1916
Died: 3rd February 1992
Seasons: 1954, 1958
Team/manufacturer(s): Emeryson, Connaught
Grands Prix: 2
Race wins: 0
Championship wins: 0

Londoner Paul Emery worked closely with his father, building racecars in the prewar years. These were called Emerysons. After the war, Emery resurrected the name and became one of only two people building 500cc Formula 3 cars – the other being Enzo Ferrari. The cars were unusual in that they were front-engined and front-wheel-drive.

Emery entered the 1956 British Grand Prix at Silverstone in one of his own cars, but retired with ignition problems. The following year, he drove a Connaught at the Monaco Grand Prix but failed to qualify.

He went on to dabble with building Formula One cars and then midget racers. His son, Peter, also built cars with the Emeryson name.

Tomáš ENGE

Nationality: Czech
Born: 11th September 1976
Seasons: 2001
Team/manufacturer(s): Prost
Grands Prix: 3
Race wins: 0
Championship wins: 0

Like many drivers, Czech-born Tomáš Enge began by racing karts, following in the footsteps of his father, Bretislav, who was a touring car driver.

He then worked his way up from Formula 3 to Formula 3000 and, in 2000 he landed a role as test driver for the Jordan Formula One team. The next year Enge joined Prost towards the end of the season to replace Luciano Burti, who had been injured.

Unfortunately, Enge didn't shine in the three Grands Prix he entered, and the following year he returned to Formula 2000, and later, sportscars. He also entered the 2005 Indy 500.

Paul ENGLAND

Nationality: Australian
Born: 28th March 1929
Seasons: 1957
Team/manufacturer(s): Cooper
Grands Prix: 1
Race wins: 0
Championship wins: 0

Australian Paul England was born in Melbourne and, as an

adult, he worked for Repco. In his spare time he raced a Holden-engined Austca in the 1957.

England competed in one Formula One event, the 1957 German Grand Prix at the Nürburgring. Driving a Formula 2 Cooper-Climax he began from 23rd on the grid but had to retire with a distributor problem.

He later set up his own engine-balancing business which he ran for many years before his son took over. England then retired to Essendon in Victoria.

Harald ERTL

Nationality: Austrian
Born: 31st August 1948
Died: 7th April 1982
Seasons: 1975-1978, 1980
Team/manufacturer(s): Hesketh, Ensign, ATS
Grands Prix: 28
Race wins: 0
Championship wins: 0

Austrian Harald Ertl bought a Formula 5 car at the age of 21 and won six races in it during his first season. The next year he came second in the European cup.

By 1971, he had moved to Touring cars and remained racing in that field throughout his career. However, he also competed in Formula 2, between 1974 and 1976.

Ertl first competed in Formula One in 1975, entering three Grands Prix for Hesketh; his best result being eighth place at Silverstone. The next year he did a full season, with his best performance again being at Silverstone, this time with a seventh place.

After a poor 1977 season with Hesketh, Ertl competed in four Grands Prix with Ensign the next year but, again, had no success. He briefly returned to Formula One in 1980, when he entered the German Grand Prix, driving for ATS, but failed to qualify.

Ertl was killed in 1982, when the plane he was flying crashed. He was with his family at the time, and his wife and son survived, albeit with serious injuries.

Nasif Moisés ESTÉFANO

Nationality: Argentinean
Born: 18th November 1932
Died: 21st October 1973
Seasons: 1960, 1962
Team/manufacturer(s): Maserati, De Tomaso
Grands Prix: 2
Race wins: 0
Championship wins: 0

Nasif Estéfano began racing in his home country of Argentina in 1955, in Turismo Carretera events. It was there that he entered his first Grand Prix, the 1960 race held at Buenos Aires. Driving a Maserati 250F, he finished in eighth place. The next year, like other South American drivers, he travelled to Europe to race in Formula Junior. Then, in 1962, he entered a De Tomaso 801 in the Italian Grand Prix, but the car was not a success and he failed to qualify.

Estéfano then returned to his home country where he won the local single-seater championship in 1963 and 1964. He also competed in sportscars, with more than a little success.

It was in the 1973 Turismo Carretera that Estéfano lost his life. His Ford Falcon crashed on a bend and his seatbelt broke, allowing him to be flung on to the road, where his car then fell on top of him. He died on the way to hospital. Estéfano was then posthumously crowned Turismo Carretera champion, on account of having won five races that season.

Philippe ÉTANCELIN

Nationality: French
Born: 29th December 1896
Died: 13th October 1981
Seasons: 1950-1952
Team/manufacturer(s): Talbot, Maserati
Grands Prix: 12
Race wins: 0
Championship wins: 0

Nicknamed 'Phi Phi', Normandy-born Philippe Étancelin was a successful businessman. He began racing with a Bugatti in 1926 and, just a year later, he won the Grand Prix de Reims. From there, he competed in various European events in Maseratis or Alfa Romeos and proved himself to be an excellent driver. As well as Grand Prix events, in 1934 he won at Le Mans.

After the Second World War, Étancelin bought a Talbot 26C and had some success in Grand Prix events, most notably winning at Paris in 1949.

His first Formula One event was the British Grand Prix at Silverstone in 1950, where he finished eighth. By now, though, his Talbot was getting dated and he didn't get the results he deserved. He did, though, gain three championship points during his three years of competing.

Étancelin slowly retired from racing from then on, spending more time at his farm in Normandy.

Robert (Bob) EVANS

Nationality: British
Born: 11th June 1947
Seasons: 1975-1976
Team/manufacturer(s): BRM, Lotus, RAM
Grands Prix: 12
Race wins: 0
Championship wins: 0

Robert Evans was born in Lincolnshire in 1947 and began racing in a Sprite as a young man. He then worked his through Formula Ford and Formula 3. It was when testing in the latter formula that Evans broke his neck, almost putting a stop to his career, but he recovered and carried on racing.

By 1974, Evans was competing in Formula 5000 and won the British Championship that year, driving a Lola T332. This was enough to give him a foothold to Formula One, where he drove for BRM in 1975. Unfortunately, the car was dated and Evans struggled to compete.

The next year saw him test for Lotus and he competed in the South African and US West Grands Prix, but without success. Later that same year he raced for RAM at the British Grand Prix but he failed to finish.

Evans then raced in the Aurora F1 Championship before retiring from the sport and running a poster business.

Tomáš Enge

F

FABI, Corrado
FABI, Teo
FABRE, Pascal
FACETTI, Carlo
FAGIOLI, Luigi
FAIRMAN, Jack
FANGIO, Juan Manuel
FARINA, Nino
FERGUSON, William
FIRMAN, Ralph
FISCHER, Ludwig
FISCHER, Rudi
FISHER, Mike
FISICHELLA, Giancarlo
FITCH, John
FITTIPALDI, Christian
FITTIPALDI, Emerson
FITTIPALDI, Wilson
FITZAU, Theo
FLINTERMAN, Jan
FLOCKHART, Ron
FOITEK, Gregor
FOLLMER, George
FONTANA, Norberto
FONTES, Azdrubal
FORINI, Franco
FOTHERINGHAM-PARKER, Phillip
FRANCIA, Giorgio
FRENTZEN, Heinz-Harald
FRERE, Paul
FRIESACHER, Patrick
FRY, Joe
FUSHIDA, Hiroshi

Pascal Fabre

Corrado FABI

Nationality: Italian
Born: 12th April 1961
Seasons: 1983-1984
Team/manufacturer(s): Osella, Brabham
Grands Prix: 18
Race wins: 0
Championship wins: 0

The younger brother of driver Teo Fabi, Corrado Fabi was born in Milan and began racing as a 12-year-old boy and, by his late teens, was competing successfully in Formula 3. Indeed, he was third in the European Formula 3 Championship in 1980, when he was just 19. And by the time he was 21, Fabi was European Formula 2 Champion.

From there, Formula One was the next natural step, and Fabi drove for Osella through the 1983 season. Unfortunately, the year was not a success, with the young Italian failing to qualify for most races, and the best result he managed was 10th place at Austria that year.

The next year, he stood in for his older brother, driving for Brabham in three Grands Prix. He retired from two, but at the third, the USA race, he came seventh and gave a hint of what he was capable of.

Sadly, though, that was the end of his Formula One career. Fabi's father died in 1984 and so he returned to Italy to take over the running of the family transport business.

Teodorico (Teo) FABI

Nationality: Italian
Born: 9th March 1955
Seasons: 1982, 1984-1987
Team/manufacturer(s): Toleman, Brabham, Benetton
Grands Prix: 71
Race wins: 0
Championship wins: 0

Born in Milan in 1955, Teo Fabi was a talented racer from an early age and, by the time he was 20, he was the European Karting Champion. From there, he worked his way through Formula 3, Formula Pacific and then Formula 2, which he competed in at the start of the 1980s.

The year 1982 saw Fabi make his Formula One debut, but it was not a good season, with him failing to start a single race driving for Toleman. After a year with Indy Cars, he returned to Formula One in 1984, driving for Brabham with mixed success; his best result was an impressive third place at the US East Grand Prix.

He then returned to Toleman for 1985 and had another poor season, before going to Benetton for the next two years. His last year in Formula One, 1987, was his most satisfying, with a sprinkling of top-five finishes.

Fabi then returned to Indy Cars, driving for Porsche and winning one race, in 1989. After a spell in Endurance racing, he competed again in Indy Cars but slowly retired from racing towards the end of the 1980s. He went on to work in the family transport business.

Pascal FABRE

Nationality: French
Born: 9th January 1960
Seasons: 1987
Team/manufacturer(s): AGS
Grands Prix: 14
Race wins: 0
Championship wins: 0

Lyon-born Pascal Fabre began racing in Formula Renault as a teenager in 1979 as part of the Volant Elf scholarship scheme. Just a year later, he came second in the French Formula 3 Championship and, by 1982, he was competing in Formula 2. That didn't last, though, and it was back to Formula 3 the next year, when Fabre also raced at Le Mans.

After a brief return to Formula 2 and some sportscar racing, Fabre graduated to Formula One in 1987, driving for the French AGS team. The car was not competitive but it was at least reliable, allowing Fabre to complete most of the Grands Prix he entered, albeit well down the field. Unfortunately, it was not enough for the team and he was replaced by Roberto Moreno towards the end of the season.

Fabre later pursued a reasonably successful career in sportscar racing before becoming an instructor.

Carlo FACETTI

Nationality: Italian
Born: 26th June 1935
Seasons: 1974
Team/manufacturer(s): Scuderia Finotto
Grands Prix: 1
Race wins: 0
Championship wins: 0

Italian driver Carlo Facetti was born in Milan. He began racing in 1953 in a Fiat 1100 8V. He then moved to a self-built Formula Junior special, which was powered by a Lancia engine and proved competitive.

Facetti later became chief test-driver for Alfa Romeo while, at the same time, racing in sportscars and other disciplines, including Formula 2 and Formula 3. In the latter, he came second in the Italian Championship in 1965.

His single Formula One appearance was not a success, though. Driving a Scuderia Finotto Brabham BT42, he failed to qualify for the 1974 Italian Grand Prix.

Facetti had more luck in 1979 when he won the FIA Touring Car Championship. When he retired from racing he became involved in racecar preparation.

Luigi FAGIOLI

Nationality: Italian
Born: 9th June 1898
Died: 20th June 1952
Seasons: 1950-1951
Team/manufacturer(s): Alfa Romeo
Grands Prix: 7
Race wins: 1
Championship wins: 0

As a child, Luigi Fagioli grew up in the pioneering days of motor racing and was soon absorbed by it. Before long, he was com-

Pascal Fabre

Jack Fairman

peting in hillclimbs and then racing. By 1930, he was driving for Maserati in Grand Prix events and rose to be one of Italy's most talented drivers, later moving to Mercedes and Auto Union, and winning a number of major races.

After the Second World War, Fagioli's health was failing but he continued to race, nevertheless. In 1950, he competed in the new World Championship series for Alfa Romeo. The following year he only competed in one Grand Prix, in France, which he won in conjunction with Fangio. At the age of 53, he was the oldest person to ever win a Formula One race.

For 1952, Fagioli raced sportscars for Lancia and came third at the Mille Miglia. Soon after, he crashed during a practice at Monaco and died in hospital three weeks later.

Jack FAIRMAN

Nationality: English
Born: 15th March 1913
Died: 7th February 2002
Seasons: 1953, 1955-1961
Team/manufacturer(s): HWM, Connaught, BRM, Cooper, Ferguson
Grands Prix: 13
Race wins: 0
Championship wins: 0

Jack Fairman hailed from Surrey and worked as an engineer, competing in his spare time from a young age. At first, he drove in trials and hillclimbs, usually in an Alvis.

After the Second World War, during which time he was in the Tank Corps, Fairman began to get involved in endurance racing and competed at Le Mans and Spa

towards the end of the 1940s. However, he didn't neglect single-seater racing altogether, and raced in a number of Grands Prix, beginning in 1953 when he competed at the British and Italian events for HWM and Connaught.

Oddly, it was only in these Grands Prix that he competed in later years, from 1955 to 1971, for various teams. His best result was fourth place at the 1956 British Grand Prix at Silverstone.

After he finally retired from racing, Fairman ran a garage in London for some years.

Juan-Manuel FANGIO

Nationality: Argentinean
Born: 24th June 1911
Died: 17th July 1995
Seasons: 1950-1951, 1953-1958
Team/manufacturer(s): Alfa Romeo, Maserati, Mercedes, Ferrari
Grands Prix: 52
Race wins: 24
Championship wins: 5

The son of an Italian immigrant, Juan-Manuel Fangio took part in his first race at the age of 18, in a Ford taxi. Soon after, the young garage owner took part in long-distance races on South American dirt roads.

After the Second World War, the Argentinean government sponsored him to travel to Europe to develop his career and promote Argentina. After proving himself in a Maserati in 1949, he was recruited by Alfa Romeo for the 1950 season. That year, he came second in the championship, but the following year he won it for the first of five times.

Fangio moved back to Maserati for 1952 and started the season well. Then he had to travel from England to Monza in Italy to compete. He drove overnight from Paris, after missing his flight, and arrived at the circuit just half an hour before the start of the race. Relegated to the back of the grid, Fangio struggled to improve his position and pushed his Maserati too hard and it went into a slide. His reactions slowed due to his lack of sleep, the normally superb driver was unable to regain control and the car hit a bank and somersaulted through the air, throwing Fangio out. His neck was broken and he was unable to race again that year.

However, Fangio was back in action for 1953, still driving for Maserati, and finished the championship in second place. 1954 saw him switch, mid-season, to Mercedes and he won six out of eight Grands Prix, taking the championship with ease. He repeated his success in 1955, driving a Mercedes W196 Monoposto, along with teammate Stirling Moss.

For 1956, Fangio moved to Ferrari and, again, he took the championship with ease, winning three races, and coming second in all the others.

Fangio returned to Maserati in 1957, and had a magnificent win at the Nüburbring, in which he passed the two leading Ferraris in his less powerful car.

He retired in 1958 and his last race was the French Grand Prix, where Mike Hawthorn slowed to let Fangio's Maserati finish before him, as a mark of respect to the Maestro. Fangio got out of his car and said simply, "It's finished".

He then returned to Argentina where he ran a Mercedes dealership. Fangio died in 1995 in Buenos Aires in 1995, at the age of 84. He is remembered as one of the true great drivers; one who won 24 of the 51 races he competed in.

Emilio Giuseppe (Nino) FARINA

Nationality: Italian
Born: 30th October 1906
Died: 30th June 1966
Seasons: 1950-1955
Team/manufacturer(s): Alfa Romeo, Ferrari
Grands Prix: 34
Race wins: 5
Championship wins: 1

Nino Farina worked as a doctor of engineering and started competing in hillclimbs in the 1920s. He then progressed to circuit racing, driving for Maserati and, later, Alfa Romeo, for which he was second driver behind Tazio Nuvolari. Racing in the Voiturette class, he was Italian Champion no less than three times between 1937 to 1939. Then, in 1940, he won the Tripoli Grand Prix.

After the Second World War, he won the 1948 Monaco Grand Prix in a private Maserati. His first Formula One season was an astounding success with him winning three out of six races and becoming the first-ever World Champion.

Sadly, Farina was unable to repeat that success, because he was second driver to Fangio the next year, although he did win at Belgium. In 1952 he moved to Ferrari and won at the Nürburgring the following season.

Farina then retired from Formula One and went on to compete in the Indy 500 in 1956, but crashed. He retired from racing soon after.

Ironically, Farina (who was nephew of Pinin Farina, the coachbuilder) was killed in a car crash while driving

to the 1966 French Grand Prix, where he was going to be a spectator.

William (Willie) FERGUSON

Nationality: South African
Born: 6th March 1940
Seasons: 1972
Team/manufacturer(s): Brabham, Surtees
Grands Prix: 1
Race wins: 0
Championship wins: 0

Usually known as Willie, Ferguson was born in Johannesburg in 1940 and very little is known of him.

In 1972, Ferguson entered the South African Grand Prix, driving a Brabham BT33 run by the local outfit, Team Gunston. However, the engine blew up during practice and he was unable to start the race.

Oddly, Ferguson was also pencilled in to drive a Surtees, again for Team Gunston, but in the end that car was driven by John Love. That was extent of Ferguson's Formula One career and he disappeared from prominence after that.

Ralph David FIRMAN

Nationality: Irish
Born: 20th May 1975
Seasons: 2003
Team/manufacturer(s): Jordan
Grands Prix: 15
Race wins: 0
Championship wins: 0

Irishman Ralph Firman was born in Norfolk, the son of Ralph Firman Senior, who ran the Van Diemen racing car company

Nino Farina

Juan-Manuel Sangio

Ralph Firman

and was himself a racing driver.

Firman started racing karts at the age of 11 and, by the time he was 17, he was competing in Formula Vauxhall Junior and won the McLaren Autosport Young Driver Award. He had soon progressed to Formula 3 and won the British Championship in 1996.

Unable to get a drive in the UK, Firman then moved to Japan for six years, to compete in Formula Nippon sportscars. He finally returned home in 2003 to drive for Jordan's Formula One team.

His one season was not great, though, with an uncompetitive car, Firman failed to finish a number of races and his best result was an eighth place at the Spanish Grand Prix. He was injured in a crash during the Hungarian Grand Prix and missed the Italian event because of this.

Firman later became involved in the A1 Grand Prix series and has competed in GT racing.

Ludwig FISCHER

Nationality: German
Born: 17th December 1915
Died: 8th March 1991
Seasons: 1952
Team/manufacturer(s): non-works AFM
Grands Prix: 1
Race wins: 0
Championship wins: 0

Born in Bad Reichenhall, Germany, in 1915, Ludwig Fischer was an enthusiastic amateur driver. He competed in hillclimbs and, later, Formula Junior and then Formula 2.

In the latter, he competed with his own 1949 AFM (Alex von Falkenhausen Motorenbau) with a BMW engine. He entered this car into the 1952 German Grand Prix at the Nürburgring, but failed to start the race, despite qualifying for it.

Fischer continued to race in other events, both in the AFM and in other cars up until the mid-1960s.

Rudolf (Rudi) FISCHER

Nationality: Switzerland
Born: 19th April 1912
Died: 30th December 1976
Seasons: 1951-1952
Team/manufacturer(s): Ferrari
Grands Prix: 7
Race wins: 0
Championship wins: 0

Born Rudolf Fischer in 1912, this enthusiastic amateur racer ran a restaurant to earn enough money to indulge his hobby. After proving himself with a Simca in the late 1940s, he treated himself to a V12 Ferrari for the 1951 season.

Fischer campaigned this car in a number of non-championship Grand Prix races and some Formula 2 races that year. He also entered the Swiss and German Grands Prix that year, finishing 11th and sixth, respectively.

The following season, Fischer bought a more advanced car, a Ferrari T500, which made him more competitive. Indeed, he finished second in Switzerland and third in Germany in it. He also competed in the French, British and Italian Grands Prix that year, but with less success. He scored a total of 10 championship points.

Despite his obvious talent, Fischer pretty much retired from racing at the end of 1952, concerned for his safety. He went back to concentrating on his restaurant business.

Michael J (Mike) FISHER

Nationality: American
Born: 13th March 1943
Seasons: 1967
Team/manufacturer(s): Lotus
Grands Prix: 2
Race wins: 0
Championship wins: 0

American Mike Fisher drove a number of cars in the early 1960s, including a Lotus 18, Porsche 906 and a Porsche 910. However, when he entered the 1967 Canadian Grand Prix, he was pretty much unknown.

The car he was driving, though, had an exciting history. It was the Lotus 33 with which Jim Clark had won the 1965 World Championship, and had been bought by Earl Chiles. Now fitted with a BRM engine, Fisher drove the car to an 11th place finish. He went on to enter the Mexican Grand Prix later that season but had to retire with fuelling problems.

Rudi Fischer

Fisher then fought in the Vietnam War as a fighter pilot and then, in the 1990s, he worked for the Pentagon. He was also executive vice-president of the CART race series for a short time.

Giancarlo FISICHELLA

Nationality: Italian
Born: 14th January 1973
Seasons: 1996-
Team/manufacturer(s): Minardi, Jordan, Benetton, Sauber, Renault
Grands Prix: 196
Race wins: 3
Championship wins: 0

Giancarlo Fisichella is nicknamed 'Fisico' or 'Fisi' and was born in Rome. He began karting as a child and moved to Formula 3 in his late teens, winning the Italian Championship in 1994 before competing in touring cars for a short time.

He began his Formula One career in 1996, racing for Minardi for part of the season. He then spent 1997 with Jordan before beginning a relationship with Benetton, which became Renault. Unfortunately, he struggled with uncompetitive cars and left to return to Jordan for 2002 and 2003.

It was in 2003 that Fisichella won his first Grand Prix, at a very wet Brazil; but only after a lot of controversy about whether he or Kimi Räikkönen had won. He went on to win again in Australia in 2005 (in which season he finished fifth in the championship) and Malaysia in 2006, now driving for Renault.

John Cooper FITCH

Nationality: American
Born: 4th August 1917
Seasons: 1953-1955
Team/manufacturer(s): HWM-Alta, Stirling Moss, Briggs Cunningham
Grands Prix: 4
Race wins: 0
Championship wins: 0

Born in Indianapolis, John Fitch built and raced cars as a teenager. During the Second World War he was a fighter pilot and spent time in the UK. After, he returned to the US and opened an MG dealership and also raced the cars.

He went on to race a variety of cars and came to Europe in the early 1950s, when he was the first American driver to make an impact there. Indeed, in 1953, he was named Sports Car Driver of the Year. It was that year that he competed in his first Grand Prix, the French event, which was followed by the Italian Grand Prix the same season.

Fitch's short Grand Prix career finished in 1965, after just four races. However, he continued to race and became an active campaigner for more safety in motorsport and started a company that developed safety equipment.

Christian FITTIPALDI

Nationality: Brazilian
Born: 18th January 1971
Seasons: 1992-1994
Team/manufacturer(s): Minardi, Footwork
Grands Prix: 43
Race wins: 0
Championship wins: 0

Giancarlo Fisichella

Christian Fittipaldi

Christian Fittipaldi is the son of Wilson and nephew of Emerson Fittipaldi, both Grand Prix drivers. His father backed him in his career, which blossomed in 1991 when he won the Formula 3000 Championship.

Fittipaldi went straight from there to Formula One, driving for the Minardi team in 1992 and 1993. He had a mixed bag of results, though, with his best result being a fourth place at South Africa in 1993. However, this was tempered by failing to finish a number of races. He left the team before the end of the 1993 season.

The next year, Fittipaldi drove for Footwork but, again, had a mixed year. He then retired from Formula One and moved to the USA to compete in Champ Car and NASCAR racing. More recently, he entered some A1 Grand Prix races.

Emerson FITTIPALDI

Nationality: Brazilian
Born: 12th December 1946
Seasons: 1970-1980
Team/manufacturer(s): Lotus, McLaren, Fittipaldi
Grands Prix: 149
Race wins: 14
Championship wins: 2

Emerson Fittipaldi's parents both raced and his father was a well-known motorsport journalist and radio com-mentator. With his brother, Wilson, he set up a custom-car spares business to raise money to build and race their own karts, with Emerson becoming the Brazilian Kart Champion by the age of 18.

He then moved to Formula Vee and won the championship in 1967. This success persuaded him to abandon his mechanical engineering course and travel to England. There, he bought a Formula Ford car and was an immediate success.

Before long, he'd moved to Formula Three, and soon drew the attention of Lotus boss, Colin Chapman, who was looking for a new Formula One driver.

Emerson made his Formula One debut in the 1970 British Grand Prix, and put in a good performance, followed by similar drives in Germany and Austria. Then came the ill-fated Italian Grand Prix at Monza, where teammate, Jochen Rindt, was killed in a practice accident. Earlier that day, Emerson had also crashed at high speed; he was shaken but unhurt. Lotus's other driver at the time, John Miles, was so affected by Rindt's death that he immediately retired from Formula One, leaving newcomer Fittipaldi as team leader, despite only racing in three Grands Prix.

He immediately rose to the challenge and won his next race, the USA Grand Prix.

The next year, 1971, was a disappointment because Fittipaldi had been badly injured in a road-car accident. However, he was back on form in 1972. He won five of the 12 races that year, securing the Constructors' Championship for Lotus and making him World Champion at the age of just 25; at the time, the youngest driver ever.

Lotus picked up the Constructors' Championship again the following year, but this time Fittipaldi was beaten by Jackie Stewart in the Drivers' Championship.

Fittipaldi left Lotus to drive for McLaren in 1974, and that year he won three races and clinched the championship for a second time. He did almost as well the following year, too, but had to make do with second place, behind Ferrari's Niki Lauda.

He then moved to the Fittipaldi team, run by his brother, Wilson. Sponsored by Brazil's state-owned sugar industry, the Fittipaldi team couldn't compete with the big players, despite their lead driver's undoubted skills. Even so, loyalty to his family and country meant that Fittipaldi stayed with the team for five years, but the best result he could manage in all that time was a second place.

Fittipaldi retired from driving in 1980, but stayed on to manage his team until it folded in 1982. He then returned to Brazil to manage the family's farm and car accessory business. However, by 1984 he was back behind the wheel of a racing car, this time in the American CART series. Fittipaldi continued to compete until 1996 when he retired again after an accident.

Wilson FITTIPALDI

Nationality: Brazilian
Born: 25th December 1943
Seasons: 1972-1973, 1975
Team/manufacturer(s): Brabham, Fittipaldi
Grands Prix: 38
Race wins: 0
Championship wins: 0

The older brother of Emerson Fittipaldi, Wilson began building and racing karts with his brother in the 1950s and 1960s. Then, again with his brother, he moved into Formula Vee. He then moved to Europe to race briefly, and unsuccessfully, in Formula 2 before returning to Brazil.

In 1970, he again came to Europe to race in British Formula 3, where he put in some good performances. The next year saw him go to Formula 2, racing alongside his brother, and again he proved himself a capable driver.

He then progressed to Formula One and drove for Brabham in 1972 and 1973, but struggled with mechanical problems for many of his races; his best result being a fifth place at the Nürburgring in 1973.

In 1974, Fittipaldi didn't compete, but spent his time setting up the Fittipaldi Formula One team, which he then drove for the following year, but he had no success.

He then retired from racing to concentrate on running the team, for which his brother, Emerson, was now driving. More recently, Fittipaldi became involved in various businesses and helped his son, Christian, get into motor racing.

Theodor (Theo) FITZAU

Nationality: East German
Born: 10th February 1923
Died: 18th March 1982
Seasons: 1953
Team/manufacturer(s): non-works AFM
Grands Prix: 1
Race wins: 0
Championship wins: 0

Theodor Fitzau was born in Köthen, East Germany and began racing in that country in the late 1940s, driving a BMW 328 EMW. At this time, there was great rivalry between East and West Germany, and Fitzau was soon driving for Rennkollektiv, the state-owned team.

He mainly raced in Formula 2 events, which often had many of the top German drivers, from East and West, entering, together with those from other parts of Europe.

In 1952, Fitzau travelled to West Germany to race and defected to the West, never returning home. This gave him the chance to compete in German Formula 3 that same year. The following season, he entered a dated AFM-BMW in the German Grand Prix at the Nürburgring, but failed to finish the race.

Jan FLINTERMAN

Nationality: Dutch
Born: 2nd October 1919
Died: 26th December 1992
Seasons: 1952
Team/manufacturer(s): Maserati
Grands Prix: 1
Race wins: 0
Championship wins: 0

Dutchman, Jan Flinterman, escaped to England in

Emerson Fittipaldi

1940, when the Germans invaded his home country. There, he joined the RAF and flew Spitfires in Malta, among other places.

After the end of the war, Flinterman remained with the RAF for some time, flying Meteor jets. He then returned to Holland to run the country's fighter pilot school.

All this flying experience must have put him in good stead to race cars. He began in Formula 3 in 1950 and, three years later, became the first Dutchman to enter a Formula One race. This was at his home event driving a Maserati. Unfortunately, he was unable to finish the race because of mechanical problems.

Flinterman later got involved in world-speed attempts and was managing director of a Dutch airline.

Ronald (Ron) FLOCKHART

Nationality: Scottish
Born: 16th June 1923
Died: 12th April 1962
Seasons: 1954, 1956-1960
Team/manufacturer(s): Maserati, BRM, Connaught, Cooper, Lotus
Grands Prix: 14
Race wins: 0
Championship wins: 0

Scotsman Ron Flockhart raced motorcycles before getting involved with MGs and JP-Vincents in the late 1940s. Then, in 1952, he bought himself an ERA D-Type with which he had plenty of success in Formula Libre.

Before long, he'd been signed to drive for BRM to race in the same formula in 1954. However, this year also gave him his first Formula One break, when he drove a Maserati briefly in the British Grand Prix before he crashed out of the race.

Flockhart made another attempt at Formula One in 1956, when he campaigned a BRM in Britain and a Connaught in Italy; finishing joint third with Fangio in the latter. The next year, he raced a BRM at the Monaco and French Grands Prix. He continued to enter Grands Prix, for various teams, until 1960.

After that, Flockhart turned his attention more to flying, and wanted to break records. Tragically, though, he was killed when his plane crashed in Australia, while he was practising for a London to Sydney record attempt.

Gregor FOITEK

Nationality: Swiss
Born: 27th March 1965
Seasons: 1989-1990
Team/manufacturer(s): EuroBrun, Rial, Brabham, Onyx, Monteverdi
Grands Prix: 22
Race wins: 0
Championship wins: 0

Swiss driver, Gregor Foitek, was born in Zurich, the son of a wealthy racing driver and sportscar dealer. In 1986, he won the Swiss Formula 3 Championship and competed in German Formula 3. At the end of the season he began racing in Formula 3000 and continued the following two years

In 1989, Foitek joined the EuroBrun Formula One team but failed to pre-qualify for all but one race, which he failed to qualify for, partly because the car was dated and uncompetitive.

He then moved to Brabham for the following season, and

Norberto Fontana

had a solitary result – seventh place at Monaco. He finished an unsuccessful season driving for Onyx.

Foitek went on to dabble in sportscar and Indy racing, but with little success. He then became involved in the family garage business.

George FOLLMER

Nationality: American
Born: 27th January 1934
Seasons: 1973
Team/manufacturer(s): Shadow
Grands Prix: 13
Race wins: 0
Championship wins: 0

Arizona-born George Follmer began racing in 1960 and took awards as Rookie of the Year and Driver of the Year. By 1965 he was SCCA US Road Racing Champion, driving a Lotus 23 with a Porsche 904 engine. A year later he won his class at the Sebring 12 Hour race.

He then moved to Can-Am and set nine records in five years, only failing to finish one race. And, in 1972, become the only person to win both the Trans-Am and Can-Am Championships.

Then, 1973, saw Follmer move into Formula One, driving for the Shadow team. At his first race, in South Africa, he finished in sixth place. His next event, the Spanish Grand Prix, saw him take third place. These were, though, the only high-

points of an otherwise lacklustre season, and he didn't return to Formula One after that. Follmer continued to race very successfully in other championships into the 1980s before retiring and working as a pilot.

Norberto Edgardo FONTANA

Nationality: Argentinean
Born: 20th January 1975
Seasons: 1997
Team/manufacturer(s): Sauber
Grands Prix: 4
Race wins: 0
Championship wins: 0

Norberto Fontana, from Argentina, won the German Formula 3 Championship in 1995, after winning no less than 10 out of 16 races that season. This was enough to win him a Formula One seat the following year, but he injured his neck in an accident and so was relegated to test-driver for Sauber.

However, for 1997 he got his chance to race for the team, after regular driver, Gianni Morbidelli, was injured. Unfortunately, though, Fontana was unable to match his Formula 3 results and, out of the four Grands Prix he entered that year, he retired from one, finished ninth in two and 14th in the last.

That was to be the extent of his Formula One career, and Fontana then competed in Formula 3000, Champ Cars and touring cars. It was in the latter that he finally returned to form, winning the Toyota Touring Car Series in 2002.

Azdrubal FONTES BAYARDO

Nationality: Uruguayan
Born: 26th December 1922
Died: 9th July 2006
Seasons: 1959
Team/manufacturer(s): Scuderia Centro Sud
Grands Prix: 1
Race wins: 0
Championship wins: 0

Azdrubal Fontes Bayardo came from Uruguay and competed, with some success, in the Argentinean Formula Libre series during the late 1950s. This series was evolving into something very like Formula One at the time.

In 1959, Fontes Bayardo entered the French Grand Prix, driving an outdated Maserati 250F. However, he failed to qualify for the race proper and returned to his homeland. And that was the full extent of his Formula One career.

Back in South America he continued to race in Formula Libre as well as taking on some endurance events. After

retiring from racing, he worked with General Motors and a company that produced pick-up trucks.

Franco FORINI

Nationality: Swiss
Born: 22nd September 1958
Seasons: 1987
Team/manufacturer(s): Osella
Grands Prix: 3
Race wins: 0
Championship wins: 0

Swiss-born Franco Forini raced karts at a national level in Italy in the late 1970s and followed that by a spell competing in Alfasuds.

By 1981, though, he was racing in Formula 3, first in the European championship, then the Italian. In the latter, he won the title in 1985. Then followed a year in Formula 3000.

Forini's Formula One career was short and unsuccessful. He drove in three Grands Prix for Osella during the 1987 season. At Italy and Portugal he had to retire with mechanical problems, while in Spain he failed to qualify.

From there, he returned to Formula 3 until 1990 when he

retired to become a production manager for a motorsport team. However, he competed briefly in rallying and continued to race karts. He also owns a number of filling stations in Switzerland.

Philip FOTHERINGHAM-PARKER

Nationality: British
Born: 22nd September 1907
Died: 15th October 1981
Seasons: 1951
Team/manufacturer(s): non-works Maserati
Grands Prix: 1
Race wins: 0
Championship wins: 0

Philip Fotheringham-Parker was a wealthy company director with the money to indulge in motor racing. Prior to the Second World War he competed in a range of machinery, including an Alvis, ERA and a Maserati 4CL single-seater racing car.

It was this same car that he continued to use after the end of the war, in various UK-based competitions. Indeed, it was the now elderly Maserati that Fotheringham-Parker

Gregor Foitek

Heinz-Harald Frentzen

entered into the 1951 British Grand Prix at Silverstone. Sadly, though, the car suffered a bad oil leak and he had to retire before the end of the race.

Fotheringham-Parker never competed in Formula One again. However, he did make an appearance at the 1953 Le Mans 24 Hour race, driving an Allard, but his team retired early. He also raced a Ford Zephyr in the 1954 Monte Carlo Rally. After that, he gradually cut down his racing activity.

Giorgio FRANCIA

Nationality: Italian
Born: 8th November 1947
Seasons: 1977, 1981
Team/manufacturer(s): Martini, Osella
Grands Prix: 2
Race wins: 0
Championship wins: 0

Giorgio Francia was born in Bologna, Italy, and began karting in his teens. He then moved on to Formula Italia and then Formula 3 and Formula 2.

With his age against him, Francia moved into sportscar racing in the mid-1970s, when he reaching his thirties. However, he also got involved in Formula One testing for

various teams. This led, in 1977, to his first Formula One attempt, at the Italian Grand Prix, driving a Brabham for Martini Racing, a race he failed to qualify for.

In 1981, a second chance came for Francia, and he drove for Osella at the Spanish Grand Prix but, again, he didn't qualify after being the slowest in practice.

Francia then continued to race sportscars and then touring cars. However, he continued to test Formula One cars for Alfa Romeo until 1985. He remained closely linked with Alfa and became a racing instructor for the company.

Heinz-Harald FRENTZEN

Nationality: German
Born: 18th May 1967
Seasons: 1994-2003
Team/manufacturer(s): Sauber, Williams, Jordan, Prost, Arrows
Grands Prix: 160
Race wins: 3
Championship wins: 0

The son of a funeral director (who also acted as his manager and mechanic) Heinz-Harald Frentzen began racing karts at the age of 13 and, by the time he was 18, he had

progressed to German Formula Ford 2000 and was runner-up in the 1987 championship.

He then went on to win the German Formula Opel Lotus Championship in his first season. Next came German Formula 3 in 1989, in which Frentzen finished joint second along with Michael Schumacher.

Frentzen's first Formula One season came in 1994, driving for Sauber. He performed well, so well that Frank Williams tried to take him to replace Ayrton Senna, but the German stayed with Sauber through 1996.

He then finally moved to Williams and got his first win in 1997 at San Marino, plus two seconds, and three fourth place finishes. Frentzen continued to do well and, now driving for Jordan, he won two races in 1999 (France and Italy) plus a good number of podium finishes.

Unfortunately, his relationship with Jordan turned sour and he moved to Prost partway through the 2001 season. He then went to Arrows for 2002 until the team went bankrupt, and then it was back to Sauber until the end of 2003. His results were less good by then, although he did finish a respectable third in the USA Grand Prix that year.

From 2004, Frentzen competed in the German DTM touring car series.

Paul FRÈRE

Nationality: Belgian
Born: 30th January 1917
Seasons: 1952-1956
Team/manufacturer(s): HWM, Simca-Gordini, Gordini, Ferrari
Grands Prix: 11
Race wins: 0
Championship wins: 0

Belgian Paul Frère is better known as a motoring journalist, which was always his main career. However, he also enjoyed racing cars and first appeared at the Spa 24 Hours in an MG, in the 1950s.

Despite not being a full-time driver, Frère managed to compete in 10 Grands Prix between 1952 and 1956, beginning with his home race (which he entered each year), where he finished a respectable fifth, driving for HWM.

Frère's best results were driving for Ferrari in 1955 and 1956. These two years, the only Grands Prix he entered were the Belgian ones and he finished fifth and then second.

Later, he won the 1960 Le Mans 24 Hours, driving a works Ferrari. That same year Frère also won the non-championship South African Grand Prix.

Frère continued to be involved in motor racing and journalism throughout his life, and wrote a seminal work on the Porsche 911.

Patrick FRIESACHER

Nationality: Austrian
Born: 26th September 1980
Seasons: 2005
Team/manufacturer(s): Minardi
Grands Prix: 11
Race wins: 0
Championship wins: 0

As a youngster, Patrick Friesacher started off riding

Patrick Friesacher

motorcycles in motocross but switched to karting when he was 11, competing at national and international level. A bad accident set him back but didn't put him off and, by the time he was 19, he was competing in French Formula 3, followed by German Formula 3 in 2000 and then Formula 3000.

Despite showing good promise in all these series, Friesacher struggled to get in with a Formula One team. However, he was employed by Minardi to drive its two-seater Formula One car that gave passenger rides at special events, and that led to him testing for the team at the end of 2004.

He proved himself good enough to get a place with Minardi for the 2005 season, but failed to achieve any decent results. However, he did finish sixth at the US Grand Prix, but only because only six drivers competed, as the other teams pulled out because of concerns over tyre safety.

Friesacher was dropped from Minardi partway through the season because of a lack of sponsorship. He spent 2006 competing in the A1 Grand Prix series.

Joseph (Joe) FRY

Nationality: British
Born: 26th September 1915
Seasons: 1950
Team/manufacturer(s): Maserati
Grands Prix: 1
Race wins: 0
Championship wins: 0

Joe Fry served in the Royal Air Force during the Second World War. Afterwards, together with his brother, he built his own single-seater car, called the Freikaiserwagen, which used an air-cooled V-twin Blackburne engine, mounted at the rear. He used this car to compete in sprints and hillclimbs.

Fry also raced a Maserati 4CL in various events, including the first ever World Championship Grand Prix, at Silverstone. He was sharing the drive with Brian Shaw-Taylor and the pair finished in 10th place.

Just a few weeks later, he was competing in his Freikaiserwagen in a hillclimb at Blandford, when he lost control and crashed the car. He died, aged just 34.

Hiroshi FUSHIDA

Nationality: Japanese
Born: 10th March 1946
Seasons: 1975
Team/manufacturer(s): Maki
Grands Prix: 2
Race wins: 0
Championship wins: 0

Japanese-born Hiroshi Fushida came from a wealthy family – his father owned the country's largest kimono manufacturing company. Fushida apparently had no great background as a successful driver when he was chosen by the Maki team as a driver.

A mix of inexperience and an uncompetitive car meant that Fushida's brief Formula One career was a disappointment, with him failing to qualify for either the Dutch or the British Grands Prix – the only two he entered.

Fushida later came to the UK to run the TOM British Formula 3 team, he then returned to Japan to work with a Formula 3 team there.

G

GABBIANI, Beppe
GACHOT, Bertrand
GAILLARD, Patrick
GALICA, Divina
GALLI, Giovannl
GALVEZ, Oscar
GAMBLE, Fred
GANLEY, Howden
GARDNER, Frank
GARTNER, Jo
GAZE, Tony
GEKI
GENDEBIEN, Olivier
GENE, Marc
GERARD, Bob
GERINI, Gerino
GETHIN, Peter
GHINZANI, Piercarlo
GIACOMELLI, Bruno
GIBSON, Dick
GIMAX
GINTHER, Richie

GIRAUD CABANTOUS, Yves
GIUNTI, Ignazio
GLOCK, Timo
GLOCKLER, Helm
GODIA, Paco
GOETHALS, Christian
GONZALEZ, José Froilán
GONZALEZ, Oscar
GORDINI, Aldo
GOULD, Horace
GOUNON, Jean-Marc
GREENE, Keith
GREGORY, Masten
GRIGNARD, Auguste
GROUILLARD, Olivier
GUBBY, Brian
GUELFI, Andre
GUERRA, Miguel Angel
GUERRERO, Roberto
GUGELMIN, Mauricio
GURNEY, Dan

Piercarlo Ghinzani

Giuseppe (Beppe) GABBIANI

Nationality: Italian
Born: 2nd January 1957
Seasons: 1978, 1981
Team/manufacturer(s): Surtees, Osella
Grands Prix: 17
Race wins: 0
Championship wins: 0

Born to a wealthy Italian family, Giuseppe – or Beppe – Gabbiani began karting when he was in his early teens. By the time he was 20, he was competing in Formula 3 and won his first-ever race in the European series, finishing the 1977 series in fourth place.

The following year, Gabbiani moved into Formula 2 for an uneventful season. However, the same year he also rented a Surtees and entered the USA and Canadian Grands Prix, but failed to qualify for either.

Gabbiani then returned to Formula 2 for the 1979 and 1980 seasons. He was, though, determined to make it in Formula One and so secured a drive with Osella for 1981. Sadly, though, he didn't have the required experience and, despite entering every race of the season, he either failed to qualify or failed to finish any of them.

It was then back to Formula 2 before trying out a variety of different series over the years.

Bertrand GACHOT

Nationality: Belgian
Born: 23rd December 1962
Seasons: 1989-1992, 1994-1995
Team/manufacturer(s): Onyx, Rial, Coloni, Jordan, Larrousse, Pacific
Grands Prix: 84
Race wins: 0
Championship wins: 0

A Belgian citizen born in Luxembourg, Bertrand Gachot began racing karts at the age of 15. By the time he was in his early twenties he was competing in Formula Ford and won the British Championship in 1986.

The following year, he came second in the British Formula 3 Championship and then went to a mixed season in Formula 3000.

Then Gachot made his Formula One debut, driving for

Onyx in 1989. However, he left the team towards the end of the season and drove for Rial in the last two Grands Prix. Throughout the year, though, he failed to perform, not qualifying for most of the races.

The next year, driving for Coloni was even less successful, with him failing to qualify for a single race. A move to Jordan in 1991 proved much better, with him getting some good finishes, including fifth place in Canada, and setting a lap record at Hungary. Unfortunately, though, he was unable to do the full season because an assault on a London taxi driver led to Gachot spending two months in prison. Unable to return to Jordan, he moved to Larrousse for the last race of the season and stayed with them for 1992.

Gachot drove for Pacific in 1994 and 1995. Again, though, he failed to qualify for most of the races. Since retiring from racing, he moved to Spain and set up various business ventures.

Patrick GAILLARD

Nationality: French
Born: 12th February 1952
Seasons: 1979
Team/manufacturer(s): Ensign
Grands Prix: 5
Race wins: 0
Championship wins: 0

Patrick Gaillard was born in Paris, the son of a businessman who ran a van-hire company. He proved himself in European Formula 3, coming third in the 1978 championship.

A move to Formula 2 the following year proved to be a step to Formula One, when he found himself driving for Ensign in five Grands Prix, starting with the French one. However, Gaillard struggled with the car and failed to qualify for three of the races, didn't finish one and came 13th at the British event.

Gaillard went on to drive for Ensign at the 1980 Spanish Grand Prix and finished a worthwhile sixth. However, this race was later downgraded from World Championship status and so didn't count as an entry.

Gaillard then returned to Formula 2, CanAm and sportscar racing. After retiring from racing he became a race instructor in France.

Divina Galica

Divina GALICA

Nationality: English
Born: 13th August 1944
Seasons: 1976, 1978
Team/manufacturer(s): Surtees, Hesketh
Grands Prix: 3
Race wins: 0
Championship wins: 0

Divina Galica was born in Hertfordshire and began her sporting career as a successful skier, competing in the 1964 Olympic Games and the 1968 and 1972 Winter Olympics.

She then became hooked on motor racing after taking part in a celebrity race at Oulton Park, where she performed well. Galica went on to compete in a variety of machinery, including karts, sportscars and even trucks.

In 1976, she entered the British Grand Prix at Brands Hatch, driving a Surtees TS16, but failed to qualify. At the time, she surprised people by driving in car number 13. This had only once been used in Grand Prix racing since Giullo Masetti died in a car so-numbered during the 1926 Targa Florio.

Galica entered two more World Championship races in 1978, driving for Hesketh, but failed to qualify for either the Argentinean or the Brazilian Grands Prix.

She then continued to race in various series before retiring. Galica later ran Skip Barber Racing and received an OBE for her sporting career.

Giovanni Giuseppe Gilberto (Nanni) GALLI

Nationality: Italian
Born: 2nd January 1940
Seasons: 1970-1973
Team/manufacturer(s): McLaren, March, Tecno, Ferrari, Williams
Grands Prix: 20
Race wins: 0
Championship wins: 0

Born in Bologna as Giovanni Giuseppe Gilberto Galli, but better known as Nanni, he came from a wealthy family

Bertrand Gachot

and didn't take up racing until he was in his twenties.

After a stint in karts, he moved to touring cars and was soon making a name for himself, finishing second in the 1966 Targa Florio, driving an Alfa Romeo.

In 1967, he moved to Formula 2 for a few years before returning to saloon cars, driving for Alfa Romeo again. It was this Alfa connection that got him his first Formula One drive, because the Italian company was supplying engines to McLaren at the time. However, at his one race with the team, the 1970 Italian Grand Prix, he failed to qualify.

From there, he drove, for various teams, in a handful of Grands Prix each season until the end of 1973, but failed to make much of an impression. He retired from racing soon after and concentrated on various business concerns, including Fruit of the Loom clothing, which was a Williams sponsor in 1978. He was also involved in getting the Benetton family into Formula One.

Oscar Alfredo GÁLVEZ

Nationality: Argentinean
Born: 17th August 1913
Died: 16th December 1989
Seasons: 1953
Team/manufacturer(s): Maserati
Grands Prix: 1
Race wins: 0
Championship wins: 0

Argentinean Oscar Gálvez was a very well-known driver in his own country since before the Second World War, and a rival of fellow countryman, Fangio.

Together with his brother, Juan, Gálvez competed in long-distance road races in South America, most notably the Turismo de Carretera, which he dominated for a number of years.

However, Gálvez was also a skilled circuit racer and, in 1953, he drove a Maserati in the Argentinean Grand Prix and finished in an impressive fifth place, scoring two championship points.

That was, though, the extent of his Formula One career, and he went back to concentrating on road racing until his retirement in 1964. He continued to be involved in the sport as a manager.

After Gálvez died in 1989, the Buenos Aires circuit was renamed after him.

Frederick (Fred) GAMBLE

Nationality: American
Born: 17th March 1932
Seasons: 1960
Team/manufacturer(s): Behra-Porsche
Grands Prix: 1
Race wins: 0
Championship wins: 0

Fred Gamble came from Pittsburgh, Pennsylvania, and enjoyed racing MGs and Triumphs in his early days. He then became involved in the Scuderia Camoradi team, for which he raced a Corvette in various European events, including the 1960 Le Mans 24 Hour race, where he finished in 10th place.

The team was based in Modena and had access to a Behra-Porsche Formula 2 car. In 1960, British teams were boycotting the Italian Grand Prix and when Gamble was offered $1000 to enter the race, he jumped at the

chance. Unfortunately, after running out of fuel, he finished the race in last place.

Gamble later returned to the USA, where he worked for tyre company Goodyear. He later retired to Colorado.

James Howden GANLEY

Nationality: New Zealander
Born: 24th December 1941
Seasons: 1971-1974
Team/manufacturer(s): BRM, Williams, March, Maki
Grands Prix: 41
Race wins: 0
Championship wins: 0

Howden Ganley grew up in New Zealand but moved to England at the age of 20 with the dream of becoming a racing driver. Strapped for cash, he worked as a mechanic for a racing school and took the cars out for a drive whenever the opportunity arose.

By 1967, Ganley was able finally to realise his dream, when he entered his first full season of Formula 3, driving his own Brabham for which he'd worked and saved hard. By 1970 he had progressed to Formula 5000 and finished a respectable second in the championship that year.

This led to an offer of a drive with BRM for 1971 and 1972, and had a mixed bag of results. However, 1973 saw a move to Iso, which proved to be a very poor season for Ganley and he left the team at the end of the season.

The next year, 1974, saw Ganley enter two races at the start of the season with March, and then with the Japanese Maki team towards the end of the year, when he entered the British Grand Prix. Then a crash in the same car in Germany led to an injury that effectively finished his Formula One career.

Ganley went on to form Tiga Race Cars and became involved in other motorsports companies as well.

Frank GARDNER

Nationality: Australian
Born: 1st October 1930
Seasons: 1964-1965, 1968
Team/manufacturer(s): Brabham, BRM
Grands Prix: 9
Race wins: 0
Championship wins: 0

Australian Frank Gardner was an active sportsman from an early age, especially as a boxer and lifesaver. He also raced motorcycles successfully and this led, in 1956, to him taking up car racing, driving a C-type Jaguar to victory in an incredible 23 out of 24 races in the New South Wales Sportscar Championship.

A move to England followed and Gardner worked as a mechanic for Brabham and this, indirectly, led to him entering the 1964 British Grand Prix at Brands Hatch. However, he had to retire from the race after an accident.

The following year, he entered six Grands Prix with Brabham, but neither he nor the team had the experience to make the season a success, and Gardner decided to move into sportscar racing instead.

He did, however, find himself behind the wheel of a BRM for the 1968 Italian Grand Prix, but he failed to qualify.

Gardner then went back to some single-seater racing, winning the 1971 and 1972 Formula 5000 Championships. In saloon cars, he won the Australian Sports Sedan Championship in 1976 and 1977.

After retiring from racing he worked as a time manager and then retired fully to Queensland.

Joseph (Jo) GARTNER

Nationality: Austrian
Born: 24th January 1954
Died: 1st June 1986
Seasons: 1984
Team/manufacturer(s): Osella
Grands Prix: 8
Race wins: 0
Championship wins: 0

Jo Gartner began his career working as an engineer on Formula Vee cars but soon moved on to driving them. By 1978 he was driving in the European Super Vee Championship and then on to German Formula 3 the following year, and Formula 2 by 1980.

All this time, Gartner was struggling for finance but nonetheless managed to get a Formula One drive with Osella for the 1984 season. Out of eight Grands Prix, he failed to finish four of them, and finished 16th in one, 12th in two and an impressive fifth at Italy that year.

Sadly, it was not enough for Osella to sign him for another season and he moved into sportscar and IMSA racing, all the time hoping to return to Formula One.

Gartner was killed when his Porsche crashed at Le Mans in 1986. He was just 32 years old.

Anthony (Tony) GAZE

Nationality: Australia
Born: 3rd February 1920
Seasons: 1984
Team/manufacturer(s): HWM
Grands Prix: 4
Race wins: 0
Championship wins: 0

Tony Gaze served in the RAF during the Second World War and was awarded the Distinguished Flying Cross. After the end of hostilities, he returned home to Australia and soon got involved in motor-racing, driving a prewar Alta, among other things.

A move to England at the start of the 1950s, led to Gaze competing in four Grands Prix, driving his own HWM. However, the only race he finished was his first, the Belgian Grand Prix, where he came a lowly 15th. He retired from the British and German events and failed to qualify in Italy.

He then moved to sportscar racing and had more success, both in Britain and Australia. Indeed, he did much to promote and develop motorsport in his home country. He retired to Victoria and remained involved in motorsport.

Giacomo RUSSO (Geki)

Nationality: Italian
Born: 23rd October 1937
Died: 18th June 1967
Seasons: 1964-1966
Team/manufacturer(s): Walker, Lotus
Grands Prix: 3
Race wins: 0
Championship wins: 0

Born in Milan, Giacomo Russo was universally known as 'Geki' in the world of motorsport. He worked his way up from Italian Formula Junior and was four-time Italian Formula 3 Champion, from 1961 to 1964.

Marc Gené

Although not a Formula One regular, Geki did appear in his home Grand Prix, each year from 1964 to 1966. The first time, he didn't qualify in a Walker, the second, his Lotus suffered mechanical failure and he had to retire, and in the third race, also in a Lotus, he finished ninth.

There may have been more entries but, tragically, Geki was killed in a Formula 3 race at Caserta in 1967. His car hit another driver who was trying to warn of a pile-up ahead and Geki then crashed into a wall and his car caught fire.

Olivier GENDEBIEN

Nationality: Belgian
Born: 12th January 1924
Died: 2nd October 1998
Seasons: 1956, 1958-1961
Team/manufacturer(s): Ferrari, Reg Parnell Racing, Emeryson
Grands Prix: 15
Race wins: 0
Championship wins: 0

Olivier Gendebien was born into a wealthy Belgian family and spent the Second World War as part of the Belgian Resistance and, later, in the British Army.

After the war, he worked in Forestry and, through that, developed an interest in rallying. By 1955 he was winning rallies and was offered a job driving for Ferrari in sportscar and Grand Prix events, the latter as a stand-in driver.

Because of this, he only competed in a handful of Formula One races but, when he did, he often performed well, starting with a fifth place at the Argentinean Grand Prix, his first event.

A move to Cooper in 1960 saw Gendebien continue to do well in the few Grands Prix he entered; most notably a second place finish in France and third in Belgium. The next year, he came fourth in Belgium for Emeryson.

However, Gendebien really excelled in sports car racing, winning at Le Mans no less than four times in the late 1950s and early 1960s. He also won the 12 Hours of Sebring and the Targa Florio three times.

Gendebien retired from racing at the age of 38, after his wife became concerned for his safety. However, he remained involved with the sport and also enjoyed skiing, tennis and horse riding.

Marc GENÉ

Nationality: Spanish
Born: 29th March 1974
Seasons: 1999-2000, 2003-2004
Team/manufacturer(s): Minardi, Williams
Grands Prix: 36
Race wins: 0
Championship wins: 0

Spaniard Marc Gené shone from an early age, coming second in the Catalan Kart Championship at the age of just 13, and going on to win both that and the National Class Spanish Kart Championship the following year.

By 1992, Gené had moved up to Formula Ford and came second in the Spanish Championship that year and runner up in the European Championship the following season. In 1996 he won the FISA Superformula Championship and the Open

Bruno Giacomelli

Fortuna Championship in 1998.

Gené's Formula One career began in 1999 with a drive with Minardi that yielded a mix of results, with his best showing being sixth place in the European Grand Prix. After a disappointing second season with Minardi, Gené moved to Williams as a test driver. However, he did compete in three Grands Prix for the team between 2003 and 2004, and came fifth at the Italian Grand Prix in 2003.

From 2004, Gené drove as a test driver for Scuderia Ferrari.

Piercarlo Ghinzani

Frederick Roberts (Bob) GERARD

Nationality: British
Born: 19th January 1914
Died: 26th January 1990
Seasons: 1950-1951, 1953-1954, 1956-1957
Team/manufacturer(s): ERA, Cooper-Bristol
Grands Prix: 8
Race wins: 0
Championship wins: 0

Born in Leicester, Bob Gerard was often referred to as 'Mr Bob' or the 'Gentleman of Motor Racing'. He began competing in trials before the Second World War, driving a Riley.

After the end of the war, he began to race more seriously, driving an ERA in various events around the UK, including finishing second in the pre-Formula One 1949 British Grand Prix.

Gerard entered the ERA in the British and Monaco Grands Prix in 1950 and came sixth both times. The next year, he just entered the British event and finished 11th.

He then competed in the French Grand Prix in 1953, then the British one in 1954, 1956 and 1957, with his best result being another sixth place in the last event.

Gerard continued to compete, mainly in Formula 2, for a number of years. Gerard's Bend at the Mallory Park circuit is named after him.

Gerino GERINI

Nationality: Italian
Born: 10th August 1914
Seasons: 1956, 1958
Team/manufacturer(s): Maserati
Grands Prix: 7
Race wins: 0
Championship wins: 0

Gerino Gerini was an Italian nobleman from a wealthy background. He began his race career with Ferrari in the postwar years, but switched to the rival Maserati team.

It was in a Maserati that he entered his seven Formula One races, starting with the Argentinean Grand Prix in 1956, where he finished fourth. His other Grand Prix that year was his home event, where he came 10th. In 1958, Gerini attempted five Grands Prix, but only completed the French race, where he came ninth.

Gerini later turned to sportscar racing for a short time, before returning to the family home in Italy and working as an agent for Lamborghini before retiring.

Peter Gethin

Peter Kenneth GETHIN

Nationality: British
Born: 21st February 1940
Seasons: 1970-1974
Team/manufacturer(s): McLaren, BRM, Hill
Grands Prix: 31
Race wins: 1
Championship wins: 0

Peter Gethin was born in Surrey and began racing a Lotus Seven in his early 20s, followed by a Lotus 23, with which he proved very competitive in various UK events.

He moved into Formula 3 in 1965, then Formula 2 three years later. By 1969, he had claimed the new Formula 5000 Championship after winning four races in a row. He went to win the championship again the following year.

In 1970, Gethin got his first chance at a drive for McLaren Formula One after the death of Bruce McLaren. After a struggling season and a bit, he moved to BRM in 1971 and it was then he really hit the headlines. He won the Italian Grand Prix at Monza, coming up from fourth place in the final lap with the fastest speed in Formula One history.

That, though, turned out to be a one-off and Gethin struggled in the few Formula One races he entered after that. He then returned to Formula 5000 and also raced

in Can-Am. After retiring from racing, he ran a racing school at Goodwood.

Piercarlo GHINZANI

Nationality: Italian
Born: 16th January 1952
Seasons: 1981, 1983-1989
Team/manufacturer(s): Osella, Toleman, Ligier, Zakspeed
Grands Prix: 111
Race wins: 0
Championship wins: 0

Italian driver, Piercarlo Ghinzani, began competing in Formula Ford when he was just 18 years old. Just three years later he had progressed to Italian Formula 3, and on to European Formula 3 by 1977, when he won the championship.

After a short and unnoteworthy spell in Formula 2, he got signed by Osella and did two Grands Prix for the team in 1981, at Belgium and Monaco. Ghinzani went on to race full seasons with the team between 1983 and 1986 (apart from a brief spell with Toleman at the end of 1985), his best result being a fifth place at the US Grand Prix in 1984.

After a disappointing spell with Ligier in 1987 and Zakspeed in 1988, Ghinzani returned to Osella for the 1989

season but he only qualified for three races that year.

Ghinzani retired from racing and formed his own Formula 3 and Formula 3000 team in Italy.

Bruno GIACOMELLI

Nationality: Italian
Born: 10th September 1952
Seasons: 1977-1983, 1990
Team/manufacturer(s): McLaren, Alfa Romeo, Toleman, Life
Grands Prix: 82
Race wins: 0
Championship wins: 0

Bruno Giacomelli began competing in Formula Italia, and then came to the UK to race in the 1976 Formula 3 Championship and finished the season in second place.

It was then on to Formula 2 for the following season, and it was then that Giacomelli had his first stab at Formula One, driving a McLaren at his home Grand Prix but retiring with engine trouble.

The next year, he became the first Italian driver to win the Formula 2 Championship and also competed in five Formula One events, again for McLaren, his best finish being seventh place at the British Grand Prix.

Giacomelli then moved to Alfa Romeo and stayed with

German race at the Nürburgring in 1953. He was driving a Cooper Formula 2 car but failed to qualify because the engine blew.

That same year and the following one, he entered a Porsche 550. Interestingly, that car was inspired by a Porsche Spyder that Glöckler's brother, Walter, had created in 1951. Glöckler ran a motorcycle dealer and other companies in Frankfurt, both during and after his racing days.

Francisco (Paco) GODIA

Nationality: Spanish
Born: 21st March 1921
Died: 28th November 1990
Seasons: 1951, 1954, 1956-1958
Team/manufacturer(s): Maserati
Grands Prix: 14
Race wins: 0
Championship wins: 0

Francisco Godia was more commonly known as Paco Godia. He was a wealthy Spanish businessman who enjoyed racing as a hobby, and had the money to do so, competing in a range of cars and events over the years.

His Formula One career was with Maserati, for which he drove whenever the cars were not wanted for more experienced drivers. That meant that he only drove on occasions.

Despite his amateur status and his cautious nature, Godia often drove well, most notably finishing in fourth place at both the German and Italian Grands Prix in 1956.

Outside of motorsport, Godia was a keen fine-art collector and founded a museum in Barcelona, which also contains mementos of his racing career.

Kurt Christian GOETHALS

Nationality: Belgian
Born: 4th August 1928
Died: 26th February 2003
Seasons: 1958
Team/manufacturer(s): Cooper
Grands Prix: 1
Race wins: 0
Championship wins: 0

Christian Goethals was, like many at the time, an amateur driver who raced purely for fun. In the mid-1950s he competed in a Porsche Spyder in various European events, with some success.

He bought a Formula 2 Cooper in 1958 with which to attempt single-seater racing. It was in this car that he entered his one Formula One race, the 1958 German Grand Prix at the Nürburgring. However, he didn't finish the race because his car developed a fuel-pump problem.

José González

Soon after, he returned to sportscar racing, this time in a Porsche RSK and did reasonably well in a number of events. He retired from racing in the early 1960s.

José Froilán GONZÁLEZ

Nationality: Argentinean
Born: 5th October 1922
Seasons: 1950-1957, 1960
Team/manufacturer(s): Maserati, Talbot-Lago, Ferrari, Vanwall
Grands Prix: 26
Race wins: 2
Championship wins: 0

José Froilán González was born and bred in Argentina and grew up enjoying a range of sports, including football, swimming and cycling. However, motor-racing was his first love and he began competing on motorcycles while in his teens.

González came to Europe with Fangio and other drivers in 1950 and drove a Maserati in the Monaco and French Grands Prix. The following year he got a works place with Ferrari and when on to win the team's first World Championship Grand Prix, at Silverstone that year, coming in ahead of Fangio.

He then switched between Maserati and Ferrari, and also drove for other teams, but never did a full season of Grands Prix, although he won again at Silverstone in 1954 and did his home race each year from 1953 to 1960, after which he pretty much retired from racing.

González was nicknamed the 'Pampas Bull' on account of his size. He went on to become a successful businessman in Buenos Aires.

Oscar GONZÁLEZ

Nationality: Uruguayan
Born: 10th November 1923
Died: 5th November 2006
Seasons: 1956
Team/manufacturer(s): Maserati
Grands Prix: 1
Race wins: 0
Championship wins: 0

Uruguayan driver Oscar González was born in Montevideo and grew up to be a successful businessman who raced for pleasure in his spare time.

In 1956, he entered the Argentinean Grand Prix, sharing a Maserati 250F with fellow countryman, Alberto Uria, who was a somewhat better-known driver in Uruguay. The pair qualified in 13th place on the grid and went on to share a sixth place finish. They were, though, the last to finish the race and were regularly lapped by the faster drivers.

González never entered another World Championship race and disappeared into racing obscurity. He continued to work in his businesses and died in Montevideo in 2006.

Aldo GORDINI

Nationality: French
Born: 20th May 1921
Died: 28th January 1995
Seasons: 1951
Team/manufacturer(s): Simca-Gordini
Grands Prix: 1
Race wins: 0
Championship wins: 0

Aldo Gordini was born in Turin but his family moved to

Peter Gethin

Peter Kenneth GETHIN

Nationality: British
Born: 21st February 1940
Seasons: 1970-1974
Team/manufacturer(s): McLaren, BRM, Hill
Grands Prix: 31
Race wins: 1
Championship wins: 0

Peter Gethin was born in Surrey and began racing a Lotus Seven in his early 20s, followed by a Lotus 23, with which he proved very competitive in various UK events.

He moved into Formula 3 in 1965, then Formula 2 three years later. By 1969, he had claimed the new Formula 5000 Championship after winning four races in a row. He went to win the championship again the following year.

In 1970, Gethin got his first chance at a drive for McLaren Formula One after the death of Bruce McLaren. After a struggling season and a bit, he moved to BRM in 1971 and it was then he really hit the headlines. He won the Italian Grand Prix at Monza, coming up from fourth place in the final lap with the fastest speed in Formula One history.

That, though, turned out to be a one-off and Gethin struggled in the few Formula One races he entered after that. He then returned to Formula 5000 and also raced in Can-Am. After retiring from racing, he ran a racing school at Goodwood.

Piercarlo GHINZANI

Nationality: Italian
Born: 16th January 1952
Seasons: 1981, 1983-1989
Team/manufacturer(s): Osella, Toleman, Ligier, Zakspeed
Grands Prix: 111
Race wins: 0
Championship wins: 0

Italian driver, Piercarlo Ghinzani, began competing in Formula Ford when he was just 18 years old. Just three years later he had progressed to Italian Formula 3, and on to European Formula 3 by 1977, when he won the championship.

After a short and unnoteworthy spell in Formula 2, he got signed by Osella and did two Grands Prix for the team in 1981, at Belgium and Monaco. Ghinzani went on to race full seasons with the team between 1983 and 1986 (apart from a brief spell with Toleman at the end of 1985), his best result being a fifth place at the US Grand Prix in 1984.

After a disappointing spell with Ligier in 1987 and Zakspeed in 1988, Ghinzani returned to Osella for the 1989 season but he only qualified for three races that year.

Ghinzani retired from racing and formed his own Formula 3 and Formula 3000 team in Italy.

Bruno GIACOMELLI

Nationality: Italian
Born: 10th September 1952
Seasons: 1977-1983, 1990
Team/manufacturer(s): McLaren, Alfa Romeo, Toleman, Life
Grands Prix: 82
Race wins: 0
Championship wins: 0

Bruno Giacomelli began competing in Formula Italia, and then came to the UK to race in the 1976 Formula 3 Championship and finished the season in second place.

It was then on to Formula 2 for the following season, and it was then that Giacomelli had his first stab at Formula One, driving a McLaren at his home Grand Prix but retiring with engine trouble.

The next year, he became the first Italian driver to win the Formula 2 Championship and also competed in five Formula One events, again for McLaren, his best finish being seventh place at the British Grand Prix.

Giacomelli then moved to Alfa Romeo and stayed with

85

Richie Ginther

However, he had to retire from the race with steering problems. The following year, he entered the same Grand Prix with the same car but, again, was forced to retire, this time with a misbehaving engine.

Gibson then travelled to New Zealand and South Africa with his car, winning the South African International Championship in 1959. However, after an accident the following year, he retired from racing.

He later moved to the USA, where he retired.

Carlo FRANCHI (Gimax)

Nationality: Italian
Born: 1st January 1938
Seasons: 1978
Team/manufacturer(s): Surtees
Grands Prix: 1
Race wins: 0
Championship wins: 0

Born in Milan as Carlo Franchi, he was always known simply as 'Gimax', which was a combination of the names of his two sons, Gigi and Massimo. He began racing sportscars in his home country in the 1970s and also competed in Formula 3.

Gimax only ever entered one Formula One Grand Prix, and that was the Italian race in 1978, when he was driving for Surtees. However, he failed to qualify.

He then returned to sportscar racing and had some success over the years, before retiring from racing at the end of the 1984 season. Back in Italy he became a successful businessman. His son went into racing, using the same nickname.

Richard (Richie) GINTHER

Nationality: American
Born: 5th August 1930
Died: 20th September 1989
Seasons: 1960-1967
Team/manufacturer(s): Ferrari, Scarab, BRM, Honda, Cooper, Eagle
Grands Prix: 54
Race wins: 1
Championship wins: 0

Born in Hollywood, Richie Ginther was a successful American driver. He began racing an MG in his twenties, and then drove a Ferrari with Phil Hill to a second-place finish in the 1954 Carrera Panamericana. This led to a drive with the American Ferrari importer, and Ginther was soon making quite an impression in local races.

By the late 1950s, he'd been offered a drive by Ferrari and so moved to Italy to take up the challenge. There, he discovered a talent for single-seater racing and competed in Formula 2 and, soon, Formula One. His first Grand Prix was at Monaco in 1960 and he finished in an impressive sixth place, and went on to come second at the Italian Grand Prix later that year.

Despite another good season with Ferrari the following year, with a number of top-five finishes, he was dropped by the team and went to BRM the following year, driving with Graham Hill. In 1963, Ginther finished second in the championship, behind his teammate.

A drive with Honda in 1965 and 1966 gave Ginther his one and only Formula One win, at the 1965 Mexican Grand Prix, despite struggling with an underdeveloped car.

After driving one race for Eagle in 1967, Ginther decided to retire from racing. He then managed race teams for a while before retiring to travel around North America in a camper van. He died on holiday in France in 1989.

Marius Aristide Yves GIRAUD (Yves Giraud-Cabantous)

Nationality: French
Born: 8th October 1904
Died: 30th March 1973
Seasons: 1950-1953
Team/manufacturer(s): Talbot-Lago, HWM
Grands Prix: 13
Race wins: 0
Championship wins: 0

Although his original name was Marius Aristide Yves Giraud, this French driver was usually known as Yves Giraud-Cabantous; the second surname came about after his father died and his mother remarried. He was a talented musician as a child and was going to make music his career, but once he'd discover cars, that was it. He worked as a mechanic in Paris and started to race cyclecars.

Giraud-Cabantous began racing cars in 1925, and was soon winning races and hillclimbs. He drove a Noel and also developed his own cars, and later competed in Bugattis and Delahayes.

After the war, he resumed his racing career, despite being in his forties, and was very successful in Delahayes and Talbot-Lagos, becoming the 1948 French Champion.

Giraud-Cabantous drove for Talbot-Lagos in the first World Championship race, the British Grand Prix, and finished in fourth place, behind three Alfa Romeos. The highlight the following year was a fifth place finish in Belgium.

He competed in the French Grand Prix only in 1952 and 1953, driving for HWM, finishing 10th and 14th respectively. After that he competed mainly in sportscar events, before retiring from the sport in 1957.

After that, Giraud-Cabantous ran his own haulage company, until he died in Paris in 1973.

Ignazio GIUNTI

Nationality: Italian
Born: 30th August 1941
Died: 10th January 1971
Seasons: 1970
Team/manufacturer(s): Ferrari
Grands Prix: 4
Race wins: 0
Championship wins: 0

Ignazio Giunti was actually born in Argentina to a wealthy family, but was brought up in Rome. He began racing as a teenager, competing in hillclimbs and local races, usually in an Alfa Romeo.

By 1966, he was driving for the Alfa Romeo team and, two years later, came second in the Targa Florio and fourth at Le Mans. By now a proven sportscar driver, Giunti was hired by Ferrari in 1970 and went on to win the 12 Hours of Sebring and the Targa Florio that year. Ferrari also gave him the opportunity to enter four Grands Prix that year. He got off to a good start, finishing fourth at Belgium, but had less luck with the other races, with a 14th, seventh and a retirement.

Giunti was signed to drive sportscars for Ferrari the following year. It was in a Ferrari that he was killed, when he crashed while leading the Buenos Aires 1000km race.

---

the team from 1979 to 1982. He gained two fourth place finishes, and one third place; the latter at the 1981 Las Vegas Grand Prix. After a disappointing season with Toleman, Giacomelli dabbled with sportscar and Indy car racing for a few years.

He did, though, make a brief return to Formula One in 1990, driving for Life, but failed to pre-qualify for any races that season. Giacomelli continued to race occasionally after that, including occasional appearances in the Porsche Supercup.

Richard (Dick) GIBSON

Nationality: British
Born: 16th April 1918
Seasons: 1957-1958
Team/manufacturer(s): Cooper
Grands Prix: 2
Race wins: 0
Championship wins: 0

Dick Gibson was born in Lincolnshire and competed in various cars, including a Cooper-Bristol and a Connaught, in the early 1950s.

Then, in 1957, he treated himself to a Formula 2 Cooper and started competing around Europe. He entered the car into the German Grand Prix at the Nürburgring that year, because it was open to Formula 2 cars in those days.

Ignazio Giunti

Timo GLOCK

Nationality: German
Born: 10th March 1982
Seasons: 2004
Team/manufacturer(s): Jordan
Grands Prix: 4
Race wins: 0
Championship wins: 0

German Timo Glock began racing karts at the age of 15 and was soon winning races and championships. He entered German Formula 3 in 2002 and then European Formula 3 the following year, finishing fifth in the championship.

In 2004, he became test driver for the Jordan Formula One team and had to step in to drive in the Canadian Grand Prix, where he finished an impressive seventh place. Towards the end of the season, he took over from Giorgio Pantano and competed in the Chinese, Japanese and Brazilian Grands Prix, tidily finishing 15th each time. Glock moved to ChampCar racing for 2005 and won the Rookie of the Year. The following year he competed in the GP2 Series.

Helmut (Helm) GLÖCKLER

Nationality: German
Born: 13th January 1909
Died: 18th December 1993
Seasons: 1953
Team/manufacturer(s): Cooper
Grands Prix: 1
Race wins: 0
Championship wins: 0

Helmut – or Helm – Glöckler was an enthusiastic amateur racer, both before and after the Second World War. In the early 1950s he campaigned a Deutsch-Bonnet in Formula 3 and was also successful in sportscar events.

Glöckler entered just one Formula One Grand Prix, the

GHI

Timo Glock

German race at the Nürburgring in 1953. He was driving a Cooper Formula 2 car but failed to qualify because the engine blew.

That same year and the following one, he entered a Porsche 550. Interestingly, that car was inspired by a Porsche Spyder that Glöckler's brother, Walter, had created in 1951. Glöckler ran a motorcycle dealer and other companies in Frankfurt, both during and after his racing days.

Francisco (Paco) GODIA

Nationality: Spanish
Born: 21st March 1921
Died: 28th November 1990
Seasons: 1951, 1954, 1956-1958
Team/manufacturer(s): Maserati
Grands Prix: 14
Race wins: 0
Championship wins: 0

Francisco Godia was more commonly known as Paco Godia. He was a wealthy Spanish businessman who enjoyed racing as a hobby, and had the money to do so, competing in a range of cars and events over the years.

His Formula One career was with Maserati, for which he drove whenever the cars were not wanted for more experienced drivers. That meant that he only drove on occasions.

Despite his amateur status and his cautious nature, Godia often drove well, most notably finishing in fourth place at both the German and Italian Grands Prix in 1956.

Outside of motorsport, Godia was a keen fine-art collector and founded a museum in Barcelona, which also contains mementos of his racing career.

Kurt Christian GOETHALS

Nationality: Belgian
Born: 4th August 1928
Died: 26th February 2003
Seasons: 1958
Team/manufacturer(s): Cooper
Grands Prix: 1
Race wins: 0
Championship wins: 0

Christian Goethals was, like many at the time, an amateur driver who raced purely for fun. In the mid-1950s he competed in a Porsche Spyder in various European events, with some success.

He bought a Formula 2 Cooper in 1958 with which to attempt single-seater racing. It was in this car that he entered his one Formula One race, the 1958 German Grand Prix at the Nürburgring. However, he didn't finish the race because his car developed a fuel-pump problem.

Soon after, he returned to sportscar racing, this time in a Porsche RSK and did reasonably well in a number of events. He retired from racing in the early 1960s.

José Froilán GONZÁLEZ

Nationality: Argentinean
Born: 5th October 1922
Seasons: 1950-1957, 1960
Team/manufacturer(s): Maserati, Talbot-Lago, Ferrari, Vanwall
Grands Prix: 26
Race wins: 2
Championship wins: 0

José Froilán González was born and bred in Argentina and grew up enjoying a range of sports, including football, swimming and cycling. However, motor-racing was his first love and he began competing on motorcycles while in his teens.

González came to Europe with Fangio and other drivers in 1950 and drove a Maserati in the Monaco and French Grands Prix. The following year he got a works place with Ferrari and when on to win the team's first World Championship Grand Prix, at Silverstone that year, coming in ahead of Fangio.

He then switched between Maserati and Ferrari, and also drove for other teams, but never did a full season of Grands Prix, although he won again at Silverstone in 1954 and did his home race each year from 1953 to 1960, after which he pretty much retired from racing.

González was nicknamed the 'Pampas Bull' on account of his size. He went on to become a successful businessman in Buenos Aires.

Oscar GONZÁLEZ

Nationality: Uruguayan
Born: 10th November 1923
Died: 5th November 2006
Seasons: 1956
Team/manufacturer(s): Maserati
Grands Prix: 1
Race wins: 0
Championship wins: 0

Uruguayan driver Oscar González was born in Montevideo and grew up to be a successful businessman who raced for pleasure in his spare time.

In 1956, he entered the Argentinean Grand Prix, sharing a Maserati 250F with fellow countryman, Alberto Uria, who was a somewhat better-known driver in Uruguay. The pair qualified in 13th place on the grid and went on to share a sixth place finish. They were, though, the last to finish the race and were regularly lapped by the faster drivers.

González never entered another World Championship race and disappeared into racing obscurity. He continued to work in his businesses and died in Montevideo in 2006.

Aldo GORDINI

Nationality: French
Born: 20th May 1921
Died: 28th January 1995
Seasons: 1951
Team/manufacturer(s): Simca-Gordini
Grands Prix: 1
Race wins: 0
Championship wins: 0

Aldo Gordini was born in Turin but his family moved to

José González

France after the First World War. His father, Amédee Gordini, was the famous sportscar builder and, naturally, the youngster soon got embroiled in cars and racing.

After the Second World War, Gordini went to work as a mechanic for his father, who was rebuilding the company after the hostilities. Naturally, he wanted to compete in the cars, rather than just build and repair them, and he took every opportunity to get behind the wheel, often in Formula 2 races.On 1st July 1951, Gordini entered his one and only Formula One Grand Prix. This was the French race at Reims, but he had to retire with engine problems after 27 laps.He continued to race and then went on to running his father's business.

Horace Harry TWIGG (Horace Gould)

Nationality: English
Born: 20th September 1918
Died: 4th November 1968
Seasons: 1954-1958, 1960
Team/manufacturer(s): Cooper, Maserati
Grands Prix: 17
Race wins: 0
Championship wins: 0

Born Horace Harry Twigg, Horace Gould always lived in Bristol, where he worked as a motor trader. A large man, he started competing in Coopers the post-war years, moving to Formula 2 in 1954, driving a Cooper-Bristol.

It was in this car that he competed in the 1954 British Grand Prix at Silverstone, where he finished in 15th place. He later bought himself a Maserati 250F and spent most of the 1955 season in Modena, Italy, where he built up a good relationship with the Maserati factory, so that he could obtain parts for his car for little or no outlay. Gould entered three Grands Prix that season but failed to finish any of them, although he did have some luck in non-championship races.

Gould continued to compete in various events in his Maserati, including a handful of Grands Prix (he finished fifth at Silverstone in 1956), but when the factory pulled out of racing he was no longer able to obtain parts so he gradually withdrew from racing. However, he did enter the 1960 Italian Grand Prix but his now tired Maserati failed to start because of a fuelling problem.

Gould returned to Bristol but died of a heart attack at the age of just 48.

Jean-Marc GOUNON

Nationality: French
Born: 1st January 1963
Seasons: 1993-1994
Team/manufacturer(s): Minardi, Simtek
Grands Prix: 9
Race wins: 0
Championship wins: 0

Jean-Marc Gounon was born in the French city of Aubenas and won the French Formula 3 Championship in his second year of competing, in 1989.

He then spent time in Formula 3000 before finally getting a break in Formula One, buying himself a drive with Minardi for the end of the 1993 season. He entered the Japanese and Australian Grands Prix that year, but failed to finish either race. The next year, Gounon took over from an injured Andrea Montermini and drove for Simtek in seven races that year. He was at the back of the grid for every

Jean-Marc Gounon

race, but managed a reasonable ninth place at his home Grand Prix, which was also the team's best-ever result.

Gounon then moved to sportscars and competed with some success over the years, including in the Le Mans Series.

Keith GREENE

Nationality: British
Born: 5th January 1938
Seasons: 1959-1962
Team/manufacturer(s): Cooper, Gilby
Grands Prix: 9
Race wins: 0
Championship wins: 0

Keith Greene was born in London, the son of Sid Greene who ran Gilby Engineering. This Essex-based garage entered Maseratis in various races and, later, competed with Coopers.

It was not surprising, then, that the young Green would get involved in motorsport, driving a Cooper-Climax and a Lotus XI in various sportscar races.

In 1959, he began competing in single-seaters, entering the Cooper in Formula 2 races, plus the British Grand Prix that year, but he failed to qualify. Greene tried the same event the following year, but had to retire when his engine overheated. For the 1961 season, Gilby Engineering built its own car, with a Coventry Climax engine. Greene raced this in

the British Grand Prix that year, and the German and Italian ones the following season, but without much success.

Greene went on to be a motorsport team manager and advisor, before retiring.

Masten GREGORY

Nationality: American
Born: 29th February 1932
Died: 8th November 1985
Seasons: 1957-1963, 1965
Team/manufacturer(s): Scuderia Central Sud, Maserati, Cooper, Behra-Porsche, Lotus, Lola, BRM
Grands Prix: 43
Race wins: 0
Championship wins: 0

Born in Kansas, Masten Gregory inherited a great deal of money at an early age, after his father died. The young Gregory promptly bought himself a Mercury-powered Allard which he drove in various US events, winning his third race. He then bought a Jaguar and won a number of races in 1953.

After a spell competing in Europe, Gregory won the Argentinean 1000km which led to a job with Scuderia Central Sud driving a Maserati. At his first Grand Prix, at Monaco in 1957, he finished an impressive third, making him the first American to gain a Formula One podium place.

Roberto Guerrero

He continued to perform well and finished the season in sixth place, despite only entering half the races.

After a short 1958 season with Maserati, Gregory moved to Cooper-Climax and his best results were a third place at the Dutch Grand Prix and a second place in Portugal. He finished eighth in the championship that year.

Gregory then drove with a number of uncompetitive teams until 1965. From then he concentrated on sportscar racing, before winding down his racing activities. He finally retired from racing in 1972 and moved to Amsterdam where he worked as a diamond merchant. He died of a heart attack in Italy in 1985.

Auguste Georges Paul (Georges) GRIGNARD

Nationality: French
Born: 25th July 1905
Died: 7th December 1977
Seasons: 1951
Team/manufacturer(s): Talbot-Zago
Grands Prix: 1
Race wins: 0
Championship wins: 0

Auguste Georges Paul Grignard, or Georges Grignard, was born near Paris in 1905. He had his own garage business and, in the late 1920s, he enjoyed rally driving and competed at Monte Carlo in 1928 and 1929.

After the Second World War, Grignard raced in a Delahaye and, from 1948, a Talbot. He made good use of this car over the next few years, winning the non-championship Paris Grand Prix in 1950. He also entered it into his only Formula One Championship race, the 1951 Spanish Grand Prix at Pedralbes. Sadly, though, he had to retire from the race with engine problems.

Grignard remained close to the Talbot marque after retiring from racing in 1955. In 1959, he bought up the company's liquidated stock and supplied parts to enthusiasts around the world.

Olivier GROUILLARD

Nationality: French
Born: 2nd September 1958
Seasons: 1989-1992
Team/manufacturer(s): Ligier, Osella, Fondmetal, AGS, Tyrrell
Grands Prix: 62
Race wins: 0
Championship wins: 0

Olivier Grouillard began racing karts at the age of 14 and progressed his career in racing with the help of the Elf Racing School in France. By 1982 he was the Formula Renault Champion.

A move to French Formula 3 the following year saw him do well in his first season, and he went on to win the championship the following year, 1984. That led to a move up the ladder to Formula 3000, where Grouillard stayed until 1988. During this time, he also competed in touring car races, driving for BMW.

Grouillard's Formula One career began in 1989 when he drove for Ligier, but with very mixed results. He only completed three Grands Prix, but finished in the top ten in each. The next year he moved to Osella and had a very poor season, and it was a similar story with Fondmetal and AGS in 1991, when he failed to qualify for most of the races. His last year in Formula One, 1992, was with Tyrrell and, again, he failed to perform well.

Grouillard then tried his hand at CART racing in the USA before moving into sportscars. He finally gave up racing around 2000 and worked as a carriage builder in France.

Brian GUBBY

Nationality: British
Born: 17th April 1934
Seasons: 1965
Team/manufacturer(s): Lotus
Grands Prix: 1
Race wins: 0
Championship wins: 0

Brian Gubby was born in Epsom, the son of a jockey. He began racing in 1959, driving a modified Austin A30. He then worked his way up to Lotuses, using money he made as a motor trader.

His first Lotus was an 11, which was followed by a Lotus 18 and then a Lotus 24 with a Coventry Climax engine. It was this last car that he rebuilt himself and then entered into the 1965 British Grand Prix at Silverstone. He failed to qualify, though, because of gearbox problems.

Gubby gave up racing seriously soon after this, and concentrated on building a chain of car dealers, a hotel and a property development company. He also trained racehorses.

André GUELFI

Nationality: French
Born: 6th May 1919
Seasons: 1958
Team/manufacturer(s): Cooper
Grands Prix: 1
Race wins: 0
Championship wins: 0

André Guelfi was born in Morocco in 1919, and it was North Africa where he did most of his racing, starting with a Delahaye in the early 1950s.

Although Guelfi was most at home driving sportscars, he did enjoy some single-seater seater racing in France and Morocco, usually in a rear-engined Formula 2 Cooper. It was in one of these cars that he entered the 1958 Moroccan Grand Prix, in which he finished last. It's interesting to note that this was the one and only World Championship Grand Prix in Morocco.

Guelfi raced into the 1960s and also worked for Elf. He was involved in a scandal with the French Government and received a suspended jail sentence and a hefty fine. He later retired to Malta.

Miguel Ángel GUERRA

Nationality: Argentinean
Born: 31st August 1953
Seasons: 1981
Team/manufacturer(s): Osella
Grands Prix: 4
Race wins: 0
Championship wins: 0

Miguel Ángel Guerra was born in Buenos Aires and worked his way up to Formula 2, in which he first competed from 1978 to 1980.

His Formula One career was brief, to say the least. Driving for Osella in 1981, he failed to qualify for the US West, Brazilian and Argentinean Grands Prix, but finally got to the start line for the fourth event, the San Marino Grand Prix.

Unfortunately, though, another car hit him on the first lap and Guerra was pushed into a wall. He broke his wrist and ankle in the accident and was unable to drive for the rest of the season. His Formula One career was over almost before it had started.

Guerra then returned to Formula 2 before moving to touring cars during the 1990s. He also ran the Argentinean Top Race V6 touring car series.

Olivier Grouillard

Mauricio Gugelmin

Roberto José GUERRERO

Nationality: Colombian
Born: 16th November 1958
Seasons: 1982-1983
Team/manufacturer(s): Ensign, Theodore
Grands Prix: 29
Race wins: 0
Championship wins: 0

Colombian Roberto Guerrero had a promising start to his career, coming second in the British Formula 3 Championship, and winning at Thruxton in his first Formula 2 race in 1981.

His performances led to a drive with the Ensign Formula One team for the 1982 season. However, problems with the underdeveloped cars meant that Guerrero either failed to qualify for, or retired from, most of the races. The only Grand Prix he completed was the German one, where he came eighth.

The following year was spent with the Theodore team and Guerrero fared slightly better, completing four races, but he was always towards the back of the pack.

At the end of the 1983 season, Guerrero couldn't find a drive for the following year, so he went to the USA to race in ChampCars, winning the CART and Indy 500 Rookie of the Year awards.

Guerrero remained in the USA after retiring from racing, and worked as a spotter and coach for racing teams.

Mauricio GUGELMIN

Nationality: Brazilian
Born: 20th April 1963
Seasons: 1988-1992
Team/manufacturer(s): March, Leyton House, Jordan
Grands Prix: 80
Race wins: 0
Championship wins: 0

Mauricio Gugelmin raced karts with Ayrton Senna as a youngster and progressed up to Formula Ford, winning the Brazilian championship in 1981. He then came to Europe

where he worked his way, through Formula 3, to Formula 3000 by 1986.

He then got a drive with March for the 1988 and 1989 season, and had mixed results, retiring from a number of races with mechanical problems, yet finishing in the top ten in others; his best result being third place at Brazil in 1989.

It was much the same story the next two years, when the team's name had changed to Leyton House. Gugelmin's final Formula One season was spent with Jordan where he again had to struggle with unreliable cars, but nonetheless performed the best he could.

Gugelmin then moved to the USA and competed in the CART Championship from 1993 to 2001. Soon after a bad crash in 2001, Gugelmin's young son, who had been suffering from cerebral palsy, died and he retired from racing at the end of the season. However, he later returned to low-level racing.

Daniel Sexton (Dan) GURNEY

Nationality: American
Born: 13th April 1931
Seasons: 1959-1968, 1970
Team/manufacturer(s): Ferrari, BRM, Porsche, Lotus, Brabham, Eagle, McLaren
Grands Prix: 87
Race wins: 4
Championship wins: 0

Daniel Gurney was born in New York but grew up in California. It was there that he began racing in a Triumph TR2, from there he worked his way up to Formula One.

He was offered a drive with the Ferrari Formula One team and achieved four podium finishes in just four races during the 1959 season. However, he left Ferrari at the end of the year and entered a BRM, with no success, the following year. During his Formula One career, Gurney won four Grands Prix.

He drove for various teams, including his own. The American Grand Prix Eagle project was an attempt to compete with the best European racecars manufacturers. He

won the 1967 Belgian Grand Prix in an Eagle.

Gurney can be thanked for starting the tradition of spraying champagne from the podium, which he first did at Le Mans in 1967. He is also known as the inventor of the Gurney flap – a device used on car and aeroplane wings to increase lift or downforce. In addition, he introduced full-face helmets to Formula One and Indy car racing.

Daniel Gurney

G
H
I

Lewis Hamilton

Hubert HAHNE

Nationality: German
Born: 13th April 1931
Seasons: 1967-1968, 1970
Team/manufacturer(s): BMW, Lola, March
Grands Prix: 3
Race wins: 0
Championship wins: 0

German Hubert Hahne was born in Moers and began racing from an early age. He became closely involved with BMW as a touring car driver and, in 1963, achieved his first major victory when he won the European Touring Car Championship.

The following year, Hahne dominated the German Circuit Championship in a BMW 1800i, winning 14 of the 15 races. And in 1965, he became the first touring car driver to lap the Nürburgring in less than 10 minutes.

Hahne moved into single-seater racing through his BMW connections, driving for the company's Formula 2 team from 1967. In this year, he entered the German Grand Prix which, at the time, had Formula 2 cars racing to fill the field, but these did not appear in the Formula One results. The next year, Hahne again entered the German Grand Prix, in a BMW-powered Lola, and finished in 10th place.

Hahne then had a third try at the same Grand Prix in 1970, this time driving a March 701. However, he failed to qualify, claiming that the car was very poor, and decided to retire from racing.

He later ran a Lamborghini specialist in Essen, Germany.

Stanley Michael Bailey (Mike) HAILWOOD, MBE, GM

Nationality: British
Born: 13th April 1931
Died: 23rd March 1981
Seasons: 1963-1965, 1971-1974
Team/manufacturer(s): Lotus, Lola, Surtees, McLaren
Grands Prix: 50
Race wins: 0
Championship wins: 0

Mike Hailwood

Mike Hailwood's father ran a motorcycle distributorship and so began riding motorbikes off-road from an early age. After leaving school, he worked for Triumph motorcycles and began racing bikes in 1957, and went on to be incredibly successful, winning 76 motorcycle Grands Prix.

His Formula One career began in 1963, when he entered the British Grand Prix driving a Lotus and finished eighth. The following year he did an almost full season with Lotus, his best result being sixth place at Monaco. Monaco was then the only race he entered in 1965.

Hailwood didn't enjoy Formula One, so returned to bike racing for a couple of years before competing in Formula 5000 and sportscar racing. He then returned to Formula One for the end of the 1971 season, finishing fourth in Italy after an impressive drive in a Surtees.

He then stayed with Surtees for the 1972 and 1973 seasons, scoring points in four races. In 1974 he drove for McLaren and, again, scored points in four races; his best result being third place in South Africa.

Hailwood made a surprise comeback to motorcycle racing in 1978, when he won the Isle of Man TT at the age of 38.

Tragically, Hailwood was killed in a road accident near Birmingham in 1981 that also claimed the life of his daughter. Every year, motorcyclists do a memorial run past the spot he was killed and on to the church where he is buried.

Mika Pauli HÄKKINEN

Nationality: Finnish
Born: 28th September 1968
Seasons: 1991-2001
Team/manufacturer(s): Lotus, McLaren
Grands Prix: 165
Race wins: 20
Championship wins: 2

Mika Häkkinen started off racing karts at the age of just five years old. He went on to win his first race when he was seven, and had won his first championship by the time he was 11 years old. He went on to be Finnish Karting Champion five times.

Häkkinen moved to Formula Ford 1600 when he was 19 and won the Finnish, Swedish and Nordic championships. The following year, he walked away with the Opel Lotus Euroseries Championship and the British GM Euroseries Championship. The next stage was Formula Three, and he won the British Championship in 1990.

It was then on to Formula One. Häkkinen was signed by Lotus for 1991 but the team was past its prime; even so, in 1992, he finished eighth in the championship.

Häkkinen then moved to McLaren as a test driver, as a foothold to racing with a top team. He achieved this sooner than he expected, taking over from Michael Andretti mid-season. In qualifying for his first race, at Estoril, Häkkinen out-performed teammate Ayrton Senna.

The Finn was McLaren's team leader in 1994 and 1995, but he failed to win any races during these seasons. At the Australian Grand Prix in 1995, a tyre failure caused Häkkinen to crash into a wall and he needed an emergency tracheotomy to save his life.

He made a full recovery for the 1996 season and stayed with McLaren. Again, though, he failed to win any races, but nonetheless finished sixth in the championship; a position he matched in 1997. That year, he won at Australia and Spain.

In 1998, Häkkinen won no less than eight races that year

Mika Häkkinen

and clinched the Drivers' Championship with ease, proving he was one man who could give Michael Schumacher a run for his money.

The following year, 1999, was less easy with the McLaren cars less reliable and Schumacher determined to fight back. The Finn struggled at the start of the season and lost points, but soon got back on form and was ahead of Schumacher on points by the time the German was injured at Silverstone and was out of the championship. Up against Ferrari's Eddie Irvine, the championship went to the final race in Japan, which Häkkinen managed to win and so claim the title for the second year in a row.

Eager to score a hat-trick in 2000, Häkkinen fought hard but was pushed into second place by a determined Schumacher. Even so, he displayed some inspired driving, especially at Spa, where he stormed to victory, overtaking both Schumacher and Ricardo Zonta in one go.

The next year was to be Häkkinen's last season in Formula One, and he put in an impressive performance, with wins at Silverstone and Indianapolis. At the end of the year, he said he was going to take a break from racing but, in mid-2003, he announced his full-time retirement. There were rumours of a comeback in 2005 and Häkkinen was in talks with Williams but nothing came of it. Instead, he took up German Touring Car racing from 2005.

Bruce HALFORD

Nationality: British
Born: 18th May 1931
Died: 2nd December 2001
Seasons: 1956-1957, 1959-1960
Team/manufacturer(s): Maserati, Lotus, Cooper
Grands Prix: 9
Race wins: 0
Championship wins: 0

Bruce Halford was born near Birmingham, but grew up in Torquay, where his family ran a hotel. After driving a Cooper-Bristol, he bought himself a second-hand Maserati 250F and began competing in various races around Europe in it.

His first Formula One championship race was the 1956 British Grand Prix at Silverstone, which he had to retire from after 22 laps because of engine problems. It was a similar story at the Italian race that year, where he only managed 16 laps.

The next year he drove the Maserati in the German Grand Prix and finished 11th before failing to finish the Pescara and Italian events.

Halford then turned to sportscar racing but had another attempt at Formula One in 1959, this time in a new Lotus 16. Sadly, he crashed out of his one championship race, the Monaco Grand Prix.

In 1960, Halford entered the Monaco and Italian Grands Prix, failing to qualify for the first and coming second in the second, driving a Cooper each time.

He then retired from racing in the mid-1960s and went back to Torquay to run the family hotel and enjoy sailing.

James (Jim) HALL

Nationality: American
Born: 23rd July 1935
Seasons: 1960-1963
Team/manufacturer(s): Lotus
Grands Prix: 12
Race wins: 0
Championship wins: 0

Texan Jim Hall inherited a fortune as a teenager after his millionaire parents were killed in a plane crash. This enabled him to start racing while still at college and start a Maserati dealership alongside Carroll Shelby.

He entered his first Grand Prix in 1960, driving a Formula 2 Lotus-Climax to a seventh place finish at the USA Grand Prix at Riverside in California. The following year the USA Grand Prix was held at Watkins Glen, where Hall had to retire with a fuel leak after 76 laps. In 1962, he failed to qualify for the race.

In 1963, Hall travelled to Europe to compete in a full season of Formula One, again driving a Lotus. His best finishes were fifth place in Germany and sixth in Britain. He then returned to the USA and competed in Can-Am until the end of the 1960s.

Hall ran his own racecar company called Chaparral Cars, and developed automatic transmissions and aerodynamic aids for racing cars. He retired fully in 1996.

Duncan HAMILTON

Nationality: Irish
Born: 30th April 1920
Died: 13th May 1994
Seasons: 1951-1953
Team/manufacturer(s): Talbot-Lago, HWM
Grands Prix: 5
Race wins: 0
Championship wins: 0

Duncan Hamilton was born in Cork but educated in Brighton. During the Second World War he was an RAF pilot

and began racing in Formula 2 and sportscars after the end of hostilities, having the wealth to indulge his hobby.

In 1951, Hamilton entered the British and German Grands Prix, driving a Talbot-Lago, and finished 12th and 7th respectively.

He then drove a HWM in the British Grand Prix the following year, but failed to finish. He did better in Holland that year, coming in seventh. Hamilton had another attempt at the British race in 1953, and again, retired with mechanical problems.

Hamilton won the Le Mans 24 Hour in 1953, driving a Jaguar C-Type with Tony Rolt, despite having been up late drinking the night before! He continued to have success in sportscar racing, but retired after the death of his friend, Mike Hawthorn, in 1959. He later ran a successful garage business in England.

Lewis Carl HAMILTON

Nationality: British
Born: 7th January 1985
Seasons: 2007
Team/manufacturer(s): McLaren
Grands Prix: 17
Race wins: 4
Championship wins: 0

Formula One fans were desperate for a new superhero after seven-time World Champion Michael Schumacher's retirement at the end of the 2006 season. And they didn't have long to wait! Rookie British driver, Lewis Hamilton, stormed in at the start of 2007, finishing third in his first race, sec-

Lewis Hamilton

ond in his next four Grands Prix, and then winning the following two races, putting him firmly at the top of the World Championship and leaving other drivers in awe of this talented upstart. No other driver has ever made such an audacious start to their Formula One career

It was an astonishing performance for a 22-year-old in his first season of Formula One. However, Hamilton was focused on competing at the top level of motorsport from an early age. When he was just nine years old, the young kart racer told McLaren boss Ron Dennis that, one day, he would drive for McLaren. And he was right!

At that time, Hamilton was already making a name for himself in the karting world. He'd started racing at the tender age of six, with the devoted support of his father, Anthony, who held down three jobs while also attending every race his son competed in.

The perseverance paid off, though, as the youngster earned a place on the McLaren driver development support programme with the option of a future Formula One drive. That effectively meant that, at the age of 14, Hamilton was the youngest driver ever to get a Formula One contract. A year later, he won the Formula A European Kart Championship.

From there, the rising star moved to racing cars, beginning in Formula Renault, where he won the UK championship in 2003. He then went on to take the 2005 Formula Three Euro series after winning no less than 15 of the 20 rounds. It was then on to GP2 the following year and Hamilton again stormed to victory, winning the championship in his first year.

The next logical step was, of course, Formula One, and Hamilton was fortunate in that McLaren was looking for a second driver to compete alongside 2006 World Champion, Fernando Alonso. Despite competition from more experienced drivers, Mika Häkkinen and Pedro de la Rosa, McLaren decided to choose Hamilton.

In doing so, Hamilton became the first black driver of Afro-Caribbean descent to compete in Formula One. Indeed, compared to some drivers, his background is distinctly modest. His father's parents emigrated from Grenada in the 1950s and his grandfather worked on the London Underground. The youngster's parents split up when he was just two years old, and he later went to school in his birth-town of Stevenage. There, he was an accomplished karateka and footballer, at the same time as pursuing his karting career.

Hamilton astounded the world at his Formula One debut, at the 2007 Australian Grand Prix. He qualified fourth and finished in third place, making him the 13th driver to finish on the podium on his Grand Prix debut. The next race at Bahrain saw Hamilton qualify and finish in second place.

Then he again finished second in Spain, putting him in the lead of the World Championship, thus becoming the youngest driver ever to do so.

Another second place, in Monaco, led to accusations that McLaren was forcing the newcomer to play second-fiddle to Alonso; claims that were rigorously denied by Hamilton and his team bosses. However, the Canadian Grand Prix saw Hamilton take his first pole position, going on to lead for most of the race and winning his first Formula One race. Just one week later, he repeated the same success at the United States Grand Prix, thus becoming only the second person ever to win more than one Grand Prix in their first season.

Hamilton went on to win at Hungary and Japan and was widely tipped to win the Championship in his first year. In the event, though, he suffered mechanical problems at the Brazilian Grand Prix, finishing in seventh place, thus missing out on the World Championship by just one point to Ferrari's Kimi Räikkönen. Even so, it was a remarkable first season in Formula One.

David HAMPSHIRE

Nationality: English
Born: 29th December 1917
Died: 25th August 1990
Seasons: 1950
Team/manufacturer(s): Maserati
Grands Prix: 2
Race wins: 0
Championship wins: 0

David Hampshire was born in Derbyshire and was a wealthy company director who raced as a hobby in his spare time. He started off in a Maserati and, after the Second World War, he campaigned an ERA with some success.

In 1950, Hampshire drove a semi-works Maserati in the British Grand Prix at Silverstone, finishing in a reasonably ninth place. At his second and last Formula One race, in France towards the end of the season he failed to finish because of engine problems.

Hampshire continued to race a Maserati and ERA the following year in various non-championship races. After that, he cut down his motorsport activities to concentrate on his business.

Walter (Walt) HANSGEN

Nationality: American
Born: 28th October 1919
Died: 7th April 1966
Seasons: 1961, 1964
Team/manufacturer(s): Lotus, Cooper
Grands Prix: 2
Race wins: 0
Championship wins: 0

American Walt Hansgen ran a Jaguar dealership in New Jersey and was an accomplished sportscar racer in the 1950s and early 1960s, often driving his own Jaguar D-Type. Although not his usual discipline, Hansgen did enter some single-seater races in the early 1960s, including the USA Grand Prix twice. The first time was in 1961 driving a Cooper but an accident put him out of the race after just 14 laps. In 1964, he competed in a Lotus-Climax and impressed by finishing in fifth place.

Hansgen continued to race sportscars after this, including at Le Mans and Daytona. He was killed while testing a Ford at Le Mans for the 1966 24 Hour race.

Michael (Mike) HARRIS

Nationality: South African
Born: 25th May 1939
Seasons: 1962
Team/manufacturer(s): Cooper
Grands Prix: 1
Race wins: 0
Championship wins: 0

Mike Harris was born in Zambia in 1939 and was a keen amateur racing driver. In 1962 he won the Rhodesian Championship and so felt well placed to enter three other races at the end of the season, culminating in the South African Grand Prix.

The race that year took place at East London, on the southeast coast. Harris drove a Cooper-Alfa Romeo T53 that had previously been owned by Reg Parnell. Unfortunately, he failed to qualify and was unable to enter the race proper.

That was Harris's last attempt at single-seater racing. He later ran an Alfa Romeo dealership in Zimbabwe.

Naoki Hattori

Thomas Cuthbert (Cuth) HARRISON

Nationality: British
Born: 6th July 1906
Died: 21st January 1981
Seasons: 1950
Team/manufacturer(s): ERA
Grands Prix: 3
Race wins: 0
Championship wins: 0

Cuth Harrison was born in Sheffield and was a keen amateur racing driver. He had his own ERA C-Tyre that he campaigned in England and Europe, in various events including some Grands Prix.

His last year with the ERA was also the first year of the World Championship, and Harrison entered three races. Beginning with the British Grand Prix at Silverstone, Harrison finished in 11th place. He then drove at Monaco, finishing 14th and, finally, took 21st place in Italy.

Soon after that, he wound down his racing activities to concentrate on building his garage business, TC Harrison. This grew into the TCH Group, which has a number of Ford and other dealerships in northern England.

Brian HART

Nationality: British
Born: 7th September 1936
Seasons: 1967
Team/manufacturer(s): Cosworth
Grands Prix: 1
Race wins: 0
Championship wins: 0

In the 1950s and early 1960s, Brian Hart competed successfully in Formula Junior and sportscar events. He then graduated to Formula 3 and Formula 2.

It was in the latter that he was able to enter the 1967 German Grand Prix which, at the time, ran a Formula 2 class. Hart finished fourth in this class but Formula 2 entries did not qualify for World Championship points.

Hart continued to compete in Formula 2 after this one Formula One appearance. He then retired from racing in 1971 to concentrate on his engine building business. In time, Brian Hart Limited grew to become an important engine manufacturer that supplied powerplants to a number of top Formula 2 and Formula One teams, including Toleman, Arrows and Yamaha. Hart sold the company to Tom Walkinshaw in 1991 and retired.

Masahiro HASEMI

Nationality: Japanese
Born: 13th November 1945
Seasons: 1976
Team/manufacturer(s): Kojima
Grands Prix: 1
Race wins: 0
Championship wins: 0

Japanese driver Masahiro Hasemi began competing in motocross at the age of 15 and went on to drive for Nissan in his late teens, in saloon car events.

Hasemi became a well-known driver in his own country, as Formula 2 champion in 1980, and also winning sportscars and touring cars championships on a number of occasions. However, he never cracked Formula One, despite making a good impression in his one and only Grand Prix. At the 1976 Japanese Grand Prix he set a fastest

lap time in heavy rain before finishing in 11th place.

It was then back to what he knew best – touring cars, in which he continued to compete successfully until retiring in 2001. Hasemi then ran his own race team.

Naoki HATTORI

Nationality: Japanese
Born: 13th June 1966
Seasons: 1991
Team/manufacturer(s): Coloni
Grands Prix: 2
Race wins: 0
Championship wins: 0

Naoki Hattori was a successful driver within his home country of Japan, winning the 1990 Formula 3 Championship and the 1993 Touring Car Championship there.

Sadly, though, he had less luck in Formula One. In 1991, he entered the Japanese and Australian Grands Prix, driving a Coloni, but failed to pre-qualify for either race.

Later, in North America, he competed with some success in Indy Lights and, after that, ChampCars. He then returned to Japan in 2000 to race in the local GT Series and Formula Nippon.

Paul HAWKINS

Nationality: Australian
Born: 12th October 1937
Died: 26th May 1969
Seasons: 1965
Team/manufacturer(s): Brabham, Lotus
Grands Prix: 3
Race wins: 0
Championship wins: 0

Australian Paul Hawkins was the son of a racing motorcyclist (who later became a church minister). He came to the UK in 1960 to find a career in racing and ended up competing in Austin Healey Sprites and, later, Formula Junior.

This led to a drive in Formula 2 from 1964 and he competed in the Formula 2 class of three Formula One Grands Prix in 1965. At the South African race he finished in ninth place whilst at Monaco he crashed into the harbour (one of only two drivers to do this, the other being Alberto Ascari), and in the German Grand Prix he retired with an oil leak.

Hawkins later turned to sportscar racing and had a successful career. He was killed at Oulton Park in 1969 when his Lola T70GT crashed and caught fire.

John Michael (Mike) HAWTHORN

Nationality: British
Born: 10th April 1929
Died: 22nd January 1959
Seasons: 1952-1958
Team/manufacturer(s): LD Hawthorn, AHM Bryde, Ferrari, Vanwall, BRM
Grands Prix: 47
Race wins: 3
Championship wins: 1

John Michael Hawthorn was brought up surrounded by cars and motorcycles. His father, Leslie, had raced motorcycles before the Second World War and also ran a garage business in Farnham. By the age of nine, Hawthorn had made up his mind that he was going to be a racing driver, and he spent all his spare time at Brooklands, dreaming of being on the circuit.

Mike Hawthorn

His father, however, sent him to public school followed by technical college. The boy then took an apprenticeship with a commercial vehicle manufacturer; the plan being that he'd eventually return to the family business and help build that up.

In the meantime, though, his father was happy to encourage his son's racing hobby, supplying him with motorcycles and then cars. Before long, his racing began to take over, as he became established on the club circuit, driving a Riley. And then, in 1952, Hawthorn had a chance to race at Goodwood, in a Formula Two Cooper-Bristol. Up against the likes of Juan Manual Fangio, Hawthorn shocked everyone by winning the Formula Two race, plus the Formula Libre event, and then came second in the main race, for Formula One cars.

Inspired by his success, Hawthorn decided to race the Cooper-Bristol in the remaining Formula One races of the season, which was dominated by Ferrari-driving Alberto Ascari. Wearing his trademark bow tie, Hawthorn finished fourth in Belgium and Holland, and third in the UK, ranking him fourth in the championship.

Enzo Ferrari was impressed and hired him for the 1953 season. Hawthorn's one win that year was at the French Grand Prix, at Reims, where he crossed the line just ahead of Fangio.

In 1954 Hawthorn was badly injured in a race in Sicily, and then his father was killed in a road accident. The only high point of the year was a win at the Spanish Grand Prix.

Hawthorn then left Ferrari to drive for Vanwell and then BRM. He made the headlines once again in 1955, when he won Le Mans in a Jaguar. This was the year that a Mercedes crashed into the crowds, killing over 80 people and Hawthorn was, for a while, blamed for the incident.

He returned to Ferrari in 1957, when he became friends with teammate Peter Williams. Tragically, though, Williams was killed at the Nürburgring in 1958 and this was the final straw for Hawthorn; he was no longer interested in racing.

Nick Heidfeld

Reluctantly, he completed the season and finished just one point in front of Stirling Moss, to become World Champion.

Hawthorn then retired from racing and was looking forward to a quiet life with his fiancée, model Jean Howarth, and running the family business in Farnham. This was not to be, though: on 22nd January 1959, his Jaguar span in the wet on the Guildford bypass and the 29-year-old was dead.

Johan (Boy) HAYJE

Nationality: Dutch
Born: 3rd May 1949
Seasons: 1976-1977
Team/manufacturer(s): non-works Penske, RAM
Grands Prix: 7
Race wins: 0
Championship wins: 0

Johan Hayje was born in the Netherlands and had the nickname 'Boy'. He had a successful career racing saloon cars and then turned to single-seaters, becoming the Dutch Formula Ford Champion.

After spells in Formula 5000 and Formula 2, he made his Formula One debut at his home Grand Prix in 1976, driving a Penske. He drove well but had to retire after 63 laps with a failed halfshaft.

The following year Hayje drove for RAM but it was not a successful season. After returning from his first Grand Prix, in South Africa, with transmission problems, he had an unclassified finish at the Belgian race, and then failed to qualify for five Grands Prix. He then left the team and finished his Formula One career.

Hayje dabbled in Formula 2 and then had some success racing Renault Five Turbos. He later retired to run a 4x4 dealership in Belgium.

Willi HEEKS

Nationality: German
Born: 13th February 1922
Died: 13th August 1996
Seasons: 1952-1953
Team/manufacturer(s): AFM, Veritas
Grands Prix: 2
Race wins: 0
Championship wins: 0

German Willi Heeks was a talented Formula 2 driver in his own country, driving a BMW-engined AFM during the early 1950s.

It was in this car that he competed in his first Grand Prix, the German event at the Nürburgring in 1952. Sadly, though, he had to retire from the race after just seven laps.

The following year, Heeks had another attempt at his home Grand Prix. This time, though, he was driving a Veritas but, again, he had to drop out of the race after eight laps. He did, however, lead the race for a short time before that.

Heeks competed in some sportscar races later in the 1950s before retiring from the sport.

Nick HEIDFELD

Nationality: German
Born: 10th May 1977
Seasons: 2000-
Team/manufacturer(s): Prost, Sauber, Jordan, Williams, BMW Sauber
Grands Prix: 135
Race wins: 0
Championship wins: 0

Born in Mönchengladbach, Nick Heidfeld started racing karts at the age of 11. Six years later he had won the German Formula Ford Championship by winning eight out of

nine races. By 1997, he had won the German Formula 3 Championship and, two years later he took the International Formula 3000 Championship.

Heidfeld began his Formula One career in 2000, driving for Prost. After a disappointing season, though, he moved to Sauber until the end of 2003. Next, he spent a year with Jordan and then with Williams in 2005.

The season with Williams was a mixed one, with two second-place finishes near the start. Later, though, he was forced to miss the end of the season after first being injured during testing and then being hit by a motorcycle when he was out cycling. However, Heidfeld was back in action for 2006, driving for BMW Sauber and achieving a number of top-ten finishes. He remained with the team for the following season. He remained with the team for 2007 and 2008.

Theo HELFRICH

Nationality: German
Born: 13th May 1913
Died: 29th April 1978
Seasons: 1952-1954
Team/manufacturer(s): Veritas, Klenk
Grands Prix: 3
Race wins: 0
Championship wins: 0

Theo Helfrich came from Germany and held a management position in the motor trade. In the early 1950s he had some success in various sportscars events, including a second-place finish at Le Mans, driving for Mercedes.

Helfrich entered his home Grand Prix, at the Nürburgring, three times, starting in 1952 when he retired in the first lap, driving a Veritas. The following year he finished 12th, again in a Veritas; that same season he won the Formula 2 Championship with the car.

Boy Hayje

For 1954 Helfrich switched to a Klenk car but had to pull out of the race with engine problems after eight laps. That was the end of his Formula One adventure, and he later raced in Formula 3 and also returned to sportscars.

Brian HENTON

Nationality: British
Born: 19th September 1946
Seasons: 1975, 1977, 1981-1982
Team/manufacturer(s): Lotus, March, British F1 Racing, Boro, Toleman, Arrows, Tyrrell
Grands Prix: 37
Race wins: 0
Championship wins: 0

Brian Henton was born in Castle Donington and didn't start racing until he was 23 years old. Before long, though, he had won the British Formula Vee Championship in 1971 and, in an attempt to gain some much-needed publicity, he announced to the press that he would be World Champion one day.

With this aim in mind, he worked his way successfully through Formula 3 and Formula 2 before achieving his Formula One debut in 1975. Driving for Lotus, he entered the British Grand Prix and finished 16th, but he failed to complete the Austrian and USA races.

Henton then returned to Formula 2 until he had another chance at Formula One in 1977, with his own team, British F1 Racing, driving a March. However, he failed to qualify for all but one race: the USA West Grand Prix, where he finished 10th.

A drive for Toleman in 1981 was similarly unsuccessful and then, the following season, he moved to Arrows and then Tyrrell. With this last team he did slightly better, with a few top-ten finishes but it was not good enough and Henton retired from racing at the end of 1983.

Henton had earned enough money from his sport over the years to by a country house in Leicestershire and he used the land to run equestrian events.

John Paul (Johnny) HERBERT

Nationality: British
Born: 25th June 1964
Seasons: 1989-2000
Team/manufacturer(s): Benetton, Tyrrell, Lotus, Ligier, Sauber, Stewart, Jaguar
Grands Prix: 165
Race wins: 3
Championship wins: 0

Johnny Herbert began racing karts at the age of just 10, supported by his parents who could see he had talent. By 1978 he was British Junior Karting Champion and went on to be Senior Champion in 1979 and 1982.

By 1983, he was competing in Formula Ford, followed by Formula Ford 2000. By 1987, he'd moved to Formula 3 and won the British Championship in his first season.

This led to a test with Benetton but Herbert had to spend a year in Formula 3000 which resulted in a bad accident that almost cost him his career. He finally broke into Formula One for the 1989 season, driving for Benetton. He got off to a good start, finishing fourth at his first Grand Prix, in Brazil, but was later dropped from the team after failing to qualify at Canada. He then had two unsuccessful races with Tyrrell at the end of the season.

A move to Lotus in 1990 saw Herbert working as a test driver for most of the next two seasons, although he did compete in a few races. By 1992, he was driving for Lotus full time and stayed with the team, with mixed success, until the end of 1994.

Then it was back to Benetton for 1995, which was a great season that saw Herbert win at the British and Italian Grands Prix and score points at a number of other races.

The 1997 and 1998 seasons were spent with Sauber and, the races he finished, he often claimed a top-ten position.

Herbert moved to Stewart for 1999 and won the European Grand Prix that year. He stayed with the team, now renamed Jaguar, for 2000. It was, though, a disappointing season and Herbert retired from Formula One at the end of it.

He then moved to sportscar racing and had success in the American Le Mans Series.

Hans HERRMANN

Nationality: German
Born: 23rd February 1928
Seasons: 1953-1955, 1957-1961
Team/manufacturer(s): Veritas, Mercedes, Maserati, Cooper, BRM, Porsche
Grands Prix: 19
Race wins: 0
Championship wins: 0

Hans Herrmann was born in Stuttgart and was a baker by trade. He raced in a number of disciplines in the early 1950s and first entered a Formula One event in 1953. This was the German Grand Prix and he finished ninth in a Veritas.

The following year he joined Mercedes and competed in five Grands Prix that season, but an accident at the start of 1955 put him out of action for the rest of that year.

Herrmann then moved around from marque to marque, entering a handful of Grands Prix up until 1961. After that, though, he only competed in minor races, driving an Abarth. However, in 1966 he made a comeback, driving for Porsche in the World Sportscar Championship and winning the 1968

Johnny Herbert

Damon Hill

24 Hours of Daytona and the Sebring 12 Hours race. And in 1970 he won the first victory for Porsche at the Le Mans 24 Hour race, driving a 917K with Richard Attwood.

Herrmann then retired from racing and concentrated on his automotive supply business.

François HESNAULT

Nationality: French
Born: 30th December 1956
Seasons: 1984-1985
Team/manufacturer(s): Ligier, Brabham, Renault
Grands Prix: 21
Race wins: 0
Championship wins: 0

François Hesnault was born in Paris to a wealthy family who ran a transport business. After school he became an officer in a parachute regiment and fought in West Africa.

It was after he left the military that Hesnault began racing. By 1980 he was competing in Formula Renault and, two years later, Formula 3; coming third in the championship that year.

In 1984, Hesnault joined the Ligier Formula One team as second driver alongside Andrea de Cesaris, and drove well through the season, despite having to retire from a number of races.

The following year Hesnault moved to Brabham, as teammate to Nelson Piquet, but was dropped after a disappointing four races. He then went to Renault for the 1985 German Grand Prix, where he made a little bit of history by being the first Formula One driver to carry an onboard camera.

That was the end of Hesnault's Formula One career and he later retired from racing. He went to live in Switzerland to run the family transport business and other companies.

Hans HEYER

Nationality: German
Born: 16th March 1943
Seasons: 1977
Team/manufacturer(s): ATS
Grands Prix: 1
Race wins: 0
Championship wins: 0

German Hans Heyer used to travel across the border to Holland so that he could race karts before he was old enough to do so in his home country. He won the Dutch Kart Championship in 1962.

Heyer went on to be a successful touring car driver in the late 1960s and early 1970s, and became known for his trademark Tyrolean hat. He was the European Touring Car Champion in 1974 and Deutsche Rennsport Meisterschaft Champion in 1975, 1976 and 1980.

His one attempt at Formula One was at the 1977 German Grand Prix in a Penske car owned by the ATS team. His lack of experience in single-seaters coupled with an uncompetitive car, meant that he did not qualify for the race. However, that did not stop him sneaking out of the pits and joining the race anyway! His car broke down after nine laps, but he would have been disqualified anyway.

Heyer won the 12 Hours of Sebring in 1985, driving a Porsche 935 and finally retired from racing in 1989.

Damon Graham Devereux HILL, OBE

Nationality: British
Born: 17th September 1960
Seasons: 1992-1999
Team/manufacturer(s): Brabham, Williams, Arrows, Jordan
Grands Prix: 122
Race wins: 22
Championship wins: 1

The son of Formula One legend, Graham Hill, the young Damon Hill was brought up in the world of motorsport but, as a child, he complained that having to attend Grands Prix was "boring adult stuff".

However, at the age of 11, Hill was in the paddock at Silverstone when he was offered a go on a 50cc Honda 'monkey' bike. The lad was so impressed, he persuaded his father to buy him a similar bike.

By 1981, after the death of his father, Hill was dabbling in motorbike racing. His mother, though, wasn't impressed and decided to wean him off dangerous motorbikes by sending him to the Winfield Racing School at Magny-Cours, France, in 1983. Here he learnt to drive single-seater racing cars but stubbornly stuck to bike racing until the end of 1984. Then, Hill switched from bikes to Formula Ford and won his first race at Brands Hatch.

Over the following years, he competed in Formula Ford and then Formula Three and Formula 3000. In 1991, Hill began working as a test driver for Williams and soon proved

to be competent behind the wheel of a Formula One car. The following season, he drove for Brabham while, at the same time, continuing to test for Williams.

Keeping in with Williams proved a good move because Hill was asked to race with that team for 1993, alongside Alain Prost. Hill won three races and was runner-up in four.

The 1994 season was marred by the death of Hill's new teammate, Ayrton Senna, which led to him being the team leader, a position at which he excelled. That season Hill won six races and came second in five, putting him just one point behind Michael Schumacher. Beating the German in Australia would have clinched the championship for Hill.

Sadly, though, it was not to be. Schumacher hit a wall and then knocked into Hill's car – some say deliberately – causing both drivers to retire. Schumacher subsequently walked away with the championship, leaving Hill with second place.

Damon Hill

Hill had to make do with second place – again behind Schumacher – in 1995. The following year, though, he won the championship with Williams. He had no less than eight wins that year and started every race of the season on the front row of the grid.

However, Hill's contract was not renewed and so he moved to the new Arrows team for 1997. Unfortunately, the cars didn't prove to be as good as Hill had expected and he spent the season plagued by mechanical problems.

Hill moved to Jordan for 1998, driving with Ralf Schumacher. Despite a bad start to the season – again, due to mechanical problems – Hill put in a good show and gave the team its first ever win, at Spa.

Hill stayed with Jordan for 1999 but the season didn't go well for him. After a crash at Montreal and a poor performance in France, he wanted to retire but his team persuaded him to see out the year. Clearly demotivated, Hill finished the season a pale shadow of his former self.

Since retiring, Hill has been involved in several business ventures, including car dealerships and a high-performance car leasing company.

Norman Graham (Graham) HILL

Nationality: British
Born: 15th February 1929
Died: 29th November 1975
Seasons: 1958-1975
Team/manufacturer(s): Lotus, BRM, Brabham, Hill
Grands Prix: 179
Race wins: 14
Championship wins: 2

Graham Hill did not even drive a car until he was 24 years old, yet went on to become a Formula One legend during the 1960s and 1970s.

When Hill finally bought a car, it was an old Austin with failing brakes. To stop, he used to scrub the tyres against the kerb, and later claimed that this was essential training in becoming a racing driver.

Hill did four laps at a new racing school at Brands Hatch and decided that was what he wanted to do. Before long, he was working as a mechanic for a similar school. Soon he was competing in races and acting as an instructor. A meeting with Colin Chapman then led to Hill working at Lotus as a mechanic.

He did some racing in Lotus's Formula Two cars, but Hill was convinced that he should be racing the cars, not maintaining them and persuaded Chapman to promote him to full-time driver. And in 1958, he made his Formula One debut.

However, he became disillusioned with the Lotuses' mechanical failures and so, in 1960, he moved to BRM. However, it wasn't until 1962, when BRM had produced a new V8-engine car, that Hill began to win races, his first being at Zandvoort. By the end of the season, he was World Champion.

Sadly, mechanical problems meant he was unable to repeat his success with BRM, although he did win the Indianapolis 500 in 1966. By 1967 he had returned to Lotus where he teamed up with Jim Clark.

After Clark's tragic death in 1968, Hill was determined to keep his friend's spirit alive and went on to win the Championship that year, clinching the title in the final round.

That, though, was the beginning of the end of Hill's Grand Prix career. He had limited success in 1969, despite a win at Monaco. A bad crash at the US Grand Prix at Watkins Glen that year led to Hill being thrown from his Lotus 49B and his injuries meant that he was confined to a wheelchair for some time after, but he returned to racing for the following season.

A brief spell with Brabham was unremarkable and then, in 1973, Hill set up his own racing team – Hill Embassy Racing – for which he also drove. Sadly, he and the team were unsuccessful and, after failing to qualify for the 1975 Monaco Grand Prix, Hill decided it was time to let another driver take his place on the team. That driver was a young talent by the name of Tony Brise.

Tragically, though, a few months after announcing his retirement, Hill was dead, along with Brise and four other members of the team. They were returning from France, with Hill at the helm of his Piper Aztec light aircraft. He was struggling to land at Elstree airfield in thick fog and the plane crashed, killing all on board.

Philip Toll (Phil) HILL

Nationality: American
Born: 20th April 1927
Seasons: 1958-1964, 1966
Team/manufacturer(s): Maserati, Ferrari, Cooper, Porsche, ATS, Lotus, Eagle
Grands Prix: 51
Race wins: 3
Championship wins: 1

Born in Florida but brought up in California, Phil Hill began racing MGs at an early age before moving to England in 1949 to work as a trainee at Jaguar.

By 1956, he was driving for Ferrari and, two years later, made his Grand Prix debut in a Maserati. This was at the French Grand Prix at Reims where Hill finished seventh.

Back in a Ferrari, Hill had his first Formula One win, at the Italian Grand Prix in 1960. The following year he won again in Italy and also in Belgium and gained points in enough other races to become World Champion that year – the only American driver to do so.

That was to be the high point of his Formula One career,

Graham Hill

Phil Hill

even though he continued competing until 1966. After that, Hill went on to be a successful sportscar racer.

After retiring from racing, Hill wrote for car magazines and enjoyed restoring vintage cars and pianos.

Peter HIRT

Nationality: Swiss
Born: 30th March 1910
Died: 28th June 1992
Seasons: 1951-1953
Team/manufacturer(s): Veritas, Ferrari
Grands Prix: 5
Race wins: 0
Championship wins: 0

Peter Hirt came from Kussnacht, near Zurich. He ran a precision tool manufacturing business which was very successful and gave him the money to indulge in motorsport.

Driving his own Veritas, he entered the Swiss Grand Prix in 1951 but had to retire at the start of the race with fuel problems.

Disappointed with the car, Hirt teamed up with Rudi Fischer to campaign Formula 2 Ferraris. This time, Hirt finished a respectable seventh at his home Grand Prix. He then went on to enter the British Grand Prix later in the season but retired after just three laps with faulty brakes.

Hirt's third and last Formula One race was the 1953 Swiss Grand Prix. Again, though, he had to retire, this time because his Ferrari developed an engine fault.

David HOBBS

Nationality: British
Born: 9th June 1939
Seasons: 1967-1968, 1971, 1974
Team/manufacturer(s): BRM, Honda, McLaren
Grands Prix: 6
Race wins: 0
Championship wins: 0

Born in Royal Leamington Spa, David Hobbs began racing in sportscars in the early 1960s before moving into single-seater racing, in Formula Junior and Formula 2.

He was not a regular Formula One driver, but did enter the odd Grand Prix, starting with the 1967 British event, where he drove a BRM to an eighth place finish. His best result was seventh place at the 1974 Austrian Grand Prix, driving a McLaren, and he did his last Grand Prix soon after, at Monza, Italy.

Hobbs had more success in other series, winning the 1971 Formula 5000 Championship and the 1983 Trans-Am Series. He also competed in the Le Mans 24 Hour no less than 20 times, finishing third three times.

Denny Hulme

After retiring from racing, Hobbs moved to the USA where he worked as a commentator for Formula One and opened his own car dealership.

Ingo HOFFMANN

Nationality: Brazilian
Born: 28th February 1953
Seasons: 1976-1977
Team/manufacturer(s): Fittipaldi
Grands Prix: 6
Race wins: 0
Championship wins: 0

Ingo Hoffmann was born in São Paulo and became a successful Super Vee and saloon car driver in his home country. He then travelled to the UK to compete in Formula 3 in 1975.

This led to a Formula One drive with Fittipaldi for the 1976 season. However, as second driver, he only entered races when the struggling team could afford to campaign two cars. Hoffmann's debut was at his home Grand Prix where he finished 11th. However, he failed to qualify for the other three Grands Prix he entered that year.

The following season, he retired from the Argentinean Grand Prix and finished seventh at Brazil before being dropped by the team because it could no longer afford to run two cars.

Despite his obvious talent, Hoffmann never again raced in Formula One. He did, though, have success in Formula 2 and sportscar and saloon car racing. He also won the Brazilian Stock Car Championship 11 times.

Kazuyoshi HOSHINO

Nationality: Japanese
Born: 1st July 1947
Seasons: 1976-1977
Team/manufacturer(s): Heros Racing
Grands Prix: 2
Race wins: 0
Championship wins: 0

Japanese driver Kazuyoshi Hoshino began racing in motocross and was 90cc and 125cc Champion in 1968. The following year, he switched to cars and drove for Nissan.

In 1976 and 1977, Hoshino entered his home Grand Prix, driving for Heros Racing. At the first race he drove a Tyrrell but had to retire after he'd used up his quota of tyres, but not before proving himself a capable driver under very wet conditions. The following year, Hoshino drove an out-dated Kojima and finished 11th in the race.

Hoshino went on to become Japanese Formula 2 Champion in 1978 and then won the local Formula 3000 Championship three times, in 1987, 1990 and 1993. He also won the Japanese Touring Car Championship in 1990.

After retiring from racing in 2002, he ran his own Super GT team.

Dennis Clive (Denny) HULME

Nationality: New Zealander
Born: 18th June 1936
Died: 4th October 1992
Seasons: 1965-1974
Team/manufacturer(s): Brabham, McLaren
Grands Prix: 112
Race wins: 8
Championship wins: 1

James Hunt

Denny Hulme grew up on a tobacco farm on New Zealand's South Island. After leaving school, he worked in a garage and used an MG TF for hillclimbing.

A move to England in 1960 saw him working for Jack Brabham as a mechanic and he was soon driving in Formula Junior for the team. He then raced in Formula 2 for Tyrrell and Brabham.

Hulme's Formula One career began in 1965, when he drove for Brabham at Monaco and finished in eighth place. He went on to score points in France that year, when he finished fourth.

The following year was Hulme's first full season in Formula One and this was followed, in 1967, by his best one. Winning at Monaco and Germany, plus three second-places, three third-places and one fourth-place, was enough to clinch the World Championship for the New Zealander.

A move to McLaren for 1968 saw Hulme just miss winning the championship for a second time, when a suspension failure put him out of the last race at Mexico City.

Hulme continued to perform well for McLaren for the rest of his Formula One career, which lasted through 1974. After that, he returned to New Zealand where he raced touring cars.

In 1992, Hulme was racing in the Bathurst 1000 in Australia, when he suffered a heart attack at the wheel. He managed to bring the car to a stop but was pronounced dead at the scene.

James Simon Wallis HUNT

Nationality: British
Born: 29th August 1947
Died: 15th June 1993
Seasons: 1973-1979
Team/manufacturer(s): Hesketh, McLaren, Wolf
Grands Prix: 93
Race wins: 10
Championship wins: 1

James Hunt grew up in Berkshire, the son of a stockbroker. After a public school education, he was to become a doctor, but a friend took him to a motor race at Silverstone when he was 18 and he was instantly hooked.

Hunt decided there and then he was going to be a Formula One World Championship, and bought a wrecked Mini, which he spent the next two years race preparing.

He made a name for himself as a good, if rather accident-prone, driver and soon graduated to Formula Ford and Formula Three. His many accidents became legendary and earned him the nickname of 'Hunt the Shunt'.

Perhaps part of the reason for his crashes was Hunt's nerves. He never conquered his pre-race worries and was known to vomit and shake uncontrollably in the pit lane. This turned to adrenaline and testosterone on the track, though, which gave him a reputation as a bit of a madman.

For this reason, his career may have ended then if it hadn't been for the intervention of his friend, Lord Alexander Hesketh, who decided to start his own racing team, with Hunt as driver.

They started off in Formula Two and Three. However, Hesketh argued that, if they were going to lose money in motorsport, they might as well do it in Formula One.

Other teams treated Hesketh Racing as a joke at the start of the 1974 season, but soon changed their minds when Hunt began to put in some spectacular performances and went on to beat Niki Lauda's Ferrari to win the 1975 Dutch Grand Prix. Sadly, at the end of the season, Hesketh decided he could no longer afford to plough money into the team.

Luckily, McLaren needed a driver for 1976, and Hunt was the only available person with any experience. By the end

of the season, Hunt was vying with Niki Lauda for the championship and it came to a showdown at the last race in Japan. Lauda, though, decided it was too wet and retired from the race, leaving Hunt to take third place, winning the championship on points.

From then on, Hunt was never able to match this achievement and retired from racing in 1979, claiming that he'd never really enjoyed it!

He then commentated on Formula One for the BBC. Working alongside Murray Walker, the two became well known for their entertaining but well-informed banter.

At the same time, Hunt's personal life began to settle down, and he married for a second time and had two children. However, his wife left him for the actor Richard Burton. He then met Helen, to whom he proposed to on 15th June 1993. She accepted but, tragically, hours later, Hunt had a massive heart attack and died. He was just 46 years old.

Gus HUTCHISON

Nationality: American
Born: 26th April 1937
Seasons: 1970
Team/manufacturer(s): Brabham
Grands Prix: 1
Race wins: 0
Championship wins: 0

Gus Hutchison was born in Atlanta but grew up in Dallas, which is where he started his racing career, while working as a chemist.

He first proved himself as a talented driver when he won the 1967 US Formula B Championship after coming first in each of the seven races he entered.

In 1969 he bought a Brabham BT26 and raced it in the SCCA Continental series the following year. It was this car that he entered in the 1970 US Grand Prix at Watkins Glen. Sadly, though, he had to retire after 21 laps because of a fuel leak.

After retiring from racing, Hutchison concentrated on running his successful solar energy and lighting company in allas.

G
H
I

James Hunt

ICKX, Jacky
IDE, Yuji
IGLESIAS, Jesus
INOUE, Taki
IRELAND, Innes
IRVINE, Eddie
IRWIN, Chris

Eddie Irvine

Jacky Ickx

Jacques Bernard (Jacky) ICKX

Nationality: Belgian
Born: 1st January 1945
Seasons: 1967-1979
Team/manufacturer(s): Cooper, Ferrari, Brabham,
McLaren, Williams, Lotus, Wolf, Ensign, Ligier
Grands Prix: 120
Race wins: 8
Championship wins: 0

Belgian driver Jacky Ickx was the son of a motoring journalist and, as a child, went to races with his father. He began
racing on a 50cc motorbike and was soon winning races
and championships.

Ickx then moved on to racing a Lotus Cortina in touring
cars, with great success, winning a national championship in 1965. Two years later, he made his Formula One
debut, driving a Cooper-Maserati at Monza in Italy and finishing in sixth place.

The following year, Ickx had his first full season, driving
for Ferrari, and also his first win, at the German Grand Prix.
He went on to have seven more wins over the following four
years, as well as many more points finishes. Sadly, though,
he was never able to clinch the championship.

A move to Lotus in 1974 marked the start of the end of
Ickx's Formula One career, as he struggled with uncompetitive cars, and drives for Wolf, Ensign and Ligier were
even worse.

At the end of 1979, Ickx retired from Formula One to concentrate on sportscar racing, which he'd been doing alongside his single-seater career. Indeed, between 1969 and
1982, he won at Le Mans no less than six times.

Yuji IDE

Nationality: Japanese
Born: 21st January 1975
Seasons: 2006
Team/manufacturer(s): Super Aguri
Grands Prix: 4
Race wins: 0
Championship wins: 0

Yuji Ide began racing karts at the age of 15 and, a year
later, won a national championship. He went on to com-

pete in Formula 3, first in Japan and then in France. By 2004, he was racing in Formula Nippon.

At the relatively old age of 31, Ide began his Formula One career in 2006, driving for the Super Aguri team. However, he retired from his first two races, at Bahrain and Malaysia, each time because of mechanical problems. He then entered the Australian Grand Prix at Melbourne and finished in 12th place, but not before spinning his car a number of times, and his team captain felt that Ide was not experienced enough to drive safely. Indeed, at the next race, the San Marino Grand Prix at Imola, Ide crashed into Christijan Albers on the first lap, causing the Dutchman's car to roll several times.

Ide was reprimanded for his driving and, subsequently, Super Aguri announced that he would be not be driving at the next Grand Prix. Soon after, though, the FIA revoked Ide's licence, which meant that he was unable to compete in any other Grands Prix in 2006.

He then returned to Formula Nippon with the aim of increasing his experience for a possible future return to Formula One.

Jesús IGLESIAS

Nationality: Argentinean
Born: 22nd February 1922
Died: 11th July 2005
Seasons: 1955
Team/manufacturer(s): Gordini
Grands Prix: 1
Race wins: 0
Championship wins: 0

Born and brought up in Argentina, Jesús Iglesias became well-known in his home country for racing a Chevrolet special to great effect in the early 1950s.

It was because of this reputation that Gordini asked him to drive a works car in the 1955 Argentinean Grand Prix, held at the Autodrome near Buenos Aires. The race was won by fellow countryman, Fangio, in a Mercedes, while Iglesias retired after 38 laps with transmission problems.

Iglesias then went back to racing his trusty Chevrolet, but made the headlines three years later when he forced Stirling Moss off the track at the non-championship Buenos Aires City Grand Prix.

Takachiho (Taki) INOUE

Nationality: Japanese
Born: 5th September 1963
Seasons: 1994-1995
Team/manufacturer(s): Simtek, Footwork
Grands Prix: 19
Race wins: 0
Championship wins: 0

Born Takachiho Inoue in Kobe, but usually known as Taki Inoue, he was a wealthy driver who began racing in 1985 in the Fuji Freshman Championship. Two years later, he came to the UK to compete in Formula Ford 1600 for one season. He then went back home and raced in Japanese Formula 3 until 1993.

Inoue then had a spell in Formula 3000 before gaining his Formula One debut in 1994. However, this was right at the end of the season and he only entered the Japanese Grand Prix, spinning his Simtek car into the pit wall on the third lap.

The following year Inoue had a full, but unsuccessful, season with Footwork. He was best remembered for two unlikely incidents during the year. First, at practice at Monaco his stalled car was being towed when it was hit by a course car. Second, at Hungary Inoue was helping to put out a fire in his engine when he was hit by another car, injuring his leg slightly.

Inoue left Formula One after 1995 and dabbled in sportscar racing until 1999. After that he worked as a manager for other drivers in Japan.

Robert McGregor Innes (Innes) IRELAND

Nationality: British
Born: 12th June 1930
Died: 22nd October 1993
Seasons: 1959-1966
Team/manufacturer(s): Lotus, BRP, BRM
Grands Prix: 53
Race wins: 1
Championship wins: 0

Innes Ireland was born in Yorkshire but brought up in Scotland. He trained as an engineer with Rolls Royce and then set up his own engineering business in Surrey.

He began racing in the early 1950s, but only began to take it seriously in 1957 racing sportscars with some success. This led to a Formula One drive with Lotus beginning in 1959. He got off to a good start, coming fourth and fifth in the two races he finished. The next year he entered, and finished more races and came fourth in the championship. Ireland's one Formula One win came in 1961, at the USA Grand Prix at Watkins Glen.

Ireland moved to BRP for the end of the 1963 season and back to Lotus for 1965. After a couple of races with BRM in 1966 his Formula One career came to an end, and he stopped racing soon after.

Ireland went on to be a motoring journalist and, of all things, a trawler skipper, as well as being involved in the BRDC. He died of cancer in 1993.

Edmund (Eddie) IRVINE

Nationality: British
Born: 10th November 1965
Seasons: 1993-2002
Team/manufacturer(s): Jordan, Ferrari, Jaguar
Grands Prix: 148
Race wins: 4
Championship wins: 0

Eddie Irvine was born in Newtownards in Northern Ireland. He made plenty of money selling cars and making various investments, which helped him kickstart his racing career.

After a spell in Formula Ford 1600, Irvine moved to Formula 3 in 1988 and Formula 3000 a year later. After driving for Jordan in Formula 3000 in 1990, he was promoted to the team's Formula One division for the 1993 season, although he only did the last two races that year.

At first he had a reputation for being reckless and earned the nickname 'Irv the Swerve'. However, in later years after he had moved to Ferrari, he was called 'Steady Eddie' for him calmer driving style.

In 1999, Irvine had his best season, winning four races and finishing in the top seven in all but one of the other races. He scored 74 points and came second in the championship, behind Mika Häkkinen.

Irvine saw out his Formula One career with Jaguar, but saw little success and retired from the series at the

Christopher Irwin

end of 2002. He built up a vast property portfolio around the world.

Christopher (Chris) IRWIN

Nationality: British
Born: 27th June 1942
Seasons: 1966-1967
Team/manufacturer(s): Brabham, Lotus, BRM
Grands Prix: 10
Race wins: 0
Championship wins: 0

Chris Irwin was born in London and began racing in the early 1960s. By 1964 he was competing successfully in Formula 3 and moved to Formula 2 a year later.

He made his Formula One debut in 1966, driving a works Brabham at the British Grand Prix, which was held at Brands Hatch. He finished in a respectable seventh place and so was offered a full-season's drive with BRM the following year. He put in some workmanlike performances and scored two championship points.

Irwin's career was cut short in 1968, when he crashed his Ford during practice for the Nürburgring 1000km. He suffered serious head injuries from which he never fully recovered, and didn't race again.

Taki Inoue

Alan Jones

J

Jean-Pierre Jarier

Jean-Pierre JABOUILLE

Nationality: French
Born: 1st October 1942
Seasons: 1974-1975, 1977-1981
Team/manufacturer(s): Williams, Surtees, Tyrrell,
Renault, Ligier
Grands Prix: 56
Race wins: 2
Championship wins: 0

Jean-Pierre Jabouille worked as a racecar engineer and began racing Formula 3 cars in 1967 and 1968, doing his own maintenance in between. He then went on to compete in Formula 2 and sportscars, coming third at the Le Mans 24 Hours in 1973 and 1974.

It was in 1974 that Jabouille made his Formula One debut, failing to qualify in a Williams at the French Grand Prix, and then at Austria later in the season. The following year he again entered the French Grand Prix, finishing 12th in a Tyrrell.

In 1977, Jabouille entered five Grands Prix with Renault, but retired from four and failed to qualify for the fifth. He then stayed with Renault for the next three seasons and had slightly more success, although he still failed to complete the majority of races he entered.

His first success was fourth place at the 1978 USA Grand Prix. The next year he won in France and, in 1980, he came in first at the Austrian Grand Prix. Between these flashes of success, though, Jabouille had very lit-

tle luck, and failed to finish most Grands Prix, usually because of reliability problems.

A move to Ligier in 1981 saw little improvement and he retired partway through the season. After spending time in sportscar racing, Jabouille formed his own sportscar team and continued to compete in GT racing.

John JAMES

Nationality: English
Born: 10th May 1914
Died 27th January 2002
Seasons: 1951
Team/manufacturer(s): Maserati
Grands Prix: 1
Race wins: 0
Championship wins: 0

John James was an engineer from Bromsgrove. He began racing in a Lea Francis just before the Second World War. After the end of hostilities, he campaigned in hillclimbs and sprints. At first, he drove a 2.3-litre Alfa Romeo, but this was soon replaced by a Type 54 Bugatti and, later, by a Sunbeam.

In 1951, James bought himself a Maserati 4CLT and entered it into the 1951 British Grand Prix at Silverstone. Sadly, though, he had to retire from the race after 23 laps with a leaking radiator.

The following year, Formula One regulations changed, which meant that the Maserati was no longer eligible for

championship races, so James used it in sprint events until he retired from the sport in 1953. James continued to work as an engineer and later moved to Malta.

Jean-Pierre JARIER

Nationality: French
Born: 10th July 1946
Seasons: 1971, 1973-1983
Team/manufacturer(s): March, Shadow, Penske, Ligier, ATS, Lotus, Tyrrell, Osella
Grands Prix: 143
Race wins: 0
Championship wins: 0

Born near Paris, Jarier had a successful time in Formula France before moving to Formula 3 and Formula 2 in 1971.

It was while he was in Formula 2 that he made his Formula One debut, in 1971, when his team rented a March 701, but he did not finish the race.

Two years later, Jarier found himself driving for March in Formula 2, and also competed in a number of Formula One Grands Prix that season, but with little success.

Jarier moved to Shadow for 1974 and stayed with the team through 1976. Despite a third-place finish at Monaco in 1974, he only picked up a handful of points during this largely uneventful time. He went on to drive for a number of teams over the years but failed to excel in Formula One. After retiring from the championship in 1983, he stopped driving for a number of years, then competed in the Porsche Supercup in 1994 and he went on to win the French GT Championship in 1998 and 1999. He has also worked as a stunt driver for the film industry.

Jean-Pierre Jabouille

JKL

Max JEAN

Nationality: French
Born: 27th July 1943
Seasons: 1971
Team/manufacturer(s): Williams
Grands Prix: 1
Race wins: 0
Championship wins: 0

Born in Marseilles, Max Jean competed in Formula Ford and was the French Champion in 1968. He then progressed to Formula 2 in 1970.

It was while he was competing in Formula 2 for Williams that Jean had the chance to compete in the 1971 French Grand Prix. Driving a March 701, he finished the race at the back of the pack and was not classified.

After that, Jean continued in Formula 2 for a while before returning to the more affordable Formula 3. Outside of motorsport, Jean ran a successful haulage business in France, which his sons took over after his retirement. Note that his name is sometimes mistakenly recorded as 'Jean Max'.

Stefan Nils Edwin JOHANSSON

Nationality: Swedish
Born: 8th September 1956
Seasons: 1980, 1983-1991
Team/manufacturer(s): Shadow, Spirit, Tyrrell, Toleman, Ferrari, McLaren, Ligier, Onyx, AGS, Arrows
Grands Prix: 103
Race wins: 0
Championship wins: 0

Swede Stefan Johansson's father was a keen racing driver, so it was not surprising that the youngster began racing karts from 1968, winning the Swedish title five years later.

He then moved to Formula Ford and won the local championship in 1977 before coming to the UK to compete in Formula 3 and winning the championship in 1980.

That same year saw Johansson's Formula One debut when he entered two Grands Prix with Shadow. He returned to Formula One in 1983 and, from then until the end of 1991, he drove for a number of teams and entered many races, but with no wins.

After that, he moved into CART racing, winning Rookie of the Year in 1992. He later drove in a variety of sportscar events before becoming a team manager.

Leslie George JOHNSON

Nationality: British
Born: 22nd March 1912
Died: 8th June 1959
Seasons: 1950
Team/manufacturer(s): ERA
Grands Prix: 1
Race wins: 0
Championship wins: 0

Born in Gloucestershire, Leslie Johnson was a successful sportscar driver, who had won the Spa 24 Hour race in an Aston Martin in 1948.

His one and only Formula One race was the first ever World Championship Grand Prix, at Silverstone in 1950. He drove an ERA E-Type but was forced to retire from the race after just two laps, when the compressor failed in his car.

Johnson then went back to competing in sportscars, mainly for Jaguar and had some success. In 1954, he collapsed with heart problems during the Monte Carlo Rally. He later became managing director of ERA but never fully recovered his health and died of a heart attack in 1959.

William Bruce Gordon (Bruce) JOHNSTONE

Nationality: South Africa
Born: 30th January 1937
Seasons: 1961
Team/manufacturer(s): BRM
Grands Prix: 1
Race wins: 0
Championship wins: 0

Bruce Johnstone was born in Durban and competed successfully in a Volvo during the late 1950s before moving into single-seaters. In 1960, he came sixth in the Formula Libre South African Grand Prix and was runner-up in the following year's South African Championship.

It was in 1961 that he entered his one World Championship race, the South African Grand Prix. Driving a works BRM, he finished in ninth place.

The following year, Johnstone came to Europe and raced in various events but he never again competed in Formula One, instead progressing to sportscar events.

Living in South Africa, he worked as a Yamaha importer after retiring from racing.

Alan JONES, MBE

Nationality: Australian
Born: 2nd November 1946
Seasons: 1975-1981, 1983, 1985-1986
Team/manufacturer(s): Hesketh, Hill, Surtees, Shadow, Williams, Arrows, Lola
Grands Prix: 117
Race wins: 12
Championship wins: 1

Born in Melbourne the son of a racing driver, Alan Jones raced a Mini as a teenager before coming to England in 1967 to race. After much struggling, he got into Formula 3 by 1974, followed by Formula Atlantic the next year.

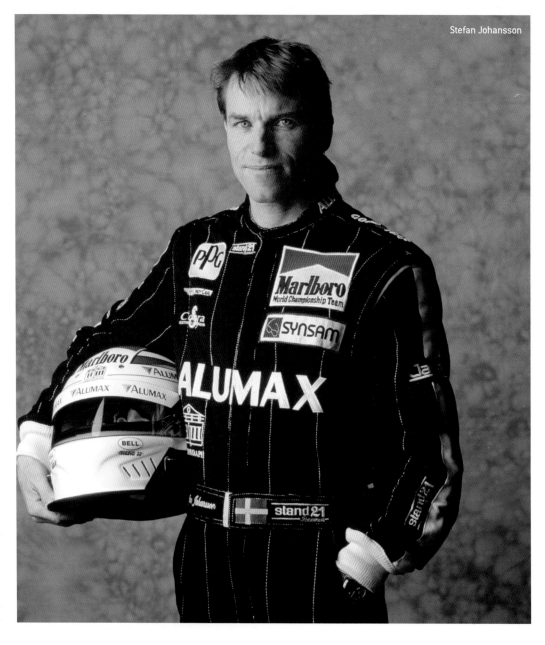

Stefan Johansson

Jones then moved to Formula One in 1975, first driving a Hesketh then for Hill. Before long he was proving to be a competitive force, winning his first race in Austria two years later.

A move to Williams in 1978 saw the start of Jones's best years, with him winning four races and coming third in the championship the following season.

The 1980 season saw Jones winning the championship after coming first in five races, second in three and third in two. He scored a total of 67 points. The following year, Jones again came third in the championship.

Jones then announced his retirement, but drove in one race for Arrows in 1983, and three for Lola in 1985. He then did a full, but unsuccessful 1986 season with Lola.

After retiring from racing, Jones worked in television and continued to compete in touring cars.

Tom JONES

Nationality: American
Born: 26th April 1943
Seasons: 1967
Team/manufacturer(s): Cooper
Grands Prix: 1
Race wins: 0
Championship wins: 0

Texan Tom Jones began racing in a Lotus Seven back in 1964 but had to stop at the end of the season to do his National Service.

He returned to the track in 1967, this time driving a Cooper T82 with a 1.5-litre V8 engine. At the time he thought this was a Formula One specification car but, in fact, the series was running 3.0-litre engines by this time.

Not to be defeated, though, he towed the car all the way to the Canadian Grand Prix at Ontario. There, his car suffered from electrical problems and Jones failed to qualify.

He returned home and raced the car in some local events, before Cooper repossessed it because Jones had lapsed on repayments. He later competed in Formula 5000 and Can Am but retired from the sport around 1980. Jones went on to run a welding and fabrication business.

Juan JOVER

Nationality: Spanish
Born: 23rd November 1903
Died: 28th June 1960
Seasons: 1951
Team/manufacturer(s): Maserati
Grands Prix: 1
Race wins: 0
Championship wins: 0

Juan Jover was a wealthy Spaniard who began racing motorcycles in the 1920s before switching to cyclecars and later, cars.

After the Second World War, Jover competed in a number of European Grand Prix races and also finished third at the Le Mans 24 Hour in 1949, driving a Delage.

Jover's one and only Formula One World Championship race was the 1951 Spanish Grand Prix. He drove a Maserati but failed to qualify.

After that, he continued to race in a variety of machinery and competitions, including hillclimbs and sportscar races. He had pretty much retired from racing by 1960, when he was driving in Spain and his car inexplicitly left the road and plunged down a cliff. Jover was killed at the scene.

Alan Jones

K

Narain Karthikeyan

Oswald KARCH

Nationality: German
Born: 6th March 1917
Seasons: 1953
Team/manufacturer(s): Veritas
Grands Prix: 1
Race wins: 0
Championship wins: 0

German Oswald Karch was born in Ludwigshafen in 1917. After the Second World War, he competed in both East and West Germany, first in a BMW-Eigenbau and then in a Veritas RS.

It was with the Veritas that he entered the 1953 German Grand Prix at the Nürburgring on 2nd August. After starting near the back of the grid he retired from the race after just 10 laps.

After that he continued to drive the Veritas in European events, and also competed in it at the 1954 Casablanca 12 Hour race, finishing in sixth place in his class.

Kumar Ram Narain (Narain) KARTHIKEYAN

Nationality: Indian
Born: 14th January 1977
Seasons: 2005
Team/manufacturer(s): Jordan
Grands Prix: 16
Race wins: 0
Championship wins: 0

Narain Karthikeyan is the son of a former Indian National Rally Champion, so became interested in racing at an early age, with the ambition of becoming India's first Formula One driver.

Starting in Formula Maruti, he then went to the UK to compete in Formula Vauxhall Junior and, later, Formula Ford. Returning to India, he won the Formula Asia International series in 1996.

Karthikeyan then worked his way through Formula 3 and Formula 3000. Then, in 2001, he became the first Indian to drive a Formula One car, when he tested for Jaguar. This was followed by tests with Jordan-Honda.

However, it was not until 2005 that Karthikeyan achieved his childhood ambition of being a full-blown Formula One driver, when he had a full season with Jordan, as a paying driver. He finished most races, albeit in low positions, with the exception of the USA Grand Prix, where he came fourth after most teams pulled out over a dispute about tyre safety.

Karthikeyan left Jordan at the end of the season and went to Williams as a test driver for 2006 and 2007, arguing that it would improve his skills for the future.

Ukyo KATAYAMA

Nationality: Japanese
Born: 29th May 1963
Seasons: 1992-1997
Team/manufacturer(s): Larrousse, Tyrrell, Minardi
Grands Prix: 97
Race wins: 0
Championship wins: 0

Born in Tokyo, Ukyo Katayama worked as a mechanic and began racing in Formula Junior 1600 in 1983, winning the title the following year. Then followed a spell in Formula 3 before Katayama moved to France to enter a racing school.

Katayama then worked his way through Formula Renault, Formula 3 and Formula 3000, not to mention a spell in the Japanese Touring Car Championship in 1989.

He finally made it to Formula One in 1992, driving for Larrousse. However, he struggled with an unreliable car and moved to Tyrrell the following year. Again, though, the car was dated and uncompetitive.

He did better in 1994, with a new car, and finished in fifth place at Brazil and San Marino, and sixth at the British Grand Prix. The following two seasons he stuck with Tyrrell but had little success.

A move to Minardi in 1997 was to be Katayama's final season in Formula One. He retired at the end of the year, admitting that he had been suffering from back cancer, from which he later recovered.

Katayama continued to race in sportscars and GTs, and also enjoyed mountaineering, climbing Mount Everest in 2001.

Kenneth (Ken) KAVANAGH

Nationality: Australian
Born: 12th December 1923
Seasons: 1958
Team/manufacturer(s): Maserati
Grands Prix: 2
Race wins: 0
Championship wins: 0

Ken Kavanagh was born in Melbourne, Australia. He was better known for his skills on two wheels, racing Norton and Moto-Guzzi motorcycles with some success.

However, he also competed in cars occasionally, which led to him entering two Grands Prix in the 1958 season, driving a Maserati 250F. The first was the Monaco Grand Prix, where he failed to qualify. Then came the Belgian race, where he qualified but was unable to enter the race proper after his engine blew up during practice.

After retiring from racing, Kavanagh settled in Italy and ran his own dry-cleaning business there.

Ukyo Katayama

Rupert Keegan

Rupert KEEGAN

Nationality: British
Born: 26th February 1955
Seasons: 1977-1978, 1980, 1982
Team/manufacturer(s): Hesketh, Surtees, RAM, March
Grands Prix: 37
Race wins: 0
Championship wins: 0

Essex-born Rupert Keegan began racing in a Ford Escort Mexico before moving on to single-seaters in the form of Formula Ford, then Formula 5. He went on to win the British Formula 3 Championship in 1976.

This led to a drive with the Hesketh Formula One team for 1977 and Keegan put in a good performance, battling with an under-developed car. Unfortunately, a move to the struggling Surtees team the following season proved very disappointing for Keegan.

With no Formula One drive for 1979, Keegan went and drove in Aurora F1 series and won the championship. Sadly, though, his return to the Formula One the following year with RAM was not as successful. Neither was his last attempt, with March, in 1982.

Keegan later raced in the USA before retiring from the sport to run various business ventures and to be a racing instructor.

Edward (Eddie) KEIZAN

Nationality: South African
Born: 12th September 1944
Seasons: 1973-1975
Team/manufacturer(s): Tyrrell, Lotus
Grands Prix: 3
Race wins: 0
Championship wins: 0

Eddie Keizan proved himself to be a talented saloon car racer in the late 1960s, winning the South African Championship on two occasions.

By 1971, he began competing in single-seater racing, first in Formula Ford then Formula 5000, winning the local championship in the latter. He then moved to the South African Formula One Championship, driving first a Tyrrell 004, then a Lotus 72.

This led to Keizan entering the South African World Championship Grand Prix three years in a row, starting in 1973. That first time, his result was not classified. However, the following year he finished 14th and, the third year he came in 13th.

Keizan later concentrated on saloon car racing. He also built up a successful alloy wheels company in South Africa.

Joseph (Joe) KELLY

Nationality: Irish
Born: 13th March 1913
Died: 28th November 1993
Seasons: 1950-1951
Team/manufacturer(s): Alta
Grands Prix: 2
Race wins: 0
Championship wins: 0

Irishman Joe Kelly left school at 13 and went on to become a successful motor dealer in Dublin, after spending time in England during the Second World War.

He began racing a Maserati 6CM in 1948 and then bought an Alta GP3 with a four-cylinder, 1490cc supercharged engine. He entered this in the first Formula One World Championship race at Silverstone in 1950 but failed to finish with a classified place. Kelly again entered the same Grand Prix the following year, in the Alta again, but was forced to retire after 75 laps. He then concentrated on Formula 2 and sportscar racing, before retiring after a crash

in 1955. Kelly later ran the Ferrari agency for Ireland and was also a property developer.

David (Dave) KENNEDY

Nationality: Irish
Born: 15th January 1953
Seasons: 1980
Team/manufacturer(s): Shadow
Grands Prix: 7
Race wins: 0
Championship wins: 0

David Kennedy was born in Sligo and went on to become a well-known Irish racing driver. He had a successful career in the Aurora F1 Championship before finally making it to Formula One.

Driving for the Shadow team, Kennedy entered eight Grands Prix during the 1980 season, starting with the Argentinean race. Unfortunately, though, the only race he qualified for and raced in was the Spanish Grand Prix, which was subsequently stripped of its World Championship status and so doesn't count.

Kennedy went on to race in sportscars before working as a Formula One television presenter in Ireland and as a manager for other drivers.

Loris KESSEL

Nationality: Switzerland
Born: 1st April 1950
Seasons: 1976-1977
Team/manufacturer(s): RAM, Apollon-Williams
Grands Prix: 6
Race wins: 0
Championship wins: 0

Loris Kessel was a garage owner who began his racing career in Alfa Romeo saloons, before getting involved in single-seaters. He worked his way through Formula 3 and Formula 2.

Kessel then drove for the RAM Formula One team in 1976, entering six Grands Prix with little success. The following season, he drove his own Apollon-Williams car at the Italian Grand Prix but failed to qualify.

After a spell in Formula 2 and sportscar racing, Kessel retired to build up his successful car dealership business, which concentrated on Ferrari and Lamborghini. He also bought and restored some of the racecars he'd driven.

Bruce KESSLER

Nationality: USA
Born: 23rd March 1936
Seasons: 1958
Team/manufacturer(s): Connaught
Grands Prix: 61
Race wins: 0
Championship wins: 0

American driver Bruce Kessler tried to enter just one Grand Prix, and that was the 1958 Monaco race. He was in a Connaught-Alta that was owned by Bernie Ecclestone, who also entered the race. Sadly, though, neither driver qualified for the race proper.

Kessler went on to compete in sportscar races, but then worked in the trawler industry with some success. Bizarrely, perhaps, he was also a successful television director, working on shows such as Knight Rider, The A Team, Ironside and Rockford Files.

Nicolas KIESA

Nationality: Danish
Born: 3rd March 1978
Seasons: 2003
Team/manufacturer(s): Minardi
Grands Prix: 5
Race wins: 0
Championship wins: 0

Nicolas Kiesa was born in Copenhagen and was a successful kart driver, winning a number of championships. In 1998, he moved into Formula Ford, winning the British Championship the following year.

Formula 3 followed, and then Formula 3000 and Kiesa proved successful in both series. His Formula One debut came towards the end of the 2003 season when he drove for Minardi in the last five races of the season, and impressed by finishing them all, albeit with a best-placed finish of 12th place.

Sadly, though, it was not enough to keep him in Formula One, although Kiesa stayed with Minardi, driving the team's two-seater promotional cars.

For 2005, he moved to Jordan as a Formula One test driver, with the chance to compete again.

Leo Juhani KINNUNEN

Nationality: Finnish
Born: 5th August 1943
Seasons: 1974
Team/manufacturer(s): AAW Racing
Grands Prix: 6
Race wins: 0
Championship wins: 0

Finnish driver, Leo Kinnunen, began competing on motorcycles as a youngster but soon moved to cars. He became

a successful rally, autocross and ice driver before getting into Formula 2 in 1967.

Next came a spell racing sportscars and, together with Pedro Rodriguez, Kinnunen won the 1969 World Sportscar Championship in a Porsche 917. He went on to win the Interserie Championship three times, from 1971 to 1973, in a 917. Kinnunen's short Formula One career was less successful. In 1974, he entered a Surtees TS16 under the AAW Racing banner but the team was underfunded and the car was under-developed. He only qualified for one race out of six, the Swedish Grand Prix, but had to retire from it with engine problems after just eight laps.

By 1977, Kinnunen had retired from racing but continued to be involved in the sport at an administrative level.

Hans KLENK

Nationality: German
Born: 29th October 1919
Seasons: 1952
Team/manufacturer(s): Veritas
Grands Prix: 1
Race wins: 0
Championship wins: 0

German Hans Klenk flew Messerschmitts during the Second World War. After, he worked as an engineer, building his own specials in Stuttgart.

He later began to race his own Veritas Meteor which had a two-litre, six-cylinder engine. It was this that he drove in his one Formula One World Championship race, the 1952 German Grand Prix. Held at the Nürburgring, Klenk finished in 11th place, after completing 14 laps of the famous circuit.

The same year, Klenk drove a works Mercedes Benz in the Mille Miglia. Along with Karl Kling, they finished second. Crucially, though, Klenk made history by making notes about the route beforehand, and these were the forerunner of today's pace notes.

Klenk went back to designing and building racecars before retiring.

Christian KLIEN

Nationality: Austrian
Born: 7th February 1983
Seasons: 2004-
Team/manufacturer(s): Jaguar, Red Bull
Grands Prix: 48
Race wins: 0
Championship wins: 0

As a child, Christian Klien met Formula One legend, Ayrton Senna, and made up his mind there and then to become a Formula One driver himself. He got off to a good start, becoming Swiss Kart Champion in his first season.

From there, Klien worked his way up through various series

Christian Klien

Karl Kling

until Jaguar signed him as a Formula One driver for the 2004 season. He had a good first year, completing all but four races and with a best result of sixth at the Belgian Grand Prix.

The following season, Klien moved to Red Bull Racing and, despite not doing the full season, finished in the top ten in most of the races he entered. For 2006, he was teamed with David Coulthard at Red Bull where he had a less successful season, and was dropped from the team before the end of the year.

Karl KLING

Nationality: German
Born: 16th September 1910
Died: 18th March 2003
Seasons: 1954-1955
Team/manufacturer(s): Mercedes Benz
Grands Prix: 11
Race wins: 0
Championship wins: 0

Karl Kling raced Mercedes in rallies and trials before the Second World War. After serving as a pilot in the German Airforce, he returned to racing and was German Sport Car Champion in 1948 and 1949, driving a Veritas.

He later returned to Mercedes Benz and raced the team's new Silver Arrows cars in the 1954 Formula One season to great success. Despite missing the first three out of nine Grands Prix that year and retiring from two, Kling still finished fifth in the championship, after gaining points in four of the five races he finished.

The following year, he again drove for Mercedes in

Formula One, but had less success, only completing one out of five Grands Prix. That was the British event, where he finished in third place.

Kling went on to be head of Daimler Benz's motorsports department, and continued to compete in long-distance races.

Ernst KLODWIG

Nationality: East German
Born: 23rd May 1903
Died: 15th April 1973
Seasons: 1952-1953
Team/manufacturer(s): non-works BMW
Grands Prix: 2
Race wins: 0
Championship wins: 0

Ernst Klodwig was born in Aschersleben and was a keen amateur racing driver. In the early 1950s he competed in a rear-engined BMW special which was based on the pre-war-design 328 sportscar. At the time, this 'Eigenbau' (self-build) was a popular and affordable choice with Germans on both sides of the border.

Klodwig entered the German Grand Prix, held at the Nürburgring, in 1952 and 1953. The first time he finished in 12th place, after completing 14 laps. The following year, he drove his BMW-based car to a disappointing 15th-place finish after 15 laps.

However, this was not typical of Klodwig who, in other-races, regularly finished in the top three.

Helmut KOINIGG

Nationality: Austrian
Born: 3rd November 1948
Died: 6th October 1974
Seasons: 1974
Team/manufacturer(s): Scuderia Finotto, Surtees
Grands Prix: 3
Race wins: 0
Championship wins: 0

Born in Vienna to wealthy parents, Helmut Koinigg began racing in a Mini Cooper before moving up to Formula Vee, winning the title in his third season, 1973.

Struggling to work his way up the single-seater route, Koinigg drove in touring cars and sportscars at the start of the 1974 season, before finally scraping together the money to buy a drive with the Scuderia Finotto team towards the end of the season. Although he failed to qualify, driving a Brabham for the team, his performance was enough to get him a seat with Surtees for the last two races of the year.

The first was the Canadian Grand Prix, where Koinigg finished in 10th place. At long last he was proving himself to be a talented driver, but it was not to be. At the USA Grand Prix his car's suspension failed, causing him to crash into the Armco, which was not properly secured. The car drove under it and Koinigg was decapitated.

Heikki KOVALAINEN

Nationality: Finnish
Born: 19th October 1981
Seasons: 2007
Team/manufacturer(s): Renault
Grands Prix: 17
Race wins: 0
Championship wins: 0

Heikki Kovalainen was born in Suomussalmi in Finland. He began racing karts in 1991, at the age of 10, and worked his way up to being runner up in the Finnish Formula A championship in 1999, then Nordic champion the following year, when he also won the Elf Masters.

Kovalainen then began racing cars, started in the British Formula Renault championship, finishing fourth in 2001. In 2003, he moved to the World Series by Nissan, winning it the following season.

In 2004, Kovalainen won the Race of Champions in Paris; the first non-rally driver to ever do so. Then it was on to the GP2 Series in 2005 where he finished in second place.

This led to a position as test-driver for Renault at the end of 2005 and through 2006. When driver Fernando Alonso moved to McLaren for the 2007 season, Kovalainen took his place.

Michael (Mikko) KOZAROWITZKY

Nationality: Finnish
Born: 17th May 1948
Seasons: 1977
Team/manufacturer(s): RAM
Grands Prix: 2
Race wins: 0
Championship wins: 0

Mikko Kozarowitzky began his sporting career playing tennis, and even represented Finland at the 1966 Davis Cup. However, he soon followed in his father's footsteps and began racing cars, starting in Formula Vee.

Kozarowitzky then spent time in Formula Super Vee, winning the Gold Cup in 1975. This gave him a break into Formula 2 but he had little success so he travelled to New Zealand the following year to compete in Formula Pacific.

On his return home, he landed a drive with RAM, which wanted a Finnish driver.

Kozarowitzky entered the Swedish and British Grands Prix but failed to qualify for either. At the latter, he broke his hand in an accident and left the team after they tried to force him to continue racing.

He retired from the sport after that and moved to Holland where he took up golf and started his own business.

Willi KRAKAU

Nationality: German
Born: 4th December 1911
Died: 26th April 1995
Seasons: 1952
Team/manufacturer(s): AFM
Grands Prix: 1
Race wins: 0
Championship wins: 0

German Willi Krakau enjoyed a number of sports before the Second World War, including skiing, sailing and scuba diving, and he represented his country at rowing in the 1936 Olympics.

After the war, he raced a home-built BMW special in Formula 2 events in Germany, constantly working on it and improving it as he went along.

However, this was not the car Krakau entered into the 1952 German Grand Prix. Instead, he borrowed a six-cylinder AFM, lending his car to fellow competitor, Harry Merke. Despite qualifying for the race, for some reason Krakau did not actually start it.

Krakau sold his trusty BMW special at the end of the 1952 season, and disappeared from the racing scene.

Rudolf KRAUSE

Nationality: East German
Born: 30th March 1907
Died: 11th April 1987
Seasons: 1952-1953
Team/manufacturer(s): BMW
Grands Prix: 2
Race wins: 0
Championship wins: 0

Rudolf Krause was one of a number of German drivers – from both sides of the border – who, after the Second World War, competed in home-built, or 'Eigenbau', BMW-engined specials.

Krause was a fast but steady driver with a reliable car, and often finished races in the top three. In 1952 and 1953, he crossed over to the West to compete in the German Grand Prix at the Nürburgring in his trusty car.

At his first attempt, though, he had to retire after just three laps. The following year, Krause did somewhat better, completing 16 laps and finishing in 14th place.

He later gave up single-seater racing and turned his hand to rally driving.

Robert KUBICA

Nationality: Polish
Born: 7th December 1984
Seasons: 2006-
Team/manufacturer(s): BMW Sauber
Grands Prix: 22
Race wins: 0
Championship wins: 0

Robert Kubica began driving a miniature car at the age of four and soon progressed to karting. Once he was old enough to race at 10, he went on to win six titles in his home country. A move to Italy saw him win the International Italian Karting Championship; the first non-Italian to do so.

After going on to win other karting events, in 2000 Kubica went on to compete in Formula Renault 2000, followed by Formula 3. Then, in 2005 he won the World Series by Renault Championship. This led to a chance to test for Renault's Formula One team.

In the event, though, he ended up signing as a test driver for BMW Sauber for the 2006 season. Towards the end of the season, he got his chance to race when teammate, Jacques Villeneuve was unfit to drive following an accident. At his debut Grand Prix, at Hungary, Kubica finished in seventh place but was later disqualified because his car was underweight.

Villeneuve then left the team and Kubica had a place as a driver proper. His best result at the end of the 2006 season was a third place finish at the Italian Grand Prix, which earned him six championship points. Kubica stayed with BMW Sauber for the 2007 and 2008 seasons.

Kurt KUHNKE

Nationality: German
Born: 30th April 1910
Died: 8th February 1969
Seasons: 1963
Team/manufacturer(s): Lotus
Grands Prix: 1
Race wins: 0
Championship wins: 0

Born in Braunschweig, Germany, Kurt Kuhnke was essentially a motorcycle racer both before and after the Second World War. However, he also dabbled in car racing, starting with a 500cc Cooper Formula 3 car in the early 1950s, with some success.

During the early 1960s, he entered a Lotus-Borgward in a number of non-championship Grands Prix but without too much luck. His one and only World Championship Grand Prix was the German event at the Nürburgring that year. Driving his Lotus, he failed dismally to qualify for the race.

Kuhnke continued to race cars and motorcycles for some time after this.

Masami KUWASHIMA

Nationality: Japanese
Born: 14th September 1950
Seasons: 1977
Team/manufacturer(s): Wolf-Williams
Grands Prix: 1
Race wins: 0
Championship wins: 0

Japanese driver, Masami Kuwashima, worked his way up the local formulae with reasonable success, starting with Formula 2000, where he came third in the championship in 1974.

After another season and a bit in Formula 2000, Kuwashima tried to get a drive with RAM for part of 1976, but the deal fell through. However, Williams suddenly found itself needing a driver for the Japanese Grand Prix that year, and Kuwashima was in the right place at the right time.

As it turned out, though, he ended up having about the shortest Formula One career ever. Kuwashima only drove in the first practice race before being replaced by Hans Binder because of a dispute over sponsorship money.

After that, he returned to Formula 2000 and then Formula 2 before retiring from racing in 1980. Kuwashima later became a team director in Japanese GT.

J
K
L

Robert Kubica

L

LA CAZE, Robert
LAFFITE, Jacques
LAGORCE, Franck
LAMMERS, Jan
LAMY, Pedro
LANDI, Chico
LANG, Hermann
LANGES, Claudio
LARINI, Nicola
LARRAURI, Oscar
LARROUSE, Gerard
LAUDA, Niki
LAURENT, Roger
LAVAGGI, Giovanni
LAWRENCE, Chris
LECLERE, Michel
LEDERLE, Neville
LEES, Geoff
LEGAT, Arthur

LEHTO, JJ
LEONI, Lamberto
LESTON, Les
LEVEGH, Pierre
LEWIS, Jackie
LEWIS-EVANS, Stuart
LIGIER, Guy
LIPPI, Roberto
LIUZZI, Vitantonio
LOMBARDI, Lella
LONDOÑO, Ricardo
LOOF, Ernst
LOUVEAU, Henri
LOVE, John
LOVELY, Pete
LOYER, Roger
LUCAS, Jean
LUCIENBONNET, Jean
LUNGER, Brett

Stuart Lewis-Evans

Robert LA CAZE

Nationality: Moroccan
Born: 26th February 1917
Seasons: 1958
Team/manufacturer(s): Cooper
Grands Prix: 1
Race wins: 0
Championship wins: 0

Robert La Caze was a Frenchman who lived and worked in Morocco. In the 1950s he was very prominent in motorsport in North Africa and had competed in various rallies and races, driving a range of machinery from Simcas to Delahayes. Most notably, he won the Moroccan International Rally in 1954, behind the wheel of a Simca.

The 1958 Moroccan Grand Prix was the only one to be part of the World Championship and, as it happened, the last one to be held in the country. La Caze entered the race in a privately run Cooper-Climax Formula 2 car and finished in 14th place after completing 48 laps.

La Caze later retired and moved back to France.

Jacques Henri LAFFITE

Nationality: French
Born: 21st November 1943
Seasons: 1974-1986
Team/manufacturer(s): Iso Marlboro, Ligier, Williams
Grands Prix: 180
Race wins: 6
Championship wins: 0

Jacques Laffite was born in Paris and began working as a race mechanic, not getting into racing seriously until he was in his late twenties.

By 1972 he had won the French Formula Renault Championship and then moved on to Formula 3 the following season, winning the French title that year.

Then, in 1974, he competed in Formula 2 and made his Formula One debut, driving for Iso Marlboro in Germany and then entering the next four Grands Prix at the end of the season.

Laffite stayed with the same team, now renamed Williams, for 1975 and then moved to Ligier, the team he drove for until the end of 1982. During this time he performed remarkably well, winning no less than six races and getting podium positions on many more. He finished fourth in the World Championship three times, in 1979, 1980 and 1981.

A move back to Williams for 1983 and 1984 was less successful and Laffite then returned to Ligier for his last two seasons in Formula One Sadly, though, a bad crash at Brands Hatch in 1986 left him with two broken legs and cut short his season.

However, he recovered and went on to compete in Touring Cars. He also worked for Ligier in a PR role. Laffite later commentated on Formula One for French television.

Franck LAGORCE

Nationality: French
Born: 1st September 1968
Seasons: 1994
Team/manufacturer(s): Ligier
Grands Prix: 2
Race wins: 0
Championship wins: 0

Frenchman Franck Lagorce was a talented kart racer as a child and won his first major title at the age of just 13. By the time he was 20, Lagorce was competing in Formula Ford 1600, finishing fifth in the championship in 1988.

After a spell in Formule Renault, Lagorce moved to French Formula 3 in 1991 and won the title the following year. In 1993 and 1994, he competed in Formula 3000 and won the championship in the second year.

Lagorce signed as a test driver for the Ligier Formula One team towards the end of the 1994 season and found himself competing in the last two Grands Prix of the year, at Japan and Australia. He retired with a driveshaft failure at the first race, and finished 11th at the second.

The following season, Lagorce returned to testing for Ligier and then did the same for Forti in 1996. When that team closed, his Formula One career was over and Lagorce went on to race in sportscar, touring cars and ice driving.

Johannes (Jan) LAMMERS

Nationality: Dutch
Born: 2nd June 1956
Seasons: 1979-1982, 1992
Team/manufacturer(s): Shadow, ATS, Ensign, Theodore, March
Grands Prix: 41
Race wins: 0
Championship wins: 0

At the age of 16, Jan Lammers entered the racing school at Zandvoort and gained his competitor licence. A year later, he won his first race, driving a Simca in touring car event. He went on to win three more times, to take the Group 1

Jan Lammers

Touring Car Championship.

By 1976, he had moved on to single-seaters, competing in Formula Ford and, the following year, Formula 3, going on to win the European Championship in 1978.

This led to a drive with the Shadow Formula One team for 1979 and he moved on to drive for ATS, Ensign and Theodore – all uncompetitive teams that didn't allow him to show his full potential.

Lammers then had a successful sportscar career, winning at Le Mans in 1988, driving a Jaguar and beating Porsche for the first time in six years.

Jacques Laffite

Pedro Lamy

Hermann Lang

In 1992, Lammers made a surprise comeback to Formula One, driving a March at the last two races of the season. He was to stay with the team for 1993, but it went bankrupt.

Lammers later formed his own sportscar team and then ran the Dutch A1 Grand Prix team.

José Pedro LAMY VIÇOSO (Pedro Lamy)

Nationality: Portuguese
Born: 20th March 1972
Seasons: 1993-1996
Team/manufacturer(s): Lotus, Minardi
Grands Prix: 32
Race wins: 0
Championship wins: 0

After racing karts as a boy, Pedro Lamy progressed to Portuguese Formula Ford at the age of 17 and won the championship that year. He then went to Formula Opel Lotus and won that title in 1991. The following year he competed in Formula 3 in Germany and, again, won the series.

All this led to a Formula One drive for Lotus at the end of the 1993 season. Lamy was then signed to drive for the team the following year, but a bad crash during testing at Silverstone put him out of action for the rest of the year and most of the next.

He finally recovered enough to drive for Minardi in the second part of 1995, and his best result was sixth place in Australia, scoring him his only championship point.

Lamy stayed with Minardi for a disappointing 1996 season, due in part to the team's lack of resources. He then moved to the FIA GT Championship where he won the GT2 class in 1998. He later won the 24 Hours Nürburgring in 2002 and 2003, and has competed in other endurance events.

Francisco Sacco (Chico) LANDI

Nationality: Brazilian
Born: 14th July 1907
Died: 7th June 1989
Seasons: 1951-1953, 1956
Team/manufacturer(s): Ferrari, Maserati
Grands Prix: 6
Race wins: 0
Championship wins: 0

Francisco or 'Chico' Landi was born in Sao Paulo and began racing in the 1930s. By the early 1940s he was considered one of the best drivers in Brazil.

However, it was not until after the Second World War that Landi began racing outside his home country. Indeed, in 1947 he became the first Brazilian to compete internationally, when he entered the Argentinean Temporada series along with top drivers from Europe.

He then became the first Brazilian to race in Europe

Claudio Langes

when he entered the 1947 Formula 2 Bari Grand Prix in Italy. He didn't finish the race that year, but returned the following to win it.

Landi entered six World Championship Grands Prix in the 1950s, in Italy, Holland, Switzerland and Argentina, driving Ferraris and, later Maseratis. He scored a total of 1.5 championship points.

He retired from racing at the end of the 1950s and went on to be a leading administrator in Brazilian motorsport.

Hermann LANG

Nationality: German
Born: 6th April 1909
Died: 19th October 1987
Seasons: 1953-1954
Team/manufacturer(s): Maserati, Mercedes
Grands Prix: 2
Race wins: 0
Championship wins: 0

Hermann Lang grew up near Stuttgart and started work as a motorcycle mechanic at the age of 14. Before long, he'd bought an old bike and began racing it. By the time he was 22 he was the German sidecar mountain race champion.

Lang went on to work for the Mercedes Grand Prix team and became head mechanic, looking after Luigi Fagioli's W25A car. This led to a chance to drive for the team and

Lang won his first race at the 1937 Tripoli Grand Prix – an event he then won again for the next two years. In 1939, Lang won five of the eight Grand Prix races he entered.

After the Second World War, Lang competed in various single-seater and sportscar races. He entered two Formula One Grands Prix, the first being the 1953 Swiss event, where he drove a Maserati to a fifth-place finish. The following year he entered the German Grand Prix, but he span out of the race after 10 laps. Lang decided then that it was time to retire and he returned to his work as a mechanic for Mercedes.

Claudio LANGES

Nationality: Italian
Born: 20th July 1960
Seasons: 1990
Team/manufacturer(s): Eurobrun
Grands Prix: 14
Race wins: 0
Championship wins: 0

Italian Claudio Langes had a promising start to his career when he became Italian 125cc Kart Champion at the age of 18.

He then worked his way through Formula 3 and then Formula 3000 with mixed results and no major wins. However, he was able to raise enough money to get himself a paid drive in 1990 for the struggling Eurobrun Formula

One team from his home country.

Driving a Judd-engined car, Langes failed to pre-qualify for any of the 14 Grands Prix he entered that season. Towards the end of the season, Eurobrun had run out of money and the team folded before the last two Grands Prix took place.

And that was the end of Langes' disastrous Formula One career. He went on to have more success in Italian touring car racing.

Nicola LARINI

Nationality: Italian
Born: 19th March 1964
Seasons: 1987-1992, 1994, 1997
Team/manufacturer(s): Coloni, Osella, Ligier, Modena, Ferrari, Sauber
Grands Prix: 75
Race wins: 0
Championship wins: 0

Italian driver Nicola Larini began racing in Formula Italia in 1983 and worked his way up to Formula 3, winning the local championship in 1986.

The following year, Larini competed in Formula 3000 driving for Coloni. Toward the end of the season the team entered a car into two Formula One Grands Prix, Italy and Spain, for which Larini drove. He did not qualify for the first

Niki Lauda

Nicola Larini

race, and retired with suspension problems in the second.

He then drove for Osella in 1988 and 1989 and proved a competent driver despite struggling with an uncompetitive car. A move to Ligier in 1990 was more promising but Larini failed to achieve better than a seventh place finish. It was a similar story with Modena in 1991.

Larini spent 1992 and 1993 testing and developing Ferrari's active suspension system. He entered the last two Grands Prix of the 1992 season but none the following year.

In 1994, Larini had his best ever finish when he came second at the San Marino Grand Prix – the event that claimed the lives of Roland Ratzenberger and Ayrton Senna. It was also the last Grand Prix that Larini would

Oscar Larrauri

enter until he did five races at the start of the 1997 season, driving for Sauber.

After that, he raced touring cars and sportscars.

Oscar Rubén LARRAURI

Nationality: Argentinean
Born: 19th August 1954
Seasons: 1988-1989
Team/manufacturer(s): Eurobrun
Grands Prix: 21
Race wins: 0
Championship wins: 0

Oscar Larrauri took up karting in his late teens and soon proved very competitive, becoming Santa Fe champion three times.

A move to Europe saw him competing in Formula 3, taking the European Championship in 1982 after winning seven races. Larrauri then moved to sportscar for some time, but remained keen to compete in Formula One.

He finally got his chance in 1988, driving for the struggling Eurobrun team. Unfortunately, the team was so underdeveloped, Larrauri failed to qualify for many of the races that season. Out of the races he did enter, he only completed two – in lowly 13th and 16th places. The following year was even worse. He only entered five Grands Prix and failed to pre-qualify for any.

Larrauri then went on to have more success in sportscar and GT racing. After retiring from racing he returned to Argentina to become a politician and to run his own cold-storage business.

Gérard LARROUSSE

Nationality: French
Born: 23rd May 1940
Seasons: 1974
Team/manufacturer(s): Brabham
Grands Prix: 2
Race wins: 0
Championship wins: 0

Gérard Larrousse came from Lyon and was a talented and successful rally driver in the 1960s. Towards the end of the decade, though, he became more and more involved in circuit racing. Endurance events were a speciality – he won the Sebring 12 Hours in 1971, driving a Porsche 917 with Vic Elford.

His Formula One career as a driver was brief and undistinguished. He drove a Brabham at the Belgian Grand Prix in 1974 but had to retire after 53 laps with a burst tyre. Larrousse then entered the French Grand Prix later in the season but failed to qualify.

He is perhaps better remembered for his own Formula One team, Larrousse, which he founded with Didier Calmels (who was later jailed for shooting his wife) in 1987. Sadly, the team struggled financially and finally folded in 1995.

Andreas Nikolaus (Niki) LAUDA

Nationality: Austrian
Born: 22nd February 1949
Seasons: 1971-1979, 1982-1985
Team/manufacturer(s): March, BRM, Ferrari, Brabham, McLaren
Grands Prix: 172
Race wins: 25
Championship wins: 3

Andreas Nikolaus Lauda was born in Vienna to a wealthy and well-respected family who were against him bringing the Lauda name into disrepute by becoming a racing driver. He spent his early teens driving around fields in an old Volkswagen Beetle convertible, and his first race was a hill-climb in a Cooper, before moving on to Formula Three.

His father refused to give Niki any financial help, so the determined youngster used his family name and connections to borrow large sums of money to fund his racing. By 1972 he had bought his way into the March Formula Two and Formula One teams. The cars, however, were uncompetitive and Lauda was unable to prove himself as a driver.

With debts to repay, and no qualifications to do anything else, Lauda had no choice but to continue racing. He spent 1973 with BRM and was offered a paid-for place on the team for the following season, but was poached by Ferrari, who repaid his substantial debts.

Lauda won the first of 26 Formula One races in that first season with Ferrari and he finished fourth in the championship, despite suffering a number of mechanical problems.

In 1975, Lauda and his Ferrari 312T dominated the season, with no less than five wins, and the championship was his. He was on track to repeat his victory the following year when disaster struck. During the German Grand Prix at the Nürburgring, his car inexplicitly swerved and crashed, catching fire in the process. Lauda suffered third-degree burns, plus several broken bones and scorched lungs.

But, despite all odds, the Austrian made a miraculous recovery and, just six weeks later, he was at the Italian Grand Prix. With blood seeping from the bandages on his head, the determined driver finished in fourth place.

Niki Lauda

J
K
L

Giovanni Lavaggi

However, the crash had shaken him to the extent that he pulled out of the Japanese Grand Prix later that year because of torrential rain, which he claimed was too dangerous to drive in. It was a decision that lost him the title to James Hunt.

However, in 1977, Lauda won the championship back, but then left Ferrari because he felt the team had not supported him after his crash the previous season.

From there, Lauda moved to Brabham where he finished fourth in the championship in 1978. The following year, though, he struggled with an uncompetitive car and announced his retirement, saying he was "tired of driving around in circles".

He then formed his own airline, Lauda Air, with him as one of the pilots. In order for this new company to grow, though, Lauda needed to raise some capital, so he returned to Formula One, after signing with McLaren for a reputed US$5 million.

In 1984, Lauda won the championship for the third time, just beating his teammate Alain Prost. Lauda then retired from racing for good in 1985.

After that, he returned to running his airline, until that was taken over by Austrian Airlines in 1999. He was in charge of the Jaguar Formula One team from 2001 to 2002 and has also been a television commentator, and has written a number of books. In 2003, Lauda formed a new, low-cost airline called Niki.

Roger LAURENT

Nationality: Belgian
Born: 21st February 1913
Died: 6th February 1997
Seasons: 1952
Team/manufacturer(s): HWM, Ferrari
Grands Prix: 2
Race wins: 0
Championship wins: 0

Roger Laurent was born in Liege and was the Belgian motor-cycle champion no less than five times. As a driver for the Ecurie Belgique team, he also proved to be successful on four wheels, and stayed with the team when it became Ecurie Francorchamps.

It was with this outfit that Laurent entered two Grands Prix in 1952. For the first, the team's Ferrari T500 wasn't available so Laurent hired an HWM and drove it to a 12th place finish at his home Grand Prix. He did somewhat better in the Ferrari, coming sixth at the German Grand Prix at the Nürburgring.

Laurent continued to compete, mainly in sportscar events until 1956, when he retired from the sport.

Giovanni LAVAGGI

Nationality: Italian
Born: 18th February 1958
Seasons: 1995-1996
Team/manufacturer(s): Pacific, Minardi
Grands Prix: 10
Race wins: 0
Championship wins: 0

Giovanni Lavaggi was born in Sicily to a respected family and grew up to be a consultant engineer in Italy before starting his own insurance business. Although he dabbled in the sport, he didn't start racing seriously until he was in his thirties.

Then, using his own money, he competed in sportscar racing, followed by a stint in Formula 3000. However, like many enthusiasts, he really wanted to race in Formula One and his chance came in 1995. It was then Lavaggi bought a drive with the Pacific team and competed in four Grands Prix that year, retiring from them all.

The next year, he moved to Minardi but had little success, with his best result of six Grands Prix being a 10th place in Hungary. He simply couldn't realise the car's true potential and drove too slowly.

Lavaggi continued to compete in sportscar events with rather more success and went on to form his own team.

Christopher J (Chris) LAWRENCE

Nationality: British
Born: 27th July 1933
Seasons: 1966
Team/manufacturer(s): Cooper
Grands Prix: 2
Race wins: 0
Championship wins: 0

London-born Chris Lawrence ran his own engine-tuning business and enjoyed racing Morgans at the weekend in the 1950s and 1960s, with more than a little success. Indeed, in 1960, he won 21 out of 22 races in the Fred Dixon Trophy.

He then moved into single-seater racing, building his own Formula Junior car for the 1960 season. By 1966, he was able to enter two World Championship Grands Prix, driving a Cooper-Ferrari special. He finished 11th at the British Grand Prix and retired from the German event with suspension failure.

Lawrence maintained his connections with Morgans, building the company engines. Later, he moved to the USA where he tuned and prepared historic racing cars. After moving back to the UK in the early 1990s he went to work for Morgan and was involved in the development of the new Aero 8 car.

Michel LECLÈRE

Nationality: French
Born: 18th March 1946
Seasons: 1975-1976
Team/manufacturer(s): Tyrrell, Wolf
Grands Prix: 8
Race wins: 0
Championship wins: 0

Michel Leclère performed well in Formule Renault and Formula 3 in the early 1970s, winning the French championship in the latter in 1973.

He then moved to Formula 2 the following year and

continued to prove himself as a talented driver, winning several races. This led to a one-off drive with the Tyrrell Formula One team at the 1975 US Grand Prix at Watkins Glen. Sadly, his Ford engine gave up after just five laps and he was out of the race.

The following year, Leclère drove for the underfunded Wolf-Williams team but without much success. Out of seven Grands Prix, the best finish he could manage was 10th place in Spain. He left the team halfway through the season.

Leclère then returned to Formula 2 where he did much better, although he had a bad year in 1977 and retired from the sport soon after. He later ran a garage in Paris and worked as a driving instructor.

Neville LEDERLE

Nationality: South African
Born: 25th September 1938
Seasons: 1962, 1965
Team/manufacturer(s): Lotus
Grands Prix: 2
Race wins: 0
Championship wins: 0

Neville Lederle came to Europe in the late 1950s and worked at a Volkswagen dealership in London. Before long, he was racing a Beetle at club level and making a good job of it. On his return to South Africa, he continued to race in a Porsche 356.

Lederle then came back to England and raced a Lotus 20

in 1960, taking it back home the following year. There he entered the South African Formula One series which gave him the chance to enter the country's World Championship Grand Prix that year. Driving the Lotus, he finished in an impressive sixth place, scoring a championship point.

Soon after, he broke his leg in an accident and wanted to retire from racing, but he found himself driving at the South African Grand Prix again in 1965. However, his heart wasn't in it and his car was dated, so he failed to qualify. Lederle went on to run his own Volkswagen dealership in South Africa before retiring.

Geoffrey (Geoff) LEES

Nationality: British
Born: 1st May 1951
Seasons: 1978-1980, 1982
Team/manufacturer(s): Ensign, Tyrrell, Shadow, RAM, Theodore, Lotus
Grands Prix: 12
Race wins: 0
Championship wins: 0

Born in Warwickshire, Geoff Lees won the Formula Ford Championship in the mid-1970s and then worked his way up through Formula 3 and Formula 2.

His Formula One career began in 1978, when he drove a non-works Ensign at the British Grand Prix but failed to qualify. The following year he entered the same race, this time for Tyrrell and impressed by finishing in seventh place.

This led to a drive with Shadow in 1980 but the team was struggling and Lees had little chance, so he moved to RAM at the end of the season. Out of eight Grands Prix, he failed to qualify for six, retired from one and came a lowly 13th at the South African Grand Prix.

He had another chance in Formula One for 1982, when he drove for Theodore at the Canadian Grand Prix but crashed out of the race. Driving a Lotus as the French Grand Prix later that year, he finished 12th.

Lees went on to have more success in sportscar racing and continued driving, on and off, into the 21st century before retiring.

Arthur LEGAT

Nationality: Belgian
Born: 1st November 1898
Died: 23rd February 1960
Seasons: 1953
Team/manufacturer(s): Veritas
Grands Prix: 1
Race wins: 0
Championship wins: 0

Arthur Legat was a garage owner from Belgium who began racing in the 1920s, and was one of the first drivers to compete on the Belgian Chimay circuit. Indeed, he ended up driving there no less than 25 times over 30 years, winning the Grand Prix des Frontieres twice in a Bugatti.

After the Second World War, Legat continued to race and bought himself a Veritas-Meteor in 1951. It was this car that he entered into the 1953 Belgian Grand Prix at the Spa-Francorchamps circuit. Unfortunately, transmission problems put him out of the race right at the start.

Legat continued to race his car for the next few years, but never again entered a World Championship Grand Prix.

Jyrki JÄRVILEHTO (JJ Lehto)

Nationality: Finnish
Born: 31st January 1966
Seasons: 1989-1994
Team/manufacturer(s): Onyx, Scuderia Italia, Sauber, Benetton
Grands Prix: 70
Race wins: 0
Championship wins: 0

His real name is Jyrki Järvilehto but this Finnish driver has always been known as simply JJ Lehto. He began karting at the age of six and was soon winning races. He then had a spell in rallying before moving on to Formula Ford and then British Formula 3 in 1988, winning the championship that year.

That success led to a test with Ferrari before joining the Onyx team for the end of the 1989 season. He then moved to Scuderia Italia for the next two years and had his best result, when he came third at the 1991 San Marino Grand Prix.

A move to Sauber in 1993 gave Lehto a mixed season but he did well enough to pick up five championship points after a fifth and a fourth place finish.

In 1994, Lehto drove for Benetton but an accident during testing at Silverstone left him injured and he missed the first two races of the season. He was then replaced after the Canadian Grand Prix and went to drive for Sauber at the end of the season.

Lehto went on to race in touring cars, GTs, sportscars and

JJ Lehto

in the CART series. He has won the Le Mans 24 Hour and the Sebring 12 Hours races. He later worked as a television commentator.

Lamberto LEONI

Nationality: Italian
Born: 24th May 1953
Seasons: 1977-1978
Team/manufacturer(s): Surtees, Ensign
Grands Prix: 5
Race wins: 0
Championship wins: 0

After winning the Formula Italia series, Lamberto Leoni worked his way through Formula 3 and Formula 2 and proved to be a competent driver.

In 1977, he had his first chance at Formula One, when he drove a hired Surtees TS19 at the Italian Grand Prix. Unfortunately, though, he failed to qualify.

The next year he drove for the Ensign team but after a disappointing start to the season he left after just four Grands Prix.

Leoni went back to racing in Formula 2 and Formula 3000, and later formed his own team. He also had a successful career as a powerboat racer.

Alfred Lazarus FINGLESTON (Les Leston)

Nationality: English
Born: 16th December 1920
Seasons: 1956-1957
Team/manufacturer(s): Connaught, Cooper, BRM
Grands Prix: 3
Race wins: 0
Championship wins: 0

Born Alfred Lazarus Fingleston, but known as Les Leston, he was born in Nottingham and began racing after the Second World War, first in a Jaguar before moving to single-seater competition. By the early 1950s he was winning races in Formula 3 and he was British Champion in 1954.

Guy Ligier

His Formula One debut came in 1956, when he raced a Connaught at the Italian Grand Prix at Monza, but he retired with suspension trouble after just six laps.

The following year he drove a Cooper-Climax at the Monaco Grand Prix but did not qualify. Later that season he entered a BRM in the British Grand Prix at Aintree but had to retire with engine failure after 44 laps.

Leston went on to race in saloon cars and rallies in the 1960s. He won the British Saloon Car Championship in 1958. He also started his own racewear and car accessory business and worked as a broadcaster in Hong Kong.

Pierre Levegh

Pierre BOUILLON (Pierre Levegh)

Nationality: French
Born: 22nd December 1905
Died 11th June 1955
Seasons: 1950-1951
Team/manufacturer(s): Lago-Talbot
Grands Prix: 6
Race wins: 0
Championship wins: 0

Born Pierre Bouillon in Paris, he took the name Levegh in memory of his uncle, who had been a racing driver in the 1900s. Pierre was a successful ice hockey and tennis player as well as a driver.

Before the Second World War, he competed in the Le Mans 24 Hour race in 1938. After the war, he continued to do the annual race at Le Mans and also enjoyed some single-seater racing.

In particular, Levegh competed in six World Championship Formula One Grands Prix, driving for Lago-Talbot between 1950 and 1951. He finished three of the races, with his best result being seventh place at the 1950 Belgian Grand Prix.

Levegh's real love, however, was Le Mans. Tragically, though, he was killed during the 1955 race, when his Mercedes Benz 300 SLR hit an earth bank and flew into a crowd of spectators, killing 82 other people. It was one of motorsport's blackest days and marked the end of Mercedes' involvement in racing for 30 years.

Jack LEWIS

Nationality: British
Born: 1st November 1936
Died: 11th June 1955
Seasons: 1961-1962
Team/manufacturer(s): Cooper, BRM
Grands Prix: 10
Race wins: 0
Championship wins: 0

Jack – or Jackie – Lewis was born in Gloucestershire to Welsh parents. His father ran a motorcycle dealership so he was exposed to all things mechanical from an early age.

Lewis's race career began in 1958 when he competed in Formula 3, winning three races that season and moving to Formula 2 the following year. By 1960 he had won the British Championship.

The following year, with sponsorship from his father's company, Lewis campaigned a Cooper-Climax in Formula One, starting at the Belgian Grand Prix. At Monza that year, he finished in a respectable fourth place.

In 1962, he continued to race his Cooper, as well as a BRM, and entered five Grands Prix. However, he didn't have much success and so didn't finish the season.

Lewis later ran a sheep farm in Wales and then his father's garage business in Stroud.

Stuart LEWIS-EVANS

Nationality: British
Born: 20th April 1930
Died: 25th October 1958
Seasons: 1957-1958
Team/manufacturer(s): Connaught, Vanwall
Grands Prix: 14
Race wins: 0
Championship wins: 0

Stuart Lewis-Evans' father was a successful Formula 3 driver, and he soon followed in his footsteps, driving in the same series and proving himself to be very talented.

Before long, Lewis-Evans was competing in Formula One, driving a Connaught at the Monaco Grand Prix and finishing in fourth place. This led to a place with the Vanwall team for the rest of the season and the following. High points included fifth place at Pescara in 1957 and Britain in 1958, and third in Belgium and Portugal in 1958.

He was undoubtedly a talented driver but, sadly, his career was cut short. At the end of the 1958 season he was racing in Morocco Grand Prix when his car's engine seized and he hit the barrier at high speed. The car burst into flames and Lewis-Evans was killed.

Guy LIGIER

Nationality: French
Born: 12th July 1930
Seasons: 1966-1967
Team/manufacturer(s): Cooper, Brabham
Grands Prix: 13
Race wins: 0
Championship wins: 0

Guy Ligier was born in Vichy and grew up an orphan, working first in a butcher's shop then in the construction industry. Before getting into motor racing he played rugby for his country.

His motorsport career began once his business, which involved building French autoroutes, gave him the money to indulge himself. After a spell in endurance racing in the early 1960s, Ligier moved to Formula 2.

He spent just two seasons in Formula One, at first driving his own Cooper-Maserati T81, but he had little success in 1966, his first year and had to sit out the tail-end of the season after breaking his kneecap in a crash.

The following year, he picked up a more competitive car, a Brabham-Repco, and entered seven Grands Prix. The highpoint of the year was finishing in sixth place at the German Grand Prix and gaining his one and only Championship point.

Ligier went on to form his own car company which also ran its own Formula One team.

Roberto LIPPI

Nationality: Italian
Born: 17th October 1926
Seasons: 1961-1963
Team/manufacturer(s): De Tomaso
Grands Prix: 3
Race wins: 0
Championship wins: 0

Roberto Lippi was born in Rome and became well-known as a sportscar driver in the 1950s, and was the Italian 750cc Sportscar Champion in 1957.

He then moved to Formula Junior and won the title in the series' inaugural season, which was 1958. Lippi stayed with Formula Junior through to 1963, but also entered some Formula One races.

However, he only competed in three World Championship events, which were his home Grands Prix each year from 1961 to 1963. For each, Lippi drove a De Tomaso OSCA 4. The first year he was out of the race after just one lap with engine problems. The second and third years, meanwhile, he failed to qualify.

Stuart Lewis-Evans

Tonio Liuzzi

Lippi retired from racing soon after that. However, he worked as a racing instructor and, in particular, worked with getting disabled people in racecars.

Vitantonio (Tonio) LIUZZI

Nationality: Italian
Born: 6th August 1981
Seasons: 2005-
Team/manufacturer(s): Red Bull, Toro Rosso
Grands Prix: 39
Race wins: 0
Championship wins: 0

Italian Vitantonio Liuzzi began racing karts at the age of 10 and won the Italian Karting Championship three years later. Then, in 2001, he won the World Karting Championship.

From there he moved on to Formula Renault, then Formula 3000. In 2004 he won seven out of 10 races in Formula 3000 series and walked away with the title.

This led to some test drives with Formula One teams and Liuzzi finally got a position with Red Bull for 2005, primarily as a test driver, but he also raced in four Grands Prix, coming a respectable eighth in his first race at San Marino.

The following year, Red Bull bought the Minardi team and renamed it Scuderia Toro Rosso (Team Red Bull) with Liuzzi as a driver. His best result in the 2006 season was an eighth place at the US Grand Prix, winning the team its one and only Championship point that year. Liuzzi remained with Toro Rosso for 2007 and 2008.

Maria Grazia (Lella) LOMBARDI

Nationality: Italian
Born: 26th March 1941
Died: 3rd March 1992
Seasons: 1974-1976
Team/manufacturer(s): Brabham, Williams, March, RAM
Grands Prix: 17
Race wins: 0
Championship wins: 0

Born Maria Grazia Lombardi but better known as Lella

Lella Lombardi

Lombardi, this Italian driver began racing from an early age, working her way through touring cars and single-seaters.

She performed well in Formula 3 and Formula 5000 in the early 1970s, and Lombardi then entered her first Grand Prix in 1974. It was the British event at Brands Hatch but she failed to qualify, driving an old Brabham. However, she did well enough in Formula 5000 that year for March to sign her for the 1975 season.

It was in that year that she came sixth in the Spanish Grand Prix and was (and still is at the time of writing) the only female Formula One driver in history to finish in the top six of a World Championship race. Sadly, because the race was shortened, Lombardi only received half a Championship point for her achievement.

After a one-off race with Williams, Lombardi stayed with March for the 1976 season but was dropped by the team after just one Grand Prix. She then entered three races later in the year with RAM but with little success.

Lombardi went on to return to sportscar racing and performed well. Sadly, she died of cancer at the age of just 50.

Ricardo LONDOÑO-BRIDGE
Nationality: Colombian
Born: 8th August 1949
Seasons: 1981
Team/manufacturer(s): Ensign
Grands Prix: 1
Race wins: 0
Championship wins: 0

You may think that Ricardo Londoño-Bridge is a joke name but, in fact, it appears to be an amalgamation of his parents' surnames, although he is also known as plain Ricardo Londoño.

In the 1970s he raced stock cars and motorcycles in his native Colombia. Later, he got involved in endurance racing and took part in the Sebring 12 Hours, Daytona 250 miles and others. He also raced in the Can-Am Championship, with his own team, Londoño-Bridge Racing.

He had the money to buy into Formula One and so got a place with the struggling Ensign team in 1981. He was entered into the second Grand Prix of the season, in Brazil, and took part in the acclimatisation practice season beforehand. However, because of his lack of experience, the FIA refused to give him the required super-licence and he was unable to enter the official practice sessions or the race. However, he was entered into the Grand Prix. Londoño-Bridge later returned to endurance racing and also competed in Formula 2.

Ernst LOOF
Nationality: German
Born: 4th July 1907
Died: 3rd March 1956
Seasons: 1953
Team/manufacturer(s): Veritas
Grands Prix: 1
Race wins: 0
Championship wins: 0

Ernst Loof was born in Neindorf and grew up to be an incredibly successful motorcycle racer before the Second World War, winning the German Motorcycle Championship eight times. After the war, he worked with Lorenz Dietrich to form Veritas, the company that produced the successful racecars of the same name, based on BMW 328s.

Loof raced one of his own creations in the 1953 German Grand Prix at the Nürburgring but retired right at the start of the race with a faulty fuel pump. It's interesting to note that seven other Veritas cars entered the same race.

He went on to do some rallying and continued to develop racecars. Sadly, though, he died of a brain tumour in 1956.

Henri LOUVEAU

Nationality: French
Born: 25th January 1910
Died: 7th January 1991
Seasons: 1950-1951
Team/manufacturer(s): Talbot
Grands Prix: 2
Race wins: 0
Championship wins: 0

Born in Paris, Henri Louveau dabbled in motorsport prior to the Second World War, while he was working as a test driver for Fiat in France. Among others, he entered the Le Mans 24 Hour and the Liege-Rome-Liege races.

After serving in the French Army, Louveau bought an old pre-war Maserati 6CM and began racing it in various races in his home country, with some success. He later acquired a Delage and continued to do well in it, including entering it in the 1949 Le Mans 24 Hour and finishing second.

Louveau's first attempt at a World Championship Grand Prix was at the end of the 1950 season, when he drove a 4.5-litre Talbot Lago in the Italian Grand Prix, but retired with brake failure after 16 laps.

The following year, he entered the same car into the Swiss Grand Prix but crashed the car on lap 30; luckily he was uninjured.

Louveau retired from racing soon after and continued to run his Paris garage which specialised in Delages and Maseratis. He also had a successful car-hire business.

John Maxwell Lineha LOVE

Nationality: Rhodesian
Born: 7th December 1924
Died: 25th April 2005
Seasons: 1962-1972
Team/manufacturer(s): Cooper, Brabham, Lotus, March, Surtees
Grands Prix: 10
Race wins: 0
Championship wins: 0

Born in Bulawayo in Southern Rhodesia, John Love raced motorcycles in the 1950s, before moving on to cars, starting with a pre-war Riley and then a Jaguar D-Type.

Love went to the UK in 1961 and 1962 to compete in Formula Junior. He then returned home and began to race in the South African Formula One series, which included the World Championship South African Grand Prix, which he first entered driving a Cooper.

In 1964 he missed the South African Grand Prix, but did enter the Italian one, but didn't qualify. However, he did much better back home and won the South African Championship that year – a feat he would go on to repeat no less than six times.

From 1965 to 1972, he entered the South African Grand Prix each year and these were the only World Championship races he did. However, despite his amazing success in the local series, he had little luck in his home Grand Prix, with the notable exception of 1967, when he drove his Cooper-

Climax to a second place finish at Kyalami.

After 1972, Love retired from the sport and returned to his hometown of Bulawayo where he ran a car and motorcycle dealership before dying of cancer in 2005.

Gerard Carlton (Pete) LOVELY

Nationality: American
Born: 11th April 1926
Seasons: 1959, 1969-1971
Team/manufacturer(s): Lotus
Grands Prix: 9
Race wins: 0
Championship wins: 0

Pete Lovely was born in Montana and first made a name for himself when he became SCCA Sportscar Champion in 1955. A couple of years later he came to Europe to race and ended up winning his class at the 1958 Reims Grand Prix.

The following year, Lovely made his Formula One debut, when he entered the Monaco Grand Prix, driving a Lotus. Sadly, though, he failed to qualify and that appeared to be the end of his Formula One career. He returned to the USA to run a Volkswagen dealership in Seattle.

However, 10 years later Lovely returned to Formula One, driving a Lotus 49 at the US Grand Prix at Watkins Glen in 1969, followed by the Mexican Grand Prix the same season. The following two seasons saw Lovely compete in selected Grands Prix around the world, but with little success. He then returned to the USA again and built up a business restoring and maintaining historic racecars, and he enjoyed racing the cars as well.

Roger LOYER

Nationality: French
Born: 5th August 1907
Died: 24th March 1988
Seasons: 1954
Team/manufacturer(s): Gordini
Grands Prix: 1
Race wins: 0
Championship wins: 0

Roger Loyer was born in Paris and grew up to be a successful motorcycle racer before the Second World War, a career he continued to excel in after the end of hostilities.

However, after the war he also competed on four wheels, starting with an Amilcar in 1945 and moving on to a Delahaye. By the early 1950s, Loyer was competing in sportscar races, driving for Gordini.

This lead to a chance to enter the 1954 Argentinean Grand Prix, driving a Gordini T16 Formula 2 car. Unfortunately, though, he was unable to finish the race because low oil pressure forced him to retire after 19 laps.

Loyer raced less after that, although he continued to compete at a low level throughout the 1950s. He later developed and patented various devices for cars.

Jean LUCAS

Nationality: French
Born: 25th April 1917
Died: 27th September 2003
Seasons: 1955
Team/manufacturer(s): Gordini
Grands Prix: 1
Race wins: 0
Championship wins: 0

Frenchman Jean Lucas must have had racing in his blood, because he was born in Le Mans. He began his sporting career as a rally driver before the Second World War. After the war, he turned to sportscar racing, with great success.

In 1953, Lucas became the manager of the Gordini team and this led to the occasion stint behind the wheel, including entering one World Championship event, the 1955 Italian Grand Prix. However, he was forced to retire with engine problems after just seven laps.

The following year, Lucas was badly injured when he crashed a Maserati 250F in Morocco and so retired from the sport. However, he continued to take an interest in racing and, in 1962, he started the French magazine, Sport-Auto, and from there built up a success publishing business.

Jean LUCIENBONNET

Nationality: French
Born: 7th January 1923
Died: 19th August 1962
Seasons: 1959
Team/manufacturer(s): Cooper
Grands Prix: 1
Race wins: 0
Championship wins: 0

Born Jean Bonnet in Nice, he changed his name to Lucienbonnet (also written as Lucien Bonnet) in deference to his brother. He competed in a variety of disciplines after the Second World War, including rallying, sportscars, Formula Junior and Formula 2. He drove for Cooper in the latter during the late 1950s and early 1960s.

Lucienbonnet's one and only World Championship race was the 1959 Monaco Grand Prix, which he entered in his own Cooper T45 but failed to qualify for the race proper.

Tragically, Lucienbonnet was killed in 1962 when he crashed during a Formula Junior race in Sicily.

Robert Brett (Brett) LUNGER

Nationality: American
Born: 14th November 1945
Seasons: 1975-1978
Team/manufacturer(s): Hesketh, Surtees, March, McLaren, Ensign
Grands Prix: 42
Race wins: 0
Championship wins: 0

Brett Lunger was part of the wealthy DuPont family in the USA and so had the money to work his way through motorsport.

After serving as a Marine in the Vietnam War, he returned to racing in 1971 and he went from Formula 5000 and Formula 2, then finally to Formula One.

His first three Grands Prix were at the end of the 1975 season, driving for Hesketh, with his best result being 10th place in Italy. Lunger then went on to drive for Surtees through the 1976 season, but had little success; he did, though, make the news as one of the drivers who helped to pull Niki Lauda from his burning car at the German Grand Prix.

The next two seasons Lunger drove Marches and McLarens for privateer teams and drove for Ensign but, again, failed to perform as well as hoped.

Lunger later tried his hand at sportscar racing before retiring from the sport to concentrate on working with DuPont and enjoying road-bike racing.

M

MACDOWEL, Mike
MACKAY-FRASER, Herbert
MACKLIN, Lance
MAGEE, Damien
MAGGS, Tony
MAGLIOLI, Umberto
MAGNUSSEN, Jan
MAIRESSE, Guy
MAIRESSE, Willy
MANSELL, Nigel
MANTOVANI, Sergio
MANZON, Robert
MARIMON, Onofre
MARKO, Helmut
MARQUES, Tarso
MARR, Leslie
MARSH, Tony
MARTIN, Eugene
MARTINI, Pierluigi
MASS, Jochen
MASSA, Felipe
MAY, Michael
MAYER, Tim
MAZZACANE, Gaston
MAZET, François
McALPINE, Kenneth
McCARTHY, Perry

McGUIRE, Brian
McLAREN, Bruce
McNISH, Allan
McRAE, Graham
MENDITEGUY, Carlos
MERKEL, Harry
MERZARIO, Arturo
MIERES, Roberto
MIGAULT, François
MILES, John
MILHOUX, Andre
MITTER, Gerhard
MODENA, Stefano
MONTAGNY, Franck
MONTEIRO, Tiago
MONTERMINI, Andrea
MONTGOMERIE-CHARRINGTON, Robin
MONTOYA, Juan Pablo
MORBIDELLI, Gianni
MORENO, Roberto
MORGAN, Dave
MOSER, Silvio
MOSS, Bill
MOSS, Stirling
MUNARON, Gino
MURRAY, David
MUSSO, Luigi

Felipe Massa

Michael George Hartwell (Mike) MACDOWEL
Nationality: British
Born: 13th September 1932
Seasons: 1957
Team/manufacturer(s): Cooper
Grands Prix: 1
Race wins: 0
Championship wins: 0

Norfolk-born Mike MacDowel was an amateur racing driver who raced a Lotus to great effect in the mid-1950s. He then went on to drive for Cooper in 1956.

It was with Cooper that he entered his one and only World Championship event, the 1957 French Grand Prix on 7th July of that year. He shared the Cooper-Climax T43 with Jack Brabham and, after qualifying in 15th place, the pair worked their way up to a very respectable seventh place finish, just missing out on Championship points.

Not long after, MacDowel had a break from competition but, in the late 1960s he became involved in hillclimbs and won the RAC Championship twice in the early 1970s, driving a 5-litre Brabham BT36X. He continued to hillclimb into the 1990s. He also worked as a property manager and has been a director of the British Racing Drivers' Club.

Herbert MACKAY-FRASER
Nationality: American
Born: 23rd June 1927
Died: 14th July 1957
Seasons: 1957
Team/manufacturer(s): BRM
Grands Prix: 1
Race wins: 0
Championship wins: 0

Herbert MacKay-Fraser was an American born in Brazil, where his father ran a coffee plantation. However, he spent most of his childhood in Connecticut, USA.

With the money to do so, MacKay-Fraser travelled to Europe in 1955 to race his Ferrari Monza and went on to drive Lotuses for the next two seasons.

In 1957, he was asked to drive for BRM in the French Grand Prix, because the team was short of a driver. He got off to a good start and was sixth in the race for a while but then had to retire after 24 laps with transmission problems.

MacKay-Fraser could have been a successful driver, but it was not to be. Just a week after his Grand Prix debut, he was racing a Lotus 11 at Reims when he crashed and was killed. He was the first team driver from Lotus to die.

Lance MACKLIN
Nationality: British
Born: 2nd September 1919
Died: 29th August 2002
Seasons: 1952-1955
Team/manufacturer(s): HWM, Maserati
Grands Prix: 15
Race wins: 0
Championship wins: 0

Lance Macklin was born in London, the son of Sir Noel Macklin who ran the Invicta car company. It was in an Invicta that Macklin started competing after the Second World War.

Before long, he was driving for HWM, from 1950, and entered his first Formula One Grand Prix in 1952. This was the Swiss race at the start of the season and he went on to

Lance Macklin

In the same year, he competed in the British and German Grands Prix, driving a Lotus-Climax and performed well enough to gain a place on the Cooper team for the next two seasons. It was a good move as he gained four podium finishes, including a second place in France, in his first season alone. He repeated the same result at the French Grand Prix the following year.

After a season with BRM in 1964, Maggs wound down his World Championship appearances and only competed in the South African Grand Prix, driving a Lotus, in 1965.

A year later, Maggs was involved in a tragic accident when his car hit a young boy who was standing in a prohibited area at a racetrack in South Africa. This episode was so upsetting that Maggs retired from racing and became a farmer in his home country.

Umberto MAGLIOLI

Nationality: Italian
Born: 5th June 1928
Died: 7th February 1999
Seasons: 1953-1956
Team/manufacturer(s): Ferrari, Maserati
Grands Prix: 9
Race wins: 0
Championship wins: 0

Italian Umberto Maglioli made his name as a sportscar driver in the early 1950s, most notably by winning the 1953 Targa Florio and then, the following year, the Carrera Panamericana.

However, he also dabbled in single-seater racing, with his first Formula One appearance being at his home Grand Prix in 1953, when he drove a Ferrari to an eighth place finish.

Over the next three years he competed in a handful of

do most of the Grands Prix that year.

He stayed with HWM but only competed in a few more Grands Prix between then and 1955, not scoring any Championship points.

During this time Macklin was also competing in endurance races and finished third at Le Mans in 1954, driving an Aston Martin. The following year he again entered the 24 Hour race but it ended in tragedy when he tried to avoid hitting Mike Hawthorn and ended up colliding with Pierre Levegh, causing the Frenchman's car to leave the track and kill 80 spectators.

Although Macklin continued to race for a short time, another accident later in the season made him decide to quit. He later spent time running a fish-and-chip shop in New Zealand and then moved to Spain as an exporter. He later returned to the UK where he died.

Damien MAGEE

Nationality: British
Born: 17th November 1945
Seasons: 1975-1976
Team/manufacturer(s): Williams, RAM
Grands Prix: 2
Race wins: 0
Championship wins: 0

Damien Magee was born in Belfast and was a successful

driver in Formula Ford during the early 1970s.

Always struggling for money and sponsorship, he competed in some non-championship Formula One races in the mid-1970s. He then finally got his chance to enter a World Championship race in 1975. That was when Williams asked him to replace Arturo Merzario for the Swedish Grand Prix. After starting 22nd on the grid in a Williams FW03, Magee worked his way up to a 14th place finish.

The following year Magee tried to enter a Brabham run by the RAM team in the French Grand Prix but he failed to qualify.

Magee continued to compete at various levels for some years before retiring to London, where he enjoyed racing in historic events.

Anthony Francis O'Connell (Tony) MAGGS

Nationality: South African
Born: 9th February 1937
Seasons: 1961-1965
Team/manufacturer(s): Lotus, Cooper, BRM
Grands Prix: 26
Race wins: 0
Championship wins: 0

Tony Maggs was born in Pretoria, the son of a wealthy farmer. After racing in an Austin Healey at home, he travelled to England in 1959, where he was joint winner of the 1961 Formula Junior Championship.

Jan Magnussen

Grands Prix, including the Italian one each season. The high point of his Formula One career was coming third in the Italian Grand Prix in 1954. The following year he shared a third place finish in the Argentinean Grand Prix.

In 1956, Maglioli drove a Maserati in just three Grands Prix, but more importantly he drove a Porsche to victory at the Targa Florio, the start of a long association with the team which would see him win the race again 12 years later.

Jan MAGNUSSEN

Nationality: Danish
Born: 4th July 1973
Seasons: 1995, 1997-1998
Team/manufacturer(s): McLaren, Stewart
Grands Prix: 25
Race wins: 0
Championship wins: 0

As a boy, Danish driver Jan Magnussen was a talented kart racer, winning the Danish Championship at the age of 12 and then going on to taking the World Championship when he was just 14 – the youngest person to do so – and won it twice more in subsequent years.

Before long, Magnussen had moved to Formula 3 and, in 1994, he took the British Championship after winning no less than 14 out of 18 races that season.

The end of the following season saw Magnussen make his Formula One debut, driving for McLaren at the 1995 Pacific Grand Prix and finishing 10th.

After a season in CART, Magnussen returned to Formula One in 1997 driving for Steward, but he failed to perform well enough for the team and he was dropped partway through the 1998 season. Ironically, this was after he'd scored his one and only Championship point, when he came sixth in Canada.

Magnussen went on to compete in sportscars and touring cars, and has been a regular at the Le Mans 24 Hour and the 12 Hours of Sebring since 1999.

Guy MAIRESSE

Nationality: French
Born: 10th August 1910
Died: 24th April 1954
Seasons: 1950-1951
Team/manufacturer(s): Talbot
Grands Prix: 3
Race wins: 0
Championship wins: 0

Frenchman Guy Mairesse ran his own haulage company and began racing soon after the end of the Second World War. Before long, he was winning races in his own Delahaye. By 1950, he had come second at the Le Mans 24 Hour race, driving a Talbot; a success he matched the following year.

Mairesse's short Formula One career was also in a Talbot. He entered the Italian Grand Prix at the end of the 1950 season and, after starting from 11th on the grid he retired after 42 laps with an oil leak. He went on to race in the Swiss and French Grands Prix the following season and finished ninth in the latter event.

After this, business matters kept Mairesse too busy to race much, although he made the occasional appearance whenever he could. Sadly, in 1954 he crashed his car during the Coupes de Paris and was killed, along with a six-year-old boy who was spectating.

Willy MAIRESSE

Nationality: Belgian
Born: 1st October 1928
Died: 9th September 1969
Seasons: 1960-1963
Team/manufacturer(s): Ferrari, Lotus
Grands Prix: 12
Race wins: 0
Championship wins: 0

Willy Mairesse was a latecomer to racing, starting at the age of 25 when he entered the 1953 Liege-Paris-Liege race with a friend. He entered it again the next two years and won his class in 1955.

Willy Mairesse

MNO

After a few more years in sportscars, Mairesse was signed by Ferrari for the 1960 Formula One season. He competed in three Grands Prix that year, and scored points in Italy, where he finished in third place.

The following year, he drove for Lotus in the Monaco Grand Prix before returning to Ferrari for two more Grands Prix that year. Again, he scored Championship points in Italy, when he finished fourth.

In 1963, Mairesse again competed in three Grands Prix before an accident at the German race put him out for the rest of the season and finished his Formula One career.

Mairesse continued to race sportscars until a bad accident at the Le Mans 24 Hour in 1968 left him badly injured. With no prospect of being able to race again, he took his own life in 1969.

Nigel Ernest James MANSELL, OBE

Nationality: British
Born: 8th August 1953
Seasons: 1980-1995
Team/manufacturer(s): Lotus, Williams, Ferrari, McLaren
Grands Prix: 187
Race wins: 31
Championship wins: 1

Nigel Mansell gained his first kart licence at the age of 10, even though the minimum age was 11, and won his first race when he was 14.

He later invested £15 in a day's Formula Ford training and, by 1977, he was Formula Ford Champion. That was despite breaking his neck in an accident during testing; an injury that doctors said would cost him his racing career. Ignoring the advice to rest, Mansell sneaked out of hospital and raced on!

Nigel Mansell

Robert Manzon

Determined to work his way up to Formula One, Mansell and his wife, sold their house and most of their belongings to fund a season in Formula Three for 1978. He came second in the championship, which secured him a place as a paid driver with Lotus the following year.

This led to a drive with the team's Formula One team from 1980. Mansell spent the next four years with Lotus, but the cars didn't perform well enough for him to realise his full potential, with a third place finish the best he could manage. He left the team to join Williams in 1985.

Armed with better cars, Mansell started to impress, gaining his first victory at Brands Hatch, followed by a second in South Africa. The following season, he performed even better, with five wins and second place in the Drivers' Championship. He missed the championship by just one point, and would have triumphed if it hadn't been for a burst tyre at Adelaide.

Mansell narrowly missed out on the Drivers' Championship again in 1987, when injuries sustained in an accident during qualifying at Suzuka caused him to miss the last race of the season.

After a disappointing 1988 season with Williams, Mansell moved to Ferrari in 1989. He won in Brazil and Hungary and finished fourth in the championship.

Mansell struggled with unreliable cars at Ferrari and returned to Williams for the 1991 season. He finished second that year, but went on to win the Championship in 1992, after a record-breaking five race wins in a row at the start of the season.

The next year, Mansell raced in the CART championship which he ended up winning, making him the only driver in history to hold both the Formula 1 World Championship and CART championship at the same time.

After the death of Ayrton Senna in 1994, Mansell returned to the Williams team for the end of the season and won the final race in Adelaide.

However, he didn't stay with Williams, choosing instead to drive for McLaren in 1995. Unfortunately, he wasn't happy with the cars and announced his retirement from Formula One after just two races.

Since then, Mansell has made some brief returns to racing, including competing in the 1998 British Touring Car Championship, and winning the Grand Prix Master Series race in Kyalami in 2005.

Sergio MANTOVANI

Nationality: Italian
Born: 22nd May 1929
Died: 23rd February 2001
Seasons: 1953-1955
Team/manufacturer(s): Maserati
Grands Prix: 8
Race wins: 0
Championship wins: 0

Born in Milan in 1929, Sergio Mantovani was a successful businessman who began racing as a hobby in sportscars and touring cars.

Before long, though, he began to take it more seriously and bought himself a Maserati. This led, in turn, to a place on the Italian company's works team, driving a 250F.

Mantovani drove in the Italian Grand Prix at the end of 1953, but had to share his car with Luigi Musso, and the pair finished joint seventh.

The following season saw Mantovani enter six Grands Prix, with him picking up Championship points in Germany and Switzerland, where he finished in fifth place both times.

In 1955, Mantovani was retained by Maserati, but he only competed in the first Grand Prix of the season, in Argentina. He crashed in a non-championship race soon after and lost a leg, thus finishing his racing career. However, he retained links with the sport through the Italian Sporting Commission.

Robert MANZON

Nationality: French
Born: 12th April 1917
Seasons: 1950-1956
Team/manufacturer(s): Simca, Gordini, Ferrari
Grands Prix: 28
Race wins: 0
Championship wins: 0

Robert Manzon came from Marseilles and ran a business selling diesel equipment, racing in his spare time. After the Second World War, he competed in a Cisitalia before joining the Gordini team in 1948.

However, for his first two Formula One seasons, he drove a Simca, entering three Grands Prix in 1950 and four the following year.

It was when he began competing in a Gordini, in 1952, that Manzon really showed his colours. He picked up Championship points with a third place finish in Belgium, a fourth in France and a fifth in Holland.

In 1953, Manzon quit the team after just one Grand Prix and went off to race sportscars. However, the following year he drove Ferraris in four Grands Prix, with his best result being a third place in France.

For 1955 and 1956 Manzon returned to Gordini to see out his Formula One career. After that he retired from racing to concentrate on running his business.

Onofre Agustín MARIMÓN

Nationality: Argentinean
Born: 23rd December 1923
Died: 31st July 1954
Seasons: 1951-1953
Team/manufacturer(s): Maserati
Grands Prix: 11
Race wins: 0
Championship wins: 0

Onofre Marimón came from Argentina and was often nicknamed 'Pinocchio' because it was said he resembled the character in the Walt Disney animation.

Like many Argentinean drivers, Marimón came to Europe to further his career. The first time was in 1951, when he competed in the French Grand Prix but retired after just three laps when his Maserati's engine failed.

Marimón then returned to Europe in 1953 and entered six Grands Prix, making a real impact when he finished third in Belgium. Sadly, the rest of the season was less successful.

It was a similar story the next year; Marimón came third in the British Grand Prix at Silverstone, but failed to finish the other three Grands Prix he entered. Tragically, he never finished the season because, during testing for the 1954

German Grand Prix at the Nürburgring, Marimón misjudged a corner and crashed. He was killed instantly and became the first person to die during a World Championship Grand Prix.

Dr Helmut MARKO

Nationality: Austrian
Born: 27th April 1943
Seasons: 1971-1972
Team/manufacturer(s): Ecurie Bonnier, BRM
Grands Prix: 9
Race wins: 0
Championship wins: 0

Helmut Marko studied law at university and gained a doctorate, but decided to pursue a career in racing instead. He worked his way through Super Vee and Formula 3 before moving to sportscars. And it was here that he made a name for himself by winning the Le Mans 24 Hour race in a Porsche in 1971.

However, he also did four Formula One races towards the end of the 1971 season, but with less success. Marko then drove five more Grands Prix the following year, driving for BRM. Then, during the French Grand Prix, a stone flew into his visor and damaged his eye.

Partially blinded, Marko had to retire from racing and so became a barrister. However, he retained links with the sport and ran various racing teams, including Red Bull.

Tarso Anibal Santanna MARQUES

Nationality: Brazilian
Born: 19th January 1976
Seasons: 1996-1997, 2001
Team/manufacturer(s): Minardi
Grands Prix: 24
Race wins: 0
Championship wins: 0

Tarso Marques came from a wealthy Brazilian family and was a talented kart racer as a boy. He then moved on to Formula Chevrolet and won the title in 1992.

By 1994, Marques had moved to Europe to compete in Formula 3000 and was soon testing for Formula One, with the added advantage of being able to bring money to the party. He had his first drives at the start of 1996 with Minardi, but retired from both the Grands Prix he entered. He then spent the rest of the season as a test driver for the team.

In 1997, he competed in 10 Grands Prix with Minardi but made little impression. Marques then left Formula One for a spell in America, racing Champ Cars.

However, he had another go at Formula One in 2001, racing for Minardi as a pay driver again. The best place finish he could manage, though, was ninth.

Marques later returned to Brazil to run and drive for a stock car team.

Leslie MARR

Nationality: British
Born: 14th August 1922
Seasons: 1954-1955
Team/manufacturer(s): Connaught
Grands Prix: 2
Race wins: 0
Championship wins: 0

Leslie Marr was born in Durham in 1922 and worked as a professional artist, racing his Connaught in his spare time

in the post-war years.

He mainly competed in Formula 2 and Libre events, sometimes with excellent results. In 1954, however, he decided to raise the standards and so entered the British Grand Prix at Silverstone. After starting 22nd on the grid he finished in 13th place.

Marr once again entered the British Grand Prix the following year. This time, though, he failed to finish the race, because his brakes failed after 18 laps. In 1956, he took the car to New Zealand where he finished fourth in the country's non-championship Grand Prix, despite starting from the back of the grid.

After retiring from racing, Marr continued to work as an artist and finally retired to Norfolk.

Anthony Ernest (Tony) MARSH

Nationality: British
Born: 20th July 1931
Seasons: 1957-1958, 1961
Team/manufacturer(s): Cooper, Lotus
Grands Prix: 5
Race wins: 0
Championship wins: 0

Tony Marsh was born in Stourbridge and became a successful hillclimber in the early 1950s, winning at championship level.

In 1957, he began to compete in single-seater races, in a Formula 2 Cooper. This led to his first Grand Prix appearance, at the German race that year, where he finished in 13th place, and fourth in the Formula 2 class.

The following year he once again entered the same car into the German Grand Prix and this time came eighth (again, fourth in his class).

After a break from Formula One, Marsh returned in 1961, now in a Lotus 18. With this new car he failed to qualify for the Belgian Grand Prix, retired from the British race and came 15th in Germany.

Marsh then returned to hillclimbs where he once again excelled, winning the British championship three more times, and continuing to compete into his seventies.

Tarso Marques

Nigel Mansell

Jochen Mass

Eugène MARTIN

Nationality: French
Born: 24th March 1915
Seasons: 1950
Team/manufacturer(s): Talbot
Grands Prix: 2
Race wins: 0
Championship wins: 0

Frenchman Eugène Martin was an engineer and a successful single-seater driver before the Second World War when

Pierluigi Martini

Pierluigi MARTINI

Nationality: Italian
Born: 23rd April 1961
Seasons: 1984-1985, 1988-1995
Team/manufacturer(s): Toleman, Minardi, Scuderia Italia
Grands Prix: 124
Race wins: 0
Championship wins: 0

Pierluigi Martini worked his way up to Formula 3, where he won the European Championship in 1983. This then led to a drive for Toleman in the 1984 Italian Grand Prix, but Martini failed to qualify.

The following year, though, Martini got a full season's drive with the then new Minardi team. However, he left them at the end of the year and went to race in Formula 3000 and came close to winning the championship.

By 1988, Martini was back in Formula One, driving for Minardi again. At his first race that season, the US East

he competed in Grand Prix races.

After the war he returned to racing, behind the wheel of a BMW/Frazer-Nash special that he'd developed himself, and won some races at Grand Prix level.

When the World Championship began in 1950, Martin competed in two of the new Formula One Grands Prix, driving a factory Lago Talbot. He began at the British Grand Prix – the first-ever World Championship race – but had to retire after just eight laps because of low oil pressure.

Next, Martin raced at the Swiss Grand Prix at Bremgarten. Sadly, though, he crashed on the 19th lap and was thrown from his car. Badly injured, he was unable to race again for some time.

Martin raced again occasionally after that, but retired for good in 1954 and became technical director of the Salmson car company.

Pierluigi MARTINI

Grand Prix, he finished sixth and scored the team its first Championship points.

Martini stayed with Minardi for most of his Formula One career, apart from a season with Scuderia Italia in 1992. Despite not winning any races, he had some good finishes and scored a total of 18 Championship points.

Partway through the 1995 season, Martini left Minardi and that was the end of his time in Formula One. After this he competed in sportscar and touring car racing, winning the Le Mans 24 Hour in 1999.

Jochen MASS

Nationality: German
Born: 30th September 1946
Seasons: 1973
Team/manufacturer(s): Surtees, McLaren, ATS, Arrows, March Engineering
Grands Prix: 138
Race wins: 1
Championship wins: 0

Munich-born Jochen Mass started off his racing career in sprints and hillclimbs before moving to touring cars and winning the European Touring Car Championship in 1972, driving a Ford Capri.

He also had a spell in Formula 3 and then Formula 2, and performed well enough to get a Formula One drive with Surtees for the second part of the 1973 season, when he drove in three Grands Prix.

The next season saw Mass start with Surtees and then move to McLaren, with whom he won the Spanish Grand Prix the following year. However, this was a strange win because the race was shortened after a tragic accident which killed four spectators, and only half the usual points were awarded, so it could be argued that Mass only won half a Grand Prix.

Mass stayed with McLaren through 1977 and then moved to ATS, followed by Arrows and March. Throughout, he performed well and scored a total of 71 Championship points throughout his Formula One career of 138 Grands Prix.

After leaving Formula One in 1982, Mass had great success in sportscar racing, winning the Spa 12 Hours in 1987 and the Le Mans 24 Hours in 1989, driving a Mercedes Benz.

After retiring from the sport, Mass continued to appear at historic events for Mercedes. He also worked in television.

Felipe MASSA

Nationality: Brazilian
Born: 25th April 1981
Seasons: 2002, 2004-
Team/manufacturer(s): Sauber, Ferrari
Grands Prix: 81
Race wins: 4
Championship wins: 0

Felipe Massa from Brazil first took an interest in racing when he was seven years old and delivered pizzas to the Brazilian Grand Prix. A year later he had begun kart racing and was soon making a name for himself.

By the time Massa was 17 he had progressed to Formula Chevrolet and won the championship in his second season. Then, in 2000, he came to Europe and won both the Italian and the European Formula Renault Championships that year. The following season he won the Formula 3000 Euro-Series.

A Formula One drive with Sauber followed in 2002. Massa performed well until he received a penalty at the US Grand Prix, after which he was dropped from the team. He then went to Ferrari as a test driver in 2003, but returned to Sauber the following year, and drove well, picking up 12 Championship points.

Massa had another reasonable season with Sauber in 2005 but it wasn't until he moved to Ferrari in 2006 that his real potential began to show. He had a superb season, finishing all but two Grands Prix in the top ten, and winning both the Turkish and the Brazilian Grands Prix (the latter being particularly important to him as it was his home event). With 80 Championship points, Massa finished the season third in the World Championship. Massa remained with Ferrari for 2007.

Massa remained with Ferrari for 2007, winning three races that year and finishing the season fourth in the Championship. He then stayed with the team for 2008.

Michael MAY

Nationality: Swiss
Born: 18th August 1934
Seasons: 1961
Team/manufacturer(s): Lotus
Grands Prix: 3
Race wins: 0
Championship wins: 0

Born in Germany but a Swiss citizen, Michael May (also spelt Michel) studied engineering and is believed to be the first person to come up with the idea of using an aerofoil on a car to include downforce. He attached such a wing to his Porsche 550 in 1956, but race organisers banned him from using it, arguing that it restricted rear visibility. It would be another 10 years before such aerodynamic aids would appear again.

Even without his wing, May proved to be a handy driver

and entered two World Championship Grands Prix in 1961, driving a Lotus 18. In Monaco he retired with a leaking oil line, in France he finished in 11th place, while at the German Grand Prix he had an accident during practice.

After this incident, he gave up racing and went to work with Porsche, developing fuel injection systems. Later he moved to Ferrari as an engineer and mooted the idea of a rear wing, which appeared on the 312 Formula One car in 1968.

Timothy (Tim or Timmy) MAYER

Nationality: American
Born: 22nd February 1938
Died: 28th February 1964
Seasons: 1962
Team/manufacturer(s): Cooper
Grands Prix: 1
Race wins: 0
Championship wins: 0

Born in Pennsylvania, Timmy Mayer studied law at university but turned to racing soon after he finished his education. He began with an Austin-Healey but soon moved to a Lotus 18 Formula Junior car which he proved to be very successful in.

By 1962, Mayer had won the 1962 Formula Junior Championship, driving a Cooper. This, in turn, led to the chance to enter the US Grand Prix with a factory Cooper. Unfortunately, though, he was unable to finish the race because of ignition problems which forced him to retire after 31 laps.

In 1963, Mayer travelled to Europe along with his elder brother, Teddy (who went on to be one of the founders of McLaren). There he competed in Formula Junior and signed with the Cooper team to race in Formula One for 1964.

Tragically, though, it was not to be. In February 1964, Mayer was practising for the Tasmin Series in Tasmania when his car left the road at high speed and hit a tree. He was killed instantly.

Felipe Massa

François Mazet

François MAZET

Nationality: French
Born: 24th February 1943
Seasons: 1971
Team/manufacturer(s): March
Grands Prix: 1
Race wins: 0
Championship wins: 0

Frenchman François Mazet was born in Paris. During the late 1960s he competed well in French Formula 3 and, in 1970, moved to Formula 2, where he had somewhat less success.

In 1971, he continued in Formula 2, by then driving for Jo Siffert's team as a second driver. It was through this connection that Mazet found himself entering his home Grand Prix that year. Driving a rented March 701 he finished in 13th place after starting 23rd on the grid.

And that was the extent of Mazet's Formula One career. After that, he continued to compete in Formula 2 for a few years.

Mazet was later involved in Essex Petroleum's sponsorship of the Lotus team at the start of the 1980s, as well as other sponsorship deals. He retired to the French Riviera to be a lemon farmer.

Gastón MAZZACANE

Nationality: Argentinean
Born: 8th May 1975
Seasons: 2000-2001
Team/manufacturer(s): Minardi, Prost
Grands Prix: 21
Race wins: 0
Championship wins: 0

Gastón Mazzacane proved to be a competent kart racer as a teenager before moving to touring cars and then Formula 3 in 1993, finishing second in the South American Championship.

A move to Italy in 1994 saw Mazzacane win the Formula 2000 Championship there. However, then followed a disappointing period in Formula 3 and Formula 3000.

Not to be discouraged, though, Mazzacane got together enough sponsorship from Argentina to be a pay driver for the Minardi Formula One team in 2000. He put in some impressive performances at times but failed to deliver any points and so was dropped at the end of the season.

Mazzacane then moved to Prost for 2001, again with tempting sponsorship, but didn't do well and was dropped from the team after just four Grands Prix.

Since then, the Argentinean driver has only appeared sporadically in competition, including Champ Cars in 2004.

Kenneth McALPINE

Nationality: British
Born: 21st September 1920
Seasons: 1952-1953, 1955
Team/manufacturer(s): Connaught
Grands Prix: 7
Race wins: 0
Championship wins: 0

Kenneth McAlpine was born in Surrey to a family that was part of the famous engineering business of the same name. With money to indulge, the young McAlpine started racing in his twenties.

Before long, he wanted more power from his Maserati 8CM so he took it to a company called Continental Cars, run by Rodney Clarke. McAlpine was so impressed with the result he agreed to invest in Clarke's plan to build his own racing car. The result was the Connaught A1 – the first of a famous marque.

McAlpine raced this and other early Connaughts with some success and went on to form the Connaught works team with, including others, Mike Hawthorn. McAlpine competed in just seven Grands Prix between 1952 and 1995 before stepping aside to let other drivers take over.

The Connaught company faded away in the late 1950s but the name was revived in 2004. McAlpine, meanwhile, concentrated on the family business and also ran a helicopter company and his own vineyard in the UK.

Perry McCARTHY

Nationality: British
Born: 3rd March 1961
Seasons: 1992
Team/manufacturer(s): Andrea Moda
Grands Prix: 7
Race wins: 0
Championship wins: 0

Londoner Perry McCarthy worked his way up through the racing ranks, including Formula Ford, Formula 3 and Formula 3000, despite struggling for money a lot of the time.

He finally made the break into Formula One; after testing for Footwork he signed with the Andrea Moda team for 1992. However, the team was poorly managed and the season was a disaster. Through no fault of his own, McCarthy failed to qualify for one of the seven Grands Prix he entered.

He went on to test for other Formula One teams, but never again raced in the series. McCarthy later competed in sportscar racing, including Le Mans in 2002. However, he shot to fame as the person behind The Stig, the masked test driver on the BBC's Top Gear programme between 2001 and

2003. He has also worked as a television presenter for various shows and has written for motoring magazines.

Brian McGUIRE

Nationality: Australian
Born: 13th December 1945
Died: 29th August 1977
Seasons: 1976-1977
Team/manufacturer(s): McGuire
Grands Prix: 2
Race wins: 0
Championship wins: 0

Australian Brian McGuire worked as a motor trader in his home town of Melbourne before moving to England in the mid 1960s, where he did the same.

While in the UK, he began racing in Formula Ford, before moving to Formula 3 and, later Formula 5000 from 1974. He did well in this series and worked his way through a variety of cars before settling on an old Williams FW04. McGuire did a lot of development work on this car and, at a minor race at Thruxton in 1976, drove it to victory – the first time a Williams car had won a race!

McGuire also entered the car into the 1976 British Grand Prix but he was on the reserve list and didn't get to compete in the event.

The following year, McGuire had done more development work on the FW04, to the extent that he'd renamed it the McGuire BM1. Again, he entered the British Grand Prix but failed to pre-qualify. Later that same year, McGuire crashed the same car at a minor meeting at Brands Hatch and he was killed, along with a marshal.

Bruce Leslie McLAREN

Nationality: New Zealander
Born: 30th August 1937
Died: 2nd June 1970
Seasons: 1959-1970
Team/manufacturer(s): McLaren, Cooper, Eagle
Grands Prix: 104
Race wins: 4
Championship wins: 0

Bruce McLaren was born in Auckland to a garage-owning father. As a teenager, he studied engineering and raced cars in his spare time, starting with an Austin Seven and moving on to Cooper-Climax racers. In 1958 he was runner up in the New Zealand Formula 2 Championship.

McLaren moved to Europe in 1958 and competed in Formula 2. This, in turn, led to a drive with the Cooper Formula One team the following season. He got off to a good start, finishing fifth in his first Grand Prix, at Monaco, and winning the last, in the USA, to finish sixth in the Championship.

He continued to perform well and won several races over the next few years with Cooper. Then, in 1996, he left the team to form his own team, Bruce McLaren Motoring Racing Limited, using Cooper chassis. The fledgling team struggled at first but, by 1968, McLaren was winning again and came fifth in the Championship. The following year he took third place with 26 Championship points.

The following season he could well have won the Championship but disaster struck. McLaren was testing a new CanAm car at the Goodwood circuit in June 1970 when the engine cover came adrift causing a loss of downforce. The car left the track and hit a building, killing its driver.

Bruce McLaren

McRae went on to continue to compete in Formula 5000 and also Can-Am in the USA. He also worked at developing his own chassis. Later, he retired from driving and returned to New Zealand. There he set up a company building replica Porsches in Wellington until ill health forced him to retire.

Carlos Alberto MENDITÉGUY

Nationality: Argentinean
Born: 10th August 1914
Died: 27th April 1973
Seasons: 1953-1958, 1960
Team/manufacturer(s): Gordini, Maserati, Cooper
Grands Prix: 11
Race wins: 0
Championship wins: 0

Born in Buenos Aires, Carlos Menditéguy was perhaps better known in his home country as a superb polo player – at one point he was said to one of the top six players in the world.

However, he was also a talented racing driver and competed regularly in his home country. From 1953 he entered the Argentinean Grand Prix each year until 1960, with the exception of 1959. The first year he drove a Gordini, but switched to Maseratis for the rest of the time, with the exception of 1960, when he used a Cooper. His best results were a third place in Argentina in 1957 and fourth at the same Grand Prix three years later. Menditéguy also travelled to Europe occasionally to compete and entered the Italian Grand Prix in 1955, coming fifth. He also entered the French and British Grands Prix in 1957. After retiring from racing, Menditéguy worked as a horse trainer.

The McLaren name lives on, not only as a motorsport legend but also as Team McLaren.

Allan McNISH

Nationality: British
Born: 29th December 1969
Seasons: 2002
Team/manufacturer(s): Toyota
Grands Prix: 17
Race wins: 0
Championship wins: 0

Scotsman Allan McNish raced motorcycles as a small boy but soon switched to karts, with which he won Scottish and British championships. He moved up to Formula Ford 1600 in 1987 and then on to Formula Vauxhall Lotus the following year, and won that championship. The next season saw McNish running up in British Formula 3.

He then spent time in Formula 3000 while, at the same time, testing for Formula One. However, try as he might, McNish was unable to get a drive in Formula One so he turned his attention to sportscars, being with Porsche in 1996. Two years later, he won the Le Mans 24 Hour race with a Porsche GT1.

Finally, he got a chance in Formula One, starting as a development driver for Toyota in 2001. The following year, he drove for the team but did not have much success, failing to pick up any Championship points.

The following season, McNish worked as a test driver for Renault. He then returned to sportscar racing, winning the 12 Hours of Sebring in 2004.

Graham McRAE

Nationality: New Zealander
Born: 5th March 1940
Seasons: 1973
Team/manufacturer(s): Iso Williams
Grands Prix: 1
Race wins: 0
Championship wins: 0

Graham McRae came from Wellington and began building his own cars in the late 1960s. He then came to Europe to race in Formula 2 in 1969. A move to Formula 5000 in the early 1970s proved a good move and he won the US series in 1972.

McRae's one and only World Championship appearance was in 1973, when he drove an Iso Williams car at the British Grand Prix. It was not a successful machine, though, and McRae started at the back of the grid and was out of the race right at the start with throttle problems.

Allan McNish

MNO

139

Arturo Merzario

Harry Erick MERKEL

Nationality: German
Born: 10th January 1918
Died: 11th February 1995
Seasons: 1952
Team/manufacturer(s): BMW-Eigenbau
Grands Prix: 1
Race wins: 0
Championship wins: 0

Harry Merkel was born in what became East Germany. There he raced in various racing events before the Second World War.

After the war, he returned to the sport and enjoyed racing in sportscar and hillclimb events. In 1952, he entered his one and only Formula One race, the German Grand Prix. Driving a BMW-Eigenbau, he did not qualify because he failed to set a time.

Merkel later moved to West Germany where he ran a number of car dealerships selling a range of cars including Lancias and Triumphs. After that he emigrated to Australia where he died in 1995.

Arturo Francesco MERZARIO

Nationality: Italian
Born: 11th March 1943
Seasons: 1972-1979
Team/manufacturer(s): Ferrari, Williams, Fittipaldi, March, Wolf, Merzario
Grands Prix: 84
Race wins: 0
Championship wins: 0

Arturo Merzario began racing Abarth sportscars in Italy in the 1960s and this led to a drive with the Ferrari factory team in 1970, driving sports cars. By 1972, he had won the Targa Florio for the team.

It was through Ferrari that Merzario had his first chance to compete in Formula One, standing in for Clay Regazzoni at the British Grand Prix, where he impressed by finishing in sixth place.

Merzario then drove for Ferrari for most of the following season and picked up six Championship points but, nonetheless, was dropped by the struggling team at the end of the year. This led to a move to Williams for 1974 and 1975.

For 1976, Merzario entered his own March into Formula One but struggled to get anywhere. The following year, he formed his own team, using March cars at first but switching to his own the next year. However, the team was underfunded and the project was a failure, with Merzario failing to qualify for or complete any races in 1978 and 1979.

After that, Merzario's team turned its hand to Formula 2 but, again, had little success. He later had more success competing in sportscars.

Roberto MIÈRES

Nationality: Argentinean
Born: 3rd December 1924
Seasons: 1953-1955
Team/manufacturer(s): Gordini, Maserati
Grands Prix: 17
Race wins: 0
Championship wins: 0

Born into a wealthy Argentinean family, Roberto Mières grew up enjoying a range of sports and began motor racing in the late 1940s, racing an MG. Before long, he'd progressed to a Mercedes SSK and then a Bugatti, with which he won the Argentinean Sportscar Championship.

A trip to Europe in 1950 saw Mières racing Gordinis and

Franck Montagny

Ferraris before, finally, being offered a drive with the Gordini works team in 1953. It was then that he entered his first three Grands Prix, as well as doing some sportscar events.

The next year, he moved to Maserati and had some good races over the next two seasons, picking up 13 Championship points from a number of top-six finishes. It was, though, the end of his Formula One career and Mières went on to concentrate on sportscar racing.

Towards the end of the 1950s, Mières gave up driving to concentrate on his other love, sailing, which he took to Olympic level in 1960. He retired to a ranch in Uruguay.

François MIGAULT

Nationality: French
Born: 4th December 1944
Seasons: 1972, 1974-1975
Team/manufacturer(s): Connew, BRM, Hill, Williams
Grands Prix: 16
Race wins: 0
Championship wins: 0

French driver François Migault was born in Le Mans and won the Volant Shell series in the late 1960s. He then had a couple of successful seasons in Formula 3 at the start of the 1970s before moving into Formula 2 in 1972.

That year also saw Migault drive in two Grands Prix for the small Connew team. However, he failed to qualify for the British Grand Prix and retired from the Austrian event.

Migault returned to Formula One in 1974, driving for BRM but struggled with an uncompetitive car. The next year he entered two Grands Prix with the Hill team but failed to finish either. Then a move to Williams saw Migault fail to qualify for the French Grand Prix.

That was the end of his Formula One career and Migault returned to Formula 2. He then competed in sportscar racing, including entering the famous 24 Hour race in his home town most years from 1971 to 2001.

John MILES

Nationality: British
Born: 14th June 1943
Seasons: 1969-1976
Team/manufacturer(s): Lotus
Grands Prix: 15
Race wins: 0
Championship wins: 0

John Miles was the son of theatre owner, Sir Bernard Miles, he grew up in London and studied engineering after leaving school.

His racing career began at club level in the early 1960s and he was soon winning races. By 1966 he had joined the Lotus works team, driving in sportscar and Formula 3 races.

In 1969 he was promoted to the team's Formula One division, primarily to help develop the Lotus 63 four-wheel-drive car. Driving alongside Jochen Rindt (who went on to win the Championship in 1970) Miles struggled with the revolutionary car and had little success.

The following season, Miles got off to a good start with a fifth place finish in South Africa but it went downhill from there. He left the team after the Italian Grand Prix which claimed the life of his teammate, Rindt, because Miles was not happy about team boss, Colin Chapman's demands.

Miles did, however, stay with Lotus as a development engineer. He also worked as a journalist.

André MILHOUX

Nationality: Belgian
Born: 9th December 1928
Seasons: 1956
Team/manufacturer(s): Gordini
Grands Prix: 1
Race wins: 0
Championship wins: 0

Born in Liege, André Milhoux was, in fact, a sportscar and production car driver for the majority of his career, beginning with large American saloon cars, including winning the 1953 Mille Miglia in a Chrysler with Paul Frère.

He then began to compete in more exotic machinery, including Ferraris, in various sportscar and endurance races.

Despite specialising in sportscars, Milhoux nonetheless found himself entering the German Grand Prix for Gordini, standing in for André Pilette, who was injured. Unfortunately, though, he was forced to retire with engine problems after 15 laps.

Milhoux then went back to what he knew, until a crash at Spa in 1958 persuaded him to retire from the sport.

Gerhard Karl MITTER

Nationality: German
Born: 30th August 1935
Died: 1st August 1969
Seasons: 1963-1967, 1969
Team/manufacturer(s): Porsche, Lotus Brabham, BMW
Grands Prix: 1
Race wins: 0
Championship wins: 0

Gerhard Mitter was born in what is now the Czech Republic and was exiled to Germany with his family at the age of 10.

After a spell racing motorcycles, Mitter moved to Formula Junior in his early twenties while, at the same time, running a garage business. Before long, he was winning races and rising to the top of the league.

It was after Mitter began working as a development engineer for Porsche that he had his Formula One debut in 1963. Driving a Porsche 781 at the Dutch Grand Prix, he had to retire with a failed clutch after just two laps. However, he had better luck at his other race that year, when he finished fourth in the German Grand Prix.

From then on, Mitter entered just the German Grand Prix each year, driving Lotuses, Brabhams and BMWs, but he never again did as well as his first attempt at the race.

Sadly, it was during practice for the 1969 German Grand Prix that Mitter met his death. He was driving a BMW and it was thought that the suspension had given way, causing him to lose control of the car.

Stefano MODENA

Nationality: Italian
Born: 12th May 1963
Seasons: 1987-1992
Team/manufacturer(s): Brabham, EuroBrun, Tyrrell, Jordan
Grands Prix: 81
Race wins: 0
Championship wins: 0

Stefano Modena was born in the city of the same name and raced karts as a boy before moving up to Formula 3 and Formula 3000, winning the championship in the latter in his first year.

This led to a one-off drive with Brabham at the Australian Grand Prix in 1987, standing in for Nigel Mansell. The next season, he signed with the new Eurobrun Formula One team but, after a disappointing season, he returned to Brabham for 1989.

That year Modena also struggled, partly because the team was short of money. However, he did finish in third place at Monaco, and fifth in the USA the next season.

Then it was on to Tyrrell for a better 1991 season before another disappointing one with Jordan in 1992. After that, Modena competed in Touring Cars until 2000. He then retired from racing to act as a test driver for Bridgestone.

Franck MONTAGNY

Nationality: French
Born: 5th January 1978
Seasons: 2003, 2005-
Team/manufacturer(s): Renault, Jordan, Super Aguri, Toyota
Grands Prix: 7
Race wins: 0
Championship wins: 0

Franck Montagny raced karts from the age of 10, winning the cadet class of the French Championship in 1992, and the National 2 class the following year.

He was just 16 when he began racing cars, winning the Renault Campus Championship. Montagny then worked his way through Formula Renault, Formula 3 and Formula 3000 before having a spell in sportscars in 2001 and 2002.

Montagny's Formula One career began in 2003 when he was a test driver for Renault. He then tested for Jordan the following year before being signed by Super Aguri as a

Stefano Modena

MNO

Tiago Monteiro

driver. Sadly, though, he had a disappointing time in the seven Grands Prix he entered, and he was demoted to the position of test driver on the team.

He was, however, then signed by Toyota for the 2007 season.

Tiago Vagaroso da Costa MONTEIRO

Nationality: Portuguese
Born: 24th July 1976
Seasons: 2005-
Team/manufacturer(s): Jordan, MF1, Spyker
Grands Prix: 7
Race wins: 0
Championship wins: 0

Portuguese driver Tiago Monteiro first shot to fame in the 1997 French Porsche Carrera Cup when he became the B-class Champion and Rookie of the Year.

The following year he moved to Formula 3 for three seasons and then on to Formula 3000 in 2002. This was followed by a year racing Champ Cars and some time in sportscars.

In 2004, Monteiro was a test driver for the Minardi Formula One team while also competing in the Nissan World Series, in which he finished second in the championship.

The next season saw Monteiro drive for Jordan in a full season of Formula One and he finished all but one race of the year – a record. His best result was third place at the US Grand Prix.

The following year, he moved to the MF1 team, which was later rename Spyker. This, though, was a less successful season, with Monteiro retiring from six races and being disqualified from the German Grand Prix because it was claimed his car's rear wing was illegal.

Monteiro signed to race with Spyker for the 2007 season.

Andrea MONTERMINI

Nationality: Italian
Born: 30th May
Seasons: 1994-1996
Team/manufacturer(s): Simtek, Pacific, Forti
Grands Prix: 28
Race wins: 0
Championship wins: 0

After starting off his career in Formula Alfa Boxer in 1987, Andrea Montermini worked his way through Formula 3 and Formula 3000 before moving to the USA to compete in Indy Cars in 1993.

A year after this, Montermini had a one-off drive in Formula One, driving a Simtek car at the Spanish Grand Prix, where he failed to qualify after crashing his car.

The next year, 1995, Montermini had a full season with the underfunded Pacific team but failed to score any points in a disappointing season. For 1996, he moved to Forti and had no more luck and he didn't finish the season.

From then, Montermini competed in sportscar circles and also had a spell in the CART series.

Robert Victor Campbell MONTGOMERIE (Robin Montgomerie-Charrington)

Nationality: British
Born: 23rd June 1915
Seasons: 1952
Team/manufacturer(s): Aston-Butterworth
Grands Prix: 1
Race wins: 0
Championship wins: 0

Born as Robert Montgomerie in London, he was educated at Eton and grew up to be wealthy farmer who enjoyed racing as a hobby. He then went by the name of Robin Montgomerie-Charrington.

Montgomerie-Charrington competed mainly in Formula

Andrea Montermini

3, driving a Cooper, which is where he got to know Bill Aston, another driver.

For the 1952 season, Aston built Montgomerie-Charrington one of his specials, a Formula 2 Aston-Butterworth, created with the input of Archie Butterworth. Rather confusingly, Montgomerie-Charrington had his car painted in the blue and white racing colours of the USA, because that is where his wife was from.

He raced the car in just one World Championship race, the 1952 Belgian Grand Prix at Spa-Francorchamps. Unfortunately, he was unable to complete the race because engine problems forced him to retire after 17 laps.

That was to be Montgomerie-Charrington's last year of serious racing and he moved to the USA soon after, although he later returned to the UK.

Juan Pablo MONTOYA (Juan Pablo Montoya-Roldan)

Nationality: Colombian
Born: 20th September 1975
Seasons: 2001-2006
Team/manufacturer(s): Williams, McLaren
Grands Prix: 95
Race wins: 7
Championship wins: 0

Juan Pablo Montoya began racing karts at the age of just six and, three years later, was the Children's National Kart Champion in Colombia. He was later the Junior Champion in 1990 and 1991.

A move to Europe in the mid-1990s saw Montoya compete in Formula Vauxhall and Formula 3 and then he was struggling to get any further when he was offered a drive in Formula 3000 and ended the season second in the championship.

This led to him being signed by Williams as a test driver from 1998 and in the same year he continued in Formula 3000, taking the title. For the 1999 season, Williams 'swapped' Montoya for Alessandro Zanardi, a CART driver and so the Colombian found himself driving in the USA, where he took the locals by storm and won the CART Championship. The following year he again surprised America by winning the Indy 500 race.

Montoya returned to Williams as a full-time driver for the 2001 season and performed well, winning the Italian Grand Prix. The following two years he did even better, coming third in the Championship both seasons, and winning in Monaco and Great Britain in 2003.

He stayed with Williams for 2004 and again did well and then moved to McLaren for 2005. In that year he won no less than three races (Britain, Italy and Brazil) and came fourth in the Championship. However, he retired from Formula One partway through the 2006 season, announcing that he was going to drive in NASCAR for 2007.

Gianni MORBIDELLI

Nationality: Italian
Born: 13th January 1968
Seasons: 1990-1997
Team/manufacturer(s): Dallara, Minardi, Ferrari, Footwork, Sauber
Grands Prix: 70
Race wins: 0
Championship wins: 0

Gianni Morbidelli's father built racing motorcycles so it was

Gianni Morbidelli

Juan Pablo Montoya

MNO

not surprising that the youngster got into karting at an early age. By 1987 he had moved on to Formula 3 and won the Italian title two years later.

At the age of just 22 he competed in his first Grand Prix, racing for Dallara in the US and Brazilian Grands Prix at the start of the 1990 season. After that, he concentrated on Formula 3000 until the end of the season, when he entered the Japanese and Australian Grands Prix for Minardi.

Morbidelli then started with Minardi for the next two season, picking up points when he came sixth at the 1991 Australian Grand Prix.

A move to Footworks in 1994 saw him achieve points at the German and Belgian Grands Prix, where he finished fifth and sixth respectively, and then he picked up another sixth place in Canada and a third in Australian the following season.

The 1997 saw Morbidelli race in only a few Grands Prix with the Sauber team because he was out of action with injuries for part of the year. This was his last Formula One season and he moved on to driving touring cars.

Roberto Pupo MORENO

Nationality: Brazilian
Born: 11th January 1959
Seasons: 1982, 1987, 1989-1992, 1995
Team/manufacturer(s): Lotus, AGS, Coloni, EuroBrun, Benetton, Andrea Moda, Forti
Grands Prix: 75
Race wins: 0
Championship wins: 0

Born in Rio de Janeiro, Roberto Moreno was a friend of Nelson Piquet and the two boys raced karts together before moving to Europe, where Moreno won the British Formula Ford 1600 Championship in 1980.

He then drove in Formula 2 and this led to his first

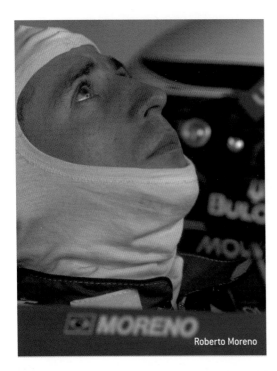

Roberto Moreno

Formula One appearance – a drive for Lotus at the 1982 Dutch Grand Prix at which he failed to qualify.

It would be five years before Moreno got another chance at Formula One, this time driving for AGS in Japan and Australia at the end of the 1987 season. In the second race he impressed by finishing in sixth place.

Two years after that, Moreno got a full season's drive with Coloni but failed to finish a single race with an uncompetitive car. It was a similar story with Eurobrun the next season, although Moreno did pull off a second place finish in Japan.

A move to Benetton for 1991 saw Moreno have a better season, picking up eight points to finish 10th in the Championship. Then it was another disappointing season in 1992 with Forti.

That was Moreno's last year with Formula One. He then turned his hand to touring cars and Champ Cars.

David (Dave) MORGAN

Nationality: British
Born: 7th August 1944
Seasons: 1975
Team/manufacturer(s): Surtees
Grands Prix: 1
Race wins: 0
Championship wins: 0

David Morgan came from Somerset and started racing a Mini in his early twenties. Before long, he'd worked his way up to Formula 3 and then Formula 2. Although by the mid-1970s he was struggling for money so went to race in the less high-profile Formula Atlantic.

By 1975, though, he had raised enough sponsorship for a one-off drive at the British Grand Prix. Behind the wheel of a Surtees TS16, Morgan finished the race in 18th place, even though – like many other cars on the wet track – he was involved in an accident.

In the early 1980s, Morgan raced saloon cars before retiring to work as a race engineer in Formula 3000 and Formula One.

SILVIO MOSER

Nationality: Swiss
Born: 24th April 1941
Seasons: 1967-1971
Team/manufacturer(s): Cooper ATS, Brabham, Bellasi
Grands Prix: 18
Race wins: 0
Championship wins: 0

Silvio Moser was born in Zurich and began racing in a Jaguar XK120 and an Alfa Romeo in the early 1960s. Before long, though, he'd switched to single-seaters, beginning with Formula Junior and then Formula 3 and Formula 2.

His Formula One debut was at the 1967 British Grand Prix, when he drove an aging Cooper ATS. The following year, Moser used a more competitive Brabham and entered four Grands Prix, picking up points when he finished fifth in Holland.

Moser then had his own Formula One car built by Guglielmo Bellasi for the 1970 season. Sadly, though, he had little success with it and dropped out of Formula One during 1971, when he entered just one race, the Italian Grand Prix.

He then returned to competing in Formula 2, driving a Brabham, while his Bellasi found its way to South America. Meanwhile, Moser was planning a return to Formula One but it was not to happen. A week before his first Grand Prix of 1974, he was driving a Lola sportscar in the Monza 1000 when he crashed. Moser died of his injuries a month later.

William (Bill) MOSS

Nationality: British
Born: 4th September 1933
Seasons: 1959
Team/manufacturer(s): Cooper
Grands Prix: 1
Race wins: 0
Championship wins: 0

William Moss was born in Luton in 1933 and began racing before the Second World War, driving an ERA R6B known as 'Remus'. This car was one of a pair (the other called 'Romulus') owned by Siamese princes, Chula and Bira, and Moss made a name for himself as a successful driver.

After the war, Moss returned to racing and worked his way up to Formula 2 by the end of the 1950s. It was in 1959 that he entered a T51 Cooper-Climax into the British Grand Prix but he failed to qualify for the race proper.

Moss was later reunited with Remus and continued to drive the car in various events at club and historic level before finally selling it to Patrick Lindsay. Moss retired to live in Wiltshire.

Sir Stirling MOSS, OBE

Nationality: British
Born: 17th September 1929
Seasons: 1950-1962
Team/manufacturer(s): Mercedes-Benz, Maserati, Vanwall, Cooper, Lotus
Grands Prix: 66
Race wins: 0
Championship wins: 0

Born in London in 1929, Moss's father, Alfred Moss, was a regular at Brooklands, and also raced in the 1924 Indianapolis 500. His mother, meanwhile, was a keen trial and rally driver. It was no surprise then, that when he was nine, the young Stirling was given an old Austin Seven, which he tore around fields in.

Despite his parents' enthusiasm for cars, they didn't expect Moss to become a full-timer driver. Instead, they wanted him to be a dentist, like his father. However, a poor academic record put paid to that plan and, at the age of 17, he went to work in a hotel.

The teenager continued to take an interest in cars, though, and ordered an Aspen-engined racecar without telling his parents. His father cancelled the order when he found out. However, when he realised his son's disappointment, he let him use his BMW sportscar for speed trial events.

Stirling Moss

Stirling Moss

Before long, Moss had proved his worth and bought a Cooper 500 racecar when he just 18. He used this for hillclimbing and racing and was soon winning regularly.

In 1950, Moss was asked to drive for the HWM Formula Two team. The following year, he was meant to be racing for Ferrari, but the team went back on their word and Moss vowed his revenge against the Italian team.

He first competed in Formula One in 1954, in a Maserati 250F. Moss created enough of an impression for Mercedes to sign him for the following season, where he was teamed with Juan-Manuel Fangio, whom Moss beat to win the British Grand Prix.

After a brief stint with Maserati in 1956, Moss signed to Vanwall for 1957, arguing that he preferred to drive for a British team. Moss went on to win six Grands Prix in 1957 and 1958. In the latter year, he was very close to winning the championship, but when his rival, Mike Hawthorn, was accused of rule-breaking in Portugal, Moss came to his defence, allowing Hawthorn to keep his points for that race. It was an admirable thing for Moss to do, but it did mean he lost the championship to Hawthorn by just one point.

Perhaps one of the reasons such a great driver never quite won the championship was because he often chose to drive British cars which, at the time, were not as competitive as some of their rivals. That said, Moss stormed to victory in the 1961 Monaco Grand Prix. Despite being in an underpowered Lotus 18, he beat his arch-rival Ferrari by just 3.6 seconds to win the race. He won the German Grand Prix in a similar fashion the same year.

In 1962, Moss suffered a bad accident at Goodwood that nearly killed him. Despite making a full recovery, he decided to retire from Formula One racing, despite being relatively young, in his early thirties. It's a reflection on his skill and charisma that Stirling Moss is still one of the best-known names in motorsport over 40 years later.

Gino MUNARON

Nationality: Italian
Born: 2nd April 1928
Seasons: 1960
Team/manufacturer(s): Maserati, Cooper
Grands Prix: 4
Race wins: 0
Championship wins: 0

Gino Munaron was born in Turin and began racing in the 1950s, mainly with sportscars and touring cars, and had some success in various events around Europe.

His first Formula One appearance was at the Argentinean Grand Prix in 1960, where he drove an elderly Maserati 250F to a 13th place finish after starting 19th on the grid.

Munaron then got behind the wheel of a Scuderia Castellotti Cooper-Ferrari later in the season and entered a handful of other Grands Prix with the less than competitive car. In France he retired after 16 laps with transmission problems, in Britain he finished in 15th place from 25th on the grid and at the Italian Grand Prix he retired with engine failure after 27 laps.

He continued to race single-seaters for a short while after this before getting back into sportscar racing, and achieving some good results at various events, including the Spa 24 Hours, where he finished fifth in 1964.

After retiring from racing, Munaron continued to drive Ferraris and Maseratis in historic events.

David MURRAY

Nationality: British
Born: 28th December 1909
Died: 5th April 1973
Seasons: 1950-1952
Team/manufacturer(s): Maserati, Cooper
Grands Prix: 4
Race wins: 0
Championship wins: 0

Scottish driver David Murray was born in Edinburgh and worked as an accountant, then as a bar owner and wine merchant. He raced cars as a hobby to begin with, although he later set up a garage business in Edinburgh that prepared vehicles for racing.

After the Second World War, Murray took up racing again with an elderly Maserati 4CLT. He entered this car into the British and Italian Grands Prix in 1950 but had to retire from both races, with engine and gearbox problems, respectively.

The following year, Murray had another attempt at the British Grand Prix but the Maserati's engine again let him down and he had to retire after 45 laps.

In 1952, he tried a different car, a Cooper-Bristol but, again, the engine failed and he was out of the race after 14 laps.

Meanwhile, Murray was building up his race-preparation business and formed the now famous Ecurie Ecosse racing team in 1952. Before long, the team's dark-blue cars were well-known and they ran Jaguar D-Types to victory at the Le Mans 24 Hour race in 1956 and 1957, much to the surprise of the more wealthy factory teams.

Sadly, the team began to struggle by the late 1960s and Murray moved to the Canary Islands where he died of a heart attack in 1973.

Luigi MUSSO

Nationality: Italian
Born: 28th July 1924
Died: 6th July 1958
Seasons: 1954-1958
Team/manufacturer(s): Maserati, Ferrari
Grands Prix: 24
Race wins: 1
Championship wins: 0

Rome-born Luigi Musso came from a wealthy family and was the youngest of three brothers who all raced cars. Before long, he was borrowing his brothers' cars and racing himself.

By 1953, all three of the brothers joined the Maserati team and Musso won the Italian 2-litre championship that year. The following year, he had his Formula One debut, at the Argentinean Grand Prix, but he failed to start the race because of an engine problem.

Musso spent most of the rest of the 1954 season in sportscar events, but he was back for the Italian and Spanish Grands Prix, still driving for Maserati, and finished second in Spain. After another season with Maserati, in which he performed well, Mosso switched to Ferrari for 1957. At the start of the season, he won the Argentinean Grand Prix but a crash put him of action for most of the year, and he then failed to qualify in the other three races he entered. He stayed with Ferrari for 1958 and came second in the Argentinean and Monaco Grands Prix at the start of the season. Then, during the French Grand Prix later in the year, his car left the track at 150mph and landed in a ditch. Musso was killed instantly.

Luigi Musso

N

Satoru Nakajima

Shinji Nakano

Satoru NAKAJIMA

Nationality: Japanese
Born: 23rd February 1953
Seasons: 1987-1991
Team/manufacturer(s): Lotus, Tyrrell
Grands Prix: 90
Race wins: 0
Championship wins: 0

Satoru Nakajima was brought up on a farm in rural Japan and his older brother taught him to drive around the fields. As soon as he was old enough, he began racing and, by the time he was 20, he was competing in the Suzuka Circuit, winning the title in his first year.

Eight years later, he had won the Japanese Formula 2 title and went on to win it again five more times. Nakajima then moved to Formula One, driving for Lotus from the start of the 1987 season and doing remarkably well for a rookie, with a best finish of fourth place at the British Grand Prix and a 12th place position in the Championship.

Unfortunately, Nakajima did less well in subsequent years, although he still held his own. For the 1990 season, he moved to the Tyrrell team for two uneventful years punctuated by moments of greatness, including a fifth place finish at the US Grand Prix.

After leaving Formula One Nakajima ran his own racing team which competed successfully in Formula Nippon.

Shinji NAKANO

Nationality: Japanese
Born: 1st April 1971
Seasons: 1997-1998
Team/manufacturer(s): Prost, Minardi
Grands Prix: 33
Race wins: 0
Championship wins: 0

Shinji Nakano was born in Osaka and began karting in his

early teens, winning several Japanese titles. When he was 18, he progressed to Formula 3 and came seventh in the local championship. Instead of staying with Formula 3, the youngster moved to the European Formula Opel Lotus Championship for two seasons.

Shinji Nakano

MN O

147

Nakano then returned to Japan to race in Formula 3000 and Formula 3 in 1992, but decided that two series was too much and so concentrated on Formula 3 for the next two years. He then raced in Formula 3000 in 1995 and 1996.

It was then into Formula One, driving for Prost in 1997 with a mixed bag of results. He failed to finish many races that season, but when he did, he finished well, picking up a couple of Championship points.

The next year saw Nakano drive for Minardi but the team was underfunded and he struggled to be competitive.

That was the end of Nakano's Formula One stint. He later went to the USA to race in CART and then returned to Japan where he competed in GTs and touring cars.

Alessandro NANNINI

Nationality: Italian
Born: 7th July 1959
Seasons: 1986-1990
Team/manufacturer(s): Minardi, Benetton
Grands Prix: 78
Race wins: 1
Championship wins: 0

Alessandro Nannini was born in Siena to a wealthy family and began racing in motocross and then rallying in his late teens.

By the early 1980s he had made the change to circuit driving and raced in Formula 2 for Minardi for the next five years. This then led to a drive in Formula One for the same team, in 1986 and 1987. They were, though disappointing years for Nannini.

Things improved when he moved to Benetton in 1988 and started to get much better results, including third places at the British and Spanish Grands Prix plus other good finishes, which earned him 12 points that season.

He did even better in 1989, with two third places, one second and a win at Japan.

These plus other point-scoring finishes left him in sixth place in the Championship at the end of the season. The following year was almost as good and he finished eighth in the Championship. He could have done better but a helicopter crash before the end of the season left him with a badly damaged hand and Nannini was unable to compete in the last two Grands Prix.

The injury spelt the end of his Formula One career, although he was able to race in touring cars afterwards. He also opened a chain of Nannini cafes around the world.

Emanuele NASPETTI

Nationality: Italian
Born: 24th February 1968
Seasons: 1992-1993
Team/manufacturer(s): March, Jordan
Grands Prix: 6
Race wins: 0
Championship wins: 0

Italian driver Emanuele Naspetti sprang to fame in 1988 when he won the Italian Formula 3 Championship at the age of 20, when he'd only been racing cars for two years. He then spent the next four years competing in Formula 3000.

In 1992, Naspetti made the jump to Formula One, driving for March for the latter part of the 1992 season. He drove reasonably well but failed to make any real impression.

The following year, Naspetti struggled to find a drive, although he did some testing for Jordan which led to him entering the Portuguese Grand Prix. Unfortunately, though,

engine problems forced him to retire from the race after just eight laps. That was the end of Naspetti's uninspiring Formula One career and he went off to drive in the Italian Superturismo series, winning the title in 1997.

Massimo NATILI

Nationality: Italian
Born: 28th July 1935
Seasons: 1961
Team/manufacturer(s): Cooper
Grands Prix: 1
Race wins: 0
Championship wins: 0

Massimo Natili was born in Roncigilione and started his career in Formula Junior in the 1950s before moving to Formula 3.

His one and only Formula One appearance was in an aging Cooper-Maserati at the British Grand Prix of 1961, held at Aintree. Starting from 28th on the grid, Natili was unable to start the race because of a gearbox problem, and that was the end of his Formula One adventure.

After that, Natili continued to compete in Formula 3 and in various sportscar events, including the 1966 Le Mans 24 Hour race.

Natili also worked as a film director and ran a BMW dealership in Italy. After retiring, he maintained close links with motorsport.

Brian NAYLOR

Nationality: British
Born: 24th March 1923
Died: 8th August 1989
Seasons: 1958-1961
Team/manufacturer(s): Cooper, JPW
Grands Prix: 7
Race wins: 0
Championship wins: 0

Brian Naylor was born in Manchester and served in the Merchant Navy during the Second World War. After the end of the war he set up a car dealership in his home town and began racing an MG in the early 1950s.

By 1957 he had progressed to Formula 2, driving a Cooper and, the following year, he entered the German Grand Prix at the Nürburgring but had to retire after just one lap with fuelling problems.

For 1958, Naylor built his own car with the help of engineer Fred Wilkinson. This was based on a Cooper with a Maserati engine and Naylor entered it into the British Grand Prix that year, but the transmission failed after 18 laps.

The next year, Naylor took his car to the Monaco, British, Italian and US Grands Prix, but only completed his home race, coming 13th. In 1961, he competed in the Italian Grand Prix only, retiring after six laps.

Naylor then gave up racing to concentrate on his business, and later moved to Spain to run a café.

Timothy (Tiff) NEEDELL

Nationality: British
Born: 29th October 1951
Seasons: 1980
Team/manufacturer(s): Ensign
Grands Prix: 2
Race wins: 0
Championship wins: 0

M
N
O

Alessandro Nannini

Born in Havant, Timothy Needell (usually called Tiff) began his career as a civil engineer. He began racing after winning a Formula Ford car in a magazine competition, which enabled him to compete in that series for 1971.

Needell worked his way successfully up through Formula 2000 and Formula 3 to the Aurora British Formula One series in 1979. The following year saw him enter two World Championship races, driving for Ensign. An engine failure forced him to retire from the Belgian race, while he failed to qualify at Monaco.

After that, Needell competed mainly in touring cars and sportscars. He also pursued a successful career as a journalist and television presenter, most notably on Top Gear and Fifth Gear.

Jacob (Jac) NELLEMAN

Nationality: Danish
Born: 19th April 1944
Seasons: 1976
Team/manufacturer(s): RAM
Grands Prix: 1
Race wins: 0
Championship wins: 0

Jacob (or Jac) Nelleman was born in Copenhagen and grew up to be Danish Formula 3 Champion no less than 11 times in the late 1960s and early 1970s.

Unfortunately his short Formula One career was somewhat less successful. Driving two Brabhams – a BT42 and a BT44B – for the underfunded RAM team, he failed to qualify for the 1976 Swedish Grand Prix.

Nelleman continued to compete in Formula 3 and then became heavily involved in historic racing. Outside of racing, he ran dealerships selling Jaguars and Honda bikes, and had his own publishing company.

Patrick Marie Ghislain Pierre Simon Stanislas NÈVE DE MÉVERGNIES (Patrick Nève)

Nationality: Belgian
Born: 13th October 1949
Seasons: 1976-1978
Team/manufacturer(s): RAM, Williams, March (P Nève)
Grands Prix: 13
Race wins: 0
Championship wins: 0

Belgian driver Patrick Nève was born in Liege to a wealthy family but had to pay his own way to becoming a racing driver, working as an instructor between races.

In 1974, he had his first full season of Formula Ford and won the UK championship before moving to Formula 3 the next year, coming fourth in the European Championship.

Raising the funds himself, Nève bought a drive in a RAM Brabham at the 1976 Belgian Grand Prix but failed to finish the race. Later that season, he drove for Ensign in France and finished 18th. The 1977 season saw Nève drive for Williams for the second part of the year, and his best result was a seventh place finish in Italy. The following year, he entered a March under his own name into the Belgian Grand Prix but failed to qualify.

That was it for Nève's Formula One career and he went on to compete in Formula 2 before moving to sportscars and touring cars. After retiring from the sport he ran a sports marketing company in Brussels.

John NICHOLSON

Nationality: New Zealand
Born: 6th October 1941
Seasons: 1974-1975
Team/manufacturer(s): Lyncar
Grands Prix: 2
Race wins: 0
Championship wins: 0

Born in Auckland, John Nicholson began racing in his home country before moving to the UK in the early 1970s. There, he worked as an engineer for McLaren, working on engine development.

He raced part-time, at first in Formula Atlantic, winning the championship in 1973 and 1974, driving a Lyncar which he partly developed himself.

In 1974, he tried to enter the British Grand Prix, driving the Lyncar, but failed to qualify. The following year, he had another attempt and finished the race in 17th place. After that, he planned to compete a full season of Formula One with a McLaren but it didn't happen.

Nicholson continued to race for a couple more years, in Formula 2 and Formula 5000, but then became involved in powerboat racing. He also continued to develop engines, at first in conjunction with McLaren, but later independently.

Helmut NIEDERMAYR

Nationality: German
Born: 29th November 1915
Died: 3rd April 1985
Seasons: 1952
Team/manufacturer(s): AFM
Grands Prix: 1
Race wins: 0
Championship wins: 0

German driver Helmut Niedermayr was born in Munich. After the Second World War he raced in various events in Europe.

His one and only World Championship appearance was at the 1952 German Grand Prix at the Nürburgring, where he drove an AFM-BMW to a ninth place finish, after starting 22nd on the grid.

That same year saw Niedermayr take second place at the Le Mans 24 Hour race, driving a Mercedes-Benz 300SL with Theo Helfich.

Less happily, though, also in 1952, Niedermayr crashed at a road circuit called Grenzlandring in the town of Wegberg. His car ploughed into a crowd of spectators, killing 14 and injuring over 40. After that tragic event, racing was banned at the circuit.

Niedermayr later moved to the Virgin Islands.

Ambraüsus (Brausch) NIEMANN

Nationality: South African
Born: 7th January 1939
Seasons: 1963, 1965
Team/manufacturer(s): Ted Lanfear/Lotus
Grands Prix: 1
Race wins: 0
Championship wins: 0

His full name was Ambraüsus Niemann but this South African driver was usually known as Brausch Niemann. Born in Durban, he enjoyed racing his own Lotus Seven in the early 1960s at local events.

He then progressed to a Lotus 22 in which he competed in Formula Junior racing with much success. Niemann also

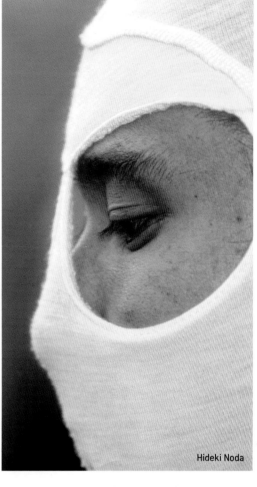

Hideki Noda

entered this car into the South African Grand Prix, held at East London, in 1963 and 1965. The first time, he finished in 14th place, after starting 15th on the grid. The second time, he failed to qualify.

Niemann continued in Formula Junior before switching to Enduro motorcycle racing, in which he won the 1979 South African Championship. After retiring from racing, he moved to Wales to start a motorcycle workshop.

Gunnar NILSSON

Nationality: South African
Born: 20th November 1948
Died: 20th October 1978
Seasons: 1976-1977
Team/manufacturer(s): Lotus
Grands Prix: 32
Race wins: 1
Championship wins: 0

Gunnar Nilsson began racing in his late teens in his home country, before moving to England in 1974 to compete in Formula Super Vee. The following year he progressed to Formula 3 and won the British championship that season, driving for March.

For 1976, Nilsson moved to Lotus to drive the new Lotus 77 alongside Mario Andretti. In his first Formula One season Nilsson made a good impression, getting two third place finishes plus a fifth and a six and picking up 11 Championship points.

The following year was even better. Nilsson won the

Gunnar Nilsson

Belgian Grand Prix and performed remarkably at many others, driving the Lotus 78 ground-effect car. With a total of 20 Championship points he was eighth in the World Championship and people spoke of him being a future champion.

Tragically, though, it was not to be. Nilsson was struck down with testicular cancer and was too ill to drive for Arrows the following season. He died in 1978 and the Gunnar Nilsson Cancer Foundation was set up in his memory.

Hideki NODA

Nationality: Japanese
Born: 7th March 1969
Seasons: 1994
Team/manufacturer(s): Larrousse, Simtek
Grands Prix: 3
Race wins: 0
Championship wins: 0

Hideki Noda was a talented kart racer as a boy, winning various Japanese championships. He then progressed to Formula Junior and won four races in his first season, aged just 18.

It was then on to Formula 3, first in Japan, then in Britain. This led to a drive in Formula 3000 for 1992 and the following two years.

As well as competing in Formula 3000, Noda was also trying to get into Formula One and he finally succeeded at the end of the 1994 season. With the help of sponsorship, he got a drive with the troubled Larrousse team. Despite outdated cars, he still managed to qualify for all three Grands Prix he entered – European, Japanese and Australian. Unfortunately, though, he failed to finish any of the races, spinning off in Japan and suffering mechanical failures at the others.

Noda signed to drive for Simtek in 1995, but nothing came of the deal and he moved to the US the following year to compete in Indy Lights. He later returned to Japan and raced GTs for some years. In 2005 and 2006 he competed in the A1 Grand Prix series.

Rodney NUCKEY

Nationality: British
Born: 26th June 1929
Died: 29th June 2000
Seasons: 1953
Team/manufacturer(s): Cooper
Grands Prix: 1
Race wins: 0
Championship wins: 0

London-born Rodney Nuckey was an amateur driver who worked for the family engineering company in Hertfordshire.

In the early 1950s, he competed in Formula 3, driving his own Cooper-Norton, and he won a number of races in the 1952 season. Nuckey then progressed to a Formula 2 Cooper-Bristol for the following season and this was the car he entered into the 1953 German Grand Prix. He finished the Nürburgring race in 11th place, after starting 20th on the grid, which was a respectable performance for a first-timer. However, Nuckey never entered another Formula One event, competing instead in Formula Libre through the 1954 season. Nuckey returned to running the family business before emigrating to Australia and then the Philippines, where he died in 2000.

MNO

O

O'BRIEN, Robert
OLIVER, Jackie
ONGAIS, Johnny
OPPITZHAUSE, Karl
OWEN, Arthur

Jackie Oliver

Robert O'BRIEN

Nationality: American
Born: 11th April 1908
Died: 10th February 1987
Seasons: 1952
Team/manufacturer(s): Simca
Grands Prix: 1
Race wins: 0
Championship wins: 0

Robert O'Brien was born in New Jersey and grew up to be a keen amateur racing driver. In the early 1950s he competed in a number of American races, including the Carrera Panamerican and various events at Watkins Glen.

In 1952, O'Brien travelled to Europe to gain experience. There, he travelled around the continent in a Cadillac, towing his Frazer Nash racecar behind him.

However, this was not the car he used in his one and only World Championship race. Instead, he borrowed a Simca-Gordini and entered it into the 1952 Belgian Grand Prix at the Spa-Francorchamps circuit. After starting in 22nd place on the grid, he finished the race in 14th place.

After that one season in Europe, O'Brien returned to his home state of New Jersey, where he worked in the motor industry.

Keith Jack (Jackie) OLIVER

Nationality: British
Born: 14th August 1942
Seasons: 1967-1973, 1977
Team/manufacturer(s): Lotus, BRM, McLaren, Shadow
Grands Prix: 50
Race wins: 0
Championship wins: 0

Jackie Oliver was born in Essex and began his racing career with a Mini and then a Lotus Elan in the early 1960s.

By 1967, he had progressed to Formula Two, driving for Lotus and in this year he made his World Championship debut, at the German Grand Prix, albeit driving in the Formula 2 class, which he won.

The following year, Oliver was promoted to the Lotus Formula One team and completed much of the season, with a fifth place finish in Belgium and a third in Mexico winning him six championship points.

From there on, though, Oliver had little success in Formula One, with a host of retirements sprinkled with the occasional points finish. In 1971 and 1972 he did not have a full-time Formula One drive, so spent time in CanAm racing.

After a season with the Shadow Formula One team in 1973, Oliver retired from Formula One, although he did make a one-off return in 1977, where he finished ninth in Sweden, again driving for Shadow.

Oliver is perhaps better known as one of the founders of the Arrows Grand Prix team, with which he remained involved until 1999, when he sold his share of the company.

Daniel (Danny) ONGAIS

Nationality: American
Born: 21st May 1942
Seasons: 1977-1978
Team/manufacturer(s): Penske, Ensign, Shadow
Grands Prix: 6
Race wins: 0
Championship wins: 0

Danny Ongais was born in Hawaii and began his career as

a drag racer in the late 1960s, before moving to circuit racing in 1974. He progressed through Formula 5000, USAC and IMSA in the USA, before making his Grand Prix debut at the 1977 USA Grand Prix, driving for Penske. He failed to finish that race, but went on to complete the Canadian Grand Prix in seventh place that season.

The following year, Ongais drove for Ensign in the Argentinean and Brazilian Grands Prix, but retired from both. He then went to the Shadow team and entered the USA West and Dutch Grands Prix, but failed to pre-qualify for either, because of very uncompetitive cars.

Ongais then retired from Formula One to concentrate on sportscar racing. He survived a horrendous crash at Indianapolis in 1981 and retired from racing six years later. However, he returned in 1996 to compete in the Indy 500, finishing seventh. He then continued to race on an occasional basis into his sixties.

Karl OPPITZHAUSER

Nationality: Austrian
Born: 4th October 1941
Seasons: 1976
Team/manufacturer(s): March
Grands Prix: 1
Race wins: 0
Championship wins: 0

Austrian Karl Oppitzhauser began racing in Formula Vee in 1963 and progressed to a Ferrari Dino in 1968, and a Lamborghini Muira three years later. He then competed in the Alfasud Cup from 1972 to 1975.

In 1976, Oppitzhauser made his one and only attempt at Formula One racing. He entered a non-works March 761 into his home Grand Prix, despite having had almost no experience in single-seater racing. Because of this lack of experience, Oppitzhauser and his teammate, Otto Stuppacher, were not allowed to race.

Unlike Stuppacher, Oppitzhauser did not make any further attempts at Formula One, but went on to race sportscars and touring cars with some success. After retiring from full-time racing, he ran a Mitsubishi dealership in his hometown of Bruck.

Arthur OWEN

Nationality: British
Born: 21st March 1915
Died: 13th April 2000
Seasons: 1960
Team/manufacturer(s): Cooper
Grands Prix: 1
Race wins: 0
Championship wins: 0

Born in London, Arthur Owen moved to Jersey, in the Channel Islands, where he ran a jewellery business. In his spare time, he enjoyed competing in hillclimb events and travelled around Europe competing in a Cooper during the 1950s.

Owen didn't usually compete in circuit racing but he was asked to enter his Cooper into the 1960 Italian Grand Prix because many of the English teams had boycotted the event because it was using a banked section of the Monza circuit.

Unfortunately, though, Owen had an accident right at the start of the race and had to retire. After that, he went back to his hillclimbing and, in 1961, won the British Championship. Owen later retired to the Algarve and then returned to England, where he died in 2000.

M
N
O

P-Q

PACE, Carlos
PAGANI, Nello
PALETTI, Riccardo
PALM, Torsten
PALMER, Jonathan
PANIS, Olivier
PANTANO, Giorgio
PAPIS, Massimiliano
PARKES, Mike
PARNELL, Reg
PARNELL, Tim
PATRESE, Riccardo
PEASE, Al
PENSKE, Roger
PERDISA, Cesare
PEREZ-SALA, Luis

PERKINS, Larry
PERROT, Xavier
PESCAROLO, Henri
PESENTI-ROSSI, Alessandro
PETERS, Josef
PETERSON, Ronnie
PIAN, Alfredo
PICARD, François
PIETERSE, Ernie
PIETSCH, Paul
PILETTE, Andre
PILETTE, Teddy
PIOTTI, Luigi
PIPER, David
PIQUET, Nelson
PIROCCHI, Renato

PIRONI, Didier
PIRRO, Emanuele
PIZZONIA, Antonio
POLLET, Jacques
PON, Ben
POORE, Dennis
POSEY, Sam
POZZI, Charles
PRETORIUS, Jackie
PRINOTH, Ernesto
PROPHET, David
PROST, Alain
PRYCE, Tom
PURLEY, David
PUZEY, Clive
QUESTER, Dieter

Nelson Piquet

José Carlos (Carlos) PACE

Nationality: Brazilian
Born: 6th October 1944
Died: 18th March 1977
Seasons: 1972-1977
Team/manufacturer(s): Williams, Surtees, Brabham
Grands Prix: 73
Race wins: 1
Championship wins: 0

Usually known as Carlos Pace, this talented Brazilian began racing karts in the 1960s and went on to be the country's Formula Vee Champion three times in a row.

Pace then travelled to Britain in 1970 to race successfully in Formula 3, followed by Formula 2 the following season, driving for Williams. He impressed enough to be promoted to the team's Formula One team in 1972, and he had a reasonable first season, picking up three championship points.

A move to Surtees for the next year saw Pace perform even better, although he then moved to Brabham partway through 1974. It was with that team that he picked up his one win – at the 1975 Brazilian Grand Prix. That season he finished sixth in the Championship.

Pace continued to perform well for Brabham through 1976 and into 1977, when he came second at the first race of the season in Argentina. But then disaster struck when the light aircraft he was flying in over Brazil crashed and Pace was killed. Today, the Brazilian Grand Prix circuit is called Autódromo José Carlos Pace in his memory.

Cirillo (Nello) PAGANI

Nationality: Italian
Born: 11th October 1911
Died: 18th October 2003
Seasons: 1950
Team/manufacturer(s): Maserati
Grands Prix: 1
Race wins: 0
Championship wins: 0

Nello Pagani was born in Milan to a wealthy family and began racing motorcycles in 1928. He proved to be a great talent on two wheels, winning a number of major events and becoming the first ever 125cc World Champion in 1949. That same year he came second in the 500cc class.

Although motorcycles were his first love, Pagani also raced cars, beginning in 1947 in a Maserati. Indeed, it was in a Maserati that he entered his one and only World Championship Grand Prix. This was the Swiss event and Pagani started from 15th on the grid and worked his way up to finish in a respectable seventh pace, in front of other more experienced drivers.

After that, Pagani continued to race bikes until he retired from the sport in 1956 to manage the MV Agusta racing team. He died in 2003 at the age of 92.

Riccardo PALETTI

Nationality: Italian
Born: 15th June 1958
Died: 13th June 1982
Seasons: 1982
Team/manufacturer(s): Osella
Grands Prix: 8
Race wins: 0
Championship wins: 0

Carlos Pace

Milan-born Riccardo Paletti began racing at the age of 19 and worked his way from SuperFord to Formula 3 and then Formula 2, driving for the Onyx team in 1981.

Despite not performing particularly well in Formula 2, Paletti managed to pick up enough sponsorship to gain a place on the small Osella Formula One team for the 1982 season.

Paletti got off to a disappointing start to the season, failing to qualify for the first three races. Then, at the San Marino Grand Prix he finally made it onto the grid, starting in 13th place, only to be forced to retired with suspension problems.

Then it was three more non-qualifiers before Paletti entered the Canadian Grand Prix. And it was here that tragedy struck. Didier Pironi stalled his Ferrari on the grid and Paletti was unable to avoid it, and slammed his car into the back of it at over 100mph. He sustained terrible chest injuries and died in hospital soon after.

As a tribute to Paletti, the racetrack at Parma in Italy was renamed Autodromo Riccardo Paletti.

Torsten PALM

Nationality: Swedish
Born: 23rd July 1947
Seasons: 1975
Team/manufacturer(s): Hesketh
Grands Prix: 2
Race wins: 0
Championship wins: 0

Swedish driver, Torsten Palm, began his career as a rally driver and navigator before moving to Formula 3 in the late 1960s, driving a Brabham. He performed well and won the Swedish Formula 3 Championship in 1970 and 1971.

Palm continued to excel in Formula 3 after that, but wanted to progress, so he entered a few Formula 2 races in 1973 and 1974. And then, in 1975, he managed to raise enough sponsorship to buy two drives with the Hesketh Formula One team.

He entered the Monaco Grand Prix first but failed to qualify. Then, at the Swedish Grand Prix, Palm ran out of fuel two

Jonathan Palmer

laps before the end of the race, but still finished in 10th place. After that, Palm's sponsorship money ran dry and he gave up with Formula One.

Palm later returned to rally driving before retiring from the sport in 1995 to run a garage in Sweden.

Dr Jonathan PALMER

Nationality: British
Born: 7th November 1956
Seasons: 1983-1989
Team/manufacturer(s): Williams, Ram, Zakspeed, Tyrrell
Grands Prix: 87
Race wins: 0
Championship wins: 0

Jonathan Palmer was born in London, the son of a doctor. He followed in his father's footsteps and studied medicine at university, but was a passionate racing driver while a student. After qualifying, he worked as a doctor in London, but realised that his first love was racing, so he competed in Formula 3 in 1981, winning the British Championship that year.

Palmer went on to win the European Formula 2 title in 1983, the same year he had his Formula One debut, driving for Williams in the European Grand Prix at the end of the season and finishing 13th.

He then drove for RAM the following season before moving to Zakspeed for 1985 and 1986, which proved a struggle because the team didn't have the resources to compete at top level. Also in 1985, Palmer competed in sportscars and finished second at Le Mans.

A move to Tyrrell in 1987 saw Palmer proving himself as a competent driver and he remained with his team throughout the rest of his Formula One career, until the end of the 1989 season. During this time, he scored a number of Championship points and consistently finished in the top ten. However, a win always eluded Palmer, with his best result being a fourth place at the 1987 Australian Grand Prix.

After working as a test driver for McLaren after that, Palmer was a television commentator for a short while and also formed a company running racetracks, including Bedford and Brands Hatch.

Olivier PANIS

Nationality: French
Born: 2nd September 1966
Seasons: 1994-1999, 2001-2004
Team/manufacturer(s): Ligier, Prost, BAR, Toyota
Grands Prix: 158
Race wins: 1
Championship wins: 0

Jonathan Palmer

Giorgio Pantano

championships. He then went on to win the Italian and World Junior titles in 1994, and the European Formula A Championship in 1995 and 1996.

From there, Pantano drove in Formula 3 and won the German championship in 2000, his first season. By this time, he was tipped to be a Formula One star and began testing for various teams. However, it was not until 2004 that he managed to land a drive, with the Jordan team.

Sadly, though, it was not a successful year for Pantano, with him struggling with an uncompetitive car and wrangles over sponsorship. In the end, he left the team before the end of the season, unable to manage better than a 13th place finish.

Since then, Pantano has driven in the GP2 Series.

Massimiliano (Max) PAPIS
Nationality: Italian
Born: 3rd October 1969
Seasons: 1995
Team/manufacturer(s): Footwork
Grands Prix: 7
Race wins: 0
Championship wins: 0

Massimiliano 'Max' Papis worked his way up through karting, Formula 3 and then to Formula 3000, where he performed well.

His short Formula One career started in the middle of the 1995 season, when he joined the struggling Footwork

team, which was tempted by the sponsorship he was able to bring to the table. Sadly, he struggled to compete and failed to complete five of the seven races he entered. However, he did manage to finish a reasonable seventh at his home Grand Prix, just missing a point.

Papis didn't finish the season and went on to race in the US CART series in 1996 and competed in that until 2003, after which he concentrated on sportscar racing.

Michael Johnson (Mike) PARKES
Nationality: British
Born: 24th September 1931
Died: 28th August 1977
Seasons: 1959, 1966-1967
Team/manufacturer(s): Fry, Ferrari
Grands Prix: 7
Race wins: 0
Championship wins: 0

Michael Parkes' father was chairman of Alvis, so motoring was in his blood from an early age. He began racing an MG TD and then a Frazer Nash, in his spare time.

By 1957, Parkes was racing a Lotus and was a reserve driver for the work's team at Le Mans. In 1959, he had his Formula One debut, entering a David Fry Formula 2 car at the British Grand Prix at Aintree. However, he failed to qualify and went on to race in sportscar events, winning the Sebring 12 Hour race in 1964, among others.

Parkes then returned to Formula One in 1966, driving for Ferrari. This time, he got off to a good start, finishing second at the French Grand Prix. He also competed in the Dutch and German events that year, before gaining another second place finish, this time in Italy.

The following year, Parkes raced in just two Grands Prix, in Holland (where he picked up points by finishing fifth) and Belgium. At the second race, though, he crashed badly and was unable to race for the rest of the season, thus ending his Formula One career.

Parkes then worked as a manager at Ferrari but continued to race sportscars on an occasional basis. He was killed in 1977 on the public road, when his car collided with a lorry.

Reginald Harold Haslam (Reg) PARNELL
Nationality: British
Born: 2nd July 1911
Died: 7th January 1964
Seasons: 1950-1952, 1954
Team/manufacturer(s): Alfa Romeo, BRM, non-works Ferrari, non-works Maserati, non-works Cooper
Grands Prix: 7
Race wins: 0
Championship wins: 0

Derbyshire-born Reg Parnell began racing an MG Magnette in the 1930s. This was followed by a successful spell behind the wheel of a Bugatti, but the Second World War drew his racing to a close, when he was still in his prime.

After the war, Parnell raced a Maserati, again very successfully, before entering the very first Formula One World Championship race, held at Silverstone. Driving a works Alfa Romeo, he stormed to a third-place finish.

Parnell then competed in a handful of other Formula One races, including his home race, which he entered three more times, and performed well.

In 1957, Parnell retired from racing to run the Aston Martin race team, and he later ran Yeoman Racing. In 1962,

Olivier Panis

Frenchman Olivier Panis began racing karts as a youngster and went on to compete in Pilote Elf and Formule Renault before making the break into Formula 3 in 1990, finishing second in the championship the following year.

Panis then moved to Formula 3000 and won the championship in 1993, which led to a drive with the Ligier Formula One team the following year. He had a good first year, scoring nine Championship points and finishing in second place at the German Grand Prix.

From there, Panis continued to perform well for Ligier, picking up 16 points in 1995 and 13 in 1996. It was 1996 that saw Panis take his one and only Formula One win, at Monaco.

Panis moved to Prost for 1997, 1998 and 1999, but missed most of the 1997 season after sustaining a broken leg at the Canadian Grand Prix, but still picked up 16 Championship points because of some good finishes at the start of the season. However, in 1998 he had a poor year and failed to get any points, followed by just two in 1999.

After a break from Formula One, Panis drove for BAR in 2001 and 2002, and then for Toyota in 2003 and 2004. He stayed on as a test driver after that before retiring from Formula One in 2006.

Giorgio PANTANO
Nationality: Italian
Born: 4th February 1979
Seasons: 2004
Team/manufacturer(s): Jordan
Grands Prix: 14
Race wins: 0
Championship wins: 0

Italian Giorgio Pantano began karting at the age of nine and, in his first year, won the Italian and the European cadet

Riccardo Patrese

came sixth in Japan.

This was followed by four seasons with Arrows, then a move to Brabham in 1982 saw Patrese take his first win, at the Monaco Grand Prix. He then won again the following season, this time in Spain.

After a couple of years with Alfa Romeo in 1984 and 1985, Patrese returned to Brabham for two seasons and then moved to Williams. It was with this team that he had his most successful seasons – in 1989 and 1991, he finished the Championship in third place, with a total of 40 and 53 points, respectively. And then, in 1992, he was runner-up in the Championship, behind Nigel Mansell.

For his last Formula One season, Patrese drove for Benetton and had another good year, finishing fifth in the Championship.

Then, at the end of the 1993 season, Patrese decided to call it a day – after a record-breaking 256 Grands Prix (six more than Michael Schumacher on his retirement). Patrese returned to racing in 2005 to compete in the Grand Prix Masters formula.

Victor (Al) PEASE
Nationality: Canadian
Born: 15th October 1921
Seasons: 1967-1969
Team/manufacturer(s): Eagle
Grands Prix: 3
Race wins: 0
Championship wins: 0

Al Pease was actually born in the north-east of England but grew up in Canada. There, he raced a Lotus 23 with some success in the early 1960s.

he formed his own team, Reg Parnell Racing. Sadly, though, he died of complications following an appendix operation in 1964, leaving his son, Tim, to run the team, in conjunction with BRM.

Reginald (Tim) PARNELL
Nationality: British
Born: 25th June 1932
Seasons: 1959, 1961, 1963
Team/manufacturer(s): Cooper, Lotus
Grands Prix: 4
Race wins: 0
Championship wins: 0

The son of racing driver, Reg Parnell, Tim Parnell (although he'd been named after his father, he preferred to be called Tim) grew up in a racing household, yet never managed to match the success of his father on the racetrack.

After starting his career in Formula Junior, the young Parnell attempted the British Grand Prix in 1959, driving a Cooper-Climax but, sadly, did not qualify.

In 1961, he had another stab at his home race, but had to retire after 12 laps with a failed clutch. However, at the Italian Grand Prix that year, he managed to finish in 10th place.

After failing to qualify for the 1963 German Grand Prix, Parnell gave up racing to concentrate on running Reg Parnell Racing, after the unexpected death of his father. He also ran the BRM Formula One team in the early 1970s.

Parnell was later chairman of the British Racing Drivers' Club and a director of Derby Country Football Club.

Riccardo PATRESE
Nationality: Italian
Born: 17th April 1954
Seasons: 1977-1993
Team/manufacturer(s): Shadow, Arrows, Brabham, Alfa Romeo, Williams, Benetton
Grands Prix: 256
Race wins: 6
Championship wins: 0

Riccardo Patrese first shot to prominence when he won the World Karting Championship at the age of 20. This was following by winning the European Formula 3 Championship two years later.

In 1977, Patrese started the season in Formula 2, but soon moved to Formula One, driving for the Shadow team, and scoring a point at the end of the season when he

Reg Parnell

Pease went on to enter the Canadian Grand Prix three times, from 1967 to 1969. He was driving a 1966 Eagle-Climax Formula One car each time. However, he had little luck. The first year, he had an unclassified finish because he was 43 laps behind. The second time, his car's engine failed in practice and he never started the race.

It was Pease's third year that proved to be his most infamous, though. He was black-flagged during the race for driving too slowly! The only driver in Formula One history to be able to claim that dubious distinction.

Pease later competed in sportscar racing before retiring from the sport. He moved to Tennessee where he enjoyed restoring cars for a hobby.

Roger PENSKE

Nationality: American
Born: 20th February 1937
Seasons: 1961-1962
Team/manufacturer(s): Cooper, Lotus
Grands Prix: 2
Race wins: 0
Championship wins: 0

Roger Penske grew up in Ohio and was obsessed by cars, even though he was badly injured when one knocked him off his motorcycle as a teenager. He started racing a Chevrolet Corvette while studying at business college and went on to win a SCCA championship in 1961.

That same year, Penske drove a Cooper-Climax in the US Grand Prix at Watkins Glen, finishing in eighth place. He then competed in the same race in 1962, this time driving a Lotus-Climax to a ninth place finish.

However, Penske really excelled in other events, winning the 1962 USAC Road Racing Championship, the Nassau TT and various other American events.

Despite his undoubted talent, Penske retired from racing at the age of 27 to concentrate on his business ventures. He went on to run a number of car dealerships around the USA and started Penske Racing in 1966 in collaboration with Mark Donohue. In time, the Penske Corporation grew to have a number of car-related businesses, including over 200 dealerships in the USA, racing teams and leasing companies.

Cesare PERDISA

Nationality: Italian
Born: 21st October 1932
Died: 10th May 1998
Seasons: 1955-1956
Team/manufacturer(s): Maserati
Grands Prix: 7
Race wins: 0
Championship wins: 0

Italian Cesare Perdisa came from a wealthy family which ran a publishing company. He began racing as a hobby in the early 1950s, driving a Maserati and showing some real talent.

His Grand Prix career was short but noteworthy. His first Formula One event was the 1955 Monaco Grand Prix, where he drove his Maserati to a third place finish. He then finished eighth at the Belgium race that season.

The following year, Perdisa entered five more Grands Prix, and finished third in Belgium, fifth in France, seventh in Monaco and Great Britain, but failing to start his last race, in Germany.

Perdisa had the odd habit of sitting in the cockpit before a race, cracking open and eating raw eggs! He retired from racing in 1957 due to family pressures, and became involved in business.

Luis PÉREZ-SALA

Nationality: Spanish
Born: 15th May 1959
Seasons: 1988-1989
Team/manufacturer(s): Minardi
Grands Prix: 32
Race wins: 0
Championship wins: 0

Luis Pérez-Sala was born in Barcelona in 1959. He began racing in earnest in 1985, when he competed in the Italian Formula 3 Championship.

The following year, Pérez-Sala moved to Formula 3000 and won two races in his first season. And then, in 1987, he came close to winning the championship, finishing in second place.

This impressive performance helped Pérez-Sala to get a place on the Minardi Formula One team for the 1988 season. It was a mixed season, with the Spaniard failing to qualify for or finish a number of races, but he did come in sixth at the Portuguese Grand Prix.

It was a similar story for 1989, when Pérez-Sala remained with Minardi and, once again, had a best place finish of sixth, this time at the British Grand Prix.

Luis Pérez-Sala

P
Q
R

Henri Pescarolo

he finished a worthwhile sixth in class.

That was Perrot's only Formula One appearance, although he continued to race in Formula 2, using a March 701. After 1972, however, he turned his attention to hillclimbing, again using the March which was ideally suited to the discipline.

After retiring, Perrot remained in his hometown of Zurich.

Henri PESCAROLO
Nationality: French
Born: 25th September 1942
Seasons: 1968, 1970-1974, 1976
Team/manufacturer(s): Matra, Williams, Iso Marlboro, BRM, Surtees
Grands Prix: 59
Race wins: 0
Championship wins: 0

After racing in a Lotus 7 in the mid-1960s, Henri Pescarolo proved himself a successful Formula 3 driver, winning the European Championship in 1967, driving for Matra.

From there, he moved to Formula 2 in 1968, still with Matra, and had his Formula One debut at the Canadian Grand Prix, although he had to retire with engine problems. He then drove in the Mexican Grand Prix that year and finished ninth.

The year 1970 saw Pescarolo do a full season in Formula One for Matra, and he finished 12th in the Championship with 8 points – the high point of the year being a third place finish at Monaco.

A move to Williams for 1971 saw Pescarolo pick up four points and finish 17th in the Championship. From there, though, it was mainly downhill, with Pescarolo concentrating more on sportscar racing than Formula One. Indeed, in 1973, he only competed in three Grands Prix.

After a disappointing 1974 season with BRM and then to Surtees for 1976, Pescarolo retired from Formula One but continued to compete in sportscars, winning at Le Mans no less than four times. He ran his own team, called Pescarolo Sport.

Alessandro PESENTI-ROSSI
Nationality: Italian
Born: 31st August 1942
Seasons: 1976
Team/manufacturer(s): Tyrrell
Grands Prix: 4
Race wins: 0
Championship wins: 0

Italian driver Alessandro Pesenti-Rossi was born in Bergamo in 1942. In the late 1960s and early 1970s he competed in Italian Formula 3 and gradually improved over the years to do reasonably well.

By 1974 and 1975 Pesenti-Rossi was also racing in Formula 2, with some success and he was encouraged enough to attempt to break into Formula One the following season.

Therefore, in 1976 Pesenti-Rossi entered four Grands Prix, driving a privately run Tyrrell. Despite his lack of experience, he managed to qualify for and finish three of the races. At the first, in Germany, he finished 14th, then he came 11th in Austria and 18th in Italy. He failed to qualify for the Dutch Grand Prix.

It was a brave attempt but, after that, Pesenti-Rossi returned to the safer world of Formula 2 for the 1977 and 1978 seasons. After that, he no longer competed seriously.

That was Pérez-Sala's last season in Formula One, after that he concentrated on touring car and GT racing in his home country.

Larry PERKINS
Nationality: Australian
Born: 18th March 1950
Seasons: 1974, 1976-1977
Team/manufacturer(s): Amon, Boro, Brabham, BRM, Surtees
Grands Prix: 15
Race wins: 0
Championship wins: 0

Australian Larry Perkins came from the small town of Cowangie in Victoria and enjoyed cars from a young age.

In the early 1970s, Perkins competed in a range of local championships, including Formula Vee, Formula Ford and Formula 2. He then travelled to the UK to further his career by racing in Formula Ford and Formula 3.

This then led to a drive with the ill-fated Amon Formula One team at the German Grand Prix, but Perkins failed to qualify and so returned to Formula 3.

He then had another go at Formula One in 1976, when he drove for the Boro team at the start of the season, with a best result of eighth place in Belgium. He later moved to

Brabham but had little success.

The following year, Perkins drove for BRM for the first two races of the season before quitting. Later in the season, he drove in three races for Surtees. Once again, though, he had little success.

That, then, was the end of Perkins' Formula One career and he returned to Australia where he became a successful touring car driver, before retiring from the sport in 2003. He also ran his own team, Perkins Engineering.

Xavier PERROT
Nationality: Swiss
Born: 1st February 1932
Seasons: 1969
Team/manufacturer(s): Brabham
Grands Prix: 1
Race wins: 0
Championship wins: 0

Born in Zurich, Xavier Perrot ran his own garage business and raced in his spare time, campaigning an Abarth-Simca and Lotus 23 in local races and hillclimbs.

By 1968, Perrot had progressed to Formula 2, driving his own Brabham BT23C and gradually improving with time. The following season saw him enter the car into the Formula 2 class of the German Grand Prix at the Nürburgring, where

Josef PETERS

Nationality: German
Born: 16th September 1914
Died: 24th April 2001
Seasons: 1952
Team/manufacturer(s): Veritas
Grands Prix: 1
Race wins: 0
Championship wins: 0

Born in Düsseldorf in 1914, Josef Peters was a regular driver in postwar Germany, driving a two-seater Veritas in various events.

Peters competed in just one World Championship event, the 1952 German Grand Prix at the Nürburgring. Driving a BMW-powered Veritas, number 129, he started from 20th on the grid. Sadly, though, he didn't get past the first lap and retired from the race, for reasons that are not recorded. Actually, it's interesting to note that seven other drivers were also out of the race on the first lap, and 18 cars failed to finish the race.

That was the extent of Peters' Formula One career. He went on to continue to campaign his trusty Veritas in a variety of races, including the 1953 Nürburgring 1000km, in which he won the 1500-2000cc class.

Bengt Ronnie (Ronnie) PETERSON

Nationality: German
Born: 14th February 1944
Died: 11th September 1978
Seasons: 1970-1978
Team/manufacturer(s): March, Tyrrell, Lotus
Grands Prix: 123
Race wins: 10
Championship wins: 0

Ronnie Peterson began karting as a child and was Swedish champion a number of times in his late teens and early twenties.

He then moved on to Formula 3 and then Formula 2, winning the European Formula 2 Championship in 1971.

While competing in Formula 2, Peterson also began entering Formula One races, starting with the 1970 Monaco Grand Prix, when he finished seventh driving for March.

The following year, Peterson drove full time for March and then moved to Lotus for 1973. It was this year that he had his first of 10 Formula One wins, driving a Lotus 72 at the French Grand Prix. He then went on to win three more races that season, at Austria, Italy and the USA.

In 1974, Peterson continued to do well, winning the French, Italian and Monaco Grands Prix for Lotus. However,

Ronnie Peterson

he had less success in 1975, because the new Lotus 76 was less competitive.

This led to a move back to March for 1976, and he won the Italian Grand Prix in a March 761 car. Peterson then went to Tyrrell for 1977 for a disappointing season and back to Lotus in 1978, when he won the South African and Austrian Grands Prix.

It was set to be another good season for Peterson, but then tragedy struck. At the Italian Grand Prix that year, there was a massive pile-up of cars at the start, and Peterson's Lotus crashed into the barriers and caught fire. His legs were badly injured and he was taken to hospital, where he died of complications the next day. The racing world lost one of its greatest drivers before he had the chance to win the World Championship.

Alfredo PIÁN

Nationality: Argentinean
Born: 21st October 1912
Died: 25th July 1990
Seasons: 1950
Team/manufacturer(s): Maserati
Grands Prix: 1
Race wins: 0
Championship wins: 0

Argentinean driver, Alfredo Pián, was born in Las Rosas in Santa Fe in 1912. Very little is known of his life, but he did have one, unsuccessful stab at a World Championship Formula One event.

This was the 1950 Monaco Grand Prix – in the first year of Formula One. Pián entered a Maserati 4CLT run by the Scuderia Achille Varzi racing team from Italy.

Unfortunately, though, things didn't go according to plan. Pián was doing well in practice, and lying in sixth place, time-wise, when his car spun in a patch of oil, which had leaked from another vehicle. The Maserati then hit the crash barrier and its hapless driver was thrown out of the cockpit. Pián suffered injuries to his legs and was unable to compete in the race proper.

And that was the extent of Pián's Formula One career.

François PICARD

Nationality: French
Born: 26th April 1921
Died: 29th April 1996
Seasons: 1958
Team/manufacturer(s): Cooper
Grands Prix: 1
Race wins: 0
Championship wins: 0

Frenchman François Picard lived in Nice and began his racing career after the Second World War. He started off modestly with a Renault 4CV before progressing to a rather more glamorous Porsche, with which he had some success.

Picard then drove a Ferrari in various long-distance races in France and North Africa, and he achieved some good results.

Sportscars, then, were what Picard knew, so it was odd that he should have driven a single-seater in the Moroccan Grand Prix in 1958. Behind the wheel of a borrowed Cooper-Climax, Picard started from 24th on the grid but, after 24 laps, he crashed into a Ferrari that had spun out of control. Picard was seriously injured and never raced again after that.

Nelson Piquet

Ernest (Ernie) PIETERSE

Nationality: South African
Born: 4th July 1938
Seasons: 1962-1963, 1965
Team/manufacturer(s): Lotus
Grands Prix: 3
Race wins: 0
Championship wins: 0

Ernest Pieterse came from Bellville in South Africa and, in the post-war years he made a name for himself racing saloon cars in his home country.

By the start of the 1960s, though, he had switched to single-seaters, and in 1961 he won the Rhodesian Grand Prix. The following season, Pieterse won the South African Championship, driving his own Lotus 21.

Also in 1962, he entered his first World Championship race, the South African Grand Prix, again in his Lotus 21, and finished in 10th place after starting 13th on the grid.

Pieterse entered his Lotus in the same Grand Prix the following year but this time retired after just three laps with engine failure. After continuing to perform well at local level, Pieterse again entered the South African Grand Prix in 1965 but failed to qualify. He then gradually left the limelight from then on.

Paul PIETSCH

Nationality: German
Born: 20th June 1911
Seasons: 1950-1952
Team/manufacturer(s): Maserati, Alfa Romeo, Veritas
Grands Prix: 3
Race wins: 0
Championship wins: 0

Paul Pietsch began racing in the 1930s, hillclimbing a Bugatti and Alfa Romeo, before switching to circuit racing when he joined the Auto Union team.

In 1935, he competed in the German Grand Prix (which was pre-Formula One World Championship days) and the Italian Grand Prix, finishing third in the latter.

However, Pietsch didn't get on with the rear-engined Auto Union cars and so, from 1937, he competed in his own Maserati.

After the Second World War, he continued to race, and entered the first World Championship Italian Grand Prix in 1950, but failed to finish.

The following year, Pietsch drove for Alfa Romeo in the German Grand Prix, but was involved in a serious accident. He had another attempt at the race in 1952, this time with Veritas, but was forced to retire with gearbox problems after just one lap.

After that, Pietsch pretty much retired from the sport to concentrate on building up his magazine publishing company, which specialised in motorcycle and car magazines.

André PILETTE

Nationality: Belgian
Born: 6th October 1918
Died: 27th December 1993
Seasons: 1951, 1953-1954, 1956, 1961, 1963-1964
Team/manufacturer(s): Talbot, Connaught, Gordini, Emeryson, Lotus, Sirocco
Grands Prix: 14
Race wins: 0
Championship wins: 0

Born in Etterbeek, André Pilette was the son of a pioneer racing driver and started racing after the Second World War.

By 1951, he had entered his first Grand Prix, driving a Talbot for Ecurie Belgique in Belgium and finishing in sixth place. He then had another go at the same race two years later and finished 11th, driving a Connaught.

Pilette went on to compete in his home Grand Prix three more times, between then and 1964. However, he also raced in other Grands Prix in this period, for various teams, and on a fairly occasional basis.

His best result was a fifth place at the 1954 Belgian Grand Prix, which scored him his only two Championship points of his career, while driving for Gordini.

After retiring from competition in 1964, Pilette when on to open his own racing school in Zolder, which was later taken over by his son, Teddy Pilette, who was also a racing driver.

Theodore (Teddy) PILETTE-VLUG

Nationality: Belgian
Born: 26th July 1942
Seasons: 1974, 1977
Team/manufacturer(s): Brabham, BRM
Grands Prix: 4
Race wins: 0
Championship wins: 0

Theodore Pilette-Vlug was born in Brussels, the son of racing driver, André Pilette. He began racing karts successfully as a boy and then moved to the UK to train at the Jim Russell Racing School. This led to him being involved in the films Grand Prix and Le Mans.

Pilette raced in GTs and saloon cars before moving to single-seaters, winning the European Formula 5000 Championship in 1973 and 1975.

His Grand Prix career was brief and undistinguished. In 1974, he drove a Brabham in the Belgian Grand Prix and finished in 17th place. And then, in 1977, he joined the ailing BRM team for three races, but failed to qualify for any of them.

After that, Pilette won the 1978 Spa 24 Hours and, in the 1990s, formed his own Formula Ford team and built and drove his own Formula 3 car. He was also involved in his father's racing school.

Luigi PIOTTI

Nationality: Italian
Born: 27th October 1913
Died: 19th April 1971
Seasons: 1956-1958
Team/manufacturer(s): Maserati, Osca
Grands Prix: 7
Race wins: 0
Championship wins: 0

Luigi Piotti was born in Milan and grew up to be a successful and wealthy businessman who had the money to indulge in his hobby of racing, which he put into his Maseratis in the early 1950s.

However, he was also a reasonable driver and found himself entering his first World Championship Grand Prix in 1956. This was the 1956 Argentinean race, where Piotti retired after an accident on the 57th lap.

Also that season, Piotti entered Monaco and Pescara Grands Prix, and then the Italian Grand Prix where he finished in a very respectable sixth place, after starting from 15th on the grid. However, he gained notoriety in Italy for nudging Stirling Moss's car into the pits after it had run out of fuel, thus allowing the Englishman to win the race!

Piotti entered just one more Grand Prix, the 1958 Monaco race, driving an Osca, but he failed to qualify in the uncompetitive car. After that, he concentrated on his business ventures and cut back on his motorsport.

David PIPER

Nationality: British
Born: 2nd December 1930
Seasons: 1959-1960
Team(s): Lotus
Grands Prix: 3
Race wins: 0
Championship wins: 0

Edgware-born David Piper began competing in hillclimbs in the 1950s before getting involved in circuit racing in his own Lotus 16.

It was in this car that he entered a handful of Grands Prix in 1959 and 1960. His first attempt was the 1959 British Grand Prix in which he managed 19 laps before having to retire with an overheating engine.

The following year, Piper travelled across the Channel to compete in the French Grand Prix, but failed to get off the grid because of engine difficulties. He then had another stab at his home Grand Prix and this time finished in 12th place, after starting 24th on the grid.

Soon after this, Piper sold his Lotus for a Ferrari and began to concentrate on sportscar racing. He then bought a Porsche 917 and was asked to use this for the Steve McQueen film, Le Mans. Unfortunately, though, he crashed the car during filming and had to have part of his leg amputated. This didn't put him off racing, though, and he continued to use the 917 in historic events. He also ran his own Ferrari garage in Surrey.

Nelson PIQUET

Nationality: Brazilian
Born: 1952
Seasons: 1978-1991
Teams: Ensign, Brabham, Williams, Lotus, Benetton
Grands Prix: 207
Race wins: 23
Championship wins: 3

The triple World Champion from Brazil was born Nelson Piquet Souto Maior and, as the son of a government minister, he had a privileged upbringing. He was a talented tennis player and was sent to sports school in San Francisco. However, while in the USA, Piquet became more interested in motor racing, something his father disapproved of.

Determined to race, though, the boy got involved in karting, using his mother's maiden name, but spelled 'Piket' at this time. Before long, he'd established himself as a competent driver and went on to win the Brazilian Championship in his second year.

His father still wasn't impressed, though, and insisted that his son returned to the USA to study engineering. However, Piquet continued racing when he could and, by 1976 he won the Brazilian SuperVee Championship.

Piquet moved to Europe in 1977 to race in Formula Three, finishing third in the championship in his first year and winning it the following season.

This led to a drive with Brabham, alongside Niki Lauda,

Didier Pironi

the following year. After a promising first season, in 1980 Piquet was promoted to team leader, and gained his first Grand Prix win, at Long Beach. By the end of the season, he was within a point of winning the championship, just behind Alan Jones. Piquet went on to win the Championship in 1981. The next year was less successful, though, because Brabham was experimenting with a new turbocharged BMW engine. Piquet won in Canada but was otherwise frustrated by mechanical problems.

It proved to be time well spent in development, though, because the next season, Piquet made good use of the powerful new engine and went head to head with Alain Prost to take the Championship for a second time.

Piquet left the team in 1986 and signed up with Williams. Sadly, his first season was marred by disagreements with teammate, Nigel Mansell, who refused to play supporting role to the Brazilian; an argument that probably cost Piquet the championship that year. In 1987, though, he managed to fight back and secured the Championship.

A move to the ailing Lotus team, in exchange for a huge salary, in 1988 was to prove disastrous for Piquet, with no wins that year, and a similarly disappointing season in 1989. He then switched to Benetton in 1990 and managed two wins that year, plus one the following season. However,

it was not a good enough performance to persuade any team to offer him the sort of money he demanded for a place in 1992, so Piquet headed off to the USA to compete there. However, he was badly injured in practice for the Indianapolis 500, so he retired from racing and went back to his home country.

Piquet pursued a number of business interests in Brazil and continued to compete in sportscar racing.

Renato PIROCCHI

Nationality: Italian
Born: 26th March 1933
Died: 29th July 2002
Seasons: 1961
Teams: Cooper
Grands Prix: 1
Race wins: 0
Championship wins: 0

Renato Pirocchi began racing sportscars in the 1950s before moving into Formula Junior, in which he excelled for a number of years.

His one and only World Championship event was the 1961 Italian Grand Prix at Monza. Driving a dated Cooper-Maserati run by the Pescara Racing Club, he put in a reason-

able performance to finish in 12th place after starting 29th on the grid. And, although he was the last to complete the race, there were 20 other cars who failed to finish at all.

Later in life, Pirocchi retired from racing and became President of the Automobile Club of Pescara, and was instrumental in reviving the Svolte di Popoli annual road race in Italy. He died from kidney problems in 2002.

Didier PIRONI

Nationality: Italian
Born: 26th March 1952
Died: 23rd August 1987
Seasons: 1978-1982
Teams: Cooper
Grands Prix: 3
Race wins: 0
Championship wins: 0

Didier Pironi grew up interested in all sorts of sports, and was a talented athlete and swimmer before gaining his pilot's licence at a young age. After a spell racing motorcycles, Pironi turned his attention to cars and was Formule Renault Champion in 1974 and Super Renault Champion the following year.

This led to a drive in Formula 2 in 1976 and, two years later,

Emanuele Pirro

Pironi was driving for the Tyrrell Formula One team. He had an impressive two years with the team, picking up a total of 21 points. For 1980, though, Pironi moved to Ligier where he did even better, winning the Belgian Grand Prix and finishing fifth in the Championship.

After that, Pironi moved to Ferrari and his career appeared to be going from strength to strength. In 1981, he finished 13th in the Championship, but the next year he won at San Marino and Holland, and picked up points in most other races. He was a front-runner to win the Championship when he crashed badly in practice for the German Grand Prix at Hockenheim. Pironi's legs were badly damaged and he was unable to race again that season, although he still finished second in the Championship.

By 1986, he had recovered from his injuries well enough to test again and, although he proved capable, he was unable to find a team to drive for. Instead, then, he competed in powerboat racing. Tragically, his boat crashed off the Isle of Wight in 1987 and Pironi was killed, along with his crew.

Emanuele PIRRO

Nationality: Italian
Born: 1st December 1962
Seasons: 1989-1991
Teams: Benetton, Dallara
Grands Prix: 40
Race wins: 0
Championship wins: 0

Emanuele Pirro was born in Rome and was fascinated by motorsport from an early age. He began racing karts at the age of 11 and was soon winning Italian championships. By 1981, he had progressed to Formula Fiat Abarth and won the title in his first year.

From there, Pirro raced successfully in Formula 3 and then Formula 2 and Formula 3000, proving himself a capable driver in every series.

After a short spell in touring cars and sportscars, Pirro finally broke into Formula One in 1989, driving for Benetton from partway through the season. The highpoint of the year was a fifth place finish at the Australian Grand Prix at the end of the season.

For 1990 and 1991, Pirro drove for the Dallara team but with little success; his best result being sixth at the 1991 Monaco Grand Prix.

That was the end of Pirro's Formula One career, afterwards he concentrated on sportscars, making history by winning at Le Mans in a diesel-powered Audi R10 in 2006.

Antônio Reginaldo PIZZONIA

Nationality: Brazilian
Born: 11th September 1980
Seasons: 2003-2005
Teams: Jaguar, Williams
Grands Prix: 19
Race wins: 0
Championship wins: 0

Brazilian driver Antônio Pizzonia came to the UK in 1997 after proving himself a talented kart racer in his home country. He soon made a name for himself, winning the F-Vauxhall Junior and F-Renault Championships before going on to win the 2000 British Formula 3 Championship.

By 2001, Pizzonia was driving in Formula 3000 and also working as a test driver for the Williams Formula One team. He was then taken on as a driver by the Jaguar team for 2003, but was dropped partway through an unsuccessful season. He then returned to Williams as a test driver and

Antonio Pizzonia

P
Q
R

Sam Posey

Pon drove for Porsche for a number of years, winning his class at Le Mans in 1961 and was an accomplished sportscar driver.

However, his one and only Formula One appearance was less than successful. Driving a Porsche in the 1962 Dutch Grand Prix, Pon hit some oil on the third lap and his car spun out of control and overturned. Luckily for Pon, he was not injured.

After that, he continued to race sportscars for Porsche until retiring from professional racing in 1965. In 1972, Pon represented his country in clay pigeon shooting at the Summer Olympics.

Pon later moved to California where he set up a respected winery, and he also ran a wine distribution company in Holland.

Roger Dennistoun (Dennis) POORE
Nationality: British
Born: 19th August 1916
Died: 12th February 1987
Seasons: 1952
Teams: Connaught
Grands Prix: 2
Race wins: 0
Championship wins: 0

Born in London, Dennis Poore came from a wealthy family. He began racing an MG before joining the RAF as Wing Commander during the Second World War.

After the war, Poore bought an Alfa Romeo with which he hillclimbed and he went on to win the 1950 RAC Hillclimb Championship.

Two years later, he joined the Connaught race team briefly and entered the British Grand Prix in 1952, finishing in fourth place and scoring three Championship points. Later that same year, Poore competed in the Italian Grand Prix and finished 12th.

After then competing in an Aston Martin sportscar, Poore retired from racing to concentrate on running the family engineering empire. He also helped found Autosport magazine and, for a time, owned several ill-fated British motorcycle companies.

ended up driving in four Grands Prix in 2004, coming seventh in three and retiring from the fourth.

Pizzonia continued in his role as test driver for 2005 and, once again, was called on to race at the end of the season in five races, and had a best finish of seventh place in Italy.

After that, though, he was unable to find a place for 2006 and so Pizzonia ended up going to the USA to compete in the CART series.

Jacques POLLET
Nationality: French
Born: 2nd July 1922
Died: 16th August 1997
Seasons: 1954-1955
Teams: Gordini
Grands Prix: 5
Race wins: 0
Championship wins: 0

Jacques Pollet drove for the Gordini team in the mid-1950s, in both sportscars and single-seaters, and this led to him appearing in five World Championship Grands Prix.

The first was the 1954 French Grand Prix, in which Pollet was out of the running after eight laps, due to engine fail-

ure. Then, later the same year, he entered the Spanish Grand Prix but, again, had to retire because of engine problems, this time after 37 laps.

The following year saw Pollet finish a respectable seventh place at the Monaco Grand Prix, after starting 20th on the grid. Then in Holland he finished in 10th place, while at the Italian Grand Prix he once again suffered engine failure and had to retire after 26 laps. Pollet had better luck in sportscars, winning his class at Le Mans in 1954, before disappearing from the racing scene.

Bernardus (Ben) PON
Nationality: Dutch
Born: 9th December 1936
Seasons: 1962
Teams: Porsche
Grands Prix: 1
Race wins: 0
Championship wins: 0

Born Bernardus Pon, but better known as plain 'Ben', his father imported Volkswagens into the USA and was closely involved in the development of the now classic Type 2 VW camper van.

Sam POSEY
Nationality: American
Born: 26th May 1944
Seasons: 1971-1972
Teams: Porsche
Grands Prix: 2
Race wins: 0
Championship wins: 0

Born in New York City, Sam Posey's first success was in 1969, when he won the Lime Rock Trans-Am in a Ford Mustang. He continued to compete in various American race series, including the Indianapolis 500.

Posey's Formula One career was short and unfulfilling, though. He entered the US Grand Prix twice, in 1971 and 1972. The first time was driving a works Surtees but he failed to finish the race. The following year, he drove a Surtees for the Champcarr Inc team and came in 12th.

After retiring from racing, Posey worked as a motor-racing commentator for American television, and later he commentated on the Tour de France cycle race. Posey also wrote books on model railways, another interest of his.

Carlos Alberto (Charles) POZZI

Nationality: French
Born: 27th August 1909
Died: 28th February 2001
Seasons: 1950
Teams: Talbot
Grands Prix: 1
Race wins: 0
Championship wins: 0

Born Carlos Alberto Pozzi in Paris to Italian parents, Pozzi grew up to be a successful luxury car dealer in the post-war years.

Unusually, he didn't start motor-racing until he was 37 years old, campaigning a Delahaye in a number of pre-World Championship Grands Prix in France and Italy.

With the coming of the Formula One World Championship in 1950, Pozzi found himself entering just one race, the French Grand Prix of that year. Driving a Talbot, he finished in sixth place. Pozzi then went on to race in endurance events, including Le Mans, and he won the Casablanca 12 Hours race in 1952. He later formed a company which was France's official importer of Ferraris and Maseratis.

Jacobus (Jackie) PRETORIUS

Nationality: South African
Born: 22nd November 1934
Seasons: 1965, 1968, 1971, 1973
Teams: LDS, Brabham, Iso
Grands Prix: 4
Race wins: 0
Championship wins: 0

South African driver Jackie Pretorius made a name for himself in his home country, driving successfully in local events.

Not surprisingly, then, he appeared in the South African Grand Prix on four occasions in the 1960s and 1970s.

The first time was in 1965, when Pretorius drove an Alfa Romeo-powered LDS but failed to pre-qualify for the race.

He tried again three years later, in 1968, this time in a Brabham Climax and managed 71 laps to finish the race at the back of the field and his time was not classified.

Pretorius's luck was no better on his third attempt, in 1971, when the engine of his Brabham Ford gave out after 22 laps.

Finally, he made one last appearance in 1973, behind the wheel of a Ford-powered Iso Marlboro. Again, though, he had to retire, this time on the 35th lap because of an overheating engine.

After retiring from racing, Pretorius continued to attend historic events in South Africa.

Ernesto PRINOTH

Nationality: Italian
Born: 15th April 1923
Died: 26th November 1981
Seasons: 1962
Teams: Lotus
Grands Prix: 1
Race wins: 0
Championship wins: 0

Italian driver Ernesto Prinoth was born in Ortisei and grew up to enjoy racing cars at a local and national level.

His one and only attempt at a Formula One World Championship race was in 1962, when he tried to enter the Italian Grand Prix, held at Monza. Prinoth was driving a Lotus 18 with a Climax straight-four engine which was being run by the Scuderia Jolly Club. Sadly, though, he failed to qualify for the race, which was won by Graham Hill.

Prinoth later moved to Austria where he ran a company that produced snow-grooming vehicles. He died of a heart attack while working at a ski resort in Innsbruck in 1981.

David PROPHET

Nationality: British
Born: 9th October 1937
Died: 29th March 1981
Seasons: 1963, 1965
Teams: Brabham
Grands Prix: 2
Race wins: 0
Championship wins: 0

David Prophet was born in Hong Kong but grew up in the English Midlands, where he became a successful motor dealer, specialising in exotic cars. This gave him the income to indulge his passion for motor racing, which he started at the age of 23.

In 1963, he bought a Brabham BT6 Formula Junior car and took it to South Africa, where he entered the Formula One Grand Prix, retiring with low oil pressure after 49 laps.

Prophet became a regular visitor to South Africa and entered the Grand Prix there again in 1965, this time finishing in 14th place after starting 19th on the grid.

After racing in Formula 2 for some years, Prophet turned his attention to sportscar racing, in a Ford T40, Lola T70 and McLaren M6A.

Tragically, he was killed in 1981 when his helicopter crashed on take-off at the Silverstone circuit, after he'd been watching a Formula 2 race.

Alain Marie Pascal PROST, OBE

Nationality: French
Born: 24th February 1955
Seasons: 1980-1991, 1993
Teams: McLaren, Renault, Ferrari, Williams
Grands Prix: 202
Race wins: 51
Championship wins: 4

As a boy, Prost wanted to be a professional footballer and probably would have done very well in that sport. Thankfully for the world of motorsport, though, he got

Alain Prost

Alain Prost

involved in karting as a teenager and soon realised that this was more fun. By the age of 18, he had won the European Junior Karting Championship and went on to compete in other karting events around Europe.

In 1975, Prost entered the Volant Elf competition and won a drive in the Formula Renault Championship the following year. He dominated the championship and walked away with the title.

This persuaded Renault to promote Prost to Formula 3 for 1978. After struggling with a substandard car in his first season, the Frenchman went on to win both the French and European Formula 3 Championships in 1979. This led to Prost being signed by the McLaren Formula One team for the 1980 season.

Sadly, Prost's debut in Formula One was marred by mechanical failures, one of which led to a minor crash that caused him to break a wrist. Despite this, the newcomer out-drove teammate, John Watson, to finish the championship in sixth place. However, Prost was not happy with McLaren and broke his contract to move to Renault the following year.

Prost won his first Formula One race on home turf at the French Grand Prix in 1981. He did well with Renault, coming second in the World Championship in 1983, behind Nelson Piquet. However, there was constant pressure on him to be the first French World Champion driving a French car, so Prost returned to McLaren for 1984.

Prost was once again runner-up at the end of 1985, second only to teammate Niki Lauda. And in 1985 he won his first Championship title; a success he repeated the following year.

Prost himself recommended that McLaren sign Ayrton Senna as his teammate for 1988, and the pair dominated the series, with Prost coming second place to Senna in the Championship. However, the following year led to confrontation between the two drivers.

The rivalry came to a head at the Japanese Grand Prix, when Prost knew that, if neither driver finished, he would win the Championship on points. The two McLarens collided and Prost retired from the race, but Senna continued, after being given an illegal push-start by the marshals, for which he was disqualified, ensuring that

Prost won the Championship.

In 1990, the tables were turned, though, and Senna deliberately drove into Prost, who was now driving for Ferrari, to ensure that Senna would clinch the title. Prost stayed with Ferrari for 1991 but he was dismissed before the end of the season for being publicly critical of the team.

There was no time to sign to another outfit for 1992, but Prost found himself driving for Williams in 1993. With seven wins that year, he easily took the Championship for a fourth time. Despite this, Williams dropped the Frenchman in favour of Ayrton Senna, and so Prost retired from Formula One.

He then became a commentator on Formula One for French television and worked as a consultant for Renault and McLaren. In 1997 he bought the Ligier team and renamed it Prost Grand Prix.

Thomas Maldwyn (Tom) PRYCE

Nationality: British
Born: 11th June 1949
Died: 5th March 1977
Seasons: 1974-1977
Teams: Token, Shadow
Grands Prix: 42
Race wins: 0
Championship wins: 0

Welshman Thomas Pryce began racing at the age of 21, after he had won a Formula Ford car in a newspaper competition. He then worked his way up through Formula Vee, Formula 3 and Formula 2.

Pryce's Formula One career began in 1974, when he joined the new Token team. He failed to qualify for his first Grand Prix, in Belgium, and then was refused entry to the Monaco Grand Prix because it was claimed he did not have enough experience.

He then moved to the Shadow team for the rest of the season and, indeed, the rest of his career. He performed well in 1975 and 1976, picking up third-place finishes in Austria and Brazil, and finishing 10th and 12th in the Championship respectively.

Pryce was then given an uncompetitive new car for the 1977 season, and got off to a poor start. And then disaster struck. At the South African Grand Prix, Pryce's car hit a teenage marshal, Jansen Van Vuuren, who had been told to cross the track to help another car, which was on fire. Van Vuuren was flung into the air and was killed instantly, and the fire extinguisher he was carrying struck Pryce on the head as the car was travelling at high speed, and he was nearly decapitated. The driver dead, the car continued along the circuit, hitting another car before coming to a standstill.

Sadly, Pryce is remembered more for this bizarre and tragic incident than his skills as a driver.

David Charles PURLEY

Nationality: British
Born: 26th January 1945
Died: 2nd July 1985
Seasons: 1973-1974, 1977
Teams: LEC, Token
Grands Prix: 11
Race wins: 0
Championship wins: 0

Born in West Sussex, David Purley's family ran the LEC Refrigeration company. He served in the army before turning his hand to motor racing, beginning with an AC Cobra and then moving on to Formula 3 in the early 1970s.

In 1973, Purley used a hired March and sponsorship from LEC to race in four Grands Prix that year. He retired from two and finished 15th in the British Grand Prix and ninth in the Italian race. At the Dutch Grand Prix he stopped his car to try to help Roger Williamson, who was trapped in a burning car. Purley received the George Medal for his actions.

The following year, Purley drove a Token in the British Grand Prix but failed to qualify. He then turned his attention to Formula 2 for the next couple of years.

He did, though, return to Formula One in 1977, this time in a specially commissioned LEC car. Sadly, he had little success in the five races he entered. Indeed, he crashed badly during pre-qualifying for the British Grand Prix and was badly injured.

Purley raced little after that and was killed when his aerobatic plane crashed into the sea off Bognor Regis.

Clive PUZEY

Nationality: Rhodesian
Born: 11th July 1941
Seasons: 1965
Teams: Lotus
Grands Prix: 11
Race wins: 0
Championship wins: 0

Clive Puzey was born in Bulawayo and began racing in local South African Formula One races in 1963, driving a Lotus 18/21. However, he only ever entered one World Championship race, and that was the 1965 South African Grand Prix. Driving his Lotus, Puzey failed to pre-qualify.

After that, Puzey continued to race with some success in the South African Formula One Championship until he retired from the sport in 1969. He then ran a garage in his hometown until 2000, when it was attacked in the Zimbabwean uprising because Puzey was instrumental in the opposition to Robert Mugabe. After that, Puzey moved to Australia.

Dieter QUESTER

Nationality: Austrian
Born: 30th May 1939
Seasons: 1969, 1974
Teams: BMW, Surtees
Grands Prix: 2
Race wins: 0
Championship wins: 0

Dieter Quester raced motorcycles and speedboats in the 1950s before turning to cars in the 1960s, first touring cars and then Formula 2, driving for BMW in both cases.

It was with BMW that Quester was entered for the 1969 German Grand Prix. However, his teammate, Gerhard Mitter was killed during practice and, because mechanical failure was suspected, the team withdrew from the race and so Quester did not actually take part in it.

In 1974, Quester had another chance at Formula One, when he drove for Surtees at the Austrian Grand Prix. Surprisingly, he finished in ninth place, ahead of double World Champion Graham Hill.

Despite this promising performance, Quester never raced in Formula One again, preferring to concentrate on touring cars. He continued to race well into his sixties and had some great successes.

Tom Pryce

David Purley

R

RABY, Ian
RAHAL, Bobby
RÄIKKÖNEN, Kimi
RAPHANEL, Pierre-Henri
RATZENBERGER, Roland
REBAQUE, Hector
REDMAN, Brian
REES, Alan
REGAZZONI, Clay
REUTEMANN, Carlos
REVENTLOW, Lance
REVSON, Peter
RHODES, John
RIBEIRO, Alex
RICHARDSON, Ken
RIESS, Fritz
RINDT, Jochen
RISELEY-PRICHARD, John

ROBARTS, Richard
RODRIGUEZ, Pedro
RODRIGUEZ, Ricardo
RODRIGUEZ LARRETA, Alberto
ROL, Franco
ROLLINSON, Alan
ROLT, Tony
ROOS, Bertil
ROSBERG, Keke
ROSBERG, Nico
ROSIER, Louis
ROSSET, Ricardo
ROTHENGATTER, Huub
RUBY, Lloyd
RUDAZ, Jean-Claude
RUTTMAN, Troy
RYAN, Peter

Clay Regazzoni

Kimi Räikkönen

Ian RABY

Nationality: British
Born: 22nd September 1921
Died: 7th November 1967
Seasons: 1963-1965
Team/manufacturer(s): Gilby, Brabham
Grands Prix: 7
Race wins: 0
Championship wins: 0

Ian Raby was born in Woolwich and became a car dealer in Brighton. He began racing in 500cc Formula 3 in the 1950s, initially with a self-built car he called 'Puddle Jumper' (because of its low ground-clearance), and later in Coopers.

He then switched to sportscars for a while and drove with Jack Brabham in the 1957 Le Mans 24 Hour race before returning to single-seater racing.

At the start of the 1960s, Raby bought a Gilby-BRM and raced in three World Championship events in 1963. At the British Grand Prix at Silverstone, he retired with gearbox failure after 59 laps, and failed to qualify for the German and Italian races.

The following year, Raby drove a Brabham-BRM in the British and Italian Grands Prix, but crashed out of the former and did not qualify for the latter.

Raby stuck with the same car for 1965 and managed to finish the British Grand Prix in 11th place, but did not qualify for the other event he entered that season: the German Grand Prix.

After that, Raby raced in Formula 2, but died in November 1967 as a result of injuries sustained during an accident at the Zandvoort circuit in Holland.

Robert Woodward (Bobby) RAHAL

Nationality: American
Born: 10th January 1953
Seasons: 1978
Team/manufacturer(s): Wolf
Grands Prix: 2
Race wins: 0
Championship wins: 0

Robert Rahal was born in Ohio and began racing in Canadian Formula Atlantic before coming to Europe in 1978 to compete in Formula 3 with the Wolf team.

Such was his performance, that the team offered him the chance to race in Formula One at the end of the 1978 season. Rahal came 12th in the US Grand Prix, but retired from the Canadian race after 16 laps with fuel problems.

After a season of Formula 2 in Europe, Rahal returned to the USA in 1980. He went on to become an accomplished CART driver, winning the Championship on three occasions.

Since retiring from driving, Rahal ran his own race team, Rahal Letterman Racing, and was also involved in the Jaguar Formula One team.

Kimi Matias RÄIKKÖNEN

Nationality: Finnish
Born: 17th October 1979
Seasons: 2001-
Team/manufacturer(s): Sauber, McLaren, Ferrari
Grands Prix: 122
Race wins: 15
Championship wins: 1

Kimi Räikkönen began karting from the age of 10 and soon proved to be very talented. He went on to win the British Formula Renault Winter series in 1999 before winning the Formula Renault UK Championship the following year.

Following these successes, Räikkönen was signed by the Sauber Formula One team for the 2001 season and had a promising first year, finishing 10th in the Championship with nine points.

The following year, Räikkönen moved to McLaren and had another good season, scoring 24 points and finishing sixth in the Championship. Then, in 2003, hr had his first win, at the Malaysian Grand Prix, and finished second in the Championship.

Räikkönen slipped back to seventh place at the end of the 2004 season, but fought back in 2005, with no less than seven wins to end the year in second place again. Then, in 2006, he came fifth in the Championship.

After Michael Schumacher's retirement, Räikkönen left McLaren and signed with Ferrari for the 2007 season and beyond. The 2007 season was a fantastic one for the Finn, with him winning six grands prix, including the Brazilian race at the end of the season. This left him with 110 points enabling him to clinch the World Championship, with a one-point lead over newcomer Lewis Hamilton.

Pierre-Henri RAPHANEL

Nationality: French
Born: 27th May 1961
Seasons: 1988-1989
Team/manufacturer(s): Larrousse, Coloni
Grands Prix: 17
Race wins: 0
Championship wins: 0

Pierre-Henri Raphanel was born in Algeria to French parents and was brought up in France. A career in karting culminated with him winning the French Championship at the age of 20.

Raphanel then moved up through Formula Renault and Formula 3, winning the latter's French Championship in 1985. He then moved around, not settling in any series for a few years. The end of the 1988 season saw Raphanel step in to drive for the Larrousse Formula One team in the Australian Grand Prix. Unfortunately, he failed to qualify because of a gearbox problem.

This was to become the pattern for the following season. Driving for Coloni, Raphanel did a full season of Formula One but failed to qualify or pre-qualify for all but one race. That was the Monaco Grand Prix, and even that Raphanel retired from with gearbox problems.

That, then, was the extent of Raphanel's Formula One career and he went on to have more success with sportscars, finishing second at Le Mans on two occasions. After retiring from racing, he ran an estate agency in Montpellier, and also worked as a test driver for Bugatti.

Roland RATZENBERGER

Nationality: Austrian
Born: 4th July 1960
Died: 30th April 1994
Seasons: 1994
Team/manufacturer(s): Simtek
Grands Prix: 3
Race wins: 0
Championship wins: 0

Pierre-Henri Raphanel

Roland Ratzenberger

Born in Salzburg, Roland Ratzenberger raced successfully in Formula Ford and Formula 3 before going to Japan to race in Formula 3000 there.

He then returned to Europe to drive for the new Simtek team for the 1994 Formula One season. His first Grand Prix was the Brazilian one, where Ratzenberger failed to qualify. He then did better at the Pacific Grand Prix, finishing in 11th place.

And then disaster struck. In qualifying for the San Marino Grand Prix at Imola, Ratzenberger's car's front wing was damaged and this led to him losing control at over 180mph and bouncing off a concrete wall. The Austrian suffered massive head injuries and was pronounced dead at the scene.

Ratzenberger was the first driver to die at a Formula One Grand Prix for 12 years, and the weekend was further marred by the death of Ayrton Senna during the race that followed.

Hector Alonso REBAQUE

Nationality: Mexican
Born: 5th February 1956
Seasons: 1977-1981
Team/manufacturer(s): Hesketh, Rebaque, Brabham
Grands Prix: 58
Race wins: 0
Championship wins: 0

Born in Mexico City to wealthy parents, Hector Rebaque came to Europe in 1974 to pursue a career in motor racing, competing in Formula Atlantic and Formula 2. He then moved to the USA to race in Formula Atlantic.

A return to Europe in 1977 saw Rebaque buy himself a drive with the Hesketh team for a disappointing season where he qualified for only one of the six Grands Prix he entered, and that he failed to finish.

The solution, Rebaque decided, was to set up his own team, called Rebaque, fielding Lotuses. In two seasons, the only worthwhile result was a sixth place finish at the German Grand Prix, which earned him one Championship point.

In 1980, Rebaque drove for Brabham for the second part of the season, doing reasonably well, and he stayed with the team for 1981, when he had three fourth-place finishes and a fifth, which gained him 11 points and left him 10th in the Championship.

After that, Rebaque went to the USA to race in CART but, after an accident in 1982, he decided to retire from racing. He later became a businessman.

Brian Thomas REDMAN

Nationality: British
Born: 9th March 1937
Seasons: 1968, 1970-1974
Team/manufacturer(s): Cooper, De Tomaso, Surtees, McLaren, Shadow
Grands Prix: 13
Race wins: 0
Championship wins: 0

Lancashire-born Brian Redman came from a wealthy family and grew up to work in the family grocery business.

In 1959, Redman began racing a Morris Minor and soon worked his way up to Jaguars and Lolas, proving himself to be a formidable talent.

A move to Formula 2 saw Redman have his Formula One debut, driving in three Grands Prix for Cooper in 1968 and finishing third in Spain.

He then moved to Porsche to compete in sportscar events, but returned to Formula One in 1970, when he entered the German Grand Prix with a De Tomaso. Redman then competed in occasional Grands Prix between then and 1974, scoring points when he finished fifth in Monaco and Germany in 1972.

However, he never really enjoyed the Formula One scene and so concentrated on sportscar racing, having great success driving for Porsche and Ferrari. After retiring from racing, Redman ran a motorsports marketing company and worked for Road & Track magazine in the USA.

Alan REES

Nationality: British
Born: 12th January 1938
Seasons: 1966-1967
Team/manufacturer(s): Winkelmann, Cooper
Grands Prix: 3
Race wins: 0
Championship wins: 0

Carlos Reutemann

Welshman Alan Rees came from a wealthy family so he was able to buy and run his own racecars, which gave his career a kickstart. He started with a Lotus 11 and worked his way up to Formula Junior, where he made quite an impression, winning the British Championship in 1961.

Rees then progressed to Formula 2 and this led to a handful of drives in Formula One Grands Prix. In 1966, he entered the Formula 2 category of the German Grand Prix, but failed to finish the race.

The following year, Rees drove in the British Grand Prix and finished a reasonable ninth. However, he then entered the German Grand Prix and came seventh, which equated to second in the Formula 2 class.

By 1969, Rees had retired from active racing and helped to set up March Engineering, before moving to Shadow and then Arrows.

Gianclaudio Giuseppe (Clay) REGAZZONI

Nationality: Swiss
Born: 5th September 1939
Died: 15th December 2006
Seasons: 1970-1980
Team/manufacturer(s): Ferrari, BRM, Ensign, Shadow, Williams
Grands Prix: 132
Race wins: 5
Championship wins: 0

Born Gianclaudio Regazzoni, but better known as Clay, this Italian-speaking Swiss driver began racing in the 1960s, driving for De Tomaso. By 1970, he had won the European Formula 2 Championship.

Regazzoni joined the Ferrari Formula One team for the second part of the 1970 season and immediately made an impression, winning in Italy and finishing third in the Championship, despite not doing a full season.

The next two years saw Regazzoni come seventh in the Championship each year for Ferrari before he moved to BRM for less successful season in 1973.

By 1974, he was back with Ferrari and won a second race, this time in German, and ended the season second in the Championship, just three points behind Emerson Fittipaldi. The next year, Regazzoni won the Italian Grand Prix and then the US West one in 1976.

Regazzoni then moved to Ensign and Shadow for 1977 and 1978 where he had less success. A move to Williams in 1979 saw him win his last race, in the UK, and finish the season in fifth place.

He then began the 1980 season driving for Ensign, but crashed at the US West Grand Prix and was left paralyzed from the waist down. Regazzoni went on to be very active in ensuring disabled people have equal opportunities and also helped developed hand-control systems for racecars.

Regazzoni died in a car accident in Italy in 2006.

Carlos Alberto REUTEMANN

Nationality: Argentinean
Born: 12th April 1942
Seasons: 1972-1982
Team/manufacturer(s): Brabham, Ferrari, Lotus, Williams
Grands Prix: 146
Race wins: 12
Championship wins: 0

Argentinean Carlos Reutemann raced touring cars and Formula 2 in his home country before coming to Europe in

1970 to compete in Formula 2, finishing the Championship in second place that year.

This led to a drive with the Brabham Formula One team in 1972 and Reutemann immediately astonished by taking pole position for his first ever Grand Prix, at Buenos Aires.

Reutemann stayed with Brabham and had a mix of excellent and disappointing results, winning no less than three races in 1974, but a number of retirements meant he finished the season in sixth place.

The following year, though, Reutemann did better overall, despite only winning one race, and took third place in the Championship.

After a disappointing 1976 season, Reutemann moved to Ferrari for 1977 and won in Brazil before finishing fourth in the Championship. He then came third the following year, still with the same time.

After a spell with Lotus, Reutemann joined Williams for 1980 and, again, finished the season in third place. However, the following year, he took second place, still with Williams.

After the first two races of 1982, Reutemann left the Williams team and that was the end of his Formula One career. He later entered politics in his home country.

Count Lance von HAUGWITZ HARDENBERG-REVENTLOW

Nationality: American
Born: 24th February 1936
Died: 24th July 1972
Seasons: 1960
Team/manufacturer(s): Reventlow, Cooper
Grands Prix: 4
Race wins: 0
Championship wins: 0

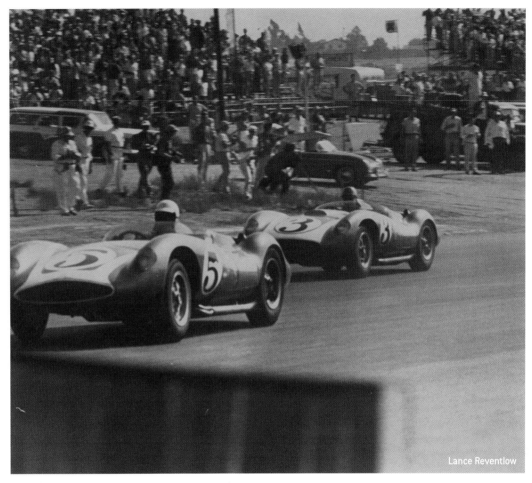
Lance Reventlow

Clay Regazzoni

Lance Reventlow was the son of a Danish nobleman and Barbara Hutton, who owned the Woolworth department stores, and who later married actor, Cary Grant.

Reventlow became hooked on cars as a teenager and bought a string of exotic cars and he became friendly with the actor James Dean, with whom he raced.

After a spell racing Formula 2 cars in Europe, Reventlow returned to the USA and set up the Scarab racecar company, which he himself raced successfully. Reventlow later moved the company to the UK and built a Formula One car. Unfortunately, its front-engined layout was uncompetitive compared to the latest rear-engined cars, and Reventlow had little luck when he raced it in a handful of Grands Prix during the 1960 season. Indeed, by the time of the British Grand Prix, he abandoned his own car in favour of a Cooper, but he still failed to qualify for the race.

By 1962, Reventlow had given up racing and concentrated on his other hobbies of flying, skiing and hiking. He was killed in a light-aircraft crash in 1972.

Peter Jeffrey REVSON

Nationality: American
Born: 27th February 1939
Died: 22nd March 1974
Seasons: 1964, 1971-1974
Team/manufacturer(s): Revson, Parnell, McLaren, Shadow
Grands Prix: 33
Race wins: 2
Championship wins: 0

PQR

Jochen Rindt

Peter Revson's family were part of the Revlon Cosmetics empire and he enjoyed a glamorous lifestyle, driving fast cars and boats, and competed in motor racing events in the US from the early 1960s. However, he wanted more so, in 1964, he travelled to Europe and competed, largely unsuccessfully, in six Grands Prix that season.

Revson then returned to the USA where he competed in various local races, including coming second at Sebring, driving a Porsche with Steve McQueen. He also competed in the 1971 US Grand Prix at Watkins Glen, but failed to finish.

The following year, though, saw Revson drive for McLaren in a full season of Formula One and had a successful year, topped off by coming second in Canada.

1973 was even better for Revson, with him winning the British and Canadian Grands Prix, and picking up points at many others, while still driving for McLaren.

Revson then moved to Shadow for the 1974 season and he was killed in practice for the South African Grand Prix when the suspension on his car failed.

John RHODES
Nationality: British
Born: 18th August 1927
Seasons: 1965
Team/manufacturer(s): Cooper
Grands Prix: 1
Race wins: 0
Championship wins: 0

Staffordshire-born John Rhodes began racing in the early 1960s, mainly in Formula Junior, a series in which he had some success.

Rhodes made just one foray into Formula One, when he entered the 1965 British Grand Prix at Silverstone, driving a V8-engined Cooper-Climax T60. After starting 21st on the grid, he had to retire with ignition problems after 38 laps.

Rhodes then returned to Formula Junior and also began racing Mini Coopers, for which he became well-known through the late 1960s. He continued to be involved with Mini racing for the rest of his career.

Alex Dias RIBEIRO
Nationality: Brazilian
Born: 7th November 1948
Seasons: 1976-1977, 1979
Team/manufacturer(s): Hesketh, March, Fittipaldi
Grands Prix: 10
Race wins: 0
Championship wins: 0

Brazilian Alex Dias Ribeiro won his country's Formula Ford Championship in 1973 and then travelled to Europe to compete in first Formula 3 then Formula 2.

Ribeiro's first Formula One race was at the US Grand Prix, where he finished in 12th place, driving a Hesketh car.

The following year, Ribeiro had his only full season of Formula One, driving for March. Unfortunately, though, the cars and the team were not up to the job and the Brazilian was not able to perform well at all, only finishing five races that season.

In 1979, Ribeiro returned to Formula One to drive in two races at the end of the season, the Canadian and US Grands Prix. However, he failed to qualify for either, driving for Fittipaldi. Ribeiro later drove the official medical car at Formula One Grands Prix and became involved in a Christian group for sports people.

William Kenneth (Ken) RICHARDSON
Nationality: British
Born: 21st August 1911
Died: 27th June 1997
Seasons: 1951
Team/manufacturer(s): BRM
Grands Prix: 1
Race wins: 0
Championship wins: 0

Ken Richardson was born and lived most of his life in Lincolnshire. An engineer by trade, he worked as a development driver for BRM in the early 1950s, and was involved in the team's V16 project.

This led to him being entered into the 1951 Italian Grand Prix, driving one of the P15 V16 cars. Richardson qualified in a respectable 10th place, but then was not allowed to start the race because it transpired he did not possess the correct racing licence.

Richardson continued to race until the late 1960s, when he then concentrated on his engineering.

Fritz RIESS
Nationality: German
Born: 11th July 1922
Died: 15th May 1991
Seasons: 1952
Team/manufacturer(s): Veritas
Grands Prix: 1
Race wins: 0
Championship wins: 0

Fritz Riess (or Rie) was born in Nuremberg in 1922 and was an active racer in his home country in the postwar years.

By the 1950s, he was driving a Veritas car in various domestic races, including the 1952 Germany Grand Prix, held at the Nürburgring. Riess qualified 12th and managed to finish a very respectable seventh, in a race that was won by Alberto Ascari.

Also in 1952, Riess won the Le Mans 24 Hour race, in a Mercedes Benz 300SL which he shared with Hermann Lang.Riess continued to race through the rest of the 1950s.

Karl Jochen (Jochen) RINDT
Nationality: Austrian
Born: 18th April 1942
Died: 5th September 1970
Seasons: 1964-1970
Team/manufacturer(s): Brabham, Cooper, Lotus
Grands Prix: 61
Race wins: 6
Championship wins: 1

German-born Jochen Rindt moved to Austria to live with his grandparents after his parents were killed in an air raid during the Second World War.

He grew up to be a successful Formula 2 driver before breaking into Formula One in 1964, when he did a one-off drive in his home Grand Prix, but failed to finish.

By 1966, Rindt was driving for Cooper and finished the Championship in a respectable third place after a successful season. Tragically, though, his best season was also to be his last. In 1970, driving a Lotus 72, Rindt won at Monaco and then, later in the season, he won an astonishing four Grands Prix in a row, in Holland, France, Britain and Germany.

And then disaster struck. During practice for the Italian Grand Prix, Rindt decided to have the wings removed from his Lotus 72, to give him a higher top speed so that he could compete better against the more powerful Ferraris. He lost control of the car coming into a corner and hit a crash barrier. Rindt's seatbelt cut into his throat and he died soon after.

Rindt was posthumously awarded the World Championship on account of the points he'd earned at the start of the season.

The trophy was presented to his widow to whom, ironically, he'd promised he'd retire from racing if he won the World Championship.

John Henry Augustin RISELEY-PRICHARD
Nationality: British
Born: 17th January 1924
Died: 8th July 1991
Seasons: 1954
Team/manufacturer(s): Connaught
Grands Prix: 1
Race wins: 0
Championship wins: 0

John Riseley-Prichard was born in Hereford in 1924 (with the surname Prichard). He began motor racing in the early 1950s, initially in a Riley.

By 1954, he had bought himself a used 2.0-litre Connaught A Type 4 racing car which he raced in various UK events, including winning a minor Formula One race in Cornwall, of all places.

Riseley-Prichard also entered the car into the 1954 British Grand Prix at Silverstone. Unfortunately, after qualifying 21st, he was involved in an accident on the 40th lap and was out of the race.

He continued to compete in the Connaught for another season, and drove an Aston Martin with Tony Brooks in the 1955 Le Mans 24 Hour race, and then retired from racing.

Riseley-Prichard worked as an insurance broker for a while, and then got accused of having links with paedophile rings, so he moved to Thailand. He died there from an AIDS-related illness in 1991.

Richard ROBARTS
Nationality: British
Born: 22nd September 1944
Seasons: 1974
Team/manufacturer(s): Brabham, Williams
Grands Prix: 4
Race wins: 0
Championship wins: 0

Richard Robarts came from an Essex farming family and started racing an Aston Martin when he was in his mid-twenties. He worked his way up to Formula 3 by 1973 and proved himself to be a talented driver.

The following year, Robarts made the jump to Formula One, paying for a drive with Brabham. However, after just three races, he was ousted to make way for another drive, Rikky von Opel, who was able to offer more money.

Robarts then found a drive with Williams and was entered into the Swedish Grand Prix, later that same season. However, before the race started, the seat was given to Tom Belso instead. That was the end of Robarts' Formula One career. He then raced in Formula 2 for a short while before going to work in coach-building in his home county of Essex.

PQR

Pedro Rodriguez

Pedro RODRIGUEZ

Nationality: Mexican
Born: 18th January 1940
Died: 11th July 1971
Seasons: 1963-1971
Team/manufacturer(s): Ferrari, Lotus, Cooper, BRM
Grands Prix: 54
Race wins: 2
Championship wins: 0

Born in Mexico City, Pedro Rodriguez was his country's national motorcycle champion in 1953 and 1954, before moving on to racing cars in 1957, in a Ferrari.

Before long, Rodriguez was competing at Le Mans, behind the wheels of a Ferrari and he went on to race there 14 times, winning in 1968.

Rodriguez began racing in Formula One Grands Prix in 1963, when he drove in the US and Mexican events for Lotus. From then on, he competed in occasional races over the years, and had his first win in 1967, driving a Cooper in South Africa.

The following year, Rodriguez did a full season of Formula One for BRM, finishing sixth in the Championship. He stayed with BRM and concentrated on Formula One after that, winning again in Belgium in 1970.

In 1971, Rodriguez was planning another full season with BRM and got off to a good start, finishing second in Holland. Then, in July of that year he was killed when driving a Ferrari 512M at a sportscar race in Germany.

Ricardo RODRIGUEZ

Nationality: Mexican
Born: 14th February 1942
Died: 1st November 1962
Seasons: 1961-1962
Team/manufacturer(s): Ferrari
Grands Prix: 5
Race wins: 0
Championship wins: 0

The younger son of Pedro Rodriguez, Ricardo Rodriguez began racing bicycles as a child before switching to motor-

cycles at the age of 14, and winning a number of Championships.

Rodriguez's car racing began with a Fiat saloon and then he turned to Porsches in the late 1950s and soon made a name as a force to be reckoned with. At the 1960 Le Mans 24 Hour race, he finished in second place, at the age of just 18.

His Formula One debut was in 1961, when Ferrari gave him a drive in the Italian Grand Prix. After astonishing everyone by qualifying in second place, Rodriguez was at the front of the pack for much of the race until he was forced to retire with fuel pump failure.

The following year, Rodriguez was given a works drive with Ferrari, but wasn't entered into every race, on account of his young age and relative inexperience. However, he performed well, finishing fourth in Belgium and sixth in Germany. That year, Rodriguez also won the Targa Florio.

The young Rodriguez had already proved he had the potential to be a champion, but it was not to be. In a non-Championship race in Mexico, he was driving a Lotus when he crashed during practice and was killed, at the age of just 20.

Alberto RODRIGUEZ LARRETA

Nationality: Argentinean
Born: 14th January 1934
Died: 11th March 1977
Seasons: 1960
Team/manufacturer(s): Lotus
Grands Prix: 1
Race wins: 0
Championship wins: 0

Alberto Rodriguez Larreta was born in Buenos Aires in 1934 and became an enthusiastic amateur racing driver who was well-known in his home country during the 1950s and 1960s. He had the nickname 'El Mosca' which means 'The Fly'.

Most of Larreta's racing took place within Argentina and it was there that he competed in his one and only Formula One event. He entered the 1960 Argentinean Grand Prix driving a Team Lotus 16. Starting in 15th place on the grid, he worked his way up to finish ninth, after 77 laps.

Larreta carried on racing until the end of the 1960s. He then became involved in various business ventures before dying of a heart attack in 1977.

Franco ROL

Nationality: Italian
Born: 5th June 1908
Died: 18th June 1977
Seasons: 1950-1952
Team/manufacturer(s): Maserati, Osca
Grands Prix: 5
Race wins: 0
Championship wins: 0

Born in Turin in 1908, Franco Rol came from a wealthy Italian family and racing was an indulgence for him.

Rol spent most of his time competing successfully in sportscar events in the immediate postwar years. However, he also dabbled in single-seater racing and this lead to handful of Grand Prix entries in the early 1950s.

In 1950, Rol drove his own Maserati A6GCM in the Monaco, French and Italian Grands Prix, but failed to finish any of them. The following year saw him drive an Osca 4500G in the Italian Grand Prix only and he finished in ninth place, after qualifying 18th.

For the 1952 Italian Grand Prix, Rol reverted to a Maserati

Keke Rosberg

but, again, was forced to retire, because of engine failure after 24 laps.

Rol was badly injured in an accident during the 1953 Tour of Sicily race and retired from racing after that.

Alan ROLLINSON

Nationality: British
Born: 15th May 1943
Seasons: 1965
Team/manufacturer(s): Cooper
Grands Prix: 1
Race wins: 0
Championship wins: 0

Alan Rollinson was born in Staffordshire and was a reasonably successful Formula 3, Formula 2 and Formula 5000 driver.

Unfortunately, he made just one attempt at Formula One without success. He entered a Ford-powered Cooper T71/73 into the 1965 British Grand Prix, which was held at Silverstone, but failed to qualify for the race.

That was the extent of Rollinson's Formula One involvement. However, he went on to have a long career as a racing driver, doing particularly well in Formula 3 and Formula 5000 in Britain. He later retired to Worcestershire.

Anthony Peter Roylance (Tony) ROLT

Nationality: British
Born: 16th October 1918
Seasons: 1950, 1953, 1955
Team/manufacturer(s): ERA, Connaught
Grands Prix: 3
Race wins: 0
Championship wins: 0

Anthony Rolt was born in Hampshire in 1918 and was a successful racing driver before the Second World War. During the war, he joined the British Army and found himself a prisoner of war in the infamous Colditz Castle, where he was involved in an audacious plan to escape using a glider. The castle was liberated by the allies before the plan was executed, though, and Rolt was awarded a Military Cross.

After the war ended, Rolt returned to the UK and resumed his racing career, driving a range of machinery, including Alfa Romeos and Delages, in a variety of mainly UK-based events.

Rolt entered the British Grand Prix three times, driving for the Peter Walker team. He was behind the wheel of an ERA in 1950, and a Connaught in 1953 and 1955. He failed to finish any of the races. However, in 1953 he won the Le Mans 24 Hour race for Jaguar.

Rolt was also instrumental in the development of four-wheel drive for cars, as part of the FF Developments company.

Bertil ROOS

Nationality: Swedish
Born: 12th October 1943
Seasons: 1974
Team/manufacturer(s): Shadow
Grands Prix: 1
Race wins: 0
Championship wins: 0

Born in Gothenburg, Bertil Roos moved to the USA in the early 1970s where he won the 1973 Super Vee Championship.

Back in Europe, he competed in Formula 2 and was asked to drive for the underperforming Shadow team in the 1974 Swedish Grand Prix. Sadly, though, the gearbox in his DN3 car gave up after just two laps of the race and Roos was forced to retire.

Roos never again raced in Formula One, instead returning to North America where he had more success in other race series.

After retiring from racing, Roos set up a drivers' school in the USA and was involved in the development of a special racing car for training purposes.

Keijo Erik (Keke) ROSBERG

Nationality: Finnish
Born: 6th December 1948
Seasons: 1978-1986
Team/manufacturer(s): Theodore, ATS, Wolf, Fittipaldi, Williams, McLaren
Grands Prix: 114
Race wins: 5
Championship wins: 1

Keijo – to give him his full name – Rosberg was born in Stockholm to Finnish parents. Back in Finland, he was the national kart champion no less than three times before moving on to Formula Vee and Super Vee, where he was also successful.

After a spell in Formula 2, Rosberg made his Formula One debut in 1978, with a relatively unsuccessful season with the Theodore team, and no more luck the following year with Wolf.

A move to Fittipaldi in 1980 saw Rosberg start the season with a third place in Argentina, and one or two other successful races, scoring him six points and putting him 10th in the Championship at the end of the year. However,

the next season with the same team was a disappointment.

For the 1982 season, Rosberg moved to Williams and had a tremendous year, scoring points in most of the races he entered, winning his first race, the Swiss Grand Prix, and finishing the season with 44 points, thus clinching the World Championship.

Rosberg stayed with Williams for the next three seasons and continued to perform well, winning at Monaco, USA (twice) and Australia. In 1985, he had his second-best season, finishing the Championship in third place with 40 points.

For the 1986 season, Rosberg moved to McLaren and, again, drove well, scoring 22 points and finishing the year in sixth place. That, though, was to be his final season in Formula One because he announced – prematurely as it happened – his retirement from the sport.

However, in 1989, he competed in the Spa 24 Hour race and continued to race in sportscar events in the early 1990s, before moving to German Touring Cars, setting up a team after he stopped racing.

Nico ROSBERG

Nationality: German
Born: 27th June 1985
Seasons: 2006-
Team/manufacturer(s): Williams
Grands Prix: 35
Race wins: 0
Championship wins: 0

Nico Rosberg was born in Wiesbaden in Germany, the son of 1982 Formula One World Champion, Keke Rosberg. Although his father is Finnish, Nico Rosberg races under the German

Nico Rosberg

flag, because that is his mother's nationality.

Rosberg began karting at the age of 11 and then, just six years later he won the German Formula BMW Championship in 2002. That same year, he tested for Williams and, in doing so, became the youngest person ever to drive a Formula One car – he was just 17.

However, he went on to race for his father's Formula 3 team in 2003 and 2004. For the 2005 season, Rosberg competed in the new GP2 Series and went on to win the Championship, driving for Williams.

This success led to a drive for the Williams Formula One team in 2006. He got off to a good start, finishing seventh in Bahrain and in the European Grand Prix. However, the rest of the season was less successful, with Rosberg retiring from many races, and finishing well down the pack in others. Rosberg remained with the Williams team for the 2007 season.

Louis ROSIER

Nationality: French
Born: 5th November 1905
Died: 29th October 1956
Seasons: 1950-1956
Team/manufacturer(s): Talbot, Ferrari, Maserati
Grands Prix: 38
Race wins: 0
Championship wins: 0

The son of a wine merchant, Louis Rosier began his working life as an apprentice in a garage and, before long, started racing motorcycles with some success.

Once he'd learned his trade, Rosier started his own garage business, selling Renaults and Talbots. Just before the outbreak of the Second World War he had begun racing cars and had even entered the Le Mans 24 Hour race.

Sadly, though, the war intervened and Rosier had to give up his work and hobby to work for the French Resistance.

After the end of hostilities, Rosier began racing again and won the French Championship in 1949 for the first of five times, before winning at Le Mans the following year.

Also in 1950, Rosier entered the inaugural season of Formula One, driving a Talbot and finishing fourth in the Championship, after a successful season.

That, though, was to be his best year of Formula One. Despite continuing to race in the series for the next five years, he never achieved such a good result, although he continued to excel in other races.

Tragically, Rosier was killed at the end of the 1956 season after a Ferrari he was racing at Montlhéry crashed.

Ricardo ROSSET

Nationality: Brazilian
Born: 27th July 1968
Seasons: 1996-1998
Team/manufacturer(s): Arrows, Lola, Tyrrell
Grands Prix: 33
Race wins: 0
Championship wins: 0

Brazilian driver Ricardo Rosset was born in Sao Paulo and first tasted success when he won a race in the 1993 British Formula 3 Championship. By 1995, he had progressed to Formula 5000 and finished the Championship in second place.

This achievement led to a drive with the Arrows Formula One team in 1996 where he had an uninspiring season.

However, that was better than his following year, when he joined the Lola team which then pulled out of Formula One after just one Grand Prix, leaving Rosset without a drive for the rest of the season.

Then, in 1998, Rosset joined Tyrrell, more on the back of his sponsorship than his skill as a driver. The season was a disaster with crashes and team arguments throughout the year. At one point, after damaging his car during practice at Monaco, Rosset's furious mechanics switched the first and last letters of his surname to say what they thought of him!

Rosset left the team at the end of the season and pretty much gave up motor racing. He returned to Brazil to develop his sportswear business.

Hubertus (Huub) ROTHENGATTER

Nationality: Dutch
Born: 8th October 1954
Seasons: 1984-1986
Team/manufacturer(s): Spirit, Osella, Zakspeed
Grands Prix: 30
Race wins: 0
Championship wins: 0

Huub Rothengatter was a successful Dutch businessman who worked his way up to Formula One after giving reasonable performances in Formula 3 in the 1970s and then Formula 2 during the early 1980s.

He finally made it into Formula One, driving for the small Spirit team from the UK, during the second part of the 1984 season. Rothengatter made little impact, though, with his best result being a reasonable eighth place in Italy.

Rothengatter then moved to Osella but, again, only for the latter part of the season and with similarly disappointing results. He did, though, manage to get a seventh place finish in Australia at the end of the year. He then moved to Zakspeed in 1986, missing the first two Grands Prix of the season but competing in all the rest, but with little success.

Rothengatter later gave up racing to concentrate on managing other drivers, including Dutchman Jos Verstappen.

Lloyd RUBY

Nationality: American
Born: 12th January 1928
Seasons: 1961
Team/manufacturer(s): Lotus
Grands Prix: 1
Race wins: 0
Championship wins: 0

Texan driver Lloyd Ruby began racing midgets after the Second World War and he also competed on motorcycles. By the end of the 1950s he had progressed to sportscars and dirt cars.

In 1960 he entered the Indy 500 race for the first time, and that was the last year the race counted towards the FIA World Championship. However, the following year Ruby attended a Grand Prix proper when he raced a Lotus 18 in the United States Grand Prix which was held for the first time at Watkins Glen. Ruby qualified 19th, at the back of the grid, but was forced to retire after 76 laps when his engine's magneto failed.

Ruby went on to be an Indy 500 regular, entering the race every year from 1960 to 1977.

Jean-Claude RUDAZ

Nationality: Swiss
Born: 23rd July 1942
Seasons: 1964
Team/manufacturer(s): Cooper
Grands Prix: 1
Race wins: 0
Championship wins: 0

Born in Sion, Swiss driver, Jean-Claude Rudaz, entered just one World Championship Formula One event, and that was the 1964 Italian Grand Prix.

The race took place at Monza and Rudaz was driving a Cooper T60 Climax run by Fabre Urbain. Rudaz qualified 20th, out of 25 entrants but, unfortunately, his engine failed during practice and so he was unable to enter the race itself.

That same year, Rudaz entered the Le Mans 24 Hour race in a Renault-Gordini with Pierre Monneret, but they were out of the race after 62 laps.

Rudaz was also an airline pilot and went on to form his own successful airline company. Transvalair now specialises in freight forwarding and cargo handling, and is based in Switzerland.

Troy RUTTMAN

Nationality: American
Born: 11th March 1930
Died: 19th May 1997
Seasons: 1958
Team/manufacturer(s): Maserati
Grands Prix: 2
Race wins: 0
Championship wins: 0

American Troy Ruttman was born in Oklahoma and was an Indy 500 regular between 1949 and 1964 (and from 1950 to 1960 these races were considered part of the Formula One World Championship – see page 236). He won the Indy 500 in 1952, driving for Kuzma-Offenhauser and, at the age of 22, was the youngest winner to do so.

However, he also participated in two 'proper' Formula One races, both in 1958. The first was the French Grand Prix, where he finished in 10th place, driving a Maserati 250F. Then, at the German Grand Prix, he failed to quality, driving the same car.

Ruttman moved into stockcar racing before retiring from the sport in 1964. He died from cancer in 1997.

Peter RYAN

Nationality: Canadian
Born: 10th June 1940
Died: 2nd July 1962
Seasons: 1961
Team/manufacturer(s): Lotus
Grands Prix: 1
Race wins: 0
Championship wins: 0

Although Peter Ryan was born in Philadelphia in the USA, he had Canadian nationality. He began racing at an early age, and first made a name for himself at the age of 19, when he drove a Porsche RSK to a second-place finish in the Carling 300 sportscar race at Harewood Acres racetrack in Ontario.

The race was won by racing legend, Roger Penske, who invited the young Ryan to team up with him in a later race, which the pair won in an RSK.

A year later, in 1961, Ryan drove a Lotus to victory in the Canadian Grand Prix sportscar race, beating Stirling Moss, who was driving a similar machine.

It was also in 1961 that Ryan made his single Formula One appearance. Driving a Lotus 18 at the US Grand Prix, he finished in ninth place.

The following year, Ryan travelled to Europe to race, and began with Formula Junior, but soon got more involved in sportscar events during that season. He competed at Daytona and Le Mans, driving Ferraris and was soon making a name for himself as a force to be reckoned with.

Sadly, though, Ryan's career was tragically cut short when he crashed his Lotus during a race at Reims in France. He was thrown from the car and died of his injuries. Ryan was just 22 years old.

Ricardo Rosset

P
Q
R

Mika Salo

SAID, Bob
SALAZAR, Eliseo
SALO, Mika
SALVADORI, Roy
SANESI, Consalvo
SARRAZIN, Stéphane
SATO, Takuma
SCARFIOTTI, Ludovico
SCARLATTI, Giorgio
SCHECKTER, Ian
SCHECKTER, Jody
SCHELL, Harry
SCHENKEN, Tim
SCHERRER, Albert
SCHIATTARELLA, Domenico
SCHILLER, Heinz
SCHLESSER, Jean-Louis

SCHLESSER, Jo
SCHNEIDER, Bernd
SCHOELLER, Rudolf
SCHROEDER, Rob
SCHUMACHER, Michael
SCHUMACHER, Ralf
SCHUPPAN, Vern
SCHWELM CRUZ, Adolfo
SCOTT-BROWN, Archie
SCOTTI, Piero
SEIDEL, Wolfgang
SEIFFERT, Gunther
SENNA, Ayrton
SERAFINI, Dorino
SERRA, Chico
SERRURIER, Doug
SERVOZ-GAVIN, Johnny

SETTEMBER, Tony
SHARP, Hap
SHAWE-TAYLOR, Brian
SHELBY, Carroll
SHELLY, Tony
SIFFERT, Jo
SIMON, André
SOLANA, Moises
SOLER-ROIG, Alex
SOMMER, Raymond
SOSPIRI, Vincenzo
SOUTH, Stephen
SPARKEN, Mike
SPEED, Scott
SPENCE, Mike
STACEY, Alan
STARRABBA, Gaetano

STEWART, Ian
STEWART, Jackie
STEWART, Jimmy
STOHR, Siegfried
STOMMELEN, Rolf
STREIFF, Philippe
STUCK, Hans
STUCK, Hans Joachim
STUPPACHER, Otto
SULLIVAN, Danny
SURER, Marc
SURTEES, John
SUTCLIFFE, Andy
SUTIL, Adrian
SUZUKI, Aguir
SUZUKI, Toshio
SWATERS, Jacques

S
T

Boris (Bob) SAID

Nationality: American
Born: 5th May 1932
Died: 24th March 2002
Seasons: 1959
Team/manufacturer(s): Connaught
Grands Prix: 1
Race wins: 0
Championship wins: 0

Born in New York to Russian and Syrian parents, his proper name was Boris Said, but he was known to most people as the rather more down-to-earth Bob Said. After a privileged upbringing and education, he gave up his Princeton University course to race cars in Europe.

After two years of successful competition, he returned to the USA in 1955 and raced a Ferrari there. At the same time he was beginning to make money in property.

In 1959, Said hired a Connaught single-seater and entered the US Grand Prix at Sebring. Sadly, though, he crashed on the first lap and was out of the race before it had really got going.

That was the end of Said's Formula One adventure, although he continued to race in other series until the early 1960s. After that, he concentrated on his property development and became very wealthy.

Said also became a competent bob-sleigher and represented his country in the 1968 and 1972 Winter Olympics. In addition, he got interested in film production and started his own company making documentaries. He died of cancer in 2002.

Eliseo SALAZAR

Nationality: Chilean
Born: 14th November 1955
Seasons: 1981-1983
Team/manufacturer(s): March, ATS, RAM
Grands Prix: 37
Race wins: 0
Championship wins: 0

Chilean driver Eliseo Salazar came to the UK in 1979 to compete in Formula 3 and performed well enough in that to switch to the British Formula One series the following season.

In 1981, he had his Formula One World Championship debut, driving for the cash-strapped March. Before long, though, Salazar had switched to Ensign. With both teams he had little success that season, apart from a worthwhile sixth-place finish in Holland, which scored him one Championship point.

It was a similar tale the following year. Driving for ATS, he made very little impression apart from a fifth place in the San Marino Grand Prix, which gave him another two points.

Unfortunately, Salazar shot to fame during the 1982 German Grand Prix when he collided with race-leader Nelson Piquet's car. The furious Piquet got out of his car and began to punch and kick Salazar – an incident that was witnessed by television viewers the world over.

Salazar gave up Formula One partway through the 1983 season after a disappointing start with RAM. He went on to be a regular competitor in the Indy 500, which he entered seven times.

Mika Juhani SALO

Nationality: Finnish
Born: 30th November 1966
Seasons: 1994-2000, 2002
Team/manufacturer(s): Lotus, Tyrrell, Arrows, BAR, Ferrari, Sauber, Toyota
Grands Prix: 111
Race wins: 0
Championship wins: 0

After starting off racing karts, Helsinki-born Mika Salo worked his way up through Formula 3 and Formula 3000, the latter in Japan. Unfortunately, his career suffered a setback when, in 1990, he was convicted of drink-driving in the UK.

Salo finally broke into Formula One in 1994, driving for Lotus at the end of the season.

The following year, he moved to Tyrrell and began to make an impression, with three point-scoring finishes. Salo stayed with Tyrrell through to the end of the 1997 season, picking up the odd points here and there.

He then moved to Arrows, where he had a disappointing season apart from a worthwhile fourth place finish in Monaco.

After a short spell with BAR in 1999, Salo moved to Ferrari and finished second in Germany and third in Italy.

Eliseo Salazar

Mika Salo

Sadly, though, the rest of his season was not so successful and he finished no better than 10th in the Championship.

In 2000, Salo drove for Sauber and it was a similar story – a handful of good finishes but not enough to make a real impact. He then joined the new Toyota team but did not compete again until 2002, when he started the season with a brace of sixth places, but then it went downhill. Salo then moved on to sportscar racing, driving for Maserati.

Roy SALVADORI

Nationality: British
Born: 12th May 1922
Seasons: 1952-1962
Team/manufacturer(s): Ferrari, Connaught, Maserati, BRM, Cooper, Lola
Grands Prix: 48
Race wins: 0
Championship wins: 0

Roy Salvadori was born in Essex but his parents were Italian, hence his surname. He began racing after the end of the Second World War – mainly in sportscars – and became known as a competent and successful driver.

He first drove in Formula One in 1952, when he piloted a Ferrari in the British Grand Prix. The following year, Salvadori did more Grands Prix around Europe, driving for Connaught.

In 1954, Salvadori drove a Maserati 250F in two Grands Prix, and then just one (in Britain) the following year, and three in 1956.

The 1957 season saw Salvadori behind the wheel of a BRM for four races, and he finished fifth at the British Grand Prix. However, he really shone in 1958, with finishes in fifth, fourth, third and second places – the latter at the German Grand Prix.

That was to be Salvadori's best year in Formula One, although he continued to compete at this level until the end of the 1962 season. He also won the 1959 Le Mans 24 Hour race, driving an Aston Martin with Carroll Shelby.

After giving up racing, Salvadori worked as a motor trader and also a team manager.

Consalvo SANESI

Nationality: Italian
Born: 28th March 1911
Died: 28th July 1998
Seasons: 1950-1951
Team/manufacturer(s): Alfa Romeo
Grands Prix: 5
Race wins: 0
Championship wins: 0

Italian Consalvo Sanesi was born in Bracciolini, Italy, and grew up to have the enviable job of test driver for the Alfa Romeo race team in the postwar years.

He also competed in races, often as a team driver for Alfa. This led to a handful of appearances in World Championship Grands Prix. The first was in 1950, when he piloted an Alfa Romeo Tipo 158/159 racecar in the Italian Grand Prix at Monza. Sadly, though, after qualifying fourth, his engine gave out after just 11 laps and he was forced to retire.

The next year, Sanesi drove the same car in four races, starting with the Swiss Grand Prix, where he finished in fourth place in a race won by Fangio. He retired from the Belgian Grand Prix, finished 10th in France and sixth in Britain.

After that, Sanesi concentrated more on sportscar racing, partly because Alfa Romeo had withdrawn from racing, and he continued to compete until the mid-1960s.

Stéphane SARRAZIN

Nationality: French
Born: 2nd November 1974
Seasons: 1999
Team/manufacturer(s): Minardi
Grands Prix: 1
Race wins: 0
Championship wins: 0

Stéphane Sarrazin was the son of an amateur French rally driver and soon picked up the bug, racing karts as a boy and becoming French Junior Champion. Then it was on to French Formula Renault which he won in 1994 before moving into Formula 3 and then Formula 3000.

Sarrazin tested for Formula One teams in the late 1990s and was asked to drive for Minardi in the 1999 Brazilian Grand Prix in place of regular driver, Luca Badoer, who had an injured wrist.

Unfortunately for Sarrazin, though, he suffered a major shunt on the startline and was out of the race before it had even started. In fact, as it turned out, his Formula One career was over before it started, too!

Sarrazin worked as a test driver for Prost in 2000 but then moved away from Formula One for a while before again working as a test driver, this time for Toyota in 2004.

However, he was by then getting more involved in rally driving and became a regular driver for Subaru. In contrast, he also raced an Aston Martin in the American Le Mans series.

Stéphane Sarrazin

Roy Salvadori

GRAND PRIX DRIVER BY DRIVER

Takuma SATO

Nationality: Japanese
Born: 28th January 1977
Seasons: 2002-
Team/manufacturer(s): Jordan, BAR, Super Aguri
Grands Prix: 88
Race wins: 0
Championship wins: 0

Japanese driver Takuma Sato began karting as a boy in Japan. At the age of 21 he came to the UK to race in Junior Formula before switching to Formula 3 the following year. He went on to win the British Formula 3 Championship in 2001.

A year later, Sato made the break into Formula One, when he got a place on the Jordan team. However, he had a mixed first season, with more than his fair share of crashes, including a bad one at the Austrian Grand Prix when he collided with Nick Heidfeld. Thankfully, Sato was not badly injured and was able to continue the season.

Sato then spent 2003 as a test driver for BAR, coming into race at his home Grand Prix at the end of the year and finishing the race in sixth place.

This led to a full season of racing with BAR in 2004, and he did well, with a best finish of third place in the USA. With 34 points that year, Sato finished eighth in the Championship.

Unfortunately the following season was less successful. Still with BAR, he had a disappointing year and only picked up one point, finishing 23rd in the Championship. This lead to him being dropped by BAR.

A move to Super Aguri in 2006 saw Sato struggle to perform and, again, it was a disappointing season for him.

He remained with the same team for 2007 and had some moments of brilliance, finishing eighth in Spain to score Super Aguri's first Championship point, and going on to take sixth place in Canada.

Ludovico SCARFIOTTI

Nationality: Italian
Born: 18th October 1933
Died: 8th June 1968
Seasons: 1963-1968
Team/manufacturer(s): Ferrari, Anglo American, Cooper
Grands Prix: 10
Race wins: 1
Championship wins: 0

Ludovico Scarfiotti came from Turin and was the nephew of Gianni Agnelli, who ran Fiat. He began racing in the early 1950s in a Fiat sportscar, and won his class in the 1957 Mille Miglia. Then, in 1963 he won the Le Mans 24 Hour, driving a Ferrari.

That same year, Scarfiotti had his Formula One debut when he drove for Ferrari in the Dutch Grand Prix and finished in sixth place. He also entered the French Grand Prix that year but crashed during practice, breaking both legs.

Scarfiotti mainly drove in sportscar events, but continued to enter the occasional Grand Prix, often with good results. This was most apparent in 1966, when he drove his Ferrari to victory in his home Grand Prix in Monza. An Italian driver winning the Italian Grand Prix in an Italian car – it made him a legend in his home country.

After entering two Grands Prix with Ferrari in 1967, he left the team. Later that season he entered the Italian Grand Prix driving an Eagle for Anglo American Racers but he did not finish the race.

Takuma Sato

Then it was on to Cooper for the 1968 season, when Scarfiotti finished in fourth place in the Spanish and Monaco Grands Prix. Scarfiotti was killed during a hillclimb in Bavaria 1968, when his Porsche crashed into some trees.

Giorgio SCARLATTI

Nationality: Italian
Born: 2nd October 1921
Died: 26th July 1990
Seasons: 1956-1961
Team/manufacturer(s): Ferrari, Maserati, Cooper, De Tomaso
Grands Prix: 15
Race wins: 0
Championship wins: 0

Born in Rome in 1921, Giorgio Scarlatti was a wealthy man and essentially a sportscar driver, racing a Maserati to a second place finish in the 1955 Tour of Sicily.

Keen to get into Formula One, Scarlatti bought a Ferrari 500 for the 1956 season and began by entering the Monaco Grand Prix. Unfortunately, though, he was too slow to qualify for the race. Later that same year, he entered the German Grand Prix with the same car but, after qualifying 17th, his engine failed him at the very start of the race.

Scarlatti then joined the Maserati team for the 1957 season and improved throughout the year, finally finishing the Italian Grand Prix in fifth place, gaining one Championship point.

The Maserati works team then closed but Scarlatti held on to his 250F and continued to enter the occasional Grand Prix race. He also drove for Cooper for part of the 1960 season and, the following year, drove a De Tomaso in the French Grand Prix.

That was the end of Scarlatti's Formula One career, although he continued to race both single-seaters and sportscars into the 1960s.

Ian SCHECKTER

Nationality: South African
Born: 22nd August 1947
Seasons: 1974-1977
Team/manufacturer(s): Lotus, Hesketh, Tyrrell, March, Williams
Grands Prix: 20
Race wins: 0
Championship wins: 0

South African Ian Scheckter was the elder brother of the 1979 World Champion, Jody Scheckter. He won the 1970 Formula Ford series in his home country before coming to Europe to race before returning to South Africa soon after.

Scheckter's Formula One debut was at his home Grand Prix in 1974, when he drove a Lotus 72 to a 13th place finish. Later that year, he attempted the Austrian Grand Prix in a Hesketh, but failed to qualify.

He had another go at the South African Grand Prix in 1975 and in 1976, driving a Williams and a Tyrrell respectively, but with no success. He also entered the Swedish and Dutch Grands Prix in 1975.

Then, in 1977, Scheckter gained a seat on the March team for a full season of Grands Prix. Unfortunately, though, he had little success and dropped out of Formula One after that.

Scheckter returned to South Africa to compete in Formula Atlantic and saloon car racing, and he also ran a service station and PR company.

Jody David SCHECKTER

Nationality: South African
Born: 29th January 1950
Seasons: 1972-1980
Team/manufacturer(s): McLaren, Tyrrell, Wolf, Ferrari
Grands Prix: 113
Race wins: 10
Championship wins: 1

Harry Schell

Jody Scheckter began racing karts as a boy in South Africa and then progressed to motorcycles and then saloon cars. After winning the local Formula Ford series he travelled to Europe to progress his career.

There, he raced in Formula Ford and Formula 3 and was soon rewarded with a drive for the McLaren Formula One team, at the age of just 22. In 1972, Scheckter debuted at the US Grand Prix and finished in ninth place.

He then drove for McLaren the following year before moving to Tyrrell, which is when he really began to shine. In 1974, Scheckter won two races and scored points in several others, finishing the season third in the Championship with 45 points.

Scheckter kept on performing well, for Tyrrell and then Wolf, with lots of point-scoring finishes. He again finished the season in third place in 1976, and came second in 1977.

Then, a move to Ferrari in 1979 saw Scheckter win three races and, again, perform well in most others. It was enough to win him 51 points and become the World Champion. Oddly, the following year with Ferrari was a disappointment and he only gained two Championship points.

Scheckter retired from Formula One after that and moved to the USA to begin his own weapons simulation business and becoming an organic farmer.

Harry O'Reilly SCHELL

Nationality: American
Born: 29th June 1921
Died: 13th May 1960
Seasons: 1950-1960
Team/manufacturer(s): Cooper, Talbot-Lago, Maserati, Gordini, Ferrari, Vanwall, BRM
Grands Prix: 56
Race wins: 0
Championship wins: 0

Harry Schell was born in Paris to wealthy American parents, who were both racing enthusiasts themselves. The family returned to the USA during the Second World War.

Schell, however, returned to Europe after the war and made his Formula One debut at the Monaco Grand Prix, driving a Cooper. From then on, he continued to enter the occasional Grand Prix, driving a variety of machinery.

By the mid 1950s Schell was competing in more Formula One races and, in 1956 he scored his first Championship points when he finished fourth at the Belgian Grand Prix, behind the wheel of a Vanwall.

The following year, Schell drove a Maserati and had a very good season, finishing fourth in Argentina, fifth in France, third in Pescara and fifth in Italy.

And 1958 was even better, with Schell coming fifth in Monaco, Belgium, Britain and Morocco, and second in Holland.

Schell was obviously a talented driver, but his life was cut short when he died after a crash during practice for a race at Silverstone in 1960.

Timothy (Tim) SCHENKEN

Nationality: Australian
Born: 26th September 1943
Seasons: 1970-1974
Team/manufacturer(s): Williams, Brabham, Surtees, Iso Marlboro, Trojan, Lotus
Grands Prix: 36
Race wins: 0
Championship wins: 0

Tim Schenken came from Sydney and began competing in hillclimbs, driving an Austin A30. Before long, he'd graduated to a Lotus 18 and was proving to be very competitive, indeed.

By 1965, Schenken had moved to the UK and racing in Formula Ford and Formula 3. He won both Championships in 1968.

This finally led to a chance to compete in Formula One, driving for Williams in the latter part of the 1970 season. However, he failed to finish any of the four races he entered.

Schenken got a drive with Brabham for 1971, and had more luck, picking up points in Germany with a sixth place finish and in Austria where he impressed by coming third.

The following year, driving for Surtees, Schenken got off to a good start with a fifth place in Argentina but then had a less successful rest of season.

By 1972, Schenken was concentrating on racing sportscars and cut down his Formula One involvement. He only drove in one Grand Prix (in Canada) that year, but did an almost full, but undistinguished season in 1974.

Schenken continued to race sportscars after this and also set up his own constructor company called Tiga. He has also acted as a clerk of the course for races in Australia.

Albert SCHERRER

Nationality: Swiss
Born: 28th February 1908
Died: 5th July 1986
Seasons: 1953
Team/manufacturer(s): HWM
Grands Prix: 1
Race wins: 0
Championship wins: 0

Born in Riehen, Albert Scherrer was a successful Swiss businessman who raced as a hobby, usually within his home country.

His main stead was a Jaguar XK120 and he had some success campaigning this in the 1940s and 1950s, on both circuits and hillclimbs.

Scherrer made just one Formula One appearance. Driving a rented HWM Atlas, he entered the Swiss Grand Prix in 1953. Starting at 18th on the grid, Scherrer survived a minor shunt and managed to complete 49 laps to finish the

Jody Scheckter

Bernd Schneider

race in ninth place – the last car to finish because the rest of the pack had retired.

Scherrer later raced in a Mercedes 300SL before retiring from the sport in the 1960s.

Domenico (Mimmo) SCHIATTARELLA

Nationality: Italian
Born: 17th November 1967
Seasons: 1994-1995
Team/manufacturer(s): Simtek
Grands Prix: 7
Race wins: 0
Championship wins: 0

Italian Domenico Schiattarella had the nickname 'Mimmo'. Born in Milan, he began competing seriously in Formula 4 and then Formula 3, in Italy.

He then went to South America to compete in Formula 3 before moving to the USA to race Champcars.

Schiattarella got together the money to buy himself a drive with the underfunded Simtek Formula One team at the end of the 1994 season, competing with little success in the European and Australian Grands Prix.

In 1995, he started the season with Simtek and entered five Grands Prix but without much luck, with a best finish of ninth place in Argentina. After the Monaco Grand Prix, Simtek ran out of money and folded, leaving Schiattarella without a drive.

He then competed in sportscars and CART later in the 1990s, and then returned to Italy to race in, among other things, the Ferrari Challenge.

Heinz SCHILLER

Nationality: Swiss
Born: 25th January 1930
Seasons: 1962
Team/manufacturer(s): Lotus
Grands Prix: 1
Race wins: 0
Championship wins: 0

Swiss driver Heinz Schiller was a successful speedboat racer in the 1950s. Later in the decade, though, he switched to car racing, campaigning in sportscar events in Italy and hillclimbs at home, where competitive racing was banned.

In 1962, Schiller was hired by the new Ecurie Nationale Suisse racing team to drive in the German Grand Prix. Behind the wheel of a Lotus 24, he qualified 20th but was forced to retire from the race after just four laps because of low oil pressure in his engine.

Schiller then returned to sportscar racing and hillclimbing, this time with a Porsche 904. He competed in the 1964 Le Mans 24 Hour race and finished 10th.

Later, Schiller retired from racing and ran a Porsche dealership in Geneva.

Jean-Louis SCHLESSER

Nationality: French
Born: 12th September 1948
Seasons: 1988
Team/manufacturer(s): RAM, Williams
Grands Prix: 2
Race wins: 0
Championship wins: 0

A nephew of racing driver, Jo Schlesser, Jean-Louis Schlesser was born in France but grew up in Morocco,

where he raced bicycles and motorcycles as a boy. He later returned to his home country and began racing cars, becoming joint winner of the French Formula 3 Championship in 1978.

He then competed in European Formula 3 and did some sportscar racing before becoming a test driver for the Williams Formula One team during the 1980s.

In 1983, Schlesser drove for RAM in the French Grand Prix but failed to qualify. It was to be another five years before he got another chance. While with Williams, he was entered into the 1988 Italian Grand Prix and finished 11th, standing in for Nigel Mansell. Schlesser continued to race sportscars, winning the World Sportscar Championship in 1989 and 1990. He also competed a number of times in the Paris-Dakar Rally, driving cars he designed himself. He won the race outright in 1999 and 2000, as well as being successful in other long-distance rallies.

Joseph (Jo) SCHLESSER

Nationality: French
Born: 18th May 1928
Seasons: 1968
Team/manufacturer(s): Matra, Honda
Grands Prix: 3
Race wins: 0
Championship wins: 0

Jo Schlesser was born in Madagascar and moved to France after the Second World War. He began racing relatively late in life, at the age of 24, but was travelling back and forth to Madagascar with his work, so was unable to pursue his new hobby.

When he could race, Schlesser had more than his fair share of accidents but was not put off, and made the decision to become a professional driver, driving a Cooper Formula 3 car.

However, the crashes continued and he flitted from one discipline to another, even moving to the USA to compete in stock cars for a while.

Schlesser entered the German Grand Prix in 1966 and 1967, in the Formula 2 class. And then, in 1968, he had his chance to drive a Formula One car in a Grand Prix. At the time, John Surtees was driving for Honda, but he refused to enter the French Grand Prix because he claimed the car Honda was testing was unsafe, so Schlesser took his place.

Tragically, after two laps, Schlesser lost control of the car and it crashed into a bank. The car caught fire and Schlesser was killed at the scene. Honda then withdrew from racing for the rest of the season.

Bernd SCHNEIDER

Nationality: German
Born: 20th July 1964
Seasons: 1988-1990
Team/manufacturer(s): Zakspeed, Arrows
Grands Prix: 34
Race wins: 0
Championship wins: 0

German Bernd Schneider was destined to become a racing driver because he was named after the legendary prewar driver, Bernd Rosemeyer, and he grew up near the Nürburgring! He began racing karts as a young boy and, by 1980, had won the German Kart Championship. He won again the following year and also picked up the World Junior Kart Championship.

Michael Schumacher

Michael Schumacher

Schneider then spent time competing in Formula Ford, Formula 2000 and Formula 3. He won the German Formula 3 Championship in 1987. This victory led to an offer of a drive with the Zakspeed Formula One team in 1988 and 1989. Unfortunately, though, the team didn't have the finances to be a success and Schneider struggled with uncompetitive cars. Indeed, in those two seasons he failed to pre-qualify or qualify for the majority of races, and only finished two – in 1988 – the British and Belgian Grand Prix, in which he finished 12th and 13th respectively.

In 1990, Schneider drove in two Grands Prix for the Arrows team, but his Formula One career was over. He went on to drive Porsche sportscars before getting involved in the German Touring Car Championship, driving for AMG-Mercedes, and winning it no less than five times up until 2006.

Rudolf SCHOELLER

Nationality: Swiss
Born: 27th April 1902
Died: 7th March 1978
Seasons: 1952
Team/manufacturer(s): Ferrari
Grands Prix: 1
Race wins: 0
Championship wins: 0

Rudolf Schoeller was born in Duren, Germany at the start of the 20th century but had Swiss nationality. He did, though,

live much of his life in Germany and was an enthusiastic amateur racing driver both before and after the Second World War

Schoeller was 50 years old when he entered his one and only Formula One Grand Prix. This was the 1952 German event at the Nürburgring. Schoeller was driving a Ferrari 212 for the Ecurie Espadon team. He started from a lowly 24th on the grid and then had to retire from the race after just three laps because of a suspension problem.

Later that season, Schoeller acted as a reserve driver for the same team but never raced in another Formula One event. At the end of the year, he bought the Ferrari for his own use.

Robert (Rob) SCHROEDER

Nationality: American
Born: 11th May 1926
Seasons: 1962
Team/manufacturer(s): Lotus
Grands Prix: 1
Race wins: 0
Championship wins: 0

Little is know of American driver Rob Schroeder both before and after his short Formula One career. He competed in just one Grand Prix, the 1962 United States Grand Prix, which was held at Watkins Glen, New York, on 7th October 1962.

Schroeder drove a Climax-engined Lotus 24 owned by John Mecom, a Texan millionaire who had made his

money from the oil industry. Schroeder started 17th on the grid and ended up finishing in 10th place in the race, seven laps behind the winner, Jim Clark, who was also driving a Lotus. Out of 18 drivers in the race that year, seven were American.

Schroeder then disappeared back into obscurity.

Michael SCHUMACHER

Nationality: German
Born: 3rd January 1969
Seasons: 1991-2006
Team/manufacturer(s): Jordan, Benetton, Ferrari
Grands Prix: 250
Race wins: 91
Championship wins: 7

Michael Schumacher started racing a homemade kart at the age of five. His father, Rolf, built the machine and was manager of the kart track at Kerpen, the family's hometown.

The youngster soon proved himself handy behind the wheel and, at the age of 12, he began racing karts competitively. Throughout his teens, Schumacher won numerous kart Championships in Germany and Europe.

In 1988, at the age of 19, Schumacher raced in Formula Ford, moving to German Formula 3 for the following two years, and winning the Championship in 1990.

Schumacher drove for Jordan in the 1991 Belgian Grand Prix as a one-off, because he'd assured team boss, Eddie Jordan, that he knew the Spa circuit well. If the truth be known, though, the young German had only ever been round the track once – on a bicycle! Still, on this, his first Formula One race, Schumacher qualified seventh. Sadly, he had to retire from the race, but his performance was good enough to persuade Benetton to sign him for the rest of the season.

In 1992, Schumacher stayed with Benetton and won his first Formula One race – at Spa. He went on to finish the season in third place.

Schumacher remained with Benetton and stormed to victory in 1994, by winning six of the first seven races of the season. It was to be a controversial season, with Schumacher sparring with Damon Hill in the last race at Adelaide, with allegations that he deliberately forced the Englishman to retire, and Schumacher won the Drivers' Championship by just one point. He repeated the success the next year, this time with a 30-point lead.

In 1996 Schumacher moved to Ferrari, an ailing team that had not won a title since 1979. The cars might have not been up to scratch, but that didn't stop the German from finishing the season in third place.

The 1997 season brought more controversy for Schumacher, with him being disqualified from the World Championship after a collision with Jacques Villeneuve. Schumacher would otherwise have taken second place.

While this was happening, the Ferrari team was improving its cars, thanks in part to efforts of the design team which Schumacher had coaxed from Benetton. Indeed, the team won the Constructors' title in 1999, but Schumacher had to wait another year before he would win the Drivers' Championship with Ferrari.

Schumacher then went on to win the Championship again for the following four years in a row. His win in 2003 was his sixth, which beat the record previously held by Juan Manuel Fangio, and the next year he won 13 races, thus breaking his own record of 11.

S
T

Ralf Schumacher

However, it was not to last. Schumacher failed to win in 2005, dogged in part by new regulations that insisted that tyres had to last for a whole race, and finished in third place at the end of the season. He did better in 2006, finishing second, behind Fernando Alonso.

Schumacher retired from Formula One in 2006, at the age of 37. He remained with Ferrari, though, as a consultant. And it will be a long time – if ever – before another driver will be able to beat the German's impressive Formula One career.

Ralf SCHUMACHER

Nationality: German
Born: 30th June 1975
Seasons: 1997-
Team/manufacturer(s): Jordan, Williams, Toyota
Grands Prix: 182
Race wins: 6
Championship wins: 0

The younger brother of seven-times World Champion, Michael Schumacher, Ralf began racing karts at the age of three. By 1995 he had finished third in the German Formula 3 Championship and, a year later, won the Japanese Formula Nippon Championship.

Schumacher tested for McLaren in 1996, but ended up driving for the Jordan Formula One team in 1997. It was a mixed first season, with him retiring from about half his races, yet finishing in the top six for more of the others, including a third place in Argentina – his third Grand Prix. He did better the following year, with a second place in Belgium and a third in Italy.

However, a move to Williams in 1999 really set Schumacher's career moving, with him finishing the year sixth in the Championship, and then fifth the following season.

Still with Williams, Schumacher had his first wins in 2001

– at San Marino, Canada and Germany. It was a good year that ended up with him fourth in the Championship, a finish he matched in 2002. More wins followed and Schumacher was fifth at the end of the 2003 season. Then an accident in the 2004 United States Grand Prix put Schumacher out for most of the season.Schumacher then moved to Toyota for 2005 and had a reasonable season, finishing sixth in the Championship. He remained with Toyota for 2006 for a less successful year, and kept with the team for 2007 but, again, had a disappointing season and left Toyota at the end of the year.

Vernon (Vern) SCHUPPAN

Nationality: Australian
Born: 19th March 1943
Seasons: 1972, 1974-1975, 1977
Team/manufacturer(s): BRM, Ensign, Hill, Surtees
Grands Prix: 12
Race wins: 0
Championship wins: 0

Born in South Australia, Vern Schuppan started his career racing karts and then came to the UK in 1969 to pursue his dream. After starting off in Formula Ford, he went on to win the 1971 Formula Atlantic Championship.

The following year saw Schuppan enter his first Grand Prix. Driving for BRM, he failed to qualify for the Belgian Grand Prix. After a couple of years in sportscars, he had a season of Formula 5000 in 1974 and also entered seven Grands Prix with the Ensign team, but with little success – he only finished one race (15th in Belgium). His one entry in 1975 was the Swedish Grand Prix, driving for Hill but, again, he failed to qualify.

Schuppan then entered four Grands Prix in 1977 and, finally, finished three of them, with a best-place of seventh in Germany. That was, though, to be the end of his Formula One career. He went on to be a successful sportscar racer, finishing second at Le Mans in 1977 and 1982, and winning the 1983 Japanese Sports-Prototype Championship.

Schuppan later became involved in property development and race team management.

Adolfo SCHWELM-CRUZ

Nationality: Argentinean
Born: 28th June 1923
Seasons: 1953
Team/manufacturer(s): Cooper
Grands Prix: 1
Race wins: 0
Championship wins: 0

Born plain Adolfo Schwelm, the 'Cruz' was added when he

Ralf Schumacher

started racing to make his name more memorable and easier to pronounce. He began racing in Italy after the Second World War before returning to Argentina, where he was Sportscar Champion in 1951.

Like other Argentinean drivers, Schwelm-Cruz travelled to Europe to compete in the early 1950s but he had little success of note. Back in his home country, he made his one and only Formula One appearance. Driving a works Cooper-Bristol at the 1953 Argentinean Grand Prix, Schwelm-Cruz qualified 13th but was out of the race on the 20th lap with a broken axle.

Schwelm-Cruz continued to compete in sportscar races, driving an Alfa Romeo and a Maserati before retiring from the sport and settling down in Buenos Aires.

William Archibald (Archie) SCOTT-BROWN

Nationality: British
Born: 13th May 1927
Died: 19th May 1958
Seasons: 1956
Team/manufacturer(s): Connaught
Grands Prix: 1
Race wins: 0
Championship wins: 0

Born in Renfrewshire, Archie Scott-Brown's mother suffered from German measles while pregnant, leaving the child with badly deformed legs and right arm. He endured 22 operations as a child and never grew taller than five feet.

However, this did not stop the young Scott-Brown from taking up motor racing, first in a small car his father built and then in an MG TD. Before long, he'd gained a reputation as a skilled driver, winning races around the UK driving cars built by Brian Lister.

Scott-Brown's abilities as a driver earned him just one Formula One drive. He entered the 1956 British Grand Prix, at Silverstone, driving a Connaught-Alta. He qualified 10th but retired after 16 laps with transmission problems.

Two years later, Scott-Brown crashed his Lister car during a sportscar race at a wet Spa and was badly injured when the car burst into flames. He died in hospital the following day, just before his 31st birthday.

Piero SCOTTI

Nationality: Italian
Born: 11th November 1909
Died: 14th February 1976
Seasons: 1956
Team/manufacturer(s): Connaught
Grands Prix: 1
Race wins: 0
Championship wins: 0

Italian Piero Scotti was born in Florence and grew up to be a successful businessman who ran a mineral water company and enjoyed racing Ferrari sportscars in the 1950s. His greatest successes were coming third in the 1951 Mille Miglia and winning the Casablanca 12 Hours the same year.

In 1956 Scotti bought himself a Connaught Formula One and entered it into just one World Championship event. That was the Belgian Grand Prix that year. Scotti qualified in 12th place and managed just 10 laps of the race before his car's gearbox gave up on him.

After that, Scotti handed the car back to Ferrari and gave up motorsport soon after, concentrating on his business concerns.

Wolfgang SEIDEL

Nationality: German
Born: 4th July 1926
Died: 1st March 1987
Seasons: 1953, 1958, 1960-1962
Team/manufacturer(s): Veritas, Maserati, Cooper, Lotus, Emerson
Grands Prix: 12
Race wins: 0
Championship wins: 0

Wolfgang Seidel was born in Dusseldorf, Germany, and became an enthusiastic amateur racing driver after the Second World War.

Between 1953 and 1962, he competed in a few Grands Prix on an intermittent basis and in a variety of machinery, beginning with the 1953 German Grand Prix, in which Seidel drove a Veritas to a lowly 16th place finish.

Then, five years later in 1958, he entered a Maserati into the Belgian and German Grands Prix, but failed to finish either race because of mechanical failures.

In 1960, Seidel entered just the Italian Grand Prix and drove his Cooper to a ninth place finish. The following year saw him enter a Lotus in four races but he only finished one – the British Grand Prix in 17th place.

The 1962 season was Seidel's last in Formula One and he competed in an Emerson in Holland, then a Lotus in Britain and Germany, but didn't finish any race.

Seidel later became a car dealer in Germany before dying of a heart attack at the young age of 60.

Günther SEIFFERT

Nationality: German
Born: 18th October 1937
Seasons: 1962
Team/manufacturer(s): Lotus
Grands Prix: 1
Race wins: 0
Championship wins: 0

German driver Günther Seiffert was born in Oldenburg in 1937 and became a keen amateur racing driver in the post-war years. However, it was not until 1962 that Seiffert had a chance to enter a World Championship race. That was his home Grand Prix, held at the Nürburgring. Seiffert drove a BRM-powered Lotus 24 run by the Autosport Team Wolfgang Seidel and he shared the drive with Seidel himself. In the event, though, they both failed to qualify for the race itself.

That was the full extent of Seiffert's Formula One adventure, although he continued to race in lesser series. Later in life, he ran classic car dealerships in Germany and Belgium.

Ayrton SENNA

Nationality: Brazilian
Born: 21st March 1960
Died: 1st May 1994
Seasons: 1984-1994
Team/manufacturer(s): Toleman Hart, Lotus, McLaren Honda, Williams
Grands Prix: 162
Race wins: 41
Championship wins: 3

Ayrton Senna

Ayrton Senna

Dorino Serafini

Ayrton Senna grew up in Sao Paulo and, encouraged by his father, began karting at the age of four, but local regulations meant he was unable to compete until his was 13. By then he was competing seriously and in 1977, at the age of 17, won the South American Kart Championship; a feat he went on to repeat the following year. He then travelled to Le Mans and came sixth in the World Championships.

By 1981, Senna was in England competing in Formula Ford 1600, and won the series in his first year. The following year he moved to Formula Ford 2000 and won both the British and European Championships.

In 1983, Senna won the Formula Three Championship and got the attention of Formula One teams. He was signed by the Toleman team (which later became Benetton and then Renault). He impressed in his first season, with an incredible performance at the very wet Monaco Grand Prix, where he worked his way up from 13th place to challenge leader, Alain Prost. However, the race was cancelled because of the weather before Senna could attempt to take the lead.

For 1985, Senna moved to Lotus, despite still being contracted to Toleman, and had his first Grand Prix victory at Portugal where, again, he showed off his wet-weather ability. He finished the season in fourth place, as he did the following year. He did slightly better with Lotus in 1987, coming third in the Championship.

Senna moved to McLaren for 1988, where he formed a formidable partnership with Alain Prost. Both superb drivers, they were often sparring with each other for victory. Indeed, that year the pair won 15 out of 16 races between them for McLaren, with Senna winning his first World Championship.

The following year, the rivalry increased, with Prost taking the Championship after blocking Senna from overtaking at Suzuka. However, in 1990 the Brazilian got his own back by bumping Prost's car at the same circuit, causing both drivers to retire, which clinched the Championship for Senna.

In 1994 Senna was racing for Williams-Renault and the San Marino Grand Prix was already turning into a nightmare, with Senna's teammate, Rubens Barrichello in hospital after an accident on the Friday. Then, on the Saturday, Austrian Roland Ratzenberger was killed in practice.

Senna almost retired there and then, but chose to continue and race at San Marino on the Sunday. He'd stuffed an Austrian flag into his cockpit, which he was going to raise in memory of Ratzenberger during his lap of honour.

However, it was not to be. During the race, Senna's car left the track at a speed of 193mph, and hit an unprotected concrete wall. He was killed instantly.

Senna's death, at the age of just 34, shocked the world, and over a million people lined the streets of Sao Paulo for his memorial service. It was a tragic and premature end to a great career.

Teodoro (Dorino) SERAFINI
Nationality: Italian
Born: 22nd July 1909
Died: 5th July 2000
Seasons: 1950
Team/manufacturer(s): Ferrari
Grands Prix: 1
Race wins: 0
Championship wins: 0

Teodoro Serafini, to give him his full name, was born and lived in Pesaro in Italy. Before the Second World War he was a talented and successful motorcycle racer.

After the war, he turned to cars but had a bad crash in 1947 when the steering wheel of his Maserati came off and he drove into a tree.

Despite being very badly injured, Serafini eventually recovered enough to start racing again and, in 1950, entered his single World Championship event. He shared a Ferrari 375 with the great Alberto Ascari in the Italian Grand Prix at Monza and the pair drove the car to an impressive second place finish, earning Serafini three Championship points.

Serafini continued to race in other classes after that and had some success over the years before slowly winding down his racing activities from the mid-1950s.

Francisco Adolpho (Chico) SERRA
Nationality: Brazilian
Born: 3rd February 1957
Seasons: 1981-1983
Team/manufacturer(s): Fittipaldi, Arrows
Grands Prix: 32
Race wins: 0
Championship wins: 0

Francisco Adolpho Serra was born in Sao Paulo and began racing karts as a boy before moving to the UK, where he worked his way up through Formula Ford and Formula 3. He went on to win the British Formula 3 Championship no less than five times.

After a season with Formula 2, Serra moved to Formula One in 1981, driving for Fittipaldi. He had a disappointing season, failing to qualify for or finish many of his races. It was a similar story the following season when, still driving for the same team, the only success Serra had was a worthwhile sixth place finish in Belgium, which won him one Championship point.

In 1983, Serra drove for Arrows in just four Grands Prix at the start of the season and had a best-placed finish of seventh at Monaco – his last Formula One race. After that, he was dropped from the team.

Serra then returned to Brazil where he built a solid career successfully racing saloon cars.

Louis Douglas (Doug) SERRURIER
Nationality: South African
Born: 9th December 1920
Died: 3rd June 2006
Seasons: 1962-1963, 1965
Team/manufacturer(s): LDS
Grands Prix: 3
Race wins: 0
Championship wins: 0

Born Louis Douglas Serrurier in Transvaal, this South African driver began his career racing speedway bikes before moving to a Triumph TR2 in the mid-1950s.

He then began building his own cars, which he called LDS (after his initials). It was these cars, which had Alfa Romeo four-cylinder engines driving Porsche five-speed gearboxes, that he entered into the South African Grand Prix on three occasions.

His first outing, in 1962, saw Serrurier qualifying in pole position but, sadly retiring after 62 laps with a leaking radiator. He then tried again the following year and finished

the race in 11th place.

Serrurier's third and last World Championship entry was in 1965, again at his home Grand Prix. This time, his car had a Climax engine in and he failed to qualify.

After this, Serrurier gave up developing his own car and bought a Lola T70 which he raced himself before getting others to drive on his behalf.

In later life, Serrurier continued to build and restore road and race cars at his Johannesburg workshop before ill health forced him to retire.

Georges-Francis (Johnny) SERVOZ-GAVIN
Nationality: French
Born: 18th January 1942
Died: 29th May 2006
Seasons: 1967-1970
Team/manufacturer(s): Matra, Cooper, March
Grands Prix: 12
Race wins: 0
Championship wins: 0

Georges-Francis Servoz-Gavin was better known as Johnny Servoz-Gavin and came from a wealthy French family. He began rallying in the early 1960s before moving on to racecars, driving in Formula 3 and Formula 2.

Servoz-Gavin was an occasional Formula One entrant and his first attempt was at the 1967 Monaco Grand Prix, where he failed to qualify his Matra. The following season he entered five Grands Prix and, astonishingly, drove his Ford-powered Matra to a second place finish at the Italian Grand Prix, earning him six Championship points. Sadly, though, he failed to finish any other race that season.

In 1969, again driving for Matra, he entered three races and finished sixth in Canada, gaining one Championship point. It was a similar story in 1970, his last season, when he entered three races and finished just one – the Spanish Grand Prix where he came fifth and picked up two points.

Servoz-Gavin gave up Formula One after that, concerned that his eyesight was failing after an accident the previous year. He later lived on a canal boat for several years before succumbing to illness and dying in 2006.

Tony SETTEMBER
Nationality: American
Born: 10th July 1926
Seasons: 1962-1963
Team/manufacturer(s): Emeryson, Scirocco
Grands Prix: 7
Race wins: 0
Championship wins: 0

Tony Settember was born in the Philippines to an Italian family and then grew up in California. He began racing sportscars in the USA before moving to Europe to try his hand at single-seater racing.

He began his Formula One career with a Climax-engined Emeryson car for the 1962 season but the car did not suit him and he only entered two races – in Britain and Italy – finishing 11th in the first and retiring from the second.

The next year Settember formed his own team, called Scirocco, and drove a V8 BRM-engined car. In this, he entered five Grands Prix in Europe but only made it to the end of the first one – the Belgian Grand Prix –where he finished eighth.

That was the end of Settember's Formula One adventure and he returned to the USA where he raced sportscars and then Can-Am before retiring to Nevada.

Jo Siffert

Brian SHAWE-TAYLOR

Nationality: British
Born: 28th January 1915
Died: 1st May 1999
Seasons: 1950-1951
Team/manufacturer(s): Maserati, ERA
Grands Prix: 2
Race wins: 0
Championship wins: 0

Brian Shawe-Taylor was born in Dublin, Ireland, to an Ulster family but was educated in England and attended Shrewsbury School, before going to university in Germany.

After serving as an anti-aircraft gunner in the Second World War, he started his own garage business in Cheltenham and also began racing his own cars. His competition career included entering the first two World Championship British Grands Prix, in 1950 and 1951.

In the first race, he was unable to enter his own car, an ERA, because it was claimed to be too old, so he shared Joe Fry's Maserati and finished joint 10th. The following year, he was allowed to race his ERA and finished the race in a respectable eighth place. Sadly, soon after, Shawe-Taylor crashed at Goodwood and was badly injured, remaining in a coma for some weeks. Although he recovered, he decided to turn his back on motor racing. He sold his garage business and went to work for GCHQ in Cheltenham. He died in 1999, aged 84.

Carroll Hall SHELBY

Nationality: American
Born: 11th January 1923
Seasons: 1958-1959
Team/manufacturer(s): Maserati, Aston Martin
Grands Prix: 8
Race wins: 0
Championship wins: 0

Texan Carroll Shelby began racing in an MG in the early 1950s and went on to compete in various sportscar events, in the USA and Europe, mainly driving Ferraris.

In 1958 he spent a season in Europe, racing a Maserati 250F and it was in this car that he entered four World Championship Grands Prix that year. He had little success but, at the Italian Grand Prix he retired and took over driving Maston Gregory's car to finish fourth, but was disqualified for doing this.

The following year, he again entered four Grands Prix, this time driving an Aston Martin. Again, though, he didn't have much luck, with his best finish being eighth at Portugal.

Back in the USA, Shelby went on to become a motoring legend as the creator of the famous AS Cobra and helping Ford win at Le Mans. For many years he suffered from heart problems and, in 1990, was given a successful heart transplant.

James (Hap) SHARP

Nationality: American
Born: 1st January 1928
Died: 7th May 1993
Seasons: 1961-1964
Team/manufacturer(s): Cooper-Climax, Lotus-BRM, Brabham-BRM
Grands Prix: 6
Race wins: 0
Championship wins: 0

His real name was James Sharp, but he picked up the nickname Hap after 'Happy New Year' on account of being born on 1st January. Sharp came from Texas and made money in the oil business, racing cars as a hobby.

Sharp only entered the United States and Mexican Grands Prix in the early 1960s. At first, he drove a Cooper-Climax car, finishing 10th at his first attempt in 1961 and 11th the following year. In 1963, he was forced to retire his Lotus from the United States Grand Prix but drove the same car to a seventh place finish in Mexico. That was to be his best finish. After disappointing races in the United States and Mexico Grands Prix of 1964, Sharp gave up on Formula One and soon retired from the sport altogether. Sadly, Sharp became terminally ill and then committed suicide in May 1993.

Anthony (Tony) SHELLY

Nationality: New Zealander
Born: 2nd February 1937
Died: 4th October 1998
Seasons: 1962
Team/manufacturer(s): Lotus
Grands Prix: 3
Race wins: 0
Championship wins: 0

Tony Shelly was born in Wellington, New Zealand, the son of the local Jaguar dealer there. He began racing after the

Second World War and soon became a big name in his home country.

However, he knew that he'd have to come to Europe to further his driving career and that's what he did in 1962. Shelly competed in a number of non-Championship races, driving a Lotus 18.

He also entered three World Championship races that year. At the British Grand Prix at Aintree, he retired after just six laps with engine failure, while in Germany and Italy he did not qualify.

That was the extent of Shelly's European adventure and he returned to New Zealand at the end of the season, where he continued to race for a couple more years before retiring from the sport.

Shelly went on to run a chain of successful car dealerships, not only in New Zealand, but also in Hawaii.

Joseph (Jo) SIFFERT

Nationality: Swiss
Born: 7th July 1936
Died: 24th October 1971
Seasons: 1962-1971
Team/manufacturer(s): Lotus, Cooper, Brabham, March, BRM
Grands Prix: 100
Race wins: 2
Championship wins: 0

Swiss driver Joseph Siffert was the son of a dairy owner and began racing motorcycles after the Second World War, becoming the Swiss 350cc champion in 1959. He then moved to Formula Junior before making the jump to Formula One.

Siffert's first Formula One season was in his own Lotus-Climax but he made little impression on any of the five events he entered that year.

A move to Brabham in 1964 saw Siffert's career start to take off, with a better season and a third place in the USA. However, he didn't really progress from then for some time. And then, in 1968, he won the British Grand Prix, driving a Lotus 49B. That season he finished eighth in the Championship. The following year, Siffert did even better, finishing fifth. However, 1968 was memorable for Siffert because of his exploits outside of Formula One – he won both the Le Mans 24 Hour and the 12 Hours of Sebring, driving a Porsche 907.

In 1971, Siffert began with a good Formula One season, with a win at Austria and a second place at the United States Grand Prix. Then, at the end of the season, he entered a non-Championship race at Brands Hatch and was killed when his BRM crashed and he was unable to get out of the burning car – he died of oxygen starvation and smoke inhalation. This tragedy led to a review of safety equipment and the adoption of on-board fire extinguishers, piped air to the driver and better fire-retardant overalls.

André SIMON

Nationality: French
Born: 5th January 1920
Seasons: 1951-1952, 1955-1957
Team/manufacturer(s): Simca, Ferrari, Mercedes, Maserati.
Grands Prix: 12
Race wins: 0
Championship wins: 0

Frenchman André Simon was born in Paris, the son of a garage owner. The youngster worked at the family garage as a teenager and soon fell in love with cars and motorsport. The Second World War forced him to put his plans on hold but, soon after, Simon was racing a Talbot Lago with great success.

By 1950, Simon was competing in Formula 2 and, a year later, he entered his first Formula One race, the 1951 French Grand Prix, although he had to retire with gearbox problems. In that year, Simon finished only one of the four Grands Prix he entered, the Italian one, where he came sixth.

The following season, Simon drove in the first and last Grands Prix of the year, in a Ferrari, and, again, came sixth in Italy. Then followed two more races in 1955 with Mercedes, neither of which he finished, although the next year he finished ninth in Italy.

The 1957 season was to be Simon's last in Formula One and he did his usual two races and, once again, only finished in Italy, this time in 11th place.

From then on, Simon competed in sportscars and touring cars, and even did some rallying. He retired from racing in 1965 and went back to running the family garage business.

Moises SOLANA

Nationality: Mexican
Born: 26th December 1935
Died: 27th July 1969
Seasons: 1963-1968
Team/manufacturer(s): BRM, Lotus, Cooper
Grands Prix: 8
Race wins: 0
Championship wins: 0

Moises Solana was born in Mexico City and was a professional Jai-Alai player – an American ballgame that involves

Raymond Sommer

volleying a ball at high speed using a wicker glove. It's claimed to be the world's fastest ballgame, with the ball travelling at up to 185mph!

So with an appetite for speed, it's perhaps no wonder that Solana also enjoyed motor racing, and his professional sport gave him the money to indulge himself.

Solana raced mainly in his home country of Mexico although he occasionally crossed the border into the USA and even went to Europe once.

His Formula One driving was confined mainly to the Mexico Grand Prix, which he entered every year from 1963 to 1968, driving a variety of machinery. However, he made little impact, with a best-placed finish of 10th, in 1964.

Solana also entered the United States Grand Prix twice, in 1965 and 1967, driving a Lotus 49 each time. Again, though, he had little success, despite qualifying seventh in 1967.

Sadly, Solana was killed when his McLaren M6B crashed and caught fire during a hillclimb in Mexico in 1969.

Alex SOLER-ROIG

Nationality: Spanish
Born: 29th October 1932
Seasons: 1970-1972
Team/manufacturer(s): Lotus, March, BRM
Grands Prix: 9
Race wins: 0
Championship wins: 0

Spaniard Alex Soler-Roig was the son of a wealthy surgeon and had a privileged upbringing. He began racing relatively late in life, enjoying some success in hillclimbs and sportscar events, before moving into European Formula 2 in 1967.

After a disappointing season, Soler-Roig went back to sportscars and had more success but was still keen to compete in Formula One. He'd proved himself as a talented driver in GT events and, crucially, was also able to bring some money to the table, so he got a drive with Lotus in 1970 at the Spanish and French Grands Prix, but failed to qualify for either race.

Then it was on to March for 1971 and five Grands Prix, none of which he finished. It was a similar story with BRM in 1973, when he retired from the two races he entered.

Soler-Roig went on to have more success in touring cars but retired from the sport at the end of 1972, after which he ran his own garage business.

Raymond SOMMER

Nationality: French
Born: 31st August 1906
Died: 10th September 1950
Seasons: 1950
Team/manufacturer(s): Ferrari, Talbot
Grands Prix: 5
Race wins: 0
Championship wins: 0

Raymond Sommer came from a wealthy carpet-making family in France and his father was a pioneer aircraft flyer in the early days of the 20th century.

Sommer went on to be a top racing driver between the wars, winning at Le Mans in 1931 and entering a number of Grand Prix events.

During the Second World War Sommer was involved in the French Resistance and returned to racing as soon as hostilities were over, winning the 1947 Turin Grand Prix, among other things.

Vincenzo Sospiri

Unfortunately, Sommer only ever competed in one season of the new Formula One World Championship – the first year it ran, 1950. He came fourth in his first race, driving a Ferrari at Monaco, but had no luck in the other four Grands Prix he entered.

Sommer was killed in September 1950, when the steering failed on his Cooper during a local Grand Prix in France. His car overturned and he was dead at the scene.

Vincenzo SOSPIRI

Nationality: Italian
Born: 7th October 1966
Seasons: 1997
Team/manufacturer(s): Lola
Grands Prix: 1
Race wins: 0
Championship wins: 0

Italian driver Vincenzo Sospiri proved himself a capable driver when, in 1995, he won the European Formula 3000 Championship, driving for Super Nova. This success led to a test with the Simtek Formula One team in 1994, but he was unable to raise enough sponsorship to get a place on the team, so he went on to be a test driver for Benetton during the 1996 season.

The following season, Sospiri was offered a chance to race for the new MasterCard Lola team. Unfortunately, the

car – which, rather ambitiously, had a Lola-built engine – was extremely slow and Sospiri failed miserably to qualify for the Austrian Grand Prix at the start of the season.

Sospiri realised that Lola was a lost cause and left the team, which folded soon after. He went on to compete in the Indy 500 and, in 1998 and 1999, won the Sports Racing World Cup, driving a Ferrari 333 SP.

After retiring from racing in 2001, Sospiri became a team manager.

Stephen SOUTH

Nationality: British
Born: 19th February 1952
Seasons: 1980
Team/manufacturer(s): McLaren
Grands Prix: 1
Race wins: 0
Championship wins: 0

Stephen South was born in Harrow and grew up to be a successful racing driver, winning the 1976 British Formula 3 Championship.

He then went on to compete in Formula 2 and also tested for Lotus in 1979. The following season South was contracted to drive for the Toleman team, but then the chance came for him to drive a McLaren M29C in the United States West Grand Prix. Unable to resist, he took up the offer but, sadly, failed to qualify for the race. Toleman, meanwhile, was not happy at South driving for another team, and promptly dropped him.

South then drove in various races, including a Can-Am race where he crashed his Lola and, as a result, had to have part of his leg amputated. He didn't race again after that, but returned to the UK to run his own engineering company.

Michael POBEREJSKY (Mike Sparken)

Nationality: French
Born: 16th June 1930
Seasons: 1955
Team/manufacturer(s): Gordini
Grands Prix: 1
Race wins: 0
Championship wins: 0

Frenchman Mike Sparken's real name was actually Michael Poberejsky and he used the pseudonym for racing. He was a wealthy man who enjoyed racing cars as a hobby.

Sparken usually competed in sportscar events, driving an Aston Martin DB2 or a Ferrari T750S. He did, though, come to England in 1955 to drive a Gordini at the British Grand Prix, which took place at Aintree that year. After starting 23rd on the grid, Sparken worked his way up to finish in seventh place. That, though, was the extent of his Formula One driving and he returned to his favoured sportscars.

In later life, Sparken enjoyed attending historic races and festivals, and even held some himself at his French home.

Scott Andrew SPEED

Nationality: American
Born: 24th January 1983
Seasons: 2006-2007
Team/manufacturer(s): Toro Rosso
Grands Prix: 28
Race wins: 0
Championship wins: 0

Mike Spence

The aptly named Scott Speed was born in California and his father was a keen racing driver. The young Speed began racing karts at the age of 10 and won seven national Championships in the USA.

In 2003, Speed came to the UK to compete in Formula 3 but a serious illness forced him to put his career on hold. The following year, though, Speed bounced back and won the Formula Renault 200 Eurocup and the German Formula Renault Championship.

By 2005, Speed was test driver for Red Bull Racing, thus becoming the first American Formula One driver since Michael Andretti in 1993. Red Bull became Toro Rosso for 2006 and made Speed one of its drivers for that season.

Speed had a steady first season and managed to finish all but five of the Grands Prix that year, with a best-place of ninth in Australia. He remained with Toro Rosso for the 2007 season.

He remained with Toro Rosso for the 2007 season but disagreements led to him being released from his contract in July. Speed then announced he would be competing in stock cars in 2008.

Michael (Mike) SPENCE

Nationality: British
Born: 30th December 1936
Died: 7th May 1968
Seasons: 1963-1968
Team/manufacturer(s): Lotus, BRM
Grands Prix: 36
Race wins: 0
Championship wins: 0

Born in Croydon, Mike Spence's family ran a garage and so he was always keen on cars and racing. He began racing a Turner in his twenties before moving to Formula Junior in 1960, driving a Cooper-Austin.

Before, long, Spence was making a name for himself on the racing circuits and was driving for the Lotus Formula Junior team. This, in turn, led to his Formula One debut in 1963, when he drove a Lotus-Climax to a 13th place finish in the Italian Grand Prix.

The following season, Spence drove in more Grands Prix for Lotus, with best finishes of sixth in Italy and fourth in Mexico. He did even better in 1965, coming fourth in South Africa and Britain, and third in Mexico.

However, Spence's best season was 1967 when, driving for BRM, he had point-scoring finishes in five Grands Prix – four fifths and one sixth place. Tragically, Spence was killed in 1968 when his Lotus 56 turbine car crashed during practice for the Indy 500 race in the USA.

Alan STACEY

Nationality: British
Born: 29th August 1933
Died: 19th June 1960
Seasons: 1958-1960
Team/manufacturer(s): Lotus
Grands Prix: 7
Race wins: 0
Championship wins: 0

Alan Stacey was born in Essex and enjoyed racing motorcycles as a teenager. Unfortunately, an accident on a bike at the age of 17 meant he had to have part of his right leg amputated. That, though, didn't stop the young Stacey from racing a Lotus 11, which he had fitted with a hand throttle. In the late 1950s he proved himself a capable driver, despite his

Scott Speed

handicap, and impressed Colin Chapman enough for him to be offered a place on the Lotus team from 1958.

Stacey made his Grand Prix debut that year, driving a Climax-engined Lotus, but was out of the race with an overheated engine after 19 laps.

The following year saw Stacey have another attempt at the British Grand Prix and this time he finished in eighth place. He also crossed the Atlantic to compete in the United States Grand Prix for Lotus but only lasted two laps before his clutch failed. In 1960, Stacey was set to do a full season of Formula One with Lotus and competed in three Grands Prix before arriving at Belgium. It was there that tragedy struck. He was driving at speed when he was hit in the face by a bird, lost control, hit a bank and was flung from the car. He died at the scene, aged just 26.

Prince Gaetano STARRABBA

Nationality: Italian
Born: 3rd December 1932
Seasons: 1961
Team/manufacturer(s): Lotus
Grands Prix: 1
Race wins: 0
Championship wins: 0

Prince Gaetano Starrabba was born in Sicily and was an Italian nobleman who enjoyed racing as a hobby, driving such cars as Maseratis and Ferraris in the 1950s.

Keen to try his hand at Formula One, Starrabba bought himself a Lotus 18 with a four-cylinder Maserati engine for the 1961 season. It was this car that he drove in his one and only World Championship appearance – his home Grand Prix at Monza in 1961. He didn't make much of an impression, though. After qualifying near the back of the grid, in 30th place, he was forced to retire after 19 laps of the race, because of engine problems. Starrabba continued to race the Lotus for a couple more seasons, although never again at the same level, before returning to sportscars.

Ian Macpherson STEWART

Nationality: British
Born: 15th July 1929
Seasons: 1953
Team/manufacturer(s): Connaught
Grands Prix: 1
Race wins: 0
Championship wins: 0

Born in Edinburgh, Ian Stewart began racing in the early 1950s with a Jaguar XK120. He later became involved with the Ecurie Ecosse team and drove a Jaguar C-Type with some success.

Stewart later moved to single-seaters, driving a Formula 2 Connaught in various events, including the 1953 British Grand Prix at Silverstone. He started the race 20th on the grid but was forced to retire after 24 laps with ignition problems.

He never again entered a World Championship race, but continued to compete, mainly in sportscar events, for a year or so.

However, a minor accident just before he got married persuaded Stewart to retire from the sport.

Stewart went on to run an agricultural business in Scotland but continued to attend historical motorsport events.

Sir John Young (Jackie) STEWART, OBE

Nationality: British
Born: 11th June 1939
Seasons: 1965-1973
Team/manufacturer(s): BRM, Matra, March, Tyrrell
Grands Prix: 100
Race wins: 27
Championship wins: 3

Jackie Stewart was born in 1939 and almost missed out on being a racing driver, because of the misfortune of his elder brother, Jimmy, who was already making a name for himself in Grand Prix racing when Jackie started work as an

Jackie Stewart

Jackie Stewart

1950s and later joined the Ecurie Ecosse team. It was with that team that, in 1953, he drove a Cooper-Bristol at the British Grand Prix – his one and only World Championship appearance.

Starting from 15th on the grid, Stewart managed to hold on for 79 laps, taking sixth place for a while, before he spun his car and was out of the race.

The following season, Stewart returned to sportscar racing, but crashed his Aston Martin at Le Mans. He was flung from the car and broke his elbow and suffered other minor injuries. It was not life-threatening, but enough to persuade his parents to try to discourage younger brother Jackie from racing – as history shows, they failed!

Stewart retired from racing in 1955, and was happy to let his brother take the limelight from then on.

Siegfried STOHR

Nationality: Italian
Born: 10th October 1952
Seasons: 1981
Team/manufacturer(s): Arrows
Grands Prix: 13
Race wins: 0
Championship wins: 0

Italian driver Siegfried Stohr (he had a German father, hence the name) was a late starter, only getting into karting in his late teens. He soon caught up, though, and won the Formula Italia title when he was 25.

After a spell in Formula 3 and then Formula 2, Stohr had a chance to move into Formula One, driving for the Arrows team for the 1981 season. Unfortunately, he had a disappointing time, only finishing three races all year – with a best placing of seventh in Holland.

A minor accident at the start of the Belgian Grand Prix appeared to shake Stohr's confidence somewhat and it was no surprise when he didn't try to do another season in Formula One. In fact, he gave up racing altogether the following year and became an instructor, starting his own racing school and writing about motorsport.

Rolf STOMMELEN

Nationality: German
Born: 11th July 1943
Died: 24th April 1983
Seasons: 1970-1976, 1978
Team/manufacturer(s): Brabham, Surtees, March, Lola, Hill, Arrows
Grands Prix: 61
Race wins: 0
Championship wins: 0

German driver Rolf Stommelen was born in Siegen and began his racing career competing in sportscars during the 1960s and 1970s, often driving for Porsche in events such as the Le Mans 24 Hour race.

He began competing in Formula One in 1970, driving a Brabham, and had a successful season, scoring points with three fifth-place finishes and one third place, the latter at Austria. That was, though, to be Stommelen's best season in Formula One.

In 1975, Stommelen was driving a Lola when he was involved in a dreadful accident at the Spanish Grand Prix at Montjuich Park in Barcelona. Stommelen was leading the race when the rear wing of his car broke, causing him to lose control and bounce off the barriers. It then flew over

apprentice mechanic at his father's garage. However, after Jimmy was injured in a crash at Le Mans, their parents decided that motor racing was not a suitable sport for their sons. Jackie, therefore, took up target shooting and almost made it to the 1960s Olympics.

However, Stewart drove at Oulton Park in 1963 and impressed Ken Tyrrell, who asked him to test for the Cooper Formula Cooper team, and soon offered the young Scot a place on his Formula Three team.

Stewart won his first race for Tyrrell the following year but he was keen to move on to Formula One, something which Tyrrell was not involved in at the time. So that meant a move to BRM. Stewart got off to a good start, picking up a Championship point in his first race, in South Africa. By the end of the season, he'd won at Monza and was honoured with the Rookie of the Year award.

After BRM, Stewart moved back to Tyrrell, which was now competing in Formula One and, in 1969, he became World Champion; an achievement he matched in 1971 and 1973. He might also have won in 1972, but missed a number of races due to illness.

After 1973 Stewart retired from Formula One, following the death of his teammate, Francois Cevert at Watkins Glen.

He then went on to be a consultant for Ford before setting up his own Formula One team in 1997. Stewart Grand Prix was run in conjunction with Ford and drivers included Rubens Barrichello and Johnny Herbert. Sadly, the team didn't achieve any notable success before being taken over fully by Ford in 2000 and renamed Jaguar Racing.

Most recently, Stewart made a name for himself as a motorsport commentator on US television, where viewers enjoyed his distinctive Scottish accent.

James (Jimmy) STEWART

Nationality: British
Born: 6th March 1931
Seasons: 1953
Team/manufacturer(s): Cooper
Grands Prix: 1
Race wins: 0
Championship wins: 0

Scotsman Jimmy Stewart was born in Dumbartonshire in Scotland, the elder brother of triple World Champion, Jackie Stewart. He began racing before his younger sibling but, in later life, never achieved the same success or recognition.

Stewart began competing in hillclimbs in the early

Rolf Stommelen

the barrier on the other side of the track into the spectators, killing five people. After this tragedy, no more Grands Prix were held at the circuit.

Stommelen was badly injured and was out of action for most of the season. After a handful of Grands Prix in 1976, he returned to sportscar racing the following year, before having an uneventful season in Formula One with Arrows in 1978.

Stommelen went on to have more successes in sportscar racing, but was killed during an IMSA event at the Riverside circuit in the USA, when his Porsche 935 crashed.

Philippe STREIFF

Nationality: French
Born: 26th June 1955
Seasons: 1984-1988
Team/manufacturer(s): Renault, Ligier, Tyrrell, AGS
Grands Prix: 54
Race wins: 0
Championship wins: 0

Philippe Streiff began racing in Formula Renault in 1978 and proved to be a talented driver. The following year he had moved up to Formula 3 and had won the French title by 1981.

This led to a move to Formula 2 for the next few years and Streiff was consistently successful, despite not winning many races. At the end of the 1984 season, he had his first chance to race in Formula One, driving a Renault at the Portuguese Grand Prix, although he didn't finish the race.

The next year, saw Streiff enter the last five Grands Prix of the season, and he finished the final one, in Australia, in third place, driving for Tyrrell. That was to be the peak of his Formula One career, although he picked up a handful of points over the following years, with Tyrrell and then AGS.

Unfortunately, Streiff was testing an AGS car for the 1989 season when he crashed badly at Rio de Janeiro and his injuries left him paralysed from the waist down. Unable to race, he devoted his time to building up a karting centre in Paris and formed a company that produced aids for disabled drivers.

Hans STUCK VON VILLIEZ

Nationality: German
Born: 27th December 1900
Died: 9th February 1978
Seasons: 1952-1953
Team/manufacturer(s): AFM
Grands Prix: 3
Race wins: 0
Championship wins: 0

Hans Stuck was born in Warsaw to Swiss parents, but he was brought up in Germany. After serving in the First World War, he started racing and hillclimbing in the early 1920s and, by 1931, had competed in his first Grand Prix, in Germany.

Stuck became well-known for his involvement with the German Auto Union cars, designed for Adolf Hitler with the help of Ferdinand Porsche. The rear-engined cars had up to 500bhp on tap and were notoriously hard to handle but Stuck mastered them and won several Grands Prix between the wars.

The Second World War forced Stuck to put his racing career on hold. After, he drove in Formula 2 and also entered three races in the new World Championship Formula One series, driving for AFM, although he had little success.

Stuck went on to drive a BMW in hillclimbs and, at the age

Siegfried Stohr

of 60, became the German Hillclimb Champion, at which point he decided to retire from racing. His son, Hans Joachim Stuck also became a racing driver.

Hans-Joachim STUCK

Nationality: German
Born: 1st January 1951
Seasons: 1974-1979
Team/manufacturer(s): March, Brabham, Shadow, ATS
Grands Prix: 93
Race wins: 0
Championship wins: 0

Hans-Joachim Stuck was the son of prewar racing legend, Hans Stuck. As a boy, not only did he race karts, but his father taught him to drive on the famed Nürburgring which put him in good stead to win the first 24-hour race there in 1970, when he was just 19 years old. Stuck went on to win the same race twice more, and also won the Spa 24 Hour race in 1972, not to mention success in a number of other sportscar challenges.

Stuck's Formula One career began in 1974 when he had the first of three seasons with March. He got off to a good start, scoring points early in the season with fifth and fourth place finishes. He was dropped from the team at the end of the year, but went back to March in the latter part of the 1975 season and stayed there until 1977. Stuck had a mixed bag of finishes, scoring points now and again.

His best Formula One season was 1977, when he picked up 12 Championship points over the year. That included two third place finishes, at Germany and Austria in the second half of the season, by which time he'd moved from March to Brabham.

It was downhill from there, though, as Stuck moved to the less-successful Shadow team for 1978 and then on to the similarly uninspiring ATS team in 1979. He did, though, finish his Formula One career with a respectable fifth place at the USA Grand Prix.

Stuck then returned to sportscar racing and was a regular at Le Mans, winning twice with a Porsche 962, and he even tried his hand at truck racing. His two sons are also racing drivers.

Otto STUPPACHER

Nationality: Austrian
Born: 3rd March 1947
Died: 13th August 2001
Seasons: 1976
Team/manufacturer(s): Tyrrell
Grands Prix: 4
Race wins: 0
Championship wins: 0

Born in Vienna, Otto Stuppacher began his career competing in hillclimbs before getting involved in sportscar racing in the early 1970s.

His short and unsuccessful Formula One career began and ended in 1976. He entered a Tyrrell into the Austrian Grand Prix that year but his entry was turned down, so he never even drove in practice or qualifying.

He did, however, manage to gain entry for the Italian Grand Prix later that season, but failed to qualify by a considerable margin. Ironically, though, three other drivers were subsequently disqualified, meaning that Stuppacher would have been able to drive in the race but, by this time, he'd left the circuit and so missed his chance.

Hans Stuck

Stuppacher then went on to enter the Canadian and United States Grands Prix, but failed to qualify for either.

He never again raced in Formula One and, indeed, appeared to do little racing of any consequence elsewhere. Stuppacher was found dead in his Vienna flat in 2001; he was just 54 years old.

Daniel John (Danny) SULLIVAN III

Nationality: American
Born: 9th March 1950
Seasons: 1983
Team/manufacturer(s): Tyrrell
Grands Prix: 15
Race wins: 0
Championship wins: 0

Danny Sullivan was born in Kentucky and came to the UK at the age of 21 with the aim of becoming a racing driver. After competing in Formula Ford and Formula 3 he returned to the USA to race in Can-Am, where his career finally began to take off.

In 1983 Sullivan returned to Europe to have a go at breaking into Formula One, driving for Tyrrell. He had an uninspiring season, though, with the one high point being a respectable fifth place finish at the Monaco Grand Prix.

Sullivan had the talent to make it in Formula One but, instead, he returned to the USA to compete in Indy car racing, after receiving a lucrative offer from a team there. It was a good move, because he went on to be a great success, winning the Indy 500 in 1985.

He later worked as a commentator for American television and was involved in the Red Bull Young Driver scheme to search for young Formula One drivers.

Marc SURER

Nationality: Swiss
Born: 18th September 1951
Seasons: 1979-1986
Team/manufacturer(s): Ensign, ATS, Arrows, Brabham
Grands Prix: 87
Race wins: 0
Championship wins: 0

Swiss-born Marc Surer began racing karts in his early twenties, which is later than usual but he soon caught up, working his way up through Formula Vee and Formula 3 to Formula 2. This culminated in him winning the European Formula 2 Championship in 1979.

That same year, Surer made his Formula One debut, driving for Ensign for the last three Grands Prix of the season, but without success. He then joined the ATS team for 1980 but broke his ankles in a crash during practice near the start of the season, so missed four Grands Prix.

In 1981, Surer picked up his first points, finishing fourth in Brazil and sixth at Monaco, but the rest of the season was disappointing. In fact, it was a similar story in the following years – he picked up a handful of points in the odd good finish, but did poorly in all other Grands Prix. His best season was 1985, when he picked up five Championship points and finished the year in 13th place, driving for Brabham. Surer moved to Arrows for the 1986 season but only did five Grands Prix before he was badly injured in a rallying accident, which put an end to his racing career. He later worked as an instructor for BMW and as a television commentator.

John SURTEES, MBE

Nationality: British
Born: 11th February 1934
Seasons: 1960-1972
Team/manufacturer(s): Lotus, Cooper, Lola, Ferrari, Honda, BRM, McLaren, Surtees
Grands Prix: 113
Race wins: 6
Championship wins: 1

John Surtees' father owned a motorcycle shop in South London and was also three-times British motorcycle sidecar champion. The young Surtees got his first motorbike at the age of 11 and learnt, not only to ride it, but also to maintain the machine himself. He left school at the age of 16 and served as an apprentice engineer for Vincent, the British motorcycle manufacturer. Before long, Surtees competed in – and won – his first motorcycle race.

Surtees then went to race for Norton in 1955 and won an incredible 68 out of 76 races that year. He moved next to the Italian MV Agusta team and won seven World Championships between 1956 and 1960.

His achievements gained the attention of car racing teams and, at his first single-seater race Surtees finished a close second to Jim Clark. Following this, Lotus's

John Surtee

Marc Surer

Colin Chapman signed him for the end of the 1960 season and Surtees came second at the British and Portuguese Grands Prix that year. He then made the decision to retire from motorcycle racing and concentrate on Formula One, racing first for Lotus.

However, it wasn't until Surtees moved to Ferrari, in 1963, that he really started to shine. As the team's number-one driver, he had his first victory at the Nürburgring; a win he repeated the following year. Indeed, 1964 was to be his finest season, with Surtees winning the Championship.

It was a great result but was also to be Surtees' last Championship title. In 1965, he moved to the USA to compete in the Can-Am series. A bad crash in Canada led to him being badly injured, but he was soon back racing at the Belgian Grand Prix, where he drove superbly in heavy rain to one of his finest wins, and his last drive for Ferrari.

Surtees joined the Cooper team in 1966 and drove their Maserati-engined car to victory in Mexico that year. Beyond that, though, he struggled with uncompetitive cars and, in 1969, moved to BRM. Again, though, the cars were not as reliable as he'd hoped and Surtees had little luck.

Fed up with other people's mechanical inadequacies, Surtees started his own Formula One team in 1970. The Surtees Racing Organisation used V8 Cosworth engines and showed promise in the early years, with Surtees himself driving for the first two seasons. Long term, the team struggled to survive and withdrew from Formula One in 1978. The following year it competed briefly in Formula 5000 before going out of business.

John Surtees retired from motorsport at that time and went on to be a property developer.

Andrew (Andy) SUTCLIFFE

Nationality: British
Born: 9th May 1947
Seasons: 1977
Team/manufacturer(s): RAM
Grands Prix: 1
Race wins: 0
Championship wins: 1

British driver Andrew Sutcliffe was born in Mildenhall, Suffolk. He worked his way up to Formula 3, where he had some success in the early 1970s.

In 1977, Sutcliffe had his one and only chance to compete in Formula One, when he drove a March 761 Cosworth for RAM in the British Grand Prix at Silverstone. Unfortunately, he wasn't up to the challenge and failed even to pre-qualify for the race.

Sutcliffe then returned to Formula 3. He also worked as a male model before becoming a plant nurseryman in Kent – a somewhat more leisurely pursuit than motorsport!

Adrian SUTIL

Nationality: German
Born: 11th January 1983
Seasons: 2007-
Team/manufacturer(s): Spyker
Grands Prix: 17
Race wins: 0
Championship wins: 0

German driver, Adrian Sutil is the son of two musicians and a talented pianist in his own right. However, motorsport was his first love since he took up karting at the age of 14.

By 2002, Sutil was competing in Swiss Formula Ford

1800 and won all ten rounds to take the championship that year. And to top that, he won five races in the Formula Masters Austria championship.

The 2004 season saw Sutil compete in the Formula 3 Euroseries and the following year he joined the ASM team alongside Lewis Hamilton. The English driver won the championship that year, but Sutil was runner up.

Sutil spent 2006 racing in Japan, winning the Formula 3 championship there. He also signed as a test-driver for MF1 Racing, which was then renamed Spyker F1. At the end of the season he was named as the team's second driver for 2007. Sadly, though, he made a disappointing start to the year, either finishing down the ranking or retiring.

Sadly, though, he had a disappointing year, either finishing down the ranking or retiring, but he had one high point, when he finished eighth in the Japanese Grand Prix, scoring a single Championship point.

Aguri SUZUKI

Nationality: Japanese
Born: 8th September 1960
Seasons: 1988-1995
Team/manufacturer(s): Lola, Zakspeed, Footwork, Jordan, Ligier
Grands Prix: 88
Race wins: 0
Championship wins: 1

Aguri Suzuki was born in Tokyo and began racing karts when he was 12, winning the Japanese Championship six years later and again two years after that.

After a season in Formula 3, Suzuki moved to touring cars and won the Japanese title in 1986. That same year he competed in Formula 2 and, the following season, in Formula 3000. In 1988, he won the Japanese Formula 3000 Championship.

Also in 1988, Suzuki had his Formula One debut, driving for Lola in the Japanese Grand Prix at the end of the season. Then followed a disastrous season in 1989, when Suzuki drove for the underfunded Zakspeed team and failed to pre-qualify for a single Grand Prix all season.

Suzuki bounced back, though, with a better season in 1990 with Lola, including a third-place finish in Japan and a total of six Championship points. That was to be his best season, though, and he made little impact from then on. An accident at the end of the 1995 season left Suzuki with bad neck injuries and he decided to retire from Formula One.

He went on to race in supercar events and, in 2006, formed the Super Aguri F1 Formula One team with the backing of Honda.

Toshio SUZUKI

Nationality: Japanese
Born: 10th March 1955
Seasons: 1993
Team/manufacturer(s): Larrousse
Grands Prix: 2
Race wins: 0
Championship wins: 1

Japanese driver Toshio Suzuki was well known in his home country. In 1979 he shot to prominence when he won the Japanese Formula 3 Championship before moving on to Formula 2 and then Formula 3000, having reasonable success in each.

At the relatively old age of 38, Suzuki had a chance to

realise his ambition of driving in a Formula One race, when he signed with the Larrousse team for the last two Grands Prix of the 1993 season. His aim was to finish the races, especially his home Grand Prix, and he did just that, coming in 12th in Japan and 14th in Australia.

Later, Suzuki became a successful sportscar driver, winning the 1992 Daytona 24 Hour race. He also competed in GT events.

Jacques SWATERS

Nationality: Belgian
Born: 30th October 1926
Seasons: 1951, 1953-1954
Team/manufacturer(s): Talbot, Ferrari
Grands Prix: 7
Race wins: 0
Championship wins: 1

Belgian driver Jacques Swaters began his race career in style, campaigning an MG in the 1948 Spa 24 Race with Paul Frère. Two years later, he was one of the founders of the Écurie Belgique race team.

It was with Écurie Belgique (or Écurie Francorchamps as it was now known) that Swaters entered the German and Italian Grands Prix in 1951, driving a Talbot-Lago.

That car was crashed by another driver, so the fledgling team bought a Ferrari T500 for the 1952 season, although Swaters didn't drive it in any World Championship races that year.

However, he did compete in 1953, driving the Ferrari in the German and Swiss Grands Prix at the end of that season. And in 1954 he entered it into the Belgian and Swiss Grands Prix.

By this time, though, Swaters was having more success in sportscar racing, driving Jaguars. However, he retired from racing in 1957 to concentrate on running the race team and other businesses, including a Ferrari dealership. The Écurie Francorchamps team, meanwhile, continued competing until 1982, racing mostly Ferraris.

Danny Sullivan

T

TAKAGI, Toranosuke
TAKARHARA, Noritake
TAKAHASHI, Kunimitsu
TAMBAY, Patrick
TARAMAZZO, Luigi
TARQUINI, Gabriele
TARUFFI, Piero
TAYLOR, Dennis
TAYLOR, Henry
TAYLOR, John
TAYLOR, Mike
TAYLOR, Trevor
TESTUT, Andre
THACKWELL, Mike
THIELE, Alfonso
THOMPSON, Eric
THORNE, Leslie
TINGLE, Sam
TITTERINGTON, Desmond
TRIMMER, Tony
TRINTIGNANT, Maurice
TRULLI, JARNO
TUERO, Esteban
TUNMER, Guy

Toranosuke (Tora) TAKAGI

Nationality: Japanese
Born: 12th February 1974
Seasons: 1998-1999
Team/manufacturer(s): Tyrrell, Arrows
Grands Prix: 32
Race wins: 0
Championship wins: 0

The son of a touring car driver, Toranosuke Takagi began racing karts when he was a boy, going on to win a number of local events before he moved on to Formula Toyota in 1992.

A year later, Takagi had a season in All Japan Formula 3 and finished 10th in the championship. His driving caught the attention of local Formula One driver, Satoru Nakajima, who took on the youngster as a driver in his own Formula 3000 team for the 1995 and 1996 seasons.

In 1997, Takagi became test driver for the Tyrrell Formula One team and, the following season, was promoted to a full-time driver. After a reasonable but unastonishing first year, Takagi moved to Arrows where, after a couple of reasonable finishes at the start of the season, he struggled to be competitive for the rest of the year.

That was the end of Takagi's Formula One career, but he went on to drive in Formula Nippon, winning the 2000 championship with an amazing eight victories out of 10 races. He later moved to the USA to race in CART and he came fifth in the 2003 Indy 500 race. Takagi then returned to Japan and Formula Nippon again.

Noritake TAKAHARA

Nationality: Japanese
Born: 6th June 1951
Seasons: 1976-1977
Team/manufacturer(s): Surtees, Kojima
Grands Prix: 2
Race wins: 0
Championship wins: 0

Noritake Takahara was born in Tokyo and began racing in the late 1960s, driving a Honda S800, before coming to Europe to compete in Formula 2 in 1973. He then returned home to race in the local Formula 2000 series, which he won in 1975 and 1976.

At the end of the 1976 season Takahara drove a Surtees TS19 in the Japanese Grand Prix and finished in a not disappointing ninth place, after starting from 15th on the grid. In fact, he was the first Japanese driver to ever complete a World Championship Grand Prix.

Takahara then moved to Formula 2 for a number of years but did make another Formula One appearance at the 1977 Japanese Grand Prix. Driving a Kojima 009, he qualified 19th but had to retire after colliding with another car on the first lap.

He retired from racing in the 1980s and moved into motorsport management in Japan.

Kunimitsu TAKAHASHI

Nationality: Japanese
Born: 29th January 1940
Seasons: 1977
Team/manufacturer(s): Tyrrell
Grands Prix: 1
Race wins: 0
Championship wins: 0

Japanese driver Kunimitsu Takahashi was born in Tokyo

Toranosuke Takagi

and started his career as a motorcycle racer. However, he was badly injured in an accident during the 1962 Isle of Man TT race and so decided to switch to four wheels from 1965, beginning with sportscars; a discipline he stuck with for many years, usually competing within his own country.

However, in 1977 Takahashi made a single Formula appearance, driving at the Japanese Grand Prix. He was in an old Tyrrell that Kazuyoshi Hoshino had driven in the previous year's event. Despite not being experienced, Takahashi still managed to finish in a respectable ninth place.

Takahashi then drove in Japanese Formula 2 for a while before returning to sportscars. He was the Japanese sportscar champion no less than four times in the 1980s. After retiring from driving at the end of the 1990s, Takahashi formed his own GT team.

Patrick TAMBAY

Nationality: French
Born: 25th June 1949
Seasons: 1977-1979, 1981-1986
Team/manufacturer(s): Surtees, Theodore, McLaren, Ligier, Ferrari, Renault, Lola
Grands Prix: 123
Race wins: 2
Championship wins: 0

Paris-born Patrick Tambay came from a wealthy family and was educated in France and the USA. His racing career began in the early 1970s when he won the Pilote Elf scheme which led to a drive in Formule Renault in 1973, where he finished the season in second place.

That excellent result was enough to get him straight into European Formula 2 for 1974 and he remained there until 1977. Then he had his first chance to compete in Formula One, when he drove a Surtees in the French Grand Prix but failed to qualify. However, he did better later that season, picking up points in three races, driving for Theodore.

Tambay then drove for a number of teams over the following years. His best two seasons were with Ferrari in 1982 and 1983, which is when he had his two Formula One wins. The first was in Germany in 1982, the second at San Marino the following year. That same season, he finished fourth in the Championship with 40 points.

After leaving Ferrari, Tambay drove for Renault and then Lola, but did not achieve the same sort of success. He retired from Formula One at the end of the 1986 season,

Gabriele Tarquini

but went on to race in sportscar events, including Le Mans. Tambay also worked in television and ran a sports promotion company.

Luigi TARAMAZZO

Nationality: Italian
Born: 5th May 1932
Died: 15th February 2004
Seasons: 1958
Team/manufacturer(s): Maserati
Grands Prix: 1
Race wins: 0
Championship wins: 0

Italian driver Luigi Taramazzo was born in Ceva in 1932 and began racing after the Second World War. He was particularly keen on hillclimbs and, in 1957, he won at a number of events, driving a rare Zagato-bodied Ferrari 250GT – a car he later bought for himself.

In 1968, Taramazzo bought a new Ferrari GT Berlinetta Scaglietti and drove it to victory at that year's Mille Miglia and a number of other races. By now, Taramazzo was well known and he was offered a large amount of money to compete in the Monaco Grand Prix, because it was thought he'd help draw the crowds. Taramazzo shared Ken Kavanagh's Maserati 250F but failed to qualify for the race itself.

That was the extent of Taramazzo's Formula One involvement, but he continued to spend money on Ferrari sportscars which he raced and hillclimbed with some success

right up until the start of the 1970s, when he decided to retire from the sport.

Gabriele TARQUINI

Nationality: Italian
Born: 2nd March 1962
Seasons: 1987-1995
Team/manufacturer(s): Osella, Cloni, AGS, Fondmetal, Tyrrell
Grands Prix: 77
Race wins: 0
Championship wins: 0

Italian Gabriele Tarquini began racing karts at the age of eight, using a track owned by his father, and went on to become World Champion. By 1983, he had progressed to Formula 3 but, after a season, he returned to karting and, again, won the World Championship.

Tarquini then moved to Formula 3000 for 1985 and also raced at Le Mans. He stayed in Formula 3000 for the next two seasons. However, at the start of 1987 he made a single Formula One appearance, driving for Osella at San Marino, but retiring from the race.

For 1988, Tarquini joined the Coloni team but he had a disappointing season. In fact, that would be the story of his Formula One career and he gained the unenviable record for being the driver to have failed to qualify or pre-qualify for the most races – no less than 40 out of 77 Grands Prix. However, to be fair, that was perhaps more a reflection on

the teams he was driving for than his ability as a driver. Tarquini's best finish was a sixth place at the 1989 Mexican Grand Prix, which earned him a single Championship point.

By 1995, Tarquini was making a name for himself as a Touring Car driver, after winning the British championship the previous year. He also he made a single Formula One appearance – his last one – at the European Grand Prix, driving for Tyrrell. After that, he pursued a successful Touring Car career, winning the European championship in 2003.

Pierino (Piero) TARUFFI

Nationality: Italian
Born: 12th October 1906
Died: 12th January 1988
Seasons: 1950-1956
Team/manufacturer(s): Alfa Romeo, Ferrari, Mercedes, Maserati, Vanwall
Grands Prix: 77
Race wins: 1
Championship wins: 0

Piero Taruffi was born in Rome and began racing motorcycles after the First World War, moving to cars later and winning the 1930 Mille Miglia as well as other events.

The Second World War meant Taruffi had to put his racing exploits on hold, but he was soon back competing in pre-World Championship Grands Prix in the late 1940s.

His first World Championship Formula One race was the 1950 Italian Grand Prix, where he drove an Alfa Romeo. The following two years he drove full seasons for Ferrari in Formula One, and with much success, too, winning in Switzerland in 1952 and picking up points in other races as well.

After that, he got more involved in racing sportscars, but still made appearances in the occasional Formula One Grand Prix, driving for Ferrari and other teams. He did well, too, finishing second in Italy and fourth in Britain in 1955.

Taruffi won the last ever Mille Miglia race, in 1957 at the age of 51, driving a Ferrari. After that, he retired from racing and started a racing school. Taruffi wrote a seminal book called The Technique of Motor Racing.

Dennis TAYLOR

Nationality: British
Born: 12th June 1921
Died: 2nd June 1962
Seasons: 1959
Team/manufacturer(s): Lotus
Grands Prix: 1
Race wins: 0
Championship wins: 0

British driver Dennis Taylor was born in Sidcup, Kent, in 1921. He began racing in Formula 3 in 1951, driving an Iota 500cc car and went on to be very successful in that series for a number of years.

In 1958, Taylor made the jump to Formula 2, behind the wheel of his own Lotus 12. It was with this car that he entered his one and only Formula One race, the 1959 British Grand Prix, which was held at Aintree that year. Unfortunately, he failed to qualify for the race.

The following year Taylor sold the Lotus and bought a front-engined Lola with which to compete in the new Formula Junior series. Then in 1961 he replaced that car with a more modern rear-engined Lola. Taylor was killed

Gabriele Tarquini

Patrick Tambay

That said, he returned to competition soon after, rallying and racing a Ford Cortina, which led to him becoming Ford's Competition manager. He later moved to the south of France to work with boats.

John TAYLOR

Nationality: British
Born: 23rd March 1933
Died: 8th September 1966
Seasons: 1964, 1966
Team/manufacturer(s): Cooper, Brabham
Grands Prix: 5
Race wins: 0
Championship wins: 0

British driver John Taylor was born in Leicester and grew up in Lancashire. He began racing in Formula Junior in the early 1960s and had some success.

Taylor also competed in some non-Championship Formula One races during the same period and this led to him driving in the 1964 British Grand Prix at Brands Hatch. Behind the wheel of a privately-run Cooper, Taylor finished the race in 14th place, after starting 20th on the grid.

Two years later saw Taylor return to World Championship racing in style, when he drove a Brabham-BRM to an impressive sixth place finish at the French Grand Prix at Reims, earning him a Championship point.

That same year, Taylor also drove the Brabham at the British and Dutch Grands Prix, finishing eighth both times. And then disaster struck. At the German Grand Prix his Brabham collided with Jacky Ickx's Matra on the first lap of

Piero Taruffi

the race. Taylor's car left the track and burst into flames and he was badly burned. He died of his injuries in hospital four weeks later.

Michael (Mike) TAYLOR

Nationality: British
Born: 24th April 1934
Seasons: 1959-1960
Team/manufacturer(s): Cooper, Lotus
Grands Prix: 2
Race wins: 0
Championship wins: 0

Michael Taylor was the son of a businessman who ran a Mayfair-based Mercedes dealership. In the late 1950s he raced at an amateur level and had some reasonable success in a Lotus 11.

He then moved to a Formula 2 Cooper-Climax for the 1959 season and, again, proved himself to be a capable driver. It was with this car that he had his Formula One debut, at the 1959 British Grand Prix at Aintree. After qualifying a lowly 24th, Taylor was forced to retire from the race with transmission problems after 17 laps.

For the 1960 season, Taylor bought himself a brand-new Lotus 18 which he took to Spa for the Belgian Grand Prix. Unfortunately, though, he crashed during practice, with the car leaving the track and smashing into some woods after the steering column failed. Taylor was badly injured and later successfully sued Lotus for damages, obtaining a substantial settlement.

After that disaster, Taylor hung up his racing helmet and went into property development and also ran his own garage. In 1980, he married Stirling Moss's former second wife, Elaine Barberino.

Trevor TAYLOR

Nationality: British
Born: 26th December 1936
Seasons: 1959, 1960-1964, 1966
Team/manufacturer(s): Lotus, BRP, Shannon
Grands Prix: 29
Race wins: 0
Championship wins: 0

Sheffield-bred Trevor Taylor was the son of a garage owner who grew up around cars. He began racing in his late teens and was soon competing in Formula 3, winning the British Championship in 1958.

From there, Taylor moved to Formula 2 and Formula Junior, and made his Formula One debut at the 1959 British Grand Prix, driving a Formula 2 Cooper-Climax, but failed to qualify.

Taylor then bought a Lotus 18 and raced for the factory team. In 1961, he won the British Formula Junior Championship, driving a Lotus 18. That same year, he entered the Dutch Grand Prix with Lotus, finishing 13th.

The following two years saw Taylor put in full Formula One seasons with Lotus, and with some success, too. At the 1962 Dutch Grand Prix, at the start of the season, he finished in second place, while in Monaco at the start of the following season he came sixth.

Taylor then left Lotus and moved to BRP for 1964. Despite struggling with the less competitive car, he did have one good result – a sixth-place finish in the USA Grand Prix.

From then on, Taylor became more involved in touring cars, driving with his sister, Anita. However, he did have one

Henry TAYLOR

Nationality: British
Born: 16th December 1932
Seasons: 1959-1961
Team/manufacturer(s): Cooper, Lotus
Grands Prix: 8
Race wins: 0
Championship wins: 0

Henry Taylor was born in Bedfordshire and was a farmer who raced as a hobby. He began at club level, winning the Autosport championship in 1955 before getting more involved in single-seaters, mainly in Formula 2 and Formula Junior.

Taylor's Formula One debut was in 1959, when he entered the Formula 2 class of the British Grand Prix at Aintree. He finished an impressive second in class, driving a Cooper-Climax. The following year saw Taylor enter five Grands Prix, again driving a Cooper-Climax, but with disappointing results.

It was a similar story for 1961, when Taylor was behind the wheel of a Lotus 18 in five Grands Prix, but with little success. Also, he crashed at the British Grand Prix and, despite not being badly injured, was shaken enough to decide to retire from racing.

when he crashed this car during the Formula Junior race that was held at Monaco on the same weekend of the Formula One Grand Prix there.

S
T

Maurice Trintignant

more Formula One drive, when he competed in the 1966 British Grand Prix in a Shannon, but he retired with engine problems at the start of the race. He also raced in Formula 5000 for a while before retiring in 1972.

André TESTUT

Nationality: French
Born: 13th April 1926
Died: 24th September 2005
Seasons: 1958-1959
Team/manufacturer(s): Maserati
Grands Prix: 2
Race wins: 0
Championship wins: 0

French racing driver André Testut came from Lyon and very little is known about him. He was active in the 1950s, mainly competing with some success in French hillclimbs, behind the wheel of an OSCA or a Porsche 356. He also competed in some GT races in the Porsche.

In 1958, Testut entered his own six-cylinder Maserati 250F into the Monaco Grand Prix but, unfortunately, failed to qualify for the race. The following year he again entered the same Grand Prix, but this time in a Maserati 250F run by the Monte Carlo Autosport team. As before, Testut failed to qualify.

After that, Testut entered his Maserati in some minor races and hillclimbs, and also competed with other cars, up until about 1960.

Michael (Mike) THACKWELL

Nationality: New Zealander
Born: 30th March 1961
Seasons: 1980, 1984
Team/manufacturer(s): Arrows, RAM
Grands Prix: 5
Race wins: 0
Championship wins: 0

New Zealander Mike Thackwell was born in Auckland, the son of a local Formula 2 driver. After competing at home, he came to England and, in 1979, was runner-up in the British Formula 3 Championship.

This led to him becoming test driver for the Tyrrell Formula One team in 1980 while, at the same time, competing in Formula 2. Partway through the season, Thackwell had a one-off drive for Arrows in the Dutch Grand Prix but failed to qualify. Then, later that same season, he drove for Tyrrell in the Canadian Grand Prix and, at the age of just 19, was the youngest driver to compete in a Formula One World Championship race. Unfortunately, a collision involving other cars meant the race was stopped and Thackwell's car was taken over by another driver when the race restarted. Thackwell then drove in the United States Grand Prix, but failed to qualify.

Thackwell then returned to Formula 2 and won the European Championship in 1984. The same year, he drove for RAM in the Canadian Grand Prix, but was forced to retire with turbocharger problems. Later that same season he returned to Tyrrell for the German Grand Prix, but failed to qualify.

That was the end of Thackwell's Formula One career, but he went on to have success in Formula 3000 and sportscar racing before retiring from the sport in 1987. Staying in the UK, he has had a variety of jobs since, including a teacher, steeplejack, miner and helicopter pilot!

Alfonse THIELE

Nationality: American
Born: 5th April 1922
Died: 1986
Seasons: 1960
Team/manufacturer(s): Cooper
Grands Prix: 1
Race wins: 0
Championship wins: 0

Although an American, Alfonse Thiele also had Italian citizenship and he spent most of his life in Italy. He began racing sportscars in the 1950s and proved himself to be a talented driver. He began with a Fiat Abarth, in which he won his class in the 1957 Mille Miglia, and then moved up to a Ferrari 250GT.

Thiele's Formula One career was short and uneventful. He entered a Centro Sud Cooper-Maserati in the 1960 Italian Grand Prix, held at Monza. However, after starting ninth on the grid, he was forced to retire after 32 laps with gearbox problems. The race, incidentally, was won by another American, Phil Hill – the first time a World Championship race had been taken by an American driver.

Thiele then went back to sportscar racing and was a works driver for Fiat Abarth and Alfa Romeo in the early 1960s.

Eric THOMPSON

Nationality: British
Born: 4th November 1919
Seasons: 1952
Team/manufacturer(s): Connaught
Grands Prix: 1
Race wins: 0
Championship wins: 0

Eric Thompson was born in Surrey and served in the army during the Second World War. After, he worked as a Lloyds insurance broker and began racing as a hobby, having some success in endurance races in the late 1940s.

By 1950, he was driving for the Aston Martin sportscar team, competing in a number of races, including Le Mans between then and 1954, when he left the team.

At the same time, Thompson was also dabbling with single-seaters and this led to his one and only Formula One appearance. At the 1952 British Grand Prix, he drove for Connaught and impressed everyone by finishing in fifth place and earning two Championship points.

Despite this success, Thompson never entered another World Championship race, preferring to concentrate on sportscar events. By the end of 1955, though, he decided to retire from racing to concentrate on his work. Later, he ran a bookshop that specialised in historic motorsport books.

Leslie THORNE

Nationality: British
Born: 23rd June 1915
Died: 13th July 1993
Seasons: 1954
Team/manufacturer(s): Connaught
Grands Prix: 1
Race wins: 0
Championship wins: 0

Scottish driver Leslie Thorne worked as a chartered accountant and raced cars has a hobby. He began in 1953 behind the wheel of a 500cc Formula 3 Cooper-Norton,

which he campaigned successfully in a variety of races.

Thorne was friendly with David Murray, the owner of the Ecurie Ecosse team, and he managed to persuade him to drive the team's Connaught Formula 2 car in selected races during 1954.

One of those races was the British Grand Prix at Silverstone. Thorne qualified 23rd and finished the race in 14th place after 78 laps – not a great result, perhaps, but at least he finished, which was something for a newcomer.

Thorne used the Connaught a few more times that season, finishing sixth in the Chichester Cup at Goodwood. He then returned to racing other cars until retiring from the sport and continuing his profession as accountant.

Sam TINGLE

Nationality: Rhodesian
Born: 24th August 1921
Seasons: 1963, 1965, 1967-1969
Team/manufacturer(s): LDS, Brabham
Grands Prix: 5
Race wins: 0
Championship wins: 0

Sam Tingle was born in Manchester, England, but grew up in Rhodesia (now Zimbabwe), with citizenship of that country. He began racing there after the Second World War, behind the wheel of, first a Bentley, then a number of MGs.

Tingle later began racing single-seaters, winning the Rhodesian Championship. He also competed in the South African Championship throughout the 1960s, which included entering the South African Grand Prix five times.

His first World Championship race was the 1963 South African Grand Prix at East London, where Tingle retired with a broken halfshaft after just two laps. Unfortunately, he didn't have much better luck in subsequent races, finishing just twice, with his best result being eighth place in 1969, driving a Brabham-Repco.

After retiring from racing, Tingle still enjoyed attending historic motorsport events in Africa and beyond.

Desmond TITTERINGTON

Nationality: British
Born: 1st May 1928
Died: 13th April 2002
Seasons: 1956
Team/manufacturer(s): Connaught
Grands Prix: 1
Race wins: 0
Championship wins: 0

Desmond Titterington was born in County Down in Northern Ireland to a wealthy family. He began racing in 1950, driving an MG in local races and, later, in mainland Europe. By 1953 he was driving with the Ecurie Ecosse team, followed by stints with Jaguar and Mercedes, and he became well-known throughout the UK.

Despite his ability, Titterington only ever made one attempt at a World Championship race, although he did enter some non-Championship events. His single Grand Prix attempt was at Silverstone in 1956, when he qualified his Connaught in 11th place, but had to retire from the race after 74 laps because of engine problems.

Titterington then returned to sportscar racing, but retired from the sport at the end of the 1956 season to concentrate on his family and yarn business, although he continued to compete at a low-level basis for a bit of fun.

He later moved from Northern Ireland to Scotland, where he died in 2002.

Tony TRIMMER

Nationality: British
Born: 24th January 1943
Seasons: 1975-1978
Team/manufacturer(s): Maki, Surtees, McLaren
Grands Prix: 6
Race wins: 0
Championship wins: 0

Tony Trimmer was born in Maidenhead in Berkshire and first shot to success in 1970 when he won the Shell British Formula 3 Championship. He then went on to compete mainly at club level.

Five years later, Trimmer entered his first World Championship race: the 1975 German Grand Prix at the Nürburgring. Unfortunately, Trimmer was driving an uncompetitive, Cosworth-engined car for the Japanese Maki team, and he failed to qualify for the race.

It was the same story for the Austrian and Italian Grands Prix that followed the same season. Maki then realised it had a problem with the car and withdrew to do some more development work. The following year, it came back with a modified car but, by this time, it was the end of the season, and it was entered only in the Japanese Grand Prix. With Trimmer driving again, the team failed to qualify once more and gave up on Formula One after that.

Trimmer, however, entered two more Grands Prix, driving cars run by Melchester Racing. In 1977 he drove a Surtees at the British Grand Prix but failed to pre-qualify. The following year he entered the same event, this time in a McLaren, but failed to qualify.

However, also in 1978, Trimmer drove the same McLaren in the BRDC International Trophy non-Championship race at Silverstone and finished in third place – ahead of many more famous drivers.

However, that was the height of his success and he went on to become a racing instructor, but continued to race in GT and historic events.

Maurice TRINTIGNANT

Nationality: French
Born: 30th October 1917
Died: 13th February 2005
Seasons: 1950-1964
Team/manufacturer(s): Gordini, Ferrari, Vanwall, Bugatti, Cooper, BRM, Aston Martin, Lotus, Lola
Grands Prix: 82
Race wins: 2
Championship wins: 0

Frenchman Maurice Trintignant was the brother of racing driver Louis Trintignant and uncle of French actor Jean-Louis Trintignant. He began racing in 1938 and, the following year, won the Grand Prix des Frontières.

After the Second World War, Trintignant joined the Gordini team to compete in the new Formula One World Championship series, which began in 1950. From then on, he raced in Formula One every season until his retirement at the end of the 1964 season, and drove an astonishing variety of cars for a number of teams.

Trintignant won two Grands Prix – each time the Monaco race, in 1955 and 1958 – becoming the first Frenchman to win a Formula One race. He finished in the top six in many more Grands Prix. Indeed, in 1954 and 1955 he finished fourth in the Drivers' Championship each season.

By 1963, Trintignant had cut down the amount of racing he did, and he only entered three World Championship Grands Prix that year. However, before retiring, he bought himself a BRM P57 and entered it privately in five Grands Prix during 1964, picking up two points when he finished fifth in Germany.

Trintignant then hung up his helmet and went back to the family business of running a vineyard and he was also the local mayor.

Jarno TRULLI

Nationality: Italian
Born: 13th July 1974
Seasons: 1997-
Team/manufacturer(s): Minardi, Prost, Jordan, Renault, Toyota
Grands Prix: 184
Race wins: 1
Championship wins: 0

Italian driver Jarno Trulli's parents were motorsport fans and he was named after Jarno Saarinen, a Finnish motorcycle champion who was killed at Monza in 1973.

Trulli began his career in karting and went on to win the Italian and European championships before moving into Formula 3, winning the German championship in 1996.

That success led to a place on the Minardi Formula One team for the 1997 season, picking up three points when he came fourth in Germany that year. Trulli then moved to Prost for 1998 and 1999, where he struggled with uncompetitive cars.

A switch to Jordan for 2001 and 2002 improved matters and then Trulli drove for Renault from 2002 to 2004 and he really began to score points. His best season was 2004, when he won at Monaco and finished the year sixth in the Championship. However, he'd fallen out with Renault by then and moved to Toyota for the last two Grands Prix of the season.

Trulli stayed with the Japanese team and again had a good season in 2005, finishing seventh in the Championship with 43 points. However, he had less success the following year, coming 12th in the Championship.

In 2007, Trulli had a mixed season, with his best finish being sixth place in the USA Grand Prix. He finished the season with 13 points, taking a respectable eighth place in the Championship.

Esteban TUERO

Nationality: Argentinean
Born: 22nd April 1978
Seasons: 1998
Team/manufacturer(s): Minardi
Grands Prix: 16
Race wins: 0
Championship wins: 0

Born in Buenos Aires to a family obsessed with motorsport, Esteban Tuero began karting at the age of seven, moving up to Formula Renault when he was just 14. The following year he was the Argentinean Formula Honda champion.

This success led to a move to Europe where the young Tuero continued to shine, winning the Italian Formula 2000 trophy in his first season.

Such a talent gained the attention of the Formula One teams and Tuero found himself testing for Minardi at the tender age of 18. The following year, he was promoted to team driver, despite concerns from some quarters about his age and lack of experience.

Tuero showed that he had skill during that season, and qualified for every race, but he failed to get the results needed, only finishing four Grands Prix all year. Tragically, though, at the Japanese Grand Prix at the end of the season, Tuero crashed badly, injuring a vertebra in his neck.

Although he recovered, the young Argentinean announced his retirement from Formula One but refused to give his reasons. He returned to his home country and raced touring cars for a while before competing in minor local championships.

Percival Guy (Guy) TUNMER

Nationality: South African
Born: 1st December 1948
Died: 22nd June 1999
Seasons: 1975
Team/manufacturer(s): Lotus
Grands Prix: 1
Race wins: 0
Championship wins: 0

His full name was Percival Guy Tunmer but this South African semi-professional driver was better known as plain Guy Tunmer. After starting off racing Minis in the late 1960s, he got involved in local Formula One races in the mid-1970s.

This led to a drive in the South African Grand Prix, which was Tunmer's one and only World Championship race. He did reasonably well, working his Team Gunston Lotus 72 up from 25th on the grid to finish the race in 11th place.

Tunmer later competed with some success in the local Formula Atlantic series, driving his own Chevron B34. He also raced touring cars.

Tragically, Tunmer died at the age of 50 after being badly injured in a motorcycle accident on public roads.

Esteban Tuero

Jarno Trulli

U-V

ULMEN, Toni
UNSER, Bobby
URIA, Alberto
VACCARELLA, Nino
VAN DE POELE, Eric
VAN DER LOF, Dries
VAN LENNEP, Gijs
VAN ROOYEN, Basil
VERSTAPPEN, Jos
VETTEL, Sebastian
VILLENEUVE, Gilles
VILLENEUVE, Jacques
VILLENEUVE, Jacques Snr
VILLORESI, Luigi
VOLONTERIO, Ottorino
VON OPEL, Ricky
VON TRIPS, Wolfgang
VONLANTHEN, Jo

Jacques Villeneuve

Toni ULMEN

Nationality: German
Born: 25th January 1906
Died: 4th November 1976
Seasons: 1952
Team/manufacturer(s): Veritas
Grands Prix: 2
Race wins: 0
Championship wins: 0

German driver Toni Ulmen was born and grew up in Dusseldorf. He began racing between the wars, yet it was after the Second World War when he really made an impact. That was in 1949 when he became German Formula 2 champion, driving for the Veritas team.

It was also with Veritas that Ulmen entered his two World Championship Grands Prix, in 1952. Right at the start of the season, he drove a Veritas BMW in the Swiss Grand Prix at Bremgarten. Starting 16th on the grid, he was forced to retire after just four laps because of a fuel leak.

Later that season Ulmen had better luck at the German Grand Prix, when he finished in eighth place from 15th on the grid, driving the same car.

Soon after that, Ulmen announced his retirement from motor racing, although he did return to drive a Jaguar in sportscar races.

Robert William (Bobby) UNSER

Nationality: American
Born: 20th February 1934
Seasons: 1968
Team/manufacturer(s): BRM
Grands Prix: 2
Race wins: 0
Championship wins: 0

Colorado-born Bobby Unser was a well-known driver in the USA and came from a family of racing drivers. He began racing stock cars as a teenager and went on to win the Indy 500 no less than three times – one of only seven drivers to achieve such a success – and he entered the race each year between 1963 and 1981.

However, Unser's short Formula One career was somewhat less successful. Perhaps tempted by the glamour, he drove for the BRM team during the 1968 season. He was entered for the Italian Grand Prix, but was unable to race because it clashed with another race. And then, at the United States Grand Prix at Watkins Glen, Unser got off to a bad start when he crashed during practice. However, he still managed to qualify (albeit 19th) but then had to retire after 35 laps when his car's engine failed.

Unser then went back to the sort of racing he knew. After retiring from the sport he worked as a television commentator and also had various business interests.

Alberto URIA

Nationality: Uruguayan
Born: 11th July 1924
Died: 4th December 1988
Seasons: 1955-1956
Team/manufacturer(s): Maserati
Grands Prix: 2
Race wins: 0
Championship wins: 0

Uruguayan driver Alberto Uria was born in Montevideo and raced in various local events over the years. And then, in

Bobby Unser

the mid-1950s he competed in international races in nearby Argentina.

These included entering the Argentinean Grand Prix twice, in 1955 and 1956. Both times Uria drove his own, rather dated, Maserati A6GCM which had been updated with a 250F engine. In 1955, he qualified 21st and then ran out of fuel after 22 laps, which forced him to retire. Then, the following year, Uria shared the drive with Oscar González and finished joint sixth; however that was the back of the pack of cars that actually finished the race.

Eric van de Poele

Nino VACCARELLA

Nationality: Italian
Born: 4th March 1933
Seasons: 1961-1962, 1965
Team/manufacturer(s): De Tomaso, Lotus, Ferrari
Grands Prix: 5
Race wins: 0
Championship wins: 0

Nino Vaccarella came from Sicily and earned his money as a lawyer, but he was also a talented racing driver. Indeed, he shot to fame when he won the 1964 Le Mans 24 Hour race. The following year, he won the Targa Florio for the first of three times (the subsequent wins were in 1971 and 1975). Vaccarella was also triumphant in various other sportscar and endurance events.

By contrast, Vaccarella's Formula One career was less impressive. He entered just five World Championship events in the early 1960s. In 1961, he drove a De Tomaso in the Italian Grand Prix but was forced to retire with engine failure.

The following year, Vaccarella competed at Monaco, Germany and Italian, with his home Grand Prix giving him his best result of ninth place. He then again entered the Italian Grand Prix in 1965, bringing his Ferrari to a 12th place finish.

Vaccarella later retired from racing and continued to work as a lawyer for some years before retiring fully.

Eric VAN DE POELE

Nationality: Belgian
Born: 30th September 1961
Seasons: 1991-1992
Team/manufacturer(s): Modena, Brabham, Fondmetal
Grands Prix: 29
Race wins: 0
Championship wins: 0

Belgian driver Eric van de Poele worked his way up to Formula 3 in 1984 before moving away from single-seaters and spending time racing touring cars and sportscars, winning the Spa 24 Race in 1987.

He then went back to single-seater racing, competing in Formula 3000 in 1989. Two years later, Van de Poele had his Formula One debut when he joined the Modena team. However, he struggled with the underfunded team and failed to qualify for all but one Grand Prix that season. The race he did compete in, the San Marino Grand Prix, he finished in ninth place.

For 1992, Van de Poele drove for the Brabham team but, again, had little success, finishing 13th in South Africa and then failing to qualify for any other races. Before the end of the season, he switched to the Fondmetal team for three Grands Prix, but didn't finish the season because, again, the team had financial problems. From there, Van de Poele returned to touring cars and sportscar and, in 2006, he competed in the Grand Prix Masters series.

Andre (Dries) VAN DER LOF

Nationality: Dutch
Born: 23rd August 1919
Died: 24th May 1990
Seasons: 1952
Team/manufacturer(s): HWM
Grands Prix: 1
Race wins: 0
Championship wins: 0

Andre 'Dries' van der Lof was a Dutch businessman who owned an electrical cable factory that made him very wealthy. He was a keen amateur driver and founded the Dutch Racing Drivers' Club, competing in various club events in his home country.

When the first World Championship Dutch Grand Prix took place, in 1952, Van der Lof was invited to compete in it. He borrowed an HWM single-seater and qualified 14th. However, he struggled with electrical problems during the race and, despite completing 70 laps, he ended up with an unclassified result.

Together with fellow countryman, Jan Flinterman, Van der Lof was the first Dutchman to race in Formula One. He went on to build an impressive collection of cars and enjoyed racing his Maserati 250F in historic events.

Gijs VAN LENNEP

Nationality: Dutch
Born: 16th March 1942
Seasons: 1971, 1973-1975
Team/manufacturer(s): Surtees, Williams, Ensign
Grands Prix: 8
Race wins: 0
Championship wins: 0

Dutchman Gijs van Lennep began racing in Formula Vee in 1965 but soon moved into sportscars, driving for the Porsche team from 1967. By 1971, he had won the Le Mans 24 Hour race in a Porsche 917 alongside Helmut Marko, breaking the record for the number of laps driven in 24 hours. He also won the Targa Florio in 1973, driving a Porsche 911.

Van Lennep had his Formula One debut in 1971, when he drove a hired Surtees TS9 in his home Grand Prix and impressed by finishing in eighth place.

From there on, Van Lennep competed in occasional Grands Prix, including the Dutch one on several occasions. In 1973, he finished sixth in Holland, scoring him a Championship point; a

success he repeated in Germany in 1975.

Despite performing well, Van Lennep did not pursue his Formula One career after this, preferring sportscars. He had another win at Le Mans in 1976 and then retired from racing. After that he became a racing instructor.

Basil VAN ROOYEN

Nationality: South African
Born: 19th March 1939
Seasons: 1968-1969
Team/manufacturer(s): Cooper, McLaren
Grands Prix: 2
Race wins: 0
Championship wins: 0

Basil van Rooyen was a South African racing driver, born in Johannesburg. During the early 1960s, he proved himself to be a talented saloon car driving, piloting machines such as Lotus Cortinas and Ford Mustangs in his home country.

In 1968, Van Rooyen tried his hand at single-seater racing, behind the wheel of a Brabham BT24. However, he didn't drive that car in his first Formula One event, instead using a Cooper T79. He raced the car in the South African Grand Prix but retired after 20 laps with engine failure.

The following year Van Rooyen had another attempt at the South African Grand Prix, this time with a McLaren M7A. Again, though, he didn't finish the race, this time because of brake failure.

He then went back to the saloon car racing that he loved, and continued with that until 1973, when he said he was retiring from racing. However, just two years later, Van Rooyen was again behind the wheel of a single-seater car, competing in Formula Atlantic for two seasons. He later retired to Australia.

Jos VERSTAPPEN

Nationality: Dutch
Born: 4th March 1972
Seasons: 1994-1998, 2001-2002, 2003
Team/manufacturer(s): Benetton, Simtek, Footwork, Tyrrell, Stewart, Arrows, Minardi
Grands Prix: 107
Race wins: 0
Championship wins: 0

Dutch driver Jos Verstappen began karting at the tender age of eight and, by the time he was 12 he was Dutch Junior champion. After further success in karts, Verstappen progressed to Formula Opel Lotus in 1991, winning the championship that year. From there, Verstappen went on to Formula 3, winning the German championship in 1993.

Verstappen made the break into Formula One in 1994, when he was taken on as a test driver for Benetton. Before long, though, he was racing for the team and took two third place finishes and a fifth in that first season. However, he went to Simtek for the start of 1995 and, after that team went bankrupt, he returned to Benetton as a test driver again. From there on, Verstappen drove for a number of teams over the years, both as a full-time driver and as a test driver. However, he had little success, often because he was struggling with uncompetitive machinery and underfunded teams. Indeed, he never again reached the highlights of his first season.

Verstappen had a disappointing career, and didn't drive in Formula One after the end of the 2003 season. He did, though, go on to join the A1 Netherlands team to drive in

the A1 Grand Prix series. He also ran his family kart circuit in Holland.

Sebastian VETTEL

Nationality: German
Born: 3rd July 1987
Seasons: 2007-
Team/manufacturer(s): BMW Sauber, Torro Rosso
Grands Prix: 8
Race wins: 0
Championship wins: 0

Born in Heppenheim, German driver Sebastian Vettel began racing cars at the age of eight, and soon proved himself to be a talented young driver, winning various races and titles. By 2003, he had moved on to cars and took the German Formula BMW championship the following year, after winning no less than 18 of the 20 races.

In 2005, Vettel competed in the Formula Three Euroseries, racing against the talented Lewis Hamilton, who dominated the series. The following year, Vettel came second in the championship. During this period, he also tested for the Williams and BMW Sauber teams, and was taken on as third driver for the latter in 2006.

Vettel made his grand prix debut at the 2007 USA Grand Prix and impressed by qualifying seventh and finishing the race in eighth place, picking up a well-deserved Championship point. At the age of 19 years and 349 days, he broke the record for being the youngest Formula One driver to score a point. He later came fourth in China, finishing the season 14th in the Championship with six points.

Gilles Villeneuve

Jos Verstappen

Joseph Gilles Henri (Gilles) VILLENEUVE

Nationality: Canadian
Born: 18th January 1950
Died: 8th May 1982
Seasons: 1977-1982
Team/manufacturer(s): McLaren, Ferrari
Grands Prix: 68
Race wins: 6
Championship wins: 0

Canadian driver Gilles Villeneuve may never have won the World Championship, but if it hadn't been for his untimely death, there's a good chance he would have done.

At the age of nine, Villeneuve's father let him drive the family's Volkswagen van along a quiet road and, from that day on, the boy was hooked on cars, and by the time he was 15 he was fixing up an old MGA, in readiness for being old enough to drive legally. In the meantime, though, he sneaked off in his father's Pontiac one night and illegally drove it to the nearby city. Travelling at speeds of over 100mph, Villeneuve lost control on the wet roads and crashed into a telegraph pole. The car was a write-off but, luckily, the teenager was unhurt.

By the time he was 16, Villeneuve was once again behind the wheel. However, one day another car started to race him along the road. The teenager rose to the challenge and the race was on. Until, that is, a herd of cows got in the way, and Villeneuve ended up in a ditch, needing 80 stitches to his head.

The high-speed pursuit had excited Villeneuve, despite his injuries, so he bought himself an old Skoda and was soon flying around the local roads.

Although fascinated by racing cars and drivers, Villeneuve didn't have the money to pursue his dream, so he turned instead to snowmobile racing. He claimed after-

wards that he learnt a lot about control, piloting snowmobiles at over 100mph on slippery surfaces.

In his early twenties Villeneuve began racing in Formula Ford and was the Quebec Champion in 1973. Next, he tried his hand at Formula Atlantic and, in 1976, he dominated the championship and took the title. This led to an offer of a Formula One drive with McLaren for 1977.

He had a good first season and showed a lot of promise,

Jacques Villeneuve

but McLaren decided not to keep him on for another year. Instead, Ferrari stepped in and signed Villeneuve for 1978. He won his first race the following year, at the Canadian Grand Prix, and finished second in the championship.

By 1982, Villeneuve was widely regarded as the best driver in Formula One and tipped to be the champion that year. However, the season got off to a bad start at San Marino when his teammate, Didier Pironi, disobeyed team orders and passed the Canadian, thus depriving Villeneuve of a win.

At the next race, the Belgian Grand Prix disaster struck. During qualifying, Villeneuve's front left wheel touched the right rear wheel of another car. Villeneuve's Ferrari flew into the air and crashed, nose first, into an embankment, before cartwheeling along the side of the track. He died in hospital shortly afterwards.

Villeneuve may have been killed before he realised his full potential, but his memory lives on, and he still has a huge following. His son, Jacques, took up where his father left off and won the World Championship in 1997.

Jacques Joseph Charles VILLENEUVE

Nationality: Canadian
Born: 9th April 1971
Seasons: 1996-2006
Team/manufacturer(s): Williams, BAR, Renault, Sauber, BMW Sauber
Grands Prix: 165
Race wins: 11
Championship wins: 1

Jacques was only 11 years old when his father, Gilles, was killed in a horrific accident at the Belgian Grand Prix in 1982. Two years later, he announced that he wanted to follow in his father's footsteps and be a racing driver. His mother told him he could go karting if he did well in his

Luigi Villoresi

maths exam. Relishing a challenge, the young Villeneuve worked hard at school, achieved good marks, and so his mother stuck to her word.

The following year found Villeneuve at the Imola kart track in Italy. The boy started off driving a 100cc kart, and the instructors were so impressed by his performance that they let him try a 135cc version. By the end of the day, the teenager was driving a Formula 4 car around the Grand Prix track. Racing was definitely in his blood!

His uncle, Jacques Villeneuve senior (often called Uncle Jacques) was also a racing driver, and enrolled his nephew on a three-day course at the Jim Russell Driving School in Quebec. Once again, the instructors were impressed by the 15-year-old's ability.

In 1989 Villeneuve began racing in Italian Formula 3. Despite some competent driving he didn't excel – probably because of the cars he was driving – so, in 1992, he left to compete in Japanese Formula 3.

In Japan, he was free of the publicity that surrounded the son of the famous Canadian and Villeneuve's driving improved immensely, with him finishing the season in second place. He then moved to the USA and took part in the Toyota Atlantic series, where he won five races. In 1994 he raced in Champ Car and was Rookie of the Year and, the following year, he won the Indy 500 as well as the championship title.

Villeneuve's success attracted the attention of Frank Williams who signed him for the 1996 season. It was a good move because Villeneuve excelled himself by achieving pole position and a podium finish (second place) in his first Grand Prix, at Melbourne. In fact, he could have won the

race, if team orders weren't to allow his teammate, Damon Hill, to pass. Villeneuve went on to win four races in his first season, gain 11 podium finishes and score 78 points – unprecedented results for a newcomer.

The next year was even better. Now the number-one driver at Williams, Villeneuve fought a season-long battle against Ferrari's Michael Schumacher, and claimed seven wins, eight podium finishes and 81 points. The battle for the championship went right to the last race, in Australia, where Schumacher tried, unsuccessfully, to force Villeneuve out of the race. The plan backfired and the German ended up in the gravel and Villeneuve went on to win the race, clinching the title.

Sadly, Villeneuve didn't again match his early achievements. After a disappointing season with Williams in 1998, he moved to BAR in 1999, where he struggled with technical problems. Even so, he stayed with the team until 2003.

With no team to compete in for in 2004, Villeneuve took time off, returning at the end of the season to drive for Renault. At the same time, he signed a two-year deal with BMW Sauber, starting in 2005. After 2006, he moved away from Formula One and towards sportscars.

Jacques (Jacquo) VILLENEUVE (Senior)
Nationality: Canadian
Born: 4th November 1953
Seasons: 1981, 1983
Team/manufacturer(s): Arrows, RAM
Grands Prix: 3
Race wins: 0
Championship wins: 0

Gilles Villeneuve's brother, Jacques, was sometimes known as 'Jacquo' or 'Uncle Jacques' to differentiate him from his nephew, the World Championship winner, Jacques Villeneuve.

Born in Quebec, he started off racing snowmobiles before getting into saloon car racing, where he had some success. Villeneuve then moved to single-seaters, competing in Formula Ford and Formula Atlantic, twice winning the title in the latter.

At the end of the 1981 season, Villeneuve drove in the Canadian and the Las Vegas Grands Prix for the Arrows team, but failed to qualify for either. Two years later, he again entered the Canadian Grand Prix, this time behind the wheel of a RAM car, but failed to qualify. However, that same year he won the Can-Am title.

Villeneuve went on to drive in CART racing and also continued to enjoy snowmobiling and powerboating.

Luigi VILLORESI
Nationality: Italian
Born: 16th May 1909
Died: 24th August 1997
Seasons: 1950-1956
Team/manufacturer(s): Ferrari, Maserati, Lancia
Grands Prix: 19
Race wins: 0
Championship wins: 0

Born in Milan, Luigi Villoresi began racing Fiats in 1931 and later drove for Maserati, winning various prewar events. Villoresi was a prisoner of war during the Second World War but, once released, began racing once more, with great success.

When the Formula One World Championship series began in 1950, Villoresi had moved from Maserati to Ferrari and at once began competing in the new Grands Prix. He had a very good 1951 season, scoring points in five out of the seven races he entered, with third and fourth places. However, he was by now in his forties and began to cut back on his racing activities, while still scoring the occasional Championship point, right up to his last season in 1956. Villoresi was a good friend of Alberto Ascari and lost interest in racing after Ascari's death.

Even so, he continued to rally for a couple of years before retiring in 1958.

Ottorino VOLONTERIO

Nationality: Swiss
Born: 7th December 1917
Died: 10th March 2003
Seasons: 1956
Team/manufacturer(s): Maserati
Grands Prix: 1
Race wins: 0
Championship wins: 0

Swiss driver Ottorino Volonterio worked as a lawyer and was an enthusiastic amateur racing driver in his spare time, having reasonable successes from time to time.

His one World Championship appearance was at the 1956 German Grand Prix, where he drove his own Maserati.

Volonterio qualified 19th on the grid – pretty much at the back – and then continued for 16 laps but was so slow his finish was unclassified.

Volonterio later bought a secondhand Maserati 250F and raced it himself as well as making it available for other, more experienced, drivers to use. Eventually, he retired from racing and concentrated on his law work.

Rikky VON OPEL

Nationality: Liechtensteiner
Born: 14th October 1947
Seasons: 1973-1974
Team/manufacturer(s): Ensign, Brabham
Grands Prix: 13
Race wins: 0
Championship wins: 0

Rikky von Opel was born in New York into the family that had made its fortune with the Opel car company. Of Liechtenstein nationality, Von Opel began racing cars under the pseudonym 'Antonio Bronco', doing well in Formula Ford and Formula 3.

In 1972, now using his real name, he bought an Ensign Formula One car and, a year later, joined the Ensign team as a driver. Unfortunately, neither the team nor the driver had a lot of experience and they only achieved modest success in the latter part of the 1973 season.

After just one race with Ensign at the start of the 1974 season, Von Opel moved to the more established Brabham

team. There, the highlights of his short season were two ninth place finishes, in Sweden and Holland. Before the year was out, though, von Opel left the team and retired from motorsport, realising he didn't have the ability to compete. He went on to work for the family business.

Wolfgang Graf Berghe VON TRIPS

Nationality: German
Born: 4th May 1928
Died: 10th September 1961
Seasons: 1956-1961
Team/manufacturer(s): Ferrari, Porsche, Cooper
Grands Prix: 29
Race wins: 2
Championship wins: 0

Wolfgang von Trips was a German aristocrat. He began racing after the Second World War and worked his way up to Formula One by the mid-1950s.

His first World Championship race was 1957, when he drove a Ferrari to a sixth place finish at the Argentinean Grand Prix. Later that season, he finished in third place in Italy, proving that he was a talented driver. Von Trips then repeated that success in France the following season, as well as fourth and fifth place finishes that same year.

In 1959, Von Trips drove a Porsche Formula 2 car at the start of the season in Monaco and crashed badly, putting him out of action for most of the year, although he drove a Ferrari to a sixth place finish in the USA at the end of the season.

Von Trips had a better season in 1960, finishing seventh in the Championship with 10 points. However, 1961 saw him really shine, with wins in Holland and Great Britain, second places in Germany and Belgium and a fourth place in Monaco earning him 33 points. This put him in second place in the Championship and a good result in Italy would have clinched it. Tragically, though, it was not to be. His Ferrari collided with Jim Clark's Lotus and the car crashed into a barrier. Von Trips was thrown out of the car and killed, along with 14 spectators.

Jo VONLANTHEN

Nationality: Swiss
Born: 31st May 1942
Seasons: 1975
Team/manufacturer(s): Williams
Grands Prix: 1
Race wins: 0
Championship wins: 0

Jo Vonlanthen was a Swiss garage owner. He began racing in Formula Vee and worked his way up to Formula 3, winning the Swiss championship in 1972.

From there, he moved to Formula 2, which he found more challenging. It was while in Formula 2 that Vonlanthen had a taste of Formula One. First, he drove for Ensign in a non-Championship race, then he raced a Williams car in the non-Championship Swiss Grand Prix in 1975.

That same year, Vonlanthen drove a Williams in his one and only World Championship race. That was the Austrian Grand Prix when he took the place of an injured Wilson Fittipaldi. After qualifying a disappointing 28th, Vonlanthen was forced to retire with engine failure after 14 laps.

Vonlanthen then went back to Formula 2 for a while and then retired from the sport to concentrate on his garage business.

Wolfgang von Trips

U
V

W-Y-Z

WACKER, Fred
WALKER, David
WALKER, Peter
WALTER, Heini
WARD, Rodger
WARWICK, Derek
WATSON, John
WEBBER, Mark
WEIDLER, Volker
WENDLINGER, Karl
WESTBURY, Peter
WHARTON, Ken
WHITEAWAY, Ted
WHITEHEAD, Graham
WHITEHEAD, Peter
WHITEHOUSE, Bill
WIDDOWS, Robin
WIETZES, Eppie
WILDS, Mike

WILLIAMS, Jonathan
WILLIAMSON, Roger
WILSON, Desire
WILSON, Justin
WILSON, Vic
WINKELHOCK, Joachim
WINKELHOCK, Manfred
WINKELHOCK, Markus
WISELL, Reine
WUNDERINK, roelof
WURZ, Alexander
YAMAMOTO, Sakon
YOONG, Alex
ZANARDI, Alessandro
ZAPICO, Emilio
ZONTA, Ricardo
ZORZI, Renzo
ZUNIÑO, Ricardo

Alexander Wurz

Frederick (Fred) WACKER

Nationality: American
Born: 10th July 1918
Died: 16th June 1998
Seasons: 1953-1954
Team/manufacturer(s): Gordini
Grands Prix: 3
Race wins: 0
Championship wins: 0

Chicago-born Fred Wacker Jr was a successful businessman who ran a company that produced tools for servicing cars and also liquid metering equipment. When he wasn't working, he was a keen amateur racing driver, and the founder of the Chicago region of the Sports Car Club of America.

Most of his racing was in sportscars, although Wacker also drove single-seaters for Gordini on an infrequent basis. This led to his three World Championship drives, starting with the 1953 Belgian Grand Prix.

The following year, he crashed badly during the Swiss Grand Prix and fractured his skull. However, he wasn't badly injured and recovered enough to impress with a sixth place finish at the following Grand Prix, in Italy.

After that, Wacker returned to the USA and his sportscar racing. He also continued to run his business.

David WALKER

Nationality: Australian
Born: 10th June 1941
Seasons: 1971-1972
Team/manufacturer(s): Lotus
Grands Prix: 11
Race wins: 0
Championship wins: 0

Australian David Walker was born in Sydney and, after studying to be an accountant, came to England in the 1960s to pursue a career in motorsport. After struggling in both Formula Ford and Formula 3, he finally joined the Lotus Formula 3 team in 1970 and went on to win the Shell and Forward Trust titles the following year.

It was also in 1971 that Walker had his Formula One debut, driving a four-wheel-drive Lotus 56B at the Dutch Grand Prix, but spun off in the rain before the end of the race.

The following year Walker had a full-time drive with the Lotus Formula One team, partnered with Fittipaldi. However, while the Brazilian went on to become World Champion that year, Walker had less success, with a ninth place finish in Spain his best result. Indeed, he was the only Formula One driver not score any points in the same season his teammate won the title!

Walker then drove in Formula 2 for a while, but was badly injured in two road accidents in one year. After trying Formula 5000 and Formula Atlantic, he returned to Australia where he ran a boat charter business.

Peter WALKER

Nationality: British
Born: 7th October 1912
Died: 1st March 1984
Seasons: 1950-1951, 1955
Team/manufacturer(s): ERA, BRM, Maserati, Connaught
Grands Prix: 4
Race wins: 0
Championship wins: 0

Peter Walker was born in Leeds and began racing and hill-climbing before the Second World War; pursuits he soon resumed after the end of hostilities.

He owned an E-Type ERA and used this at the inaugural World Championship British Grand Prix at Silverstone. However, he was forced to retire after just two laps.

The following year, though, Walker had another attempt at the British Grand Prix, this time in a supercharged BRM, and finished a respectable seventh. Also in 1951, he won at Le Mans, driving a Jaguar C-Type with Peter Whitehead.

Walker's next Formula One attempts were in 1955, when he drove a Maserati in the Dutch Grand Prix and then a Connaught in the British Grand Prix. He was forced to retire from both races.

The next year, Walker crashed his Aston Martin badly at Le Mans and decided to retire from motorsport after that and later worked as a farmer.

Heini WALTER

Nationality: Swiss
Born: 28th July 1927
Seasons: 1962
Team/manufacturer(s): Porsche
Grands Prix: 1
Race wins: 0
Championship wins: 0

Swiss driver Heini Walter was a car dealer and restaurant owner, and also an enthusiastic amateur racing driver.

He competed in Porsche Carreras and RSKs in circuit racing and hillclimbs in the 1950s and 1960s. The peak of his career was perhaps winning the European Mountain-climb Championships in 1961.

A year after this Walter entered his only World Championship race – the 1962 German Grand Prix at the Nürburgring. He was behind the wheel of a Porsche 718 Formula 2 car, run by the Ecurie Filipinetti team. He started 14th on the grid, completed 14 laps and finished in 14th place!

After that, Walter concentrated on hillclimbing, both in Porsches and also, for a while, a Ferrari 250LM. He was later involved with the resurrection of Enzmann, a classic Swiss car marque.

Rodger WARD

Nationality: American
Born: 10th January 1921
Died: 5th July 2004
Seasons: 1959, 1963
Team/manufacturer(s): Kurtis Kraft-Offenhauser, Lotus-BRM
Grands Prix: 2
Race wins: 0
Championship wins: 0

American Rodger Ward was born in Kansas and began racing midgets and stock cars in the 1940s. He then went on to be a regular in the AAA and USAC championships, and entered the Indy 500 15 times between 1951 and 1966.

Ward won the Indy 500 in 1959 and, that same year, entered his Kurtis Kraft car into the United States Grand Prix at Sebring. However, he had less success than he did at Indianapolis, qualifying 19th on the grid and then retiring with a failed clutch after 20 laps.

He then went on to win the Indy 500 again in 1962 and, the following year, had another attempt at the United States Grand Prix. This time he was behind the wheel of a Lotus-BRM but didn't qualify well, at 17th, and retired with gearbox problems after 44 laps.

Ward retired from racing after 1966 and worked as a television commentator. Note that his results in the Indy 500 counted towards Formula One World Championship points between 1950 and 1960.

Peter Walker

Derek Warwick

Derek Warwick

Derek Stanley Arthur WARWICK
Nationality: British
Born: 27th August 1954
Seasons: 1981-1993
Team/manufacturer(s): Toleman, Renault, Brabham, Arrows, Lotus, Footwork
Grands Prix: 147
Race wins: 0
Championship wins: 0

Hampshire man Derek Warwick first tasted success in 1978 when he won the British Formula 3 championship.

He first drove in Formula One three years later, when he joined the Toleman team. He stayed with them for three years, having some reasonable success and proving himself a very capable driver. Indeed, he was tipped to be a future World Champion.

A move to Renault in 1984 was to be a stepping stone to this ambition, and Warwick continued to drive well, with a number of point-scoring finishes, but a win eluded him.

In retrospect, Warwick perhaps made a mistake in turning down an offer to drive for Williams in 1985 – Nigel Mansell took the seat and went on to be World Champion. After Renault withdrew from Formula One at the end of the 1985, Warwick struggled to get a place, joining Brabham partway through the 1986 season.

Then it was on to Arrows for three seasons, where

Warwick did his best with uncompetitive cars. It was a similar story with Lotus and then Footwork. He never did win a Formula One race, but it was not for a lack of ability.

Warwick also raced sportscars and, after retiring from Formula One, touring cars. He later ran a garage in Dorset and drove in the GP Masters series.

John Marshall (Wattie) WATSON, MBE
Nationality: British
Born: 4th May 1946
Seasons: 1973-1984, 1985
Team/manufacturer(s): Penske, Brabham, McLaren
Grands Prix: 152
Race wins: 05
Championship wins: 0

John Watson was born in Belfast, the son of a car dealer, and began racing an Austin Healey Sprite in the early 1960s. This was followed by a spell in single-seaters in Northern Ireland before he came to England to further his career.

There, he worked his way up to Formula 2 where he proved himself a capable driver. By 1973, he had his first Formula One drive in an old Brabham BT37 at the British Grand Prix. This was followed, later in the season, by the United States Grand Prix. He retired from both races.

The following season saw Watson score his first points at three Grands Prix but this success was followed by a poor

John Watson

Mark Webber

1975. Then a year with Penske Racing led to his first win – at the Austrian Grand Prix. Together with other good finishes, this led to him finishing the year seventh in the Championship.

Watson then had a mix of results over the following few years until his best season – 1982. Driving for McLaren he finished third in the Championship with two wins (Belgium and US East), two second places, a third place, fourth place and two sixth places.

This was followed by a reasonable 1983 season and then Watson retired from Formula One, although he did step in to do one race in 1985. He went on to run his own racing school and worked as a television commentator.

Mark Alan (Webbo) WEBBER

Nationality: Australian
Born: 27th August 1976
Seasons: 2002-
Team/manufacturer(s): Minardi, Jaguar, Williams, Red Bull
Grands Prix: 105
Race wins: 0
Championship wins: 0

The son of an Australian motorcycle dealer, Mark Webber began competing in motocross as a boy before switching to karts, winning his local championship.

By 1995, Webber had moved to Europe to further his career driving in first Formula Ford then Formula 3. He then had a spell in sportscar racing but was put off when he crashed his Mercedes at high speed at Le Mans in 1999.

So it was back to single-seater racing, in Formula 3000, and he did well enough to be signed by the Minardi Formula One team for the 2002 season. Again, he performed well and was promptly signed by Jaguar for 2003 and 2004, where he continued to give reliable drivers.

A move to Williams in 2005 saw Webber gain his first podium finish: third place at the Monaco Grand Prix. That year, he picked up 36 points and finished 10th in the Championship. However, he had less success in 2006, with

just seven points at the end of the season. Webber then signed to drive with Red Bull Racing for 2007, alongside David Coulthard. His best result was third place in the European Grand Prix and he finished the season 12th in the Championship.

Volker WEIDLER

Nationality: German
Born: 18th March 1962
Seasons: 1989
Team/manufacturer(s): Rial
Grands Prix: 10
Race wins: 0
Championship wins: 0

Volker Weidler

German Volker Weidler began racing seriously in the early 1980s, first in Formula Ford 2000 and then Formula 3, winning the German championship in 1985, while at the same time competing in sportscars with some success.

After switching between sportscars and single-seaters for a while, Weidler made it into Formula One in 1989, driving for the Rial team. However, it was a painful season, with him failing to pre-qualify for the first six races, then he was excluded from the German Grand Prix after he stopped on the track during practice so his team could work on the car! After failing to qualify for the Hungarian Grand Prix, Weidler left Rial and drew a line under his Formula One career.

Weidler then went back to Formula 3000 and sportscar racing, winning the 1991 Le Mans 24 Hour in a rotary engine Mazda 787 – the highlight of his career. Sadly, he was forced to retire from racing soon after because he was suffering from tinnitus. He moved right away from motorsport after that.

Karl WENDLINGER

Nationality: Austrian
Born: 20th December 1968
Seasons: 1991-1995
Team/manufacturer(s): Leyton House, March, Sauber
Grands Prix: 42
Race wins: 0
Championship wins: 0

Karl Wendlinger worked his way up through karting, Formula Ford and then Formula 3, winning the German championship in 1989. From there, he became involved in sportscar racing, while keeping his hand in single-seaters with some Formula 3000 driving.

Wendlinger's Formula One debut came at the end of the 1991 season, when he drove for the Leyton House team at the Japanese Grand Prix, but crashed on the first lap.

The next season Wendlinger stayed with the team, now renamed March, and had one good result, when he came fourth in Canada, scoring three Championship points.

A move to Sauber in 1993 brought more success, with Wendlinger having a best place finish of fourth at the Italian

Grand Prix, and picking up a total of seven points through this, his best season.

The 1994 season got off to a good start for Wendlinger, with sixth and fourth place finished but then disaster struck. He crashed badly at a wet Monaco and remained in a coma for some weeks, putting him out of action for the rest of the season.

Wendlinger then continued to drive for Sauber at the start of the next season but didn't perform and was dropped from the team after four races. He did, however, return for the last two Grands Prix of the year.

After that, Wendlinger saw more success in sportscars and touring cars, winning the FIA GT Championship in 1999.

Peter WESTBURY

Nationality: British
Born: 26th May 1938
Seasons: 1969-1970
Team/manufacturer(s): Brabham, BRM
Grands Prix: 2
Race wins: 0
Championship wins: 0

London-born Peter Westbury was a keen hill-climber in the 1960s, competing in his own-design, V8-powered four-wheel-drive Felday cars, which proved to be very competitive. He then branched out into single-seater racing in 1967, driving a Brabham BT21 in Formula 3 with some

success. Two years later he upgraded to a Brabham BT50 which he used to compete in Formula 2. This led to him entering the Formula Two class of the German Grand Prix that year, where he finished ninth and fifth in class.

The following year, Westbury travelled across the Atlantic to enter the United States Grand Prix with a BRM P153 but he failed to qualify because of a blown engine.

Westbury then turned his hand to Formula 2 and sports-car racing for a couple of seasons before retiring from the sport in 1973. He continued to run his engineering business before retiring.

Kenneth (Ken) WHARTON

Nationality: British
Born: 21st March 1916
Died: 12th January 1957
Seasons: 1952-1955
Team/manufacturer(s): Frazer Nash, Cooper, Maserati, Vanwall
Grands Prix: 15
Race wins: 0
Championship wins: 0

Englishman Ken Wharton came from a middleclass family and began racing and hillclimbing in his late teens, until the Second World War put a stop to his fun.

After the end of the war, Wharton worked as a mechanic in Birmingham and built his own cars which he used in hill-climbs and club races. He also tried his hand at Formula 3 but his forte was hillclimbing.

Wharton's first World Championship appearance was in the 1952 Swiss Grand Prix where he impressed by driving his Frazer Nash to a fourth place finish. A result was never going to match again. He later bought a Cooper and then, in 1954, joined the Maserati team and competed with a 250F in four World Championship Grands Prix that season.

He then moved to the Vanwall team for 1955 but crashed badly at a non-Championship race at Silverstone. That was the end of his Formula One career, but Wharton continued to race sporadically until he was killed in 1957, when his Ferrari Monza crashed in New Zealand.

Edward (Ted) WHITEAWAY

Nationality: British
Born: 1st November 1928
Died: 18th October 1995
Seasons: 1955
Team/manufacturer(s): HWM
Grands Prix: 1
Race wins: 0
Championship wins: 0

Ted Whiteaway was born in Middlesex and raced professionally after the Second World War. Little is known about him, but he did enter a number of non-Championship Formula One races in 1954, driving his own HSM-Alta, but had little success.

In 1955, Whiteaway entered his car into the Monaco Grand Prix but failed to qualify. He never again entered a World Championship race.

He did, though, reappear in 1959 when he drove an AC Ace Bristol at Le Mans, together with John Turner. The pair finished seventh overall and, crucially, first in class.

Whiteaway then disappeared from the racing scene and died in Perth, Australia, in 1995.

Ken Wharton

Karl Wendlinger

Graham Whitehead

Graham WHITEHEAD

Nationality: British
Born: 15th April 1922
Died: 15th January 1981
Seasons: 1952
Team/manufacturer(s): Alta
Grands Prix: 1
Race wins: 0
Championship wins: 0

The half brother of racing driver Peter Whitehead, Graham Whitehead was born into a wealthy Harrogate family and began racing his brother's ERA in the early 1950s.

He again borrowed Peter's car, this time a Formula 2 Alta, to compete in the 1952 British Grand Prix. Whitehead finished the race in 12th place, after qualifying 12th. His more experienced brother drove a Ferrari to a 10th place finish in the same race. That was as far as Graham Whitehead's Formula One career went. He later became involved in sportscars, coming second in the 1958 Le Mans 24 Hour race. Soon after, he competed with his brother in the Tour de France and their Jaguar crashed badly, killing Peter. Graham, however, survived and continued racing until 1961.

Peter WHITEHEAD

Nationality: British
Born: 12th November 1914
Died: 21st September 1958
Seasons: 1950-1954
Team/manufacturer(s): Ferrari, Alta, Cooper
Grands Prix: 12
Race wins: 0
Championship wins: 0

Yorkshire-born Peter Whitehead began racing in his early twenties, beginning with a Riley but quickly upgrading to an ERA. It was with this car that he won the 1938 Australian Grand Prix.

The Second World War saw Whitehead serve as a pilot but he soon returned to racing after the end of hostilities. Indeed, he was so keen, he persuaded Enzo Ferrari to sell him a Formula One car – making Whitehead the first private buyer of such a Ferrari.

Whitehead drove this car to a very impressive third place finish in the 1950 French Grand Prix – his first World Championship event. In fact, he was on track to win the race but was slowed down by a gearbox problem. It was a result that he would never again match, though, as he continued to enter the occasional Grand Prix over the next four years. However, Whitehead's greatest victory was winning the 1951 Le Mans 24 Hour race, driving a Jaguar with Peter Walker.

Whitehead was killed in 1958 at the Tour de France, when the Jaguar he was sharing with his brother, Graham, plunged off a bridge into a ravine.

William (Bill) WHITEHOUSE

Nationality: British
Born: 1st April 1909
Died: 14th July 1957
Seasons: 1954
Team/manufacturer(s): Connaught
Grands Prix: 1
Race wins: 0
Championship wins: 0

Londoner Bill Whitehouse made his money as a car dealer and by running an off-licence, racing in his spare time. In the 1950s he proved himself to be a very capable 500cc Formula 3 driver.

Before long, he'd bought himself a Formula 2 Connaught and he raced this in various events, including the 1954 British Grand Prix at Silverstone – his only World Championship event. Whitehouse qualified a poor 19th and then retired with fuelling problems after 63 laps.

Whitehouse later retired from racing after an accident, but returned in 1957 to compete in Formula 2. Tragically, though, he was killed during a race at Reims in 1957, when his car flipped over and caught fire.

Robin WIDDOWS

Nationality: British
Born: 27th May 1942
Seasons: 1968
Team/manufacturer(s): Cooper
Grands Prix: 1
Race wins: 0
Championship wins: 0

Robin Widdows began his career of speed as a talented bob-sleigh rider, competing for Britain in the 1964 and 1968

Olympics. At around the same time, he started racing cars, first an MG Midget, then a Lotus 23.

By 1966, he was competing in Formula 3 and doing well enough to set up his own Formula 2 team – Witley Racing Syndicate – which he funded with friends. He had some success that year and went on to drive for the Chequered Flag team in 1968.

The 1968 season also saw Widdows drive in his one and only Formula One World Championship race – the British Grand Prix. Behind the wheel of a factory Cooper-BRM, he qualified a lowly 18th and retired after 34 laps with ignition trouble.

Widdows then raced in Formula 2 and sportscars events before retiring from the sport in 1970. He later worked for a champagne company which led to links with Formula One.

Egbert (Eppie) WIETZES

Nationality: Canadian
Born: 28th May 1938
Seasons: 1967, 1974
Team/manufacturer(s): Lotus, Brabham
Grands Prix: 2
Race wins: 0
Championship wins: 0

Eppie Wietzes was born in Holland but grew up in Canada with Canadian nationality. He began racing in the 1950s and soon became competitive in sportscars and GTs.

Wietzes hired a Lotus in 1967 to compete in the first World Championship Canadian Grand Prix, driving alongside Lotus's Jim Clark and Graham Hill, but he failed to finish the race.

He did, however, go on to have more success in Formula 5000 over the next few years. Wietzes also had another attempt at the Canadian Grand Prix in 1974, when he drove a rented Brabham. However, he fared no better, retiring after 33 laps with engine trouble.

Wietzes continued racing for some years more, winning the CRC championship in 1981, driving a Corvette.

Michael (Mike) WILDS

Nationality: British
Born: 7th January 1946
Seasons: 1974-1976
Team/manufacturer(s): March, Ensign BRM, Shadow
Grands Prix: 8
Race wins: 0
Championship wins: 0

Born in London, Mike Wilds worked for Firestone and raced at club level during the 1960s and early 1970s. Eventually, he made it into Formula 3 in 1972.

By 1975, Wilds was competing in Formula 5000, when he had a chance to move up to Formula One, driving a March run by the Dempster Racing team at the British Grand Prix. He then moved to Ensign and entered four races at the end of the season but failed to qualify for all but one. Wilds did start the United States Grand Prix but he was too slow to be classified.

Wilds then entered the first two Grands Prix of 1975, driving for BRM, but failed to finish either. A one-off appearance in 1976 at the British Grand Prix saw Wilds fail to qualify his privately entered Shadow.

He then went back to Formula 5000 and other race series, before getting involved with historic events. He also worked as a flying instructor.

Jonathan WILLIAMS

Nationality: British
Born: 26th October 1942
Seasons: 1967
Team/manufacturer(s): Ferrari
Grands Prix: 1
Race wins: 0
Championship wins: 0

Jonathan Williams was born in Cairo, Egypt, where his father was serving in the Royal Air Force. After a public school education, Williams began racing with friends, driving Minis and the like. He then moved up to Formula 3 and ended up moving to Italy to compete there, where he proved successful.

This led to an offer to drive for the Ferrari Formula 2 team in 1967, and Williams won the Monza Lottery race that year. At the end of the season, he drove for Ferrari in the Mexican Grand Prix, qualifying 16th and finishing eighth; two laps behind the winner, Jim Clark.

That was the extent of William's Formula One career, though, and he went back to Formula 2 for a year or two before doing some sportscar racing in the early 1970s. He later gave up racing, trained as a pilot and went on to fly executive jets in the South of France.

Peter Whitehead

Roger WILLIAMSON

Nationality: British
Born: 2nd February 1948
Died: 29th July 1973
Seasons: 1973
Team/manufacturer(s): March
Grands Prix: 2
Race wins: 0
Championship wins: 0

Roger Williamson was born in Ashby-de-la-Zouch in Leicestershire and raced karts as a boy. He then went on to racing a Mini and proved himself very talented and, before long, had progressed to Formula 3, winning the British championship in 1971 and 1972.

Williamson then moved to Formula 2 in 1973, winning the Monza Lottery race and establishing himself as a force to be reckoned with. The next step was, of course, Formula One and, in anticipation of a full season's racing in 1974, he hired an STP March in which to compete in the British Grand Prix in 1973. However, he was caught up in a multiple pile-up at the start of the race and had to retire.

The next Grand Prix was the Dutch one at the Zandvoort circuit, which had just reopened after receiving extensive safety upgrades. During the race, Williamson's March suffered a burst tyre and it ploughed into the barrier on one side and then bounced across to the other side of the track, coming to a rest upside down. Williamson appeared uninjured but was unable to get out of the car. Fellow driver David Purley came to his help but was unable to right the car, so he grabbed a fire extinguisher and tried to quell the flames but to no avail. Some onlookers – including fire marshals – thought that Purley was the car's driver and so didn't rush to help. By the time the car was turned over and the fire extinguished, Williams had died of asphyxiation.

Desiré Randall WILSON

Nationality: South African
Born: 26th November 1953
Seasons: 1980
Team/manufacturer(s): Williams
Grands Prix: 1
Race wins: 0
Championship wins: 0

South African driver Desiré Wilson was one of only five woman to date who have competed in Formula One, and the only woman to have one a Formula One race, albeit a minor non-Championship event.

The win was in round two of the Aurora AFX F1 Championship held at Brands Hatch, where Wilson was driving a Wolf WR4.

Her one World Championship entry was in the 1980 British Grand Prix at Brands Hatch. Driving a non-works Williams FW07 prepared by Brands Hatch Racing, Wilson failed to qualify for the race itself.

The following year, Wilson drove in the non-Championship (at that time) South African Grand Prix. She later tried her hand at other race disciplines, including Indycar and sportscar racing.

Wilson also ran a company with her husband, designing racetracks.

Justin WILSON

Nationality: British
Born: 31st July 1978
Seasons: 2003
Team/manufacturer(s): Minardi, Jaguar
Grands Prix: 16
Race wins: 0
Championship wins: 0

Joachim Winkelhock

Justin Wilson

Yorkshire-born Justin Wilson began racing karts at the age of nine, progressing to cars when he was 16. That season he won the Junior Challenge Cup.

Wilson's problem was always his height – he grew to 6 foot 3 inches, which made him, not only tall for a single-seat racecar, but also heavy. He therefore moved to Formula Palmer Audi in 1998, winning the title with six race wins under his belt. The prize was a drive in Formula 3000 the following season. Wilson then won the Formula 3000 championship in 2001.

This success led to an offer of a drive with the Minardi Formula One team for 2003, using a car specially made for Wilson's height. Wilson then proved himself capable by qualifying for every race he entered, although mechanical problems caused him to retire from many, through no fault of his own.

Indeed, he was poached by Jaguar for the last five races of the season, scoring a single Championship point when he finished eighth in the USA.

That was to be the end of Wilson's Formula One career, because Jaguar didn't have the funds to retain him. From there, he moved to Champ Car racing and proved very successful.

Victor (Vic) WILSON

Nationality: British
Born: 14th April 1931
Died: 14th January 2001
Seasons: 1960
Team/manufacturer(s): Cooper
Grands Prix: 1
Race wins: 0
Championship wins: 0

Although he was born in Yorkshire, Vic Wilson grew up in South Africa, where he began racing in his twenties. He then returned to England and acquired a Cooper-Climax T43 from fellow racer Dick Gibson, who was recovering from an accident he'd had with the car.

Wilson repaired the Cooper and began racing it, including entering the 1960 Italian Grand Prix. Many of the larger British teams had boycotted the event because of the fact it was being held on a combined road/oval course, so Formula 2 cars were invited to race, which is how Wilson got in. However, after qualifying 16th, he was forced to retire after 23 laps with a damaged sump.

That was the extent of his Formula One adventure, although Wilson continued to race in other events for some years after. He later worked as a car dealer.

Joachim WINKELHOCK

Nationality: German
Born: 24th October 1960
Seasons: 1989
Team/manufacturer(s): AGS
Grands Prix: 7
Race wins: 0
Championship wins: 0

The younger brother of racing driver Manfred Winkelhock, Joachim Winkelhock began racing seriously in the Renault 5 championship in 1979, moving to Formula Ford in 1982. However, when his elder brother, Manfred, was killed in a race, he paused his career for a while and then went back to sportscars.

Winkelhock had some success in the mid-1980s, winning the European Touring Car Championship in 1988 as well as the 24 Hours Nürburgring in 1990 and 1991.

In 1989, Winkelhock had a short foray into Formula One when he drove for the small French AGS team for the first half of the 1989 season. However, he failed to qualify for any of the seven Grands Prix he entered, so he left the team mid-way through the season.

He then returned to what he was good at, winning the British Touring Car Championship in 1993 and various other events over the next few years. By 2003, he retired from motorsport to run the family's truck business, although he remained involved with the Opel racing team.

Manfred WINKELHOCK

Nationality: German
Born: 6th October 1951
Seasons: 1980, 1982-1985
Team/manufacturer(s): Arrows, ATS, RAM
Grands Prix: 56
Race wins: 0
Championship wins: 0

German driver Manfred Winkelhock was a mechanic who raced in his spare time, winning the VW Junior Cup in 1976. This led to a place with the new BMW Junior race team and then on to Formula 2 during the late 1970s and early 1980s.

It was in Formula 2 that Winkelhock first shot to fame, when his car flipped backwards during a race at the Nürburgring in 1980. Although it was a dramatic crash, the driver walked away unharmed.

Winkelhock's first Formula One attempt was towards the end of the 1980 season when he failed to qualify for the Italian Grand Prix in an Arrows car.

He then spent the next three seasons with the small ATS Formula One team, where he had mixed success; the high

point being a fifth place finish at the 1982 Brazilian Grand Prix, which scored him his only Championship points.

Winkelhock then drove for RAM for part of the 1985 season but without making much of an impression. By then he was concentrating more on sportscar and touring car racing.

In 1985, Winkelhock was driving a Porsche 962C in Canada when he lost control and hit a wall. He was killed instantly. His son, Markus, became a racing driver and was a Formula One test driver for MF1 Racing in 2006.

Markus WINKELHOCK

Nationality: German
Born: 13th June 1980
Seasons: 2007-
Team/manufacturer(s): Spyker
Grands Prix: 1
Race wins: 0
Championship wins: 0

Markus Winkelhock is the son of Manfred Winkelhock and nephew of Joachim Winkelhock, both of whom had been Formula One drivers in the 1980s, so racing is well and truly in his blood.

The German worked his way up the ranks to Formula 3, where he stayed from 2001 to 2003, having a best result of finishing fourth in the championship in 2003.

Winkelhock then tried his hand at touring cars, driving a Mercedes in the DTM during the 2004 season, but with little to show for his efforts. It was then back to single-seaters in 2005, competing in the World Series by Renault and winning three races that season.

In 2006, Winkelhock became test and reserve driver for the Midland F1 team, which was later renamed Spyker F1. He finally made his Formula One debut at the 2007 European Grand Prix. And what a extraordinary experience it was! After qualifying last, Winkelhock switched tyres at the start of the race to cope with the pouring rain, and found himself in the lead while the rest of the cars were in the pits swapping tyres. This is probably the first time that a driver has managed to go from last to first place on their maiden grand prix.

Later, the race was red-flagged because of the bad weather, and later restarted. Winkelhock then became the only Formula One driver to start last and first on the grid in the same grand prix! Sadly, his luck ran out and he retired from the race with hydraulic problems.

Reine WISELL

Nationality: Swedish
Born: 30th September 1941
Seasons: 1970-1974
Team/manufacturer(s): Lotus, Marlboro, March
Grands Prix: 23
Race wins: 0
Championship wins: 0

Swede Reine Wisell began racing Minis in the early 1960s and, by 1966, had worked his way up to Formula 3, winning the Swedish championship the following season. He then went on to compete on an international level in Formula 3.

Wisell had his chance to race in Formula One after the death of Jochen Rindt left a place open to him with Team Lotus. Wisell's first race was at the 1970 United States Grand Prix where he impressed everyone by finishing in third place – the best result he'd ever have.

For 1971, Wisell stayed with Lotus and had a reasonable

Alexander Wurz

year, picking up nine points and finishing 12th in the Championship. It was not enough for Lotus to retain him, though, so he moved to Marlboro for 1972, although he went back to Lotus at the end of a disappointing season. He then just had occasional Formula One drives in 1973 and 1974 before giving up on the series.

Wisell then drove for Porsche and won the European GT series in 1975. Soon after, though, he retired from competition to concentrate on being a racing instructor in Sweden.

Roelof WUNDERINK

Nationality: Dutch
Born: 12th December 1948
Seasons: 1975
Team/manufacturer(s): Ensign
Grands Prix: 6
Race wins: 0
Championship wins: 0

Roelof Wunderink was born in Eindhoven in Holland and began racing a Simca in 1970. Within two years he had progressed to Formula Ford and won the Dutch championship.

Then Wunderink drove in Formula 3 and Formula 3000 for the next couple of seasons and then got the chance to compete in Formula One, because his sponsor was involved with the Ensign team.

However, he struggled with an uncompetitive car and out of six races, failed to qualify for three and didn't finish the other three. At the end of the season Wunderink gave up, not only on Formula One, but on motorsport in general. He later became a property developer in Holland.

Alexander WURZ

Nationality: Austrian
Born: 15th February 1974
Seasons: 1997-2000, 2005, 2007
Team/manufacturer(s): Benetton, McLaren, Williams
Grands Prix: 69
Race wins: 0
Championship wins: 0

The son of rallycross champion, Franz Wurz, Alexander Wurz's first success was in 1986, when he became a

Alexander Wurz

BMW champion. He also enjoyed racing karts, though, and worked his way up through Formula Ford and Formula 3, before switching to touring cars in 1996. That same year, Wurz won the Le Mans 24 Hour race, the youngest driver ever to do so. The following year saw Wurz have his Formula One debut, as a stand in driver for Benetton in three Grands Prix mid season. He impressed by

finishing in third place at the British Grand Prix.

Wurz then drove full time for Benetton for the next three seasons, with 1998 being his best year, with 17 points and eighth in the Championship at the end of the season. However, his performances went downhill and he was dropped by the team at the end of 2000, to be replaced by Jenson Button.

From then on, Wurz was unable to get a race seat so he became test driver for McLaren for the next four years. He drove in just one Grand Prix in that time – the 2005 San Marino race, in which he proved his worth by finishing in third place – a record eight years after his last podium finish. For 2006, Wurz worked as a test driver for Williams and was then promoted to a race driver for 2007.

He had a reasonable season, taken third place in Canada and finishing 11th in the Championship. However, he announced his retirement from Formula One in the October, saying he may return to other forms of racing in the future.

Sakon YAMAMOTO

Nationality: Japanese
Born: 9th July 1982
Seasons: 2006-
Team/manufacturer(s): Super Aguri
Grands Prix: 14
Race wins: 0
Championship wins: 0

Japanese driver Sakon Yamamoto began racing karts at the age of 12 and was soon winning races and championships in his home country. By 2001 he was competing in Formula 3, first in Japan and then in Germany.

Yamamoto then returned to Japan and ended up competing in Formula Nippon and winning the championship in 2005, while also competing in Super GT. That same year, he was asked by Jordan to be the team's test driver at the Japanese Grand Prix, because he knew the Suzuka circuit well.

Sakon Yamamoto

Partway through the 2006 season, Yamamoto joined the new Super Aguri team, initially as test driver. However, he was called to drive in the German Grand Prix, where he qualified near the back of the pack and then was forced to retire with a broken driveshaft after just one lap.

Yamamoto then competed for the rest of the 2006 season, but without making much of an impact, with a best finish of 16th in China and Brazil. He lost his drive at the end of the season but was retained by Super Aguri as a test driver for 2007, and entered seven grands prix at the tail-end of the season.

Alex YOONG

Nationality: Malaysian
Born: 20th July 1976
Seasons: 2001-2002
Team/manufacturer(s): Minardi
Grands Prix: 18
Race wins: 0
Championship wins: 0

Malaysian driver Alex Yoong was born in Kuala Lumpur to a Malaysian father and British mother. After racing saloon cars in his teens, Yoong went on to win the first ever single-seater race in China, in 1994. The following year he won the Malaysian Formula Asia Championship.

A move to Europe saw Yoong competing in Formula Renault, Formula 3 and Formula 3000. He then won backing from the Malaysian lottery company to drive three Formula One races in 2001 with Minardi: the Italian, United States and Japanese Grands Prix. Although only finishing the last race, in 16th place, Yoong impressed enough to be retained by the team for a full season in 2002.

Yoong got off to a good start, taking seventh place in Australia at the start of the season, but he had less success for the rest of the year. He then left Formula One at the end of 2002 and competed in a variety of series including Champcar, Le Mans and A1 GP.

Alex Yoong

GRAND PRIX DRIVER BY DRIVER

Alessandro (Alex) ZANARDI
Nationality: Italian
Born: 23rd October 1966
Seasons: 1991-1994, 1999
Team/manufacturer(s): Jordan, Minardi, Lotus, Williams
Grands Prix: 43
Race wins: 0
Championship wins: 0

Italian Alex Zanardi was born in Bologna and began racing karts in his early teens before moving into Formula 3 in 1988, followed by Formula 3000 in 1991. Also in 1991, Zanardi made his Formula One debut, driving for Jordan in the last three Grands Prix of the season, and finishing ninth in two of them. The following season, he drove as a guest driver for Minardi in three Grands Prix, but failed to qualify for two and retired from the third.

Then came two seasons with Lotus in 1993 and 1994, where Zanardi's best result was a point-scoring sixth place at the 1993 Brazilian Grand Prix. A bad crash during practice in Belgium that year put him out for the rest of the season and part of the next.

Zanardi then left Formula One at the end of 1994 and competed in sportscars and CART. In the latter he initiated the habit of performing 'doughnuts' on the track after winning a race.

In 1999 Zanardi returned to Formula One, driving for Williams in a disappointing season. He then returned to CART racing and then was involved in a horrific crash in Germany which resulted in him losing both legs. Against all odds, though, he returned to racing, in modified touring cars, and even drove a Formula One car again, during testing in 2006.

Emilio Rodríguez ZAPICO
Nationality: Spanish
Born: 27th May 1944
Died: 6th August 1996
Seasons: 1976
Team/manufacturer(s): Williams
Grands Prix: 1
Race wins: 0
Championship wins: 0

Spaniard Emilio Zapico began racing seriously in the early 1970s, competing in Formula Seat. He then moved to touring cars and sportscars and had some local success.
In the mid-1970s, the Williams Formula One team was struggling for money, so when Zapico turned up with a sponsor and offered to pay for a drive, he was quickly accepted. That, then, is how Zapico made his one and only Formula One drive. He drove a dated Williams FW04 in the 1976 Spanish Grand Prix but just failed to qualify for the race itself.

After that, Zapico returned to touring cars and sportscars, although he did have a brief return to single-seaters in 1984, when he competed in Formula 3 for a short time. Zapico was killed in a road traffic accident in Spain in 1996.

Ricardo Luiz ZONTA
Nationality: Brazilian
Born: 23rd March 1976
Seasons: 1997-2001, 2003-2006
Team/manufacturer(s): Williams
Grands Prix: 1
Race wins: 0
Championship wins: 0

Alessandro Zanardi

Ricardo Zonta started karting in 1987, at the age of 11 and won his first ever race, going on to win his local championship in 1991. By 1995, he had won both the Brazilian and the South American Formula 3 championships.

Next came a move to Europe where Zonta competed in Formula 3000 and in touring cars, becoming the 1997 International Touring Cars Champion. This led to him being signed by the Jordan Formula One team as test driver, followed by McLaren and BAR.

It was with BAR that Zonta had his Formula One debut, driving in the Australian Grand Prix in 1999. He stayed with the team for two season, scoring three Championship points in 2000, with three sixth place finishes.

He then moved to Jordan as test driver in 2001, but competed in two Grands Prix, coming seventh in Canada. Then it was on to Toyota as test driver in 2004 and 2005, during which time Zonta competed in six Grands Prix, but

without making much impression.
Zonta continued as test driver for Toyota in 2006 and then moved to Renault in the same role for 2007.

Renzo ZORZI
Nationality: Italian
Born: 12th December 1946
Seasons: 1975-1977
Team/manufacturer(s): Williams, Shadow
Grands Prix: 7
Race wins: 0
Championship wins: 0

Italian driver Renzo Zorzi was born in the mountains near Turin and grew up to work for Pirelli, racing in his spare time.

By 1972 he was competing in Formula 3 and beginning to make a name for himself. Indeed, he caused a surprisr in 1975 when he won the Monaco Formula 3 race, driving a car powered by a Lancia engine that he'd helped to develop.

It was also in 1975 that Zorzi had his Formula One debut, driving for Williams at the Italian Grand Prix and finishing a lowly 14th. He then drove again for Williams at the start of the 1976 season, finishing ninth in Brazil.

Then, in 1977, he joined the Shadows team and entered five grands prix at the start of the season before his sponsorship money ran out. The only race he finished was the Brazilian Grand Prix where he came sixth and picked up one Championship point.

Tragically, Zorzi was involved in an accident at the South African Grand Prix, where his car caught fire. Two marshals ran across the track to help him and one was struck and killed by Tom Pryce's car; Pryce was also killed in the incident.

Zorzi later retired from racing and went on to run a Pirelli driving school in Italy.

Ricardo ZUNIÑO
Nationality: Argentinean
Born: 13th April 1949
Seasons: 1979-1981
Team/manufacturer(s): Williams
Grands Prix: 11
Race wins: 0
Championship wins: 0

Argentinean driver Ricardo Zuniño was born in Buenos Aires to a wealthy farming family. He began racing sportscars in his early twenties and proved himself to be a competent driver.

He then moved to Europe in 1977 to race in single-seaters, starting in Formula 2. Zuniño had ambitious plans and, while racing in Formula 2, he pushed to get a drive in Formula One. This led to a chance to compete in the last two Grands Prix of 1979, with Brabham – basically because he was the only person available for the Canadian Grand Prix. However, he managed to finish in seventh place, which was not bad for a rookie.

Zuniño then stayed with Brabham for the first part of the 1980 season, but his performances went downhill and he was dropped from the team. He did, though, drive in two Grands Prix the following year, for Tyrrell.

Zuniño gave up racing soon after and returned to Argentina where he ran his own hotel and became involved with the local tourist board.

Ricardo Zonta

INDIANAPOLIS 500 COMPETITORS

The Indianapolis 500 Mile Race, or Indy 500 for short, is a popular American race held at the Indianapolis Motor Speedway in Indiana, over the Memorial Day weekend at the end of May every year, beginning in 1911.
Although the Indy 500 is essentially a one-off race each year, from 1950 to 1960 it was part of the FIA World Championship, in that drivers competing at Indy were credited with World Championship points and participation. These are the American drivers who competed in the Indy 500 during that period but don't have an entry in the main part of the book because they didn't compete in a World Championship Grand Prix. Note that the seasons refer only to those that counted towards the World Championship — some drivers competed in the Indy 500 before and/or after this time.

Walter (Walt) ADER
Born: 15th December 1913
Died: 25th November 1982
Seasons: 1950

Fred AGABASHIAN
Born: 21st August 1913
Died: 13th October 1989
Seasons: 1950-1957

George AMICK
Born: 24th October 1924
Died: 4th April 1959
Seasons: 1958

Richard (Red) AMICK
Born: 19th January 1924
Died: 16th May 1995
Seasons: 1959-1960

Keith ANDREWS
Born: 15th June 1920
Died: 15th May 1957
Seasons: 1955-1956

Frank ARMI
Born: 12th October 1918
Died: 28th November 1992
Seasons: 1954

Charles (Chuck) ARNOLD
Born: 30th May 1926
Died: 4th September 1997
Seasons: 1959

Manuel (Manny) AYULO
Born: 20th March 1921
Died: 16th May 1955
Seasons: 1951-1954

Robert (Bobby) BALL
Born: 26th August 1925
Died: 27th February 1954
Seasons: 1951-1952

Henry BANKS
Born: 14th June 1913
Died: 18th December 1994
Seasons: 1951-1952

Melvin (Tony) BETTENHAUSEN
Born: 12th September 1916
Died: 12th May 1961
Seasons: 1950-1960

Arthur (Art) BISCH
Born: 10th November 1926
Died: 6th July 1958
Seasons: 1958

Jonathan (Johnny) BOYD
Born: 19th August 1926
Died: 27th October 2003
Seasons: 1955-1960

Donald (Don) BRANSON
Born: 2nd June 1920
Died: 12th November 1966
Seasons: 1959-1960

Walter (Walt) BROWN
Born: 30th December 1911
Died: 29th July 1951
Seasons: 1950-1951

James Ernest (Jimmy) BRYAN
Born: 28th January 1926
Died: 19th June 1960
Seasons: 2004

Willard (Bill) CANTRELL
Born: 31st January 1908
Died: 22nd January 1996
Seasons: 1950-1953

Duane CARTER
Born: 5th May 1913
Died: 8th March 1993
Seasons: 1950-1955, 1959-1960

William (Bill) CHEESBOURG
Born: 12th June 1927
Died: 6th November 1995
Seasons: 1957-1959

George Rice (Joie) CHITWOOD
Born: 14th April 1912
Died: 3rd January 1988
Seasons: 1950

Robert (Bob) CHRISTIE
Born: 4th April 1924
Seasons: 1956-1960

George CONNOR
Born: 16th August 1908
Died: 29th March 2001
Seasons: 1950-1952

Raymond (Ray) CRAWFORD
Born: 26th October 1915
Died: 1st February 1996
Seasons: 1955-1956, 1959

Larry CROCKETT
Born: 23rd October 1926
Died: 20th March 1955
Seasons: 1954

Arthur (Art) CROSS
Born: 24th January 1918
Died: 15th April 2005
Seasons: 1952-1955

James (Jimmy) DAVIES
Born: 18th August 1929
Died: 11th June 1966
Seasons: 1950-1951, 1953, 1955

James (Jimmy) DAYWALT
Born: 28th August 1924
Died: 4th April 1966
Seasons: 1953-1957, 1959

J Carlyle (Duke) DINSMORE
Born: 10th April 1913
Died: 12th October 1985
Seasons: 1950-1951, 1956

Leonard (Len) DUNCAN
Born: 25th July 1911
Died: 1st August 1998
Seasons: 1954

Donald (Don) EDMUNDS
Born: 23rd September 1930
Seasons: 1957

Edward Gulbeng (Ed) ELISIAN
Born: 9th December 1926
Died: 30th August 1959
Seasons: 1954-1958

Walter (Walt) FAULKNER
Born: 16th February 1920
Died: 22nd April 1956
Seasons: 1950-1953, 1955

George Francis (Pat) FLAHERTY
Born: 6th January 1926
Died: 9th April 2002
Seasons: 1950, 1953, 1955-1956, 1959

Myron FOHR
Born: 17th June 1912
Died: 14th January 1994
Seasons: 1950

George FONDER
Born: 22nd June 1917
Died: 14th June 1958
Seasons: 1952

Carl FORBERG
Born: 4th March 1911
Died: 17th January 2000
Seasons: 1951

Gene FORCE
Born: 15th June 1916
Died: 21st August 1983
Seasons: 1951, 1960

Anthony Joseph (A J) FOYT
Born: 16th January 1935
Seasons: 1958-1960

Donald (Don) FREELAND
Born: 25th March 1925
Seasons: 1953-1960

DRIVER BY DRIVER

William (Billy) GARRETT
Born: 24th April 1933
Died: 15th February 1999
Seasons: 1956-1958

Elmer GEORGE
Born: 15th July 1928
Died: 31st May 1976
Seasons: 1957

Paul GOLDSMITH
Born: 15th July 1928
Died: 31st May 1976
Seasons: 1958-1960

Cecil GREEN
Born: 30th September 1919
Died: 29th July 1951
Seasons: 1950-1951

Clifford (Cliff) GRIFFITH
Born: 6th February 1916
Died: 23rd January 1996
Seasons: 1951-1952, 1956

Robert (Bobby) GRIM
Born: 4th September 1924
Died: 14th June 1995
Seasons: 1959-1960

Samuel (Sam) HANKS
Born: 13th July 1914
Died: 27th June 1994
Seasons: 1950-1957

Leslie (Gene) HARTLEY
Born: 28th January 1926
Died: 13th March 1993
Seasons: 1950, 1952-1954, 1956-1957, 1959-1960

Ronald (Mack) HELLINGS
Born: 14th September 1915
Died: 11th November 1951
Seasons: 1950-1951

Albert (Al) HERMAN
Born: 15th March 1927
Died: 18th June 1960
Seasons: 1955-1960

William (Bill) HOLLAND
Born: 18th December 1907
Died: 19th May 1984
Seasons: 1950-1953

Jack (Jackie) HOLMES
Born: 4th September 1920
Died: 1st March 1995
Seasons: 1950

William (Bill) HOMEIER
Born: 31st August 1918

Jeremy (Jerry) HOYT
Born: 29th January 1929
Died: 10th July 1955
Seasons: 1950, 1953-1955

James (Jim) HURTUBISE
Born: 5th December 1932
Died: 6th January 1989
Seasons: 1960

James (Jimmy) JACKSON
Born: 25th July 1910
Died: 24th November 1984
Seasons: 1950

Joseph (Joe) JAMES
Born: 23rd May 1925
Died: 5th November 1952
Seasons: 1951-1952

Edward (Eddie) JOHNSON
Born: 10th February 1919
Died: 30th June 1974
Seasons: 1952-1960

A I KELLER
Born: 11th April 1920
Died: 19th November 1961
Seasons: 1955-1960

Daniel (Danny) KLADIS
Born: 10th February 1917
Seasons: 1954

Clarence Walter (Jud) LARSON
Born: 21st January 1923
Died: 11th June 1966
Seasons: 1958-1959

Bayliss LEVRETT
Born: 14th February 1914
Died: 13th March 2002
Seasons: 1950

Andrew (Andy) LINDEN
Born: 5th April 1922
Died: 10th February 1987
Seasons: 1951-1957

William GRETSINGER (Bill Mackey)
Born: 15th December 1927
Died: 29th July 1951
Seasons: 1951

Charles Michael (Mike) MAGILL
Born: 8th February 1920
Died: 31st August 2006
Seasons: 1957-1959

Jonathan (Johnny) MANTZ
Born: 18th September 1918
Died: 25th October 1972

Ernest (Ernie) MCCOY
Born: 19th February 1921
Died: 4th February 2001
Seasons: 1953-1954

Jonathan (Johnny) MCDOWELL
Born: 29th January 1915
Died: 8th June 1952
Seasons: 1950-1952

Jack MCGRATH
Born: 8th October 1919
Died: 6th November 1955
Seasons: 1950-1955

James (Jim) MCWITHEY
Born: 4th July 1927
Seasons: 1959-1960

Chet MILLER
Born: 19th July 1902
Died: 15th May 1953
Seasons: 1951-1952

Dennis (Duke) NALON
Born: 2nd March 1913
Died: 26th February 2001
Seasons: 1951-1953

Michael (Mike) NAZARUK
Born: 2nd October 1921
Died: 1st May 1955
Seasons: 1951, 1953-1954

Cal NIDAY
Born: 29th April 1914
Died: 14th February 1988
Seasons: 1953-1955

Patrick (Pat) O'CONNOR
Born: 9th October 1928
Died: 30th May 1958
Seasons: 1954-1958

John (Johnnie) PARSONS
Born: 4th July 1918
Died: 8th September 1984
Seasons: 1959-1958

James (Dick) RATHMANN
Born: 6th January 1924
Died: 1st February 2000
Seasons: 1950, 1956,1958-1960

Richard (Jim) RATHMANN
Born: 16th July 1928
Seasons: 1950, 1952-1960

James (Jimmy) REECE
Born: 17th November 1929
Died: 28th September 1958
Seasons: 1952, 1954-1958

James (Jim) RIGSBY
Born: 6th June 1923
Died: 31st August 1952
Seasons: 1952

Mauri ROSE
Born: 26th May 1906
Died: 1st January 1981
Seasons: 1950-1951

Edward (Eddie) RUSSO
Born: 19th November 1925
Seasons: 1955, 1957, 1960

Edward (Eddie) SACHS
Born: 28th May 1927
Died: 30th May 1964
Seasons: 1957-1960

Carl SCARBOROUGH
Born: 3rd July 1914
Died: 30th May 1953
Seasons: 1951, 1953

William (Bill) SCHINDLER
Born: 6th March 1909
Died: 20th September 1952
Seasons: 1950-1952

Robert (Bob) SCOTT
Born: 4th October 1928
Died: 5th July 1954
Seasons: 1952-1953

Charles (Chuck) STEVENSON
Born: 15th October 1919
Died: 21st August 1995
Seasons: 1951-1954, 1960

Leonard (Len) SUTTON
Born: 9th August 1925
Died: 4th December 2006
Seasons: 1958-1960

Robert Charles (Bob) SWEIKERT
Born: 20th May 1926
Died: 17th June 1956
Seasons: 1952-1956

Marshall TEAGUE
Born: 22nd February 1922
Died: 11th February 1959
Seasons: 1953, 1957

Clarke (Shorty) TEMPLEMAN
Born: 12th August 1919
Died: 24th August 1962
Seasons: 1955, 1958, 1960

John (Johnny) THOMSON
Born: 9th April 1922
Died: 24th September 1960
Seasons: 1953-1960

Bud TINGELSTAD
Born: 4th April 1928
Died: 30th July 1981
Seasons: 1960

John (Johnny) TOLAN
Born: 22nd October 1917
Died: 6th June 1986
Seasons: 1956-1958

Jack TURNER
Born: 12th February 1920
Died: 12th September 2004
Seasons: 1956-1959

Jeremy (Jerry) UNSER
Born: 15th November 1932
Died: 17th May 1959
Seasons: 1958

Robert (Bob) VEITH
Born: 1st November 1926
Died: 29th March 2006
Seasons: 1956-1960

William (Bill) VUKOVICH
Born: 13th December 1918
Died: 30th May 1955
Seasons: 1951-1955

Lee WALLARD
Born: 8th September 1911
Died: 28th November 1963
Seasons: 1950-1951

Travis (Spider) WEBB
Born: 8th October 1910
Died: 27th January 1990
Seasons: 1950, 1952-1954

Wayne WEILER
Born: 9th December 1934
Died: 13th October 2005
Seasons: 1960

Charles (Chuck) WEYANT
Born: 3rd April 1923
Seasons: 1955, 1957-1959

Dempsey WILSON
Born: 11th March 1927
Died: 23rd April 1971
Seasons: 1958, 1960

The pictures in this book were provided courtesy of the following:

GETTY IMAGES
101 Bayham Street, London NW1 OAG

PA Photos
www.paphotos.com

LAT Photographic
www.latphoto.co.uk

Design and artwork by David Wildish

Creative Director Kevin Gardner

Image Research Ellie Charleston

Published by Green Umbrella Publishing

Publishers Jules Gammond and Vanessa Gardner

Written by Philip Raby